Working with Distressed
Young People

Titles in the Series

To order, please contact our distributor: BEBC Distribution, Albion Close, Parkstone, Poole, BH12 3LL. Telephone: 0845 230 9000, email: **learningmatters@bebc.co.uk**. You can also find more information on each of these titles and our other learning resources at **www.learningmatters.co.uk**

Working with Distressed Young People

BOB HARRIS

Series Editors: Janet Batsleer and Keith Popple

LEARNING
RESOURCES
CENTRE

LearningMatters

First published in 2011 by Learning Matters Ltd

British Library Cataloguing in Publication Data
A CIP record for this book is available from the British Library.

ISBN 978 1 84445 205 7

This book is also available in the following ebook formats:

Adobe ebook ISBN: 978 1 84445 637 6
EPUB ebook ISBN: 978 1 84445 636 9
Kindle ISBN: 978 1 84445 959 9

Cover and text design by Code 5 Design Associates Ltd
Project management by Swales & Willis Ltd, Exeter, Devon
Typeset by Swales & Willis Ltd, Exeter, Devon
Printed and bound in Great Britain by TJ International Ltd, Padstow, Cornwall

Learning Matters Ltd
20 Cathedral Yard
Exeter EX1 1HB
Tel: 01392 215560
info@learningmatters.co.uk
www.learningmatters.co.uk

FSC
www.fsc.org
MIX
Paper from
responsible sources
FSC® C013056

To my daughter, Layla Jade Redway-Harris

Contents

Foreword from the Series Editors

Youth work and community work has a long, rich and diverse history that spans three centuries. The development of youth work extends from the late nineteenth and early twentieth century with the emergence of voluntary groups and the serried ranks of the UK's many uniformed youth organisations, through to modern youth club work, youth project work and informal education. Youth work remains in the early twenty-first century a mixture of voluntary effort and paid and state sponsored activity.

Community work also had its beginnings in voluntary activity. Some of this activity was in the form of 'rescuing the poor', whilst community action developed as a response to oppressive circumstances and was based on the idea of self-help. In the second half of the twentieth century the state financed a good deal of local authority and government sponsored community and regeneration work and now there are multi-various community action projects and campaigns.

Today there are thousands of people involved in youth work and community work both in paid positions and in voluntary roles. However, the activity is undergoing significant change. National Occupation Standards and a new academic benchmarking statement have recently been introduced and soon all youth and community workers undertaking qualifying courses and who successfully graduate will do so with an honours degree.

Empowering Youth and Community Work Practice is a series of texts primarily aimed at students on youth and community work courses. However, more experienced practitioners from a wide range of fields will find these books useful because they offer effective ways of integrating theory, knowledge and practice. Written by experienced lecturers, practitioners and policy commentators each title covers core aspects of what is needed to be an effective practitioner and will address key competences for professional JNC recognition as a youth and community worker. The books use case studies, activities and references to the latest government initiatives to help readers learn and develop their theoretical understanding and practice. This series then will provide invaluable support to anyone studying or practising in the field of youth and community work as well as a number of other related fields.

Janet Batsleer
Manchester Metropolitan University

Keith Popple
London South Bank University

Preface

This book is about the problems and creative possibilities in working with distressed young people. The book is about all young people, and certainly not just those from poorer backgrounds.

My first professional job was as a youth and community worker at a London youth centre that just happened to draw most of its membership from quite a wealthy area. A year or two later I was running a project working with young people, some of whom were homeless and destitute. It was clear that psychological distress knew no boundaries of class or income bracket.

After several years full-time youth work, I was accepted for training as a group analyst, but still maintained my work with the most difficult young people, remaining a part-time youth worker for probably far too long – I wanted to learn all I could. My subsequent career as a psychotherapist took me for many years into the NHS, with consultancy to children's homes, therapeutic communities for very disturbed young people and direct therapeutic work with individuals and groups.

Over the course of this time I began slowly to realise that, although the symptoms – the outward manifestations – of distress and disturbance were many, the conditions that gave rise to them were in fact few. That is the good news; the not so good news is that the predisposing psychological conditions can be difficult, although not impossible, to change and manage. Many young people have suffered multiple traumas in the course of their formative years, perhaps stemming from broken relationships, absent, addicted or dysfunctional unempathic parents and multiple misattuned caretakers. This can present a complex picture.

Understanding the causes of distress in young people is largely the topic of this book, on the grounds that if you do not know what is causing a problem you are much less well equipped to come up with a creative solution to alleviate it. Very recently a young woman who had come to see me because she was suffering from severe panic attacks said thoughtfully: "You know, I really need to let my parents know that I need to feel looked after better . . . I don't want to feel so scared all the time. . . ." This was a spontaneous idea that came into her mind when mulling over with me how she felt about her parents' acrimonious separation and divorce.

There is an increasing mass of evidence that children really do need to feel securely attached to at least one adult with whom they feel safe and protected. The adult in this relationship must also possess the qualities of empathy and attunement, and be able to empathically attune to the mind and rhythms of the child. This provides the context of nurturance in which the child's psychological growth and development occur.

The most significant aspects of a young person's growth and development in this context are the nurturing of their own capacities for empathy and attunement with others. It is not hard to see that this aspect of psychological growth is an absolutely essential prereq-uisite for being able to function in relation to other people, especially in groups; and, human beings being the social animals that we are, we all need to be able to function in groups.

This is not a book about psychotherapy as such, although insights from individuals, and especially group therapy, have long influenced all sorts of professional workers who find themselves dealing with psychological distress in the course of their everyday practice. This book will help you to understand more about distressed young people you are working with and offer some guidance as to how to proceed safely and with good results.

You might want to take this a stage further and think about and design some interven-tions specifically aimed at alleviating distress in the young people you work with. Psychotherapy is, at its most elemental, a specific intervention designed to provide an enriched psychological environment that includes reliable safe attachment, empathic attunement, and the possibility for social and emotional learning. You might like to think about how these elements can be adapted into your work, in whatever setting you work in. There are some examples of such adaptation given in the book, alongside practical advice on how to begin and sustain your initiatives.

Adapting the elements of holding, containing, empathy and attunement into different set-tings is part of the art of skilled work with distressed young people. These elements are explained and elaborated more fully in the course of this book.

If you want to extend your knowledge and skills, and work safely, I strongly recommend that you get some help from an experienced practitioner who is skilled in group work, and preferably trained in psychodynamic psychotherapy. Further training, when you feel ready, is of course a good idea.

Finally, may I wish you every success in using this book. I hope that you find the concepts and ideas helpful both in specific projects and in everyday situations.

If you are successful in your work with distressed young people, and can offer them some genuine safe attachment, and a 'holding environment' in which they are able to think about their emotions in the context of relationships that provide empathy and attune-ment, then there is every chance that you will not only be of help to them, but will also influence, even if in a small way, the mental heath of future generations.

And what could be more rewarding than that?

Bob Harris
Contact me at: **www.bobharrispsychotherapy.com**

Acknowledgements

I would like to thank Orith Abittan, Professor Barry Curnow and Chris Heaume for their help and support in the course of writing this book.

Part One

Setting the scene

Chapter 1

Young people in their social, relational and cultural context

CHAPTER OBJECTIVES

By the end of this chapter you will have:

- understood how the young person's social, relational and cultural environment affects their development;
- understood the major causes of distress in young people;
- explored some of the manifestations of distress in young people;
- understood why an understanding of groups and group work skills are essential in work with distressed young people.

Introduction

Distressed young people often exhibit difficult and problematic behaviour and they are frequently miserable, angry, anxious and unhappy. Their behaviour is disturbed and disturbing for others close to them. They can be deeply troubling and worrying to those in contact with them, especially parents and others who have family, community or professional responsibility for them. Suffering the consequences of a child's disturbed and disturbing behaviour is always painful and difficult.

Some distressed young people become very quiet and compliant, silent and withdrawn. They do not make their feelings heard and do not complain. They may become almost mute and invisible. Sometimes they develop a strange symptom such as self-starvation, self-harm, maybe an obsessive preoccupation, or perhaps odd or delinquent behaviour that both calls attention to their pain and distress – and hides its true nature at the same time.

Problems may be hidden or pushed out of awareness because they are too difficult to articulate or too painful to face.

In this chapter, we will explore the nature of a child's basic needs, and the distress that is caused to the growing child and young person when these needs are not met. We shall look at some of the ways in which distress is expressed behaviourally and psychologically, and outline some basic approaches to helping distressed children. These approaches will be discussed in more detail later on in the book.

Throughout, I take the view that human psychological needs are primarily *relational,* that is, they are in relation to and connected to relationships with other people. This is part and parcel of the fact that human beings exist in complex societies, which are made up of many interrelated parts.

This is not a new idea.

> *This thou must always bear in mind, what is the nature of the whole, and what is your nature, and how this is related to that, and what kind of part it is to what kind of a whole . . .*

(Marcus Aurelius, about AD 121, quoted in Long, 1982)

Trust and safety
Young people need the experience of being able to get close to and maintain a relationship with an adult who they can trust and feel safe with. The relational context in which this essential connection can occur is largely the topic of this book.

The group comes first

During the course of this chapter, you will be invited to consider the viewpoint that young people, and human beings generally, are primarily *social,* a word which in this context is used to describe the way people in groups behave and interact. Young people grow up and learn how to behave in a social environment that develops and shapes them, and which can produce outcomes both good and bad.

The immediate social and relational environment that a child grows up in is also in the context of a wider culture, which in turn carries ideas about behavioural norms, beliefs and values. This social and cultural environment exerts a powerful influence on social learning, and consequently, social behaviour.

Distress in young people is the result of problems that the growing child experiences in relating to other people in the child's immediate environment. This includes difficulties in relationships with parents, other children and problematic aspects of the wider social and cultural network of which the child and their immediate caretakers are a part.

> *. . . a baby is formed in the womb, an individual is formed in a relationship.*

(Rifkin, 2010)

Rifkin might have said, 'within a matrix of relationships'.

Or we might say, along with Winnicott, that there is no such thing as a mother and baby as separate beings. You can only really think about a mother and baby pair, and that pair is intimately connected to the wider network that supports it (Winnicott, 1965).

I will use occasional case studies in this text, which will be discussed, and which will then be used to raise questions for the reader to consider. The case studies are, of course, modified and condensed to protect confidentiality and for the sake of brevity, but the situations are all taken from real experiences in real encounters in professional work with real young people. They are selected from work with young people from different socioeconomic classes and cultural backgrounds in order to show that, although the apparent and 'surface' features may appear to be very different, the psychological fundamentals are very much the same.

A boy who has spent much of his life as a boarder at a top public school may experience the same sort of feeling of disconnection, rejection and depression as a girl who has spent much of her life in care.

A developmental 'cascade'

I've come to realise, as I get older, that actually, at any one time, I am all the ages I have ever been.

(Youth work trainee in his late 40s)

Throughout this book it is assumed that child and adolescent development is best thought of in terms of *cascade* of developmental processes. The development of an individual human being may appear to have a linear trajectory in terms of chronological age and 'developmental tasks', but in fact proceeds in a far more complex manner as each developmental stage, or competence, always involves navigating a complicated set of fluid and often unpredictable series of relationships and processes. It is not a 'one-off' learning event.

Fortunately for us, although the day-to-day picture is complicated, the underlying principles are quite easy to understand. For instance, it was observed decades ago (Kohlberg *et al.*, 1972) that some indicators of childhood problems consistently predicted adult adjustment across multiple domains of outcome, especially 'socialised conduct' versus 'anti-social behaviour'. 'Anti-social behaviour' is indexed by persistent rule-breaking behaviours.

It is easy to grasp the fundamental assertion that effectiveness in one domain of competence in one period of life effectively becomes the scaffold on which later competence in newly emerging domains develops; in other words, competence at one stage of life creates the conditions for competence in later stages. It is an incremental process.

For instance, behavioural problems arising in the family in pre-school years, in response to inept unempathic or misattuned parenting, are carried forward into the school context by the child, leading to problems in new domains of academic and especially social competence. Failure in these domains contribute significantly towards depressive responses. Especially in the case of social competence, this frequently causes rejection by peers (who may have helped to normalise problematic behaviour) which in turn amplifies depression and raises the risk of a drift into relationships with deviant peers who may reinforce anti-social, depressive, avoidant or self-destructive behaviour (Masten and Cicchetti, 2010).

The concept of developmental cascades is of great help when assessing what kinds of interventions one might choose to make with distressed young people, so that any intervention is targeted as precisely as possible at the developmental 'domain' that needs attention. It can help us be more precise with our interventions.

Plumber to customer: 'I know I've just charged you £75 to whack your pipe with a hammer to clear the blockage. But it's taken me 25 years to learn where to whack it'.

You will almost certainly be required to explain to fund-holders and others exactly why you need money for a certain type of intervention or activity, so precise thinking in this area is very important. It is not enough any more to justify expenditure in terms of rectifying a perceived developmental deficit or vague ideas about countering the effect of social deprivation; you may have to show with evidence how your intervention impacts on the wider picture and possibly on political policy and ideology, especially if there are resource implications.

For instance, it is known that problems in peer relating has an impact on academic achievement and delinquent behaviour. So if academic achievement or delinquent behaviour is an issue with the young people that you are involved with, you may consider that an intervention that specifically addresses peer relations in depth would be a good idea. This will almost certainly involve groupwork of some kind.

This book is primarily about the domain that could be called 'social relationships' rather than academic or other learning. In work with young people, peer relationships are, of course, mainly what we are working with in one form or another.

We are social animals

Human beings are intrinsically social animals. It is probable that we evolved in smallish tribal groups that wandered, hunted and gathered food. Couplings and marriages were made, children born, old and young would die, there would be fighting with competing tribes and groups; young and old would work, hunt and gather. Babies and young children would be looked after by parents and grandparents, sometimes by older brothers and sisters and when they could walk would tag along with anyone who would make them feel safe and protected from predators of various kinds, human and animal.

Growing a little older they would play in groups, probably largely of their own sex, and when they were strong enough, joining in with the men or women in their particular activities, maybe going through some sort of initiation ceremony before being recognised as full adults. Children had plenty of opportunity to see what adults did, as life was visible and communal in most aspects. Parenting, sexuality, coping with death and birth, dealing with conflicts and relationships with other people generally, finding, preparing and eating food, rituals and ceremonies would be, by today's standards, relatively visible and social. They would be group experiences. All human cultures have evolved to deal with basic aspects of human existence. And all human cultures are based around relationships in groups in relation to the environment in which they live.

How we learn and develop

Human children learn by watching and imitating; learning from experience, exploring the nature of the world and learning from others how to cope with life. As Marcus Aurelius observed earlier, humans are the most social of animals and the most complex, especially in their mental abilities. It is the ability to learn and play with ideas that enables humans to adapt imaginatively to complex, changing environments and it is the ability to learn that creates new possibilities. Human cultures have evolved to deal with the most diverse and challenging environments; this is one of the most remarkable aspects of our species.

It is a wise African saying that 'It takes a village to raise a child', and it is worth reflecting on the kind of 'villages' that we are currently creating in our globalised culture that will shape and influence the growth of children and young people.

Children have amazing powers of social learning that enables each one to become part of a family and a wider culture, cultures that in their turn have evolved to deal with a wide variety of human habitats and environments. In most of Europe, America and large parts of the world we now live in increasingly materially adequate global and 'virtual' conditions that are characterised by very rapid technological and social change, a world that brings with it constant challenges to learn, adapt and create. The brave new Western world of plenty and instant communication also brings with it challenges of resource management, global citizenship and personal proximity that have never been faced before in human history.

Does the group come first?

We are first and foremost social animals. The group could be considered to be prior to the individual; some would say the group comes first! It is inconceivable to consider any human being without placing them in the context of other people. Even a hermit on a Himalayan hillside is only a hermit by virtue of his avoidance of groups of other people. He is still in a relationship to other people, even if it is one of avoidance.

Children are designed to learn

Children are thus born equipped to be highly adaptive to their particular social group. Human groups and cultures are very diverse, so each human child must be able to absorb the particular ways of its particular cultural group. Except in broad categories of behavioural tendencies or attributes, for instance, sucking behaviour in infants, children are not born pre-programmed like ants or birds, and even animals learn by experience far more than we might like to think. For instance, it has been discovered that horses who have early problematic relationships with their mothers have difficulty later on in relating to other horses in the herd at a time in their lives when they would normally tend to group together as 'adolescents'. Human beings learn and adapt psychologically with great complexity and sophistication according to the physical and relational environment in which they find themselves.

The minds (and brains) of humans are extremely *plastic*: that is, they are shaped by experience. There is even evidence from epigenetics that genes are switched on and off by emotional experience (Jensen, 2009). However children are, in the main, not able to choose what to learn; *they learn from whatever they experience, good or bad*. This ability to learn also creates the difficulties that young people experience. We can create good, nourishing learning experiences, or bad, destructive ones.

Differentiating distressed responses from learned behaviour

It is very important to remember that although cognitive learning is a key element in human development, not all behaviour is learnt. Emotional development – or damage – is acquired largely through experience.

If young people are *responding or reacting* to disrupted, damaged or frightening relationships by expressing various mixtures of protest, anger, anxiety and despair, then treating young people who are essentially frightened and feeling unprotected as if they are simply behaving badly is likely to be irrelevant and pointless (Bowlby, 1973, p375).

Young people who are emotionally distressed because their safe, trusted relationships are disrupted or dislocated, or because they have experienced frightening, abusive or neglectful early lives, need special understanding and help. They may also need firm behavioural boundaries to help them feel safe. In the case of distress being the result of damaged attachment and bonding, it is pointless trying to 'teach' young people better behaviour or to punish them when they are, in fact, responding with distress to their predicament.

Do remember, though, that in working with young people, *appropriate limit setting and insistence upon ordinary social norms is a necessary expression of adult care and protection.* It is part of the 'holding environment', which will be discussed in more detail later. Establishing boundaries and limit setting is not an end in itself; in work with distressed young people it is a means to an end. Reliable boundaries and limit setting are very important in the process of helping young people to develop the ability to self-regulate.

CASE STUDY

Dafydd

Dafydd comes for help because he is feeling increasingly isolated and suicidal. He drinks with his companions, who are becoming more and more irritated by his aggressive behaviour towards them when he is drunk. He has spent a large part of his early life at a sports-mad boarding school where he felt safe and secure; good at sports, he was respected and appreciated. Having left school, he is lonely and disconnected, feels out of step with his new companions, not part of any group and having lost the impressive status he had in his sports teams. He feels diminished and belittled. He finds it difficult to cope without the 'reliable rhythms' of school routines and the safe and protected camaraderie, intense relationships, boundaries and rules of his sporting life. He now lives with parents whom he doesn't really know, and towards whom he feels a vague (though powerful) resentment for having sent him away . . . and then removing him from his deep attachments at school. This provokes a complex and overwhelming mix of feelings. In many ways he does not know who he is any more.

Key question: How can you tell if a young person is responding or reacting with distress to a disrupted or damaged attachment or if they have simply 'learned' bad behaviour?

ACTIVITY **1.1**

How do young people show distress?

In a group, brainstorm the manifest signs of distress. For example, anger, anxiety, depression, self-harm . . . Can you imagine or recall a situation where a young person is distressed, but there are few outward signs?

Can you imagine or recall a situation where a young person has difficulties in relating to peers, but that this is masked in some way? What ways might this masking occur?

Safe attachments

We now know that it is fundamentally important for children to feel safely attached to **at least one significant adult**, usually a parental figure, **by whom the child feels protected**, and that this is essential for the child's emotional and cognitive growth (Bowlby, 1973). There is a vast amount of hard evidence that confirms this fact (Schore, 1994; Gerhardt, 2004).

Good learning is about developing physical and mental capacities; and also, crucially, learning to understand and feel concern for the difficulties of others. In other words, a vital aspect of the capacity to engage in social learning and group life is the development of empathy. Safe attachments also make it possible for the child to explore the world with curiosity and engagement. Exploration of our global community requires a highly developed capacity for empathy.

Problems in empathic connection will result in various forms of isolation and disconnection from others. Isolation and disconnection from others are certain ways of producing distressed individuals.

The development of empathy

Emotionally healthy children with secure attachments and attuned, empathic relationships with adults become able to empathise with the feelings of other people. This enables them to act in a way which takes the feelings and needs of others into account and, when things go wrong as they inevitably occasionally do, accept responsibility for any hurt and damage done to oneself and others.

Children who have had secure attachments and attuned, empathic relationships with adults are able to empathise with the feelings of other people because they have been empathised with themselves.

This is a new concept in the psychosocial development of human beings. The term 'empathy', in English, only dates from around 1909 (Rifkin, 2010, p12), although, of course, it has antecedents and the word itself derives from the German 'Einfuhlung', a term borrowed from aesthetics to describe the process by which one person enters into the being of another and comes to know how they feel and think. The gross and well-documented failures of human fellow-feeling in the genocides of the twentieth century went some way to hastening awareness of the need to develop this increasingly essential part of the human psyche.

At the end of the First World War, for instance, it came as a genuine surprise to soldiers of both sides that the enemy, whom they had spent four years slaughtering in their millions, were ordinary people, just like themselves. And it is only in the last 50 years or so, from about half way through the last century, that animals began to be seen as fellow beings who inhabit the planet and who need protection, rather than things to be hunted and killed for fun, or used for food or amusement.

It is increasingly necessary to develop empathy due to the global nature of communications; see **http://vodpod.com/watch/3625992-rsa-animate-the-empathic-civilisation** (Rifkin, 2010).

The context of attachment

Attachment to a 'safe' parental figure who maximises our empathic potential is set firmly in the context of a wider set of social relationships in the family, and in the broad social and cultural context of which the family is a part.

Problematic or anti-social learning takes place in an environment of anxiety and distress, where children feel exposed to dangers, where they feel isolated, frightened and unable to play and safely explore the world with other children and adults, where adults cannot be trusted to help and protect them as the child takes risks and explores the world outside the home. Bad social learning leaves a child no option but to be solely concerned with its own self and its own survival, which is a default position if a child feels unprotected and that nobody else cares.

This retreat into an essentially self-centred orientation of false self-sufficiency and independence is sometimes termed 'narcissism' and also has a clear social and *cultural context* (Lasch, 1986).

Attunement

Alongside empathy as an essential building block of a healthy relationship is attunement. Attunement is the capacity to tune in to the individual 'rhythms' of the young person . . . or the group.

Our capacity to engage in relationships at any given moment is determined by the internal rhythms and the dynamics of whatever relationship we happen to be in. In some states, we are alert, excited and attentive and in others, tired, sad, afraid, hungry . . . if we are attuned to someone, we are sensitive to their internal state; this defines whether or not they are able to 'hear' our communications and are able to respond so that we can 'hear' their internal worlds. We 'tune in' and resonate (usually without being aware of it) to the symphony of dozens of patterns of rhythmic biological activity that create, at any given moment, a person's internal state. It is partly by this process that feelings are induced in others.

Sometimes communication of emotion is more by induction than anything else. This is a familiar process in art, where the artist, actor, musician or writer attempts to induce feelings in the audience. It also occurs on an everyday level between people.

Attunements help to establish the transmission of information from one person to another; from one sensory system to another. This is extremely important in the development of the capacity to 'translate' feelings and emotions from bodily experience into sound and words that can be used to communicate at a more sophisticated and symbolic level.

Attunement is one of the bedrocks of successful relationships.

The music of the group

When working with groups, although you might have a sense of where each individual member is coming from, it is impossible and inadvisable to try to 'tune in' to each individual separately. Like an orchestral conductor in a somewhat improvisational orchestra or the members of a 'free form' band or a DJ at a Psy-trance gig, we listen to the 'music of the group' and adjust our interventions, words, rhythms and beats according to the rhythms, beats and movements of the group in an interplay of resonance and recognition.

The best sort of social learning

Good social learning takes place best in a comfortable, reliable environment where young people feel safe and protected from:

- physical harm;

- too much overwhelming emotional stress, or long periods of high emotional turbulence.

Young people also need:

- plenty of opportunity for exciting physical and mental play;

- plenty of opportunity for face-to-face play and interaction with other children *and adults* in groups.

It is important to remember that 'virtual' play on computers and faceless digital interaction is **not** the same as, or a substitute for, face-to-face contact with real people in real time. The reasons why this is so will be discussed in a later chapter.

Good and bad

I am using the terms 'good' and 'bad' here in their self-evident, common sense way, and also in the sense that 'good' tends towards nurturance, the growth of understanding, awareness of and concern for others, personal and group development, and 'bad' tends towards destructiveness, depersonalisation, disdain or carelessness of the feelings and needs of others, and personal and social stagnation.

Our current culture is very confused about what is good and bad in the social context. Unscrupulous and damaged people will misuse this confusion; for instance mothers who encouraged their toddlers to hit each other, and then videoed their toddlers fighting, presented this behaviour in court as 'character building'. They were from families in the armed forces who were used to the concept of mock battles and physical hardship in military training. They misused this idea, perversely, to justify their activities (see **http://news.bbc.co.uk/1/hi/england/devon/6574907.stm** and also **http://news.bbc.co.uk/media/avdb/news/uk/video/89000/bb/89988_16x9_bb.asx**).

CASE STUDY

Awareness, empathy and concern for others

Jamie, a 14-year-old boy, habitually stole cars and drove crazily around the area where he lived. Sometimes he took other boys and girls for exciting, but frightening, rides in his stolen cars. He injured a number a people as a result, caused a great deal of damage and inconvenience and was thoughtless of the disruption he caused to the car owners.

Once, when he was caught, and he was caught repeatedly, he was asked if he ever considered that it was a dangerous thing to do; to drive a car containing other young people at high speed in a densely populated area and racing the police chasers. He considered the question carefully for a moment or two, then replied, 'Dangerous . . . no; I never thought they'd catch me'. He was only concerned about the danger to himself of being caught. He had little or no conception of the effect he was having on others.

Jamie came from a home where his mother and father had argued and physically fought each other since his unplanned and unwanted birth. The violence would often spill over into unprovoked attacks on the boy by both parents. The father repeatedly left home, returning intermittently, leaving the mother in a state of anger and depression and unable to give much love and attention to her son, often needing the boy to comfort her, which was an impossible demand on a small and often frightened child.

Upon the father's return the fights would begin again. For most of his early years, Jamie was constantly in a state of fear with no reliable figure whom he felt protected by. Preoccupied with their own problems, his parents were oblivious to the effect that their behaviour was having on their son and they punished him if he showed distress or if he asked to be comforted, thus humiliating him further.

It is humiliating for a child to be punished and rejected when he naturally turns to parents for love and protection. Children almost invariably blame themselves as being bad or unlovable.

Traumatised by his parents' dismissive and denigrating treatment, Jamie grew up to be similarly oblivious of the effect of his behaviour on others. He verbally denigrated and sometimes physically attacked other children who showed fear or anxiety, in the same way that his parents treated him when he was fearful and anxious. This meant that his ability to relate to other children was severely impaired, and thus he was unable to join in and play with others. Although he had a deep desire to be valued and to belong, due to his dysfunctional ways of relating he was unable to gain and sustain a place in a group with other children and adults where he felt accepted, could join in and feel a part of something valuable and creative.

Consequently, one effect of his problems in relating to others was that he constantly felt inadequate and marginalised in the groups of children of which he was a part. Jamie was miserable and angry, lashing out at other children at the slightest upset, unable to translate his painful feelings into words. His teachers found him irritating and exasperating; he became generally disliked. He became a 'hanger on' on the edges of groups rather than someone who was welcomed and valued for their contribution to play or other activity.

CASE STUDY *continued*

But stealing cars and taking other children with him gave Jamie instant power and kudos, albeit a frightening sort of power. However, he gained recognition from others, and also gained temporary friends by being seen as the provider of excitement and danger; he was for a short while both creator and master of this danger, and a protector of sorts. Being persistently chased and caught by the police also gave him the recognition he craved; at last he had some importance in the world, and some adult attention!

Also, and we will consider this aspect in more detail later in the book, Jamie induces feelings of fear, extreme danger and terror, confusion and ambivalence in his friends in the car and in others who experience his actions. These are the same type of feelings that he himself experiences within his home environment. Impaired in his capacity to identify and talk about these feelings himself, he unwittingly induces these feelings in others as a form of primitive communication.

Learning outcomes

Groups and gangs

The impairment of Jamie's psychological and social development meant that he found it very difficult to join in constructive activities with other people. He could only cope if he was in some sort of dominant position, where he did not have to rely on others.

If he could create a temporary group for himself based around an exciting delinquent activity, this temporarily met his needs to feel wanted and for inclusion in a group

This is a situation ripe for gang formation. For the purposes of this book I shall use the term 'gang' to refer to groups that have an anti-social or delinquent purpose, and 'group' to refer to a collection of people sharing some commonly agreed socially useful purpose, where there is some sense of attunement and connection between the members of the group.

In the joyriding example given above, Jamie created small gangs that gave him the identity, sense of belonging, status and attention he did not get at home. Being constantly chased by the police was strangely satisfying; although he didn't consciously relish getting caught he actually found the attention from the police satisfied a need to be taken seriously by 'authority' and given firm, adult limits to his behaviour.

There are few deep emotional links amongst people engaged in 'gang' type activities, as the main aim of a gang is the production of a sense of connection, identity, belonging and perhaps material gain through the creation of excitement and conflict, often expressed in 'fight or flight' and 'leader dependent' types of behaviour (Bion, 1962).

At this juncture, I would like to make the rather obvious point that the attempt to understand behaviour, delinquent or otherwise does not imply excusing or condoning it. Children and young people who have taken a destructive path, however impossible the conditions that have shaped them, need to be helped to change their behaviour by firm limit setting and immersion in cultures, largely defined by adults, that will nourish and sustain them and that can bring rewards from socially constructive and co-operative ways of being.

Action or depression?

In the example above, Jamie attempts to deal with his problems by becoming active and creating his own group/gang where he has identity, belonging, power and status, and where he achieves temporary importance in the eyes of powerful authority figures.

If this option had not been open to him – and the delinquent culture of some housing estate environments is one opportunity for distressed children to gain some sort of status – he could well have lapsed into a deep depression, fuelled largely by overwhelming and unarticulated feelings of failure, humiliation, powerlessness and isolation. Depression is frequently covered up by angry outbursts or delinquency.

Acute, but barely articulated feelings of failure, lack of status and belonging can lead either to depression, or the angry 'acting out' of feelings, or both. These are two sides of the same coin, and dealing with such feelings are especially difficult for young men and women. Related to the problem of the high incidence of depression amongst young people is the worrying incidence of serious alcohol and drug abuse and self-harm.

The dynamics of abuse: an impossible situation

An especially salient point in cases such as Jamie's is the way in which the young person is placed in an impossible situation. He naturally seeks the love and protection of his parents, but instead is attacked by them.

In families where the parents are effectively at war with each other, the child will suffer the added impossibility of split loyalties. How can a small child possibly make sense of and manage this situation? Interparental conflict is a reliable predictor of problems in young people (Kouros *et al.*, 2010).

What happens is that the child 'internalises' these relationships and *repeats them in relation to others* later on. Children will absorb whatever are the social environmental and relational qualities that surround them. Jamie will find ways of repeating his impossible dilemmas in his relationships with others. In the case outlined above, forcing the police into high-speed car chases is one example. The police cannot ignore him; on the other hand, if they give chase they will be creating further danger as he increases his speed in trying to escape; an impossible dilemma for them. The 'impossible dilemma' has been 'put into' the police.

This introduces a difficult but intriguing therapeutic phenomenon. Children will create in adults the very problem that they themselves cannot solve. So the adults must solve it first . . .

The problem in this case is 'how can I manage an impossible dilemma'? It is as if the young person needed somewhere to put their problem so that it could be understood.

Vignette: *Zak, a distressed young man in a discussion group at a youth centre, is quite disturbing for a while. He is irritating and distressing to the others in the group. Gradually he calms down and begins to communicate more lucidly with the other group members, and begins to speak about things in his life that are disturbing and distressing him. Someone remarks that it's good that Zak is now making more sense and not being so annoying. He says with a smile: 'yes . . . I needed a place to put my thoughts'.*

A reversal of power

Central to the construction of abuse dynamics is the reversal of power. The young person finds a way of repeating the abusive relationship, but *this time they are in control*. In the example of Jamie, above, it is the police, the car owners and the boy's 'friends' who are now in *his* control, although temporarily.

It can thus be seen that the creation and expression of distress is a social phenomenon, and that the repetitive effects of distressed behaviour in children and young people are both caused by and readily extend into the surrounding social matrix.

The dynamics of abuse and ways of thinking about and working with abuse dynamics will be discussed in more detail later.

Complexity

You can see that any one 'event' or problem such as 'joy riding' can have extremely complex causes that have a multiplicity of origins and current influences. Identifying and exploring one 'problem' almost always leads to the revelation of a highly complex picture. This makes work with distressed young people both fascinating and difficult as our knowledge-base will be tested and we may be required to use thinking from several different disciplines.

I emphasise again that ordinary social and practical measures including policing and restraint must be applied to control dangerous and anti-social behaviour.

Culture matters

The way in which children are treated differs from place to place and consequently from culture to culture. For instance, many people from mainland Europe and other countries are perplexed by Britain's binge drinking culture and the way in which young people appear to be out of control around alcohol. Attitudes to childcare also differ across cultures.

Recently (2008), in the busy shopping centre of an affluent Buckinghamshire town in the heart of suburban England, I saw a middle aged woman hitting a child of about 7 years of age with a stick, shouting 'I've told you not to do that three times'. The boy looked terrified, hurt, angry and forlorn all at once. Bystanders either turned away or looked horrified – and then turned away. We know only too well the likely effect on a child of such treatment. Sooner or later he is likely to find someone else to abuse, or lapse into depression.

Such behaviour by an adult would be unthinkable – and in many cases illegal – in most other European countries.

It causes *trauma* to the child when a parent or other adult whom the child needs to trust abuses the child. The manifestations and treatment of trauma will be discussed in more detail later in the book.

Class issues

In the case of Jamie above, the boy came from a 'working class' housing estate, but it should be borne in mind that all social classes can fail their children in their own way. For a superb exploration of 'upper class' family and social dysfunction and its effect on a growing child, see the film 'Wah-Wah' by Richard E. Grant (Grant, 2002), and the book about the making of the film (Grant, 2006). The main character in the film comes from a wealthy and powerful but extremely disturbed family. Whilst presenting a 'public face' the politician father is a violent alcoholic and the mother is narcissistic, neglectful and sexually abusive. The upper class child's salvation was the creation of his own group/gang of puppets over whom, of course, he had complete omnipotent control.

In Jamie's case, he did not have the opportunity to symbolise or safely re-enact his trauma, or to find another form of reparative experience where he could gain some respect and status in a socially constructive form, so unfortunately he used real people instead!

A scientific view of the development of empathy and concern for others

There is increasing scientific evidence that people like Jamie in the case study above are *not able* to be concerned for others, that this failure to develop empathy, and therefore the capacity to relate to others in groups, occurs at a fairly specific time in the individual's early life, between the ages of about one and three (Schore, 1994; Gerhardt, 2004) and is related to the child's experience of an attached, empathic, attuned relationship with a reliable caretaking adult by whom the child feels protected.

The effects of empathic failure and emotional neglect at this time of life are known to be profound and long lasting. There is evidence that a lack of emotionally attuned and empathic relating in the early years causes problems in the actual physical neurological development of the brain (Schore, 1994). This functionally affects the way in which the growing child is able to relate to others empathically, which as we know is an essential prerequisite for a healthy group life, and therefore essential for the mental health of individuals.

Anxiety and distress also functionally affects the way in which an individual is able to empathise with others. Some young people, who are extremely distressed and anxious, learn very early on to cover this up and to push aside their feelings. They may appear on the surface to be *lacking* in anxiety, and even to be cheerful and coping, but at the same time may exhibit callous and anti-social behaviour in relation to others, sometimes engaging in self-harming behaviour and self-sabotage (Behr and Hearst, 2005). This cover up is sometimes referred to as the construction of a *'false self'* (Winnicott, 1965).

Emotional neglect can happen in overprotected as well as underprotected environments and as noted above bears no relation to social class or the economic circumstances of the parents. However, the pervasiveness of electronic 'soothers' like TV and video games, and the growth of 'virtual' computer-based relationships rather than real relationships also has a part to play (Palmer, 2006).

A child who has been failed by adults, who has had to become precociously self-reliant, perhaps developing a 'false self' and who has problems in relating to others, will tend to see attempts by adults to offer help as incomprehensible, and threatening to their precarious sense of safety, a safety that is maintained by the avoidance of dependent relationships, which makes the transition toward mature interdependence very problematic.

It is very important to remember that it is not only structured, school based teaching that children learn from; this is a relatively small part of the child's experience. By far the greater influence is home, early relationships and the wider social context of which the family is a part. The social permeates the individual to the core (Foulkes, 1990).

That is the bad news. The good news is that the human mind is to some extent 'plastic' and can be 'reshaped' by better experiences.

RESEARCH SUMMARY

Over the past 80 years or so, a great deal of research has been done into the nature of human development and the consequences of childhood experiences in particular, some of which has been referred to above (Bowlby, 1973; Schore, 2003; Gerhardt, 2004; Palmer, 2006). There are some things, notably empathic and attuned parenting in the context of safe and reliably attached relationships, that we now know for a fact to be definitive and powerful influences, not simply one way of seeing things amongst a variety of different but equally valid opinions.

Know thyself . . .

As well as the issues to do with interpersonal relationships and the development of empathic responses to others referred to above, there is a growing body of evidence that infants who have experienced unempathic or mis-attuned parenting develop problems in understanding and regulating *their own* feelings and emotions. Their own internal world is a mystery to them; they have great difficulty in identifying and thinking about their own feelings. These children are at great risk of developing serious personality problems as they try desperately to find ways of coping with this impairment of their ability to experience, make sense of and articulate their own emotional lives.

Such a child not only finds other people somewhat incomprehensible, but is also a stranger to himself!

CASE STUDY

Tamsin

Thirteen-year-old Tamsin's parents are high earners and high achievers. Her father travels the world on business, and her mother is a top barrister, often preoccupied with complex cases. Both parents, although not overtly neglectful, have almost completely lost touch with their daughter. She feels lonely and alone, and struggles to make friends. She was born prematurely, spent her first days in an incubator and her mother found it difficult to bond with her baby daughter.

Tamsin has great difficulty in identifying and expressing in words her feelings of distress, abandonment and depression. But she realises that she can gain the attention she craves from her parents by not eating.

She sees that women like Victoria Beckham gain an enormous amount of attention in magazines and the media for little other than being thin and apparently thus being able to attract an enormous amount of attention. She craves attention and approval.

She finds a like-minded collection of girls who see an absence of body fat as the key to successfully gaining the concern of parents and adults, and the admiration of others (a sort of gang). This is exciting and gives her a feeling of belonging and a chance to compete, win and gain status. However, her self-starvation also affects her cognitive capacity, that is, her ability to think realistically about her problems, and launches her into a world where reality is at best tenuous.

ACTIVITY 1.3

Have you come across anyone who fits this description?

How might you work with them?

CASE STUDY

Sammy

15-year-old Sammy realises that he gains far more attention by not working at school than by doing his work and being part of the group who just get along in an ordinary way. He sees young men around him who get out of school early (preferably dramatically 'kicked out') and live 'on the streets', fight other boys, get away with tricks and lies, own weapons and are prepared to use them. He sees that they get what they want in gaining status and admiration from girls and other young men. He joins this gang. It is exciting and gives him a feeling of belonging and a chance to compete, win and gain status.

If he cannot achieve this, he can always retreat into his virtual world of video games, Internet chat rooms and pornography, where the problems of bodies being attached to real persons are temporarily solved.

Do you know anyone like this?

How might you understand and work with them?

Consumerism

Modern consumerism and marketing powerfully implies that having more things brings happiness. We know, however, that the competition to have more and better things, to earn ever more money and to constantly measure up to the perceived success of others is a sure pathway to misery and depression (James, 2007).

'Globalisation' and the internet foster the idea that we are creatures of the world; world citizens. Paradoxically, but not surprisingly, in environments where real contact and interactions are minimised, where even new tastes and smells are treated with suspicion, many children are terrified of anything unfamiliar, and feel inadequate to take up the important developmental challenge of getting to know others and becoming known themselves.

Groupwork and working in groups

At the beginning of this chapter we asserted that human beings are essentially social animals, and that the ability to co-operate and communicate constructively with others is a basic necessity. In order to do this we must enable children to develop the quality of empathy, and we learned that this is not in-built or inherent, but develops in early life in the context of an empathic, attuned relationship with a reliable, protective adult, most often a parent.

The ability to be a part of a group and also to *attach* to a group is therefore as essential to mental well-being today as it was in the time when human psychology first evolved as part of an essential group survival strategy. Although Bowlby and others were quite specific about the need for individuals to enjoy a firm attachment to a reliable and protective individual, there is little doubt that this is best achieved in the context of a stable group environment. With the rapid demise of the extended family, which, if things went well, provided a wider and stable group to hold and contain parental couples, many parents today do not enjoy the support of a broad family group around them to help provide continuity and stability.

Attachment to a group

As large numbers of individuals become more geographically mobile, perhaps moving to several different towns or even countries in the course of a lifetime, the ability to find safe attachments to groups remains a very useful and functional ability.

Young people, if not given the opportunity to attach to useful and productive social groups, will create or find their own groups – gangs – based around anti-social, dangerous and destructive behaviour of various kinds. Because these groups do not contain mature adult influence, they will be subject to excess; violent bravado, for instance can all too easily go badly wrong. Young people need challenge, fun and excitement, physical and intellectual. They also need to gain a sense of limits and boundaries, and to feel that there are trustworthy adults around who they can turn to for help if need be.

Although they might not always show it, young people are highly sensitive to the approval or disapproval of adults they respect.

Groupwork approaches, which emphasise thoughtfulness, reflection, consistency, inclusion, tolerance, reliability, free group discussion and which take fully into account the interconnectedness and complexity of modern life can help in the alleviation of distress (Harris, 2007).

Groupwork is the treatment of choice for distressed adolescents who need 'ego training in action' (Foulkes, 1990) rather than insight-oriented help; if necessary, that can be provided later.

Later chapters will explore these issues in more detail so that experiences with adolescents can be seen in a more informed light. Both causes and effects of distress will be discussed more thoroughly with a view to thinking about best courses of action. This is not so that excuses can be found for bad or anti-social behaviour, or so that wrong-thinking can be easily put right by carefully chosen educational programmes. This approach takes into account the many influences on the growth and development of young people, and is advocated so that the nature of problems can be understood as fully as possible and suitable interventions chosen as a result.

The Institute of Public Policy Research report (Margo *et al.*, 2006) indicates that, apart from a few impoverished ex-Soviet states, Britain is the worst place in the Western world to grow up in. British children also face more tests and 'achievement targets' than anywhere else in the world. We are surrounded by a relentless culture of winning and competitiveness, which only serves to increase stress and unhappiness amongst the young.

Our global village currently encourages a culture of competitiveness and narcissistic individualism; consumerism and rivalrous isolation produce large numbers of troubled young people. Eating disorders and depression, addictions, aggressive and self-harming behaviour are all too common. Suicide rates, especially amongst young men are still high, although they have shown a recent decline, possibly due to depression becoming more socially acceptable as an 'ailment', and treatment for depression becoming less stigmatised.

Did you consider the 'matrix' of relationships that a young person is a part of?

ACTIVITY *1.5*

Some things to reflect upon:

- *What is the difference between a gang and a group?*

- *Think of your own childhood. Who were your most important attachment figures. Why? Was there a relational network that contained and supported your parents?*

- *When you were growing up, which groups were important to you?*

- *Get a selection of today's papers. What do they tell you about young people in our culture?*

- *Take a look at the section in a bookstore which contains magazines aimed at girls and young women. What do they tell you?*

- *Think of some parents that you know. What are their concerns for their children?*

- *What do you think of the binge drinking culture? Is it something to be concerned about, or just youthful exuberance that most people grow out of?*

- *If you could change one thing about your experience of being parented, what would it be?*

C H A P T E R R E V I E W

There is no question that children need safety and emotional security in order to grow and flourish and develop social skills and the capacity to understand and relate to others. These desirable attributes only develop in the context of safe, attached relationships to trustworthy and helpful adults, and these relationships grow best in the context of families who are themselves part of wider social networks which support secure, empathically attuned attachments.

If children are not raised in a psychosocial context which supports this sort of growth and development, they will become distressed and develop difficulties in understanding and articulating their own feelings. In turn, their capacity to empathise with and relate to others will be impaired. This is a 'cascade' effect in that difficult and problematic behaviours will create further problems in peer relationships and schoolwork. Young people may attempt to belong to groups that form around 'gang' mentalities rather than engaging in socially useful, creative or constructive activities.

As in the case of Jamie, where the distress is deepened by physical, sexual or emotional abuse leading to trauma, especially difficult relational processes are set in motion that require special thought and attention.

This will be the subject of a later part of the book, but the next chapter will extend our picture of healthy childhood development.

FURTHER READING

Gerhardt, Sue (2010) *Why Love Matters*. London: Routledge.

An excellent introduction to the way in which early experience affects psychosocial development. Makes the complex work of Allan Schore easier to digest.

James, O (2010) *How Not to F*** Them Up*. London: Vermilion.

Very well written, sometimes humorous and well-researched account of good childrearing practice.

Palmer, S (2006) *Toxic Childhood*. London: Orion.

Shows how 'modern life' affects child development. An easy read.

Rifkin, J (2010) *The Empathic Civilisation*. Cambridge: Polity.

For a brilliant animation that explains the book in about ten minutes, go to **http://vodpod.com/watch/3625992-rsa-animate-the-empathic-civilisation**

USEFUL WEBSITES

Depersonalisation **http://dictionary.reference.com/browse/depersonalisation**

http://news.bbc.co.uk/1/hi/england/devon/6574907.stm

http://news.bbc.co.uk/media/avdb/news/uk/video/89000/bb/89988_16x9_bb.asx

Chapter 2

Growing up: a good
enough childhood

CHAPTER OBJECTIVES

By the end of this chapter you will have:

- explored 'healthy' development;
- examined evidence-based processes that are essential for the optimal development of young people;
- discussed the importance of the concepts of 'holding' and 'containment';
- explored the concepts of denial and dissociation as ways of coping with painful feelings.

Introduction

There are many basic aspects of parenting and child development that are now known to be helpful in enabling children to grow and flourish. This chapter outlines some of the essential social and psychological elements that we know to be of importance in providing the keystones to healthy development.

In exploring what we know to be optimal conditions, we can also think more deeply and try to understand what may be causing distress to a young person. The concepts of holding and containment are examined in some detail as they are basic to work of any depth with distressed and disturbed young people. A good understanding of these concepts and their practical application will enable you to construct settings that have the resilience and flexibility to work with turbulent emotions.

Complex interrelations

There is now a significant amount of evidence about what constitutes the best possible upbringing for children and what is an optimally psychologically healthy childhood. It is also generally accepted now, backed up by vast amounts of research, that the lived experiences of favourable, early, intersubjective family relationships (Schore, 2003) are a key to satisfactory development. These are complex interrelationships, heavily influenced by contextual cultural and environmental conditions.

Genetic influences and predispositions play a part, but nurture far outweighs nature in the creation of a person. Recent research in the field of epigenetics indicates that life stresses affect the ways in which genes are structured and transmitted, so there is a *lateral* (present day, here and now) influence on genetic transmission, as well as the more obvious longitudinal one.

A child's environment, family constellation and relational experiences are far more important than other influences. In the first chapter we saw that each of us is a 'nodal point' in a network of relationships. A child grows up in a complex network of social and personal relationships that may well be fluid and difficult to control and positively influence, even by the most caring of adults. As such, healthy growth – and the creation of distress – is influenced by a variety of factors, which determine the development and creation of a person. Distress is usually *multidetermined*; that is, determined by more than one cause.

More on attachment

Bowlby and others (1973), in the chaos of the aftermath of the Second World War, studied the effects of parental separation on young children. Bowlby and his colleagues began to organise their thinking into what has become known as *Attachment Theory*, and came up with findings which have not only stood the test of time, but also have been developed, refined and subsequently largely confirmed by research. Human attachment to parents and need for parental support is not only a childhood phenomenon. Many people remain psychologically dependent and 'attached' to parents, to varying degrees, until well into middle age and beyond.

CASE STUDY

Kellie

Kellie, a 21-year-old student, who had been living independently for two or three years, came to a young people's counselling service complaining of depression and anxiety.

She had recently been home over the holiday period and found that her parents had changed her childhood bedroom into a bathroom without informing her, and didn't seem able to understand that she had feelings about this. She was deeply disappointed and angry. The part of the house containing her bedroom had, in fact, been completely destroyed and rebuilt as a spa room.

For Kellie, the removal of her bedroom felt as if a major aspect of her childhood experience had been destroyed, even negated. It connected, linked and resonated with other experiences where she felt that her needs had been overlooked. She still needed an experience of parental care and a safe base where she felt that her feelings were recognised and understood. This was especially important during her transition to the more fluid and less structured college environment, which was stressful and confusing in itself.

Her problems, however, predated the incident during the college vacation. Unfortunately, Kellie's parents had never been able to relate to her with the empathy and attunement that she needed. Prior to this she had experienced long-term very deep depressions where she had been unable to get out of bed for weeks and felt disconnected and cut off from others. She stayed in bed to feel comfort and security, and protection from what she felt to be a hostile world. However, when she joined a discussion group at college with other students who were experiencing emotional difficulties, she gradually found, to her surprise, that others were not only interested in her life, but also able to resonate with her feelings and experiences.

The group was 'open ended' and was expected to be there for the duration of Kellie's stay at college, so had a feeling of reliability and consistency about it that Kellie needed.

The music of the group

In physics and music, resonance describes a harmonic sympathetic vibration. In this context, resonance describes how the group was able to tune in to Kellie's feelings and empathise with her in a way that her mother had not been able to. In the group, she was able to engage and connect with others and begin to think about her problems in a way that she had not been able to do before. She felt less alone, more 'just like other people' and less inclined to regressively hide under the duvet when things got tough.

Emotional difficulties, trauma and distress that have earlier causes tend to re-emerge at times of stress. Young people who are going through the challenges and turbulence of adolescence often experience a re-emergence of earlier problems. Sometimes they start to behave like little children again. This 'going backwards' is sometimes called 'regression' to an earlier stage of development.

In Kellie's case, going to college, leaving her home town and joining the competitive academic environment, in other words, a loosening of her safe attachments, precipitated a regression to a childlike state of hiding from the world. Her earlier experiences with a mis-attuned, unempathic family had not prepared her to deal with stresses in life and she found it hard to find a comforting place within herself.

Some young people, instead of becoming depressed and withdrawn, become very agitated and 'speedy' or develop an obsession of some kind. All these types of responses are termed 'affect dysregulation' (Schore, 2003) and are frequently linked to problems in the parent/child intersubjective field.

What's in a word . . .

Consider the meaning of the word responsible. To be responsible we need to become response-able: that is, able to deal with our own responses. Remember that these problematic behaviours are *responses and reactions* and not just 'bad' behaviours to be ritually punished or simply behaviourally controlled or managed by adults, although, of course, children and young people need adult insistence on ordinary behavioural norms.

Adult responses must be reflected upon and thought about, and decisions made about how we deal with problematic and challenging behaviour.

Young people do need to learn to be able to think about their responses and reactions in a safe and supportive environment.

We are creatures of 'cause and effect', dependent for our growth and well-being on causes and conditions and circumstances. One of these factors is how we internally, that is, in our minds, *experience and manage* our emotional life in relation to our day-to-day experience of our surrounding environmental circumstances and the interpersonal matrix and culture of which we are a part.

ACTIVITY **2.1**

Discuss as a group:

Is there a difference between a strong emotional response to an attachment or relationship difficulty and just bad or disruptive behaviour? If there is a difference, how can you tell? Is there any point in making a distinction?

Introjection

Kellie grew up with a depressed and unempathic mother and an emotionally distant father who both had great difficulty in tuning in to the needs of their child. Kellie's parents were not unkind to her or deliberately cruel in their behaviour or attitudes, in fact, she experienced them as broadly supportive of her. But they were emotionally unavailable and unable to connect with her feelings and thoughts. She became attached to the reliability of books and the structure of school as her means of feeling safe in a confusing and perplexing world.

Parents who have problems in attuning to their children are actually experienced by the small child as confusing and chaotic. The parent does things – from feeding to giving hugs and cuddles or even chastising – that bear little relation to the child's needs at the time. The parent may be doing things that make sense to them as adults, but make no sense or are even shocking and intrusive to the child.

The concept of *introjection* helps us to understand something of Kellie's inner world. All children *absorb* their parents' caretaking and psychological makeup. It is as if the parental care (or lack of it) becomes *installed inside* the growing child and then becomes *the main way in which the child relates to herself*. Caretaking patterns are taken inside the child and live on as the way in which the child tunes in to and relates to her own feelings.

This internal caretaking model becomes the way in which young people take care of themselves.

In Kellie's case, she had great difficulty in identifying and thinking about her own feelings; she could barely tune in to her own inner world. It was only when the group began to empathise with her that she was able to get the process going of understanding herself better.

CASE STUDY

Taking the weight of thinking off my mind

Chris, a young man in a discussion group in a youth project, had a severely depressed mother who was frequently hospitalised, and a father who left before Chris was born. Chris spent much time with very old, frail grandparents who were unable to really connect with him. Consequently, although very bright academically, he had almost no sense of his own identity, and was almost unable to think about himself in any context at all, which caused him an enormous amount of distress trying to think about and work out who he was.

Throughout his teens Chris became more and more isolated and began to feel as if a transparent wall separated him off from others.

On starting the group, he told a story about standing in a playground watching the other children playing and it occurring to him that the only logical conclusion he could possibly draw would be that he must be a child like them. During his teenage years he also gradually developed other ideas that grew more and more bizarre and violent. After some time in the group and taking the risk of allowing himself to become known to the other members, he made the comment: 'I like this group. It takes the weight of thinking off my mind'.

Chris stayed in the group for over a year and became a valued member, partly for a new found skill of being able to express succinctly and helpfully what was going on inside him.

He was gradually internalising the group as a helpful internal object that could get to know him and help him to form a sense of himself. Towards the end of his time in the group he told a story about how he had been invited to a party the previous weekend and, very warily, had accepted. He described talking with a small group of boys whom he had known slightly some years before at school but had felt excluded from. Very movingly, he said, 'for the first time I felt as if I were inside the conversation'. He could also have been talking about the development of his experience in the discussion group. It was as if he now had a space, or perhaps an 'internal group', that could receive and think about his thoughts.

Environmental influences not only include material well-being and material comforts. The *psychological environment* that surrounds a child is profoundly important in shaping the personality of the child, and consequently the adult. It is the psychological environment that is absorbed by the growing child. Material well-being, in itself, is by no means sufficient, and in some respects, material aspects of modern life, which are commonly thought to be beneficial, may in fact carry within them experiences that are actually harmful. Some potentially harmful aspects of modern life will be discussed in more detail in a following chapter (see also Palmer, 2006).

It is worth emphasising at this point that groups and cultures can, of course, be profoundly destructive, as well as constructive in their activities. A healthy group culture needs to develop an active aversion to damaging and destructive aspects of group life, in much the same way as an individual needs to pay attention to their individual physical and emotional health.

Although there are some who believe in Utopian visions of perfectibility, most of us would probably settle for the mixed bag of experiences which are, to borrow Winnicott's term, 'good enough'. See **http://changingminds.org/disciplines/psychoanalysis/concepts/good-enough_mother.htm** for a good, simple explanation of this term.

Some depressing facts

However, what is not in doubt is that even a relatively loosely defined problem like 'depression' in young people is on the increase. Though it can be argued that the increase is due to more effective diagnosis, even if this were true, the incidence is still alarming and cannot in itself be due solely to genetic predisposition.

Recent figures show that seven per cent of Harvard students are taking anti-depressant medication (**www.thecrimson.com/article/2006/12/14/alarm-over-antidepressants-antidepressants-may-cause/**). In the USA, data from various studies indicate the use of antidepressants among young people grew three- to tenfold between 1987 and 1996, and a newer survey found a further 50 per cent rise in prescriptions between 1998 and 2002.

In the UK, University of London researchers compared prescribing rates between 2000 and 2002 in countries in Europe, South America and North America. During that period, we saw a 68 per cent rise in children in the UK being prescribed drugs to 'stimulate or calm the brain'. This research is published in Archives of Disease in Childhood.

This explosion in antidepressant and psychoactive drug use occurred even though many professionals are concerned about the marketing claims and procedures employed by the pharmaceutical industry. However, we do know that about one in four Britons is affected by mental health problems at some point in their lives, with one in six suffering at any one time. The cost of mental ill-health is estimated at £77bn a year. In 1996, there were 31 million prescriptions issued for anti-depressants, including 631,000 for children, a staggering total.

When it is taken into account that there is overwhelming evidence that childhood experiences are highly influential in the psychogenesis of adult mental health problems, we can see that the treatment of young people is of the greatest concern on that count alone. It is also fairly obvious that something is going badly wrong for distress to be experienced on such a scale.

But of greatest importance is the fact that emotional problems arise in the context of interpersonal and social relationships. Interpersonal, emotional and psychological difficulties clearly cannot be solved by medication; the best that can be hoped for is that the symptoms may be alleviated whilst changes are made in, or adjustments made to, the relational matrix of which each of us is a part.

We may feel better after swallowing a chemical of some kind, be it alcohol, a 'recreational drug', or Prozac, or even by gaining an 'endorphine high' after vigorous exercise, but the underlying causes of our unhappiness will remain the same. Ways of making ourselves feel better, including various treatments such as psychotherapy, are all very well, but it surely would be even better if we didn't get so sick in the first place.

If we do not attend to the underlying causes of distress, we will be engaged in an endless cycle of symptom management and treatment; never-ending therapies of various kinds and long-term prescription drug use. Some psychological treatments appear to deal effectively with the symptoms of distress, but we need to become far more aware of the causes in order to make any real change in the overall picture.

We come now to an important point. The decline into the more serious area of clinical depression rather than ordinary unhappiness seems to be influenced by the production of certain hormones in the body *which are released as the direct result of distress*. An over-production of the hormone cortisol, caused by over-exposure to fight/flight type stress, seems to be the main culprit in driving a vicious circle, or downward spiral.

This is how it works. Long-term chronic or severe temporary distress causes a biochemical reaction in the body, resulting in over-production of cortisol. This in turn causes a constant state of stress and an increase in depressive symptoms. This can become a rapidly increasing spiral; the depressive symptoms, for instance, over-eating or drinking too much, cause further problems in self esteem, relationship difficulties and biochemical imbalances, which in turn cause further depression and further distress. So whilst it is true to say that there is a biochemical involvement in the development of depressive and anxiety states, this biochemical 'push' in itself is highly likely to be caused by stressful life events, specifically problems in relationships. A depressed person may then develop further problems in relationships caused by the depression, which cause more chronic stress and make a downward spiral more likely. This is a vicious circle, or, more accurately, a vicious downward spiral. Problems caused by over production of the stress hormone cortisol can begin very early in life (see Leach 2010).

The most common (and very good) advice for depressed young people (and adults) is to counter this spiral with exercise and relaxation. This combination has almost magical effects in reducing the symptoms of depression and makes it much easier to begin to tackle the causes.

It is not difficult to see that unless the causes are tackled, for instance, social isolation, poor capacity for empathy, over-attachment to a possessive and intrusive mother, or perhaps an abusive distant father, all the symptom relief in the world will not make much difference in the long run.

Denial is a word in common usage that has a specific meaning in psychology.

Remember that depression does not always make someone look 'sad'. A depressed person may be 'in denial' and have blocked off awareness of their stressful circumstances because they are too painful, or perhaps impossible to deal with. They may indeed be 'in denial' of the fact that they are depressed. For instance, it is not uncommon for young people who have been seriously abused by a parent to tell you that the abusing parent is a wonderful person and everything is fine.

It is often the case that the more 'ill' a person is, the more they are likely to be unaware of the nature of their illness. For example severe anorexics, who are literally starving to death, will frequently tell you that there is nothing the matter with them. Their illness has solved the problem of controlling their lives and others around them, so as far as they are concerned, there is no problem. The fact that they are unable to feed themselves normally and are so dependent that they need other people to keep them alive is subject to 'denial'. They become the controllers and dictators of 'reality'.

This somewhat paradoxical effect of serious mental illness is understandable when you consider that remaining unaware of a painful, overwhelming, or impossible to manage reality enables a person to remain functional to some extent. Danger points occur when a person starts to become more aware of the reality of their situation; when the 'denial' or dissociation begins to fail and awareness seeps through (see Resnik 2005).

'Denial' is a term borrowed from psychodynamic psychotherapy and refers to the process by which we keep ourselves unaware of a causative factor in our mental distress, or the fact that there is something that needs attention. A heavy drinker, for instance, may be 'in denial' of the amount they really drink, 'genuinely' making themselves believe that it is an ordinary or safe amount. Another example is the recent (2009) global 'Credit Crunch' in which the underlying causative factors were ignored until a 'meltdown' occurred. 'Denial' is a form of self-deception.

Dissociation is another term that you might like to familiarise yourself with. It can be thought of as an extreme form of 'denial' where the subject becomes unaware of their own mental contents and, in a sense, does not know their own mind. It is a common feature of psychosis and the more severe forms of mental illness. Sometimes, dissociated feelings are referred to as 'split off' from awareness.

Just because someone is unaware of their own thoughts and feelings does not mean that these thoughts and feelings are not still active. We could say that there is an 'active out-of-awareness'. Very strong and poisonous feelings like severe jealousy and envy are the kind of feelings and emotions most commonly subject to dissociation.

Bear in mind, though, that all of these mental processes are present in varying degrees in all of us at some time. If you want to work with distressed young people it will help you to begin to think about what the young person is having difficulty in holding in mind, and to start to differentiate between ordinary thinking and thinking that is subject to high levels of denial and dissociation; but do get some skilled help and further training if you want to engage in such work in any depth.

This all may appear to be rather grim news (although remember that the mind is 'plastic' and capable of change) so let us turn for a moment to a more optimistic version of events. Of course human life being what it is, there are no perfect environments or perfect families to produce perfectly happy people, but it occurred to me that, in order to make a point of reference, it would be handy to have a model of a 'good enough family', by which we can get a sense of proportion.

So what follows, whilst not quite being a fairy story, represents only the bare bones or structure within which a healthy child might grow. I stress again that this is for demonstration purposes only, not in any sense as an achievable ideal, still less something to measure yourself or your children personally up against. But don't try this at home! Measuring yourself up against others is nearly always a failure strategy . . . you're bound to fail.

I have used a boy's name to avoid the s/he term, but with some modifications, the story below could just as easily apply to a girl. The term 'parents' has been left with unspecific genders and indeterminate numbers, as virtually all healthy psychological functions can be fulfilled by either men or women, single or together. Actual situations have been left deliberately somewhat vague as I am only illustrating a few specific points at the moment. You can insert the story into any setting you like, or any income bracket.

CASE STUDY

A good enough childhood

Sam is born to a man and a woman who are physically healthy with little history of physical or mental illness in their respective families. His parents have a warm, safe home with enough to eat, and they are not overly stressed or concerned about their jobs, money or immediate environment. The parents have a good network of local friends and feel a sense of belonging and connection to their local community. They do not feel envious of people who earn more than they do, but feel content that they do well enough and are much the same as most of their neighbours, and that that is more or less ok.

As a baby, Sam is well looked after physically and his parents spend a lot of time playing with him and 'tuning in' to his attempts to communicate his needs. At first, before he is able to speak, he communicates by crying and moving his limbs, and his parents start to understand what he is trying to say by being sensitive to the feelings that are stirred up or induced in them.

Sam's distress is felt as their distress, although the adults are not overwhelmed by these strong feelings, and are able to think about what is going on. They sometimes take appropriate actions, if possible, so that Sam starts to feel that there is a presence 'out there' that can help and understand him and respond to his needs, especially as he is helpless and hardly able to do anything for himself.

Very gradually, over time, Sam becomes able to articulate his needs and feelings in words, just as his parents are able to. It is as if he takes inside himself his parents' capacity to translate feelings into words and internalises the ability to communicate his feelings in words to others. He also learns to 'tune in' to the feelings of others and to listen to their attempts to describe their feelings in words, just like his parents do with him.

He also discovers, to his disappointment, that not all feelings can be alleviated; some unpleasant and painful feelings, like those which arise when his parents are not there when he wants them, or when things don't go the way he wants . . . just have to be tolerated and thought about.

He learns to deal with the frustration and disappointment when his parents fail him, as will happen in the ordinary course of events, and thereby becomes accepting of imperfections in himself and others.

Through this process of being understood by others, by his parents especially, Sam crucially begins to develop the ability to understand himself and others. At least one of his parents is usually around, so he gets the idea that there is almost always a safe person in his immediate environment who can be trusted to look after him and protect him. Thus he grows in confidence and the ability to trust others. Feeling safe, his anxiety levels are low, and thus he is in a good frame of mind to learn and think and empathise with others.

There is some evidence that this capacity for 'empathy' is actually 'hard-wired' into the developing brain of the infant in the right pre-frontal hemisphere during the first two years of life (Schore, 2003). The development of empathy is dependent on the child's having been empathised with itself. If this 'window' is as precise as it appears, the implications for childcare are profound.

When he is 3 years old, his parents have another child. Sam feels angry at losing the full and total attention of his parents, but is helped to understand that although his feelings are understandable, he must not act on them; instead, it is better to help look after a helpless baby, as he was looked after himself, and not to hurt it out of anger and jealousy.

He is already able to understand, to some extent, the feelings and vulnerabilities of others and is able to begin to feel and express a benign, tolerant and considerate attitude. He learns to keep his hatred under control, and, feeling sure of the safe attention of his loving and protective parents, his angry feelings gradually pass into curiosity about the new arrival and compassion for the baby's weakness and vulnerability.

So, when Sam gets to meet and play with other children, he is not only equipped to join in with them and communicate with them, but also able to share with them and help them whilst not losing a sense of his own self. He doesn't need to 'buy friends' or bully anyone to make himself feel better. He already knows from experience that selfishness leads to unpleasant experiences all round; it is better for everyone if he is generous with his attention to others and helps them because it is, in itself, a good thing to do.

He also feels entitled to expect good treatment from others and will defend his right to be treated with respect.

CASE STUDY *continued*

Gradually, Sam begins to feel and express a genuine concern for others and a real connection with them, and feels entitled to the same in return.

He is also able to trust others to help him, as he generally trusts their motives, but also knows that other people – and he himself – do not always give the full picture, and he becomes resilient enough to accept disappointment if he feels deceived, failed, or let down by others. He likes to win at games, but doesn't worry too much if he loses, often dealing with defeat by figuring out ways to perform better next time, or just accepting that others are better than he is at that particular game.

He is allowed a good deal of freedom to explore new things and new objects, and there is usually a parent somewhere around to prevent the worst of the inevitable knocks and bumps that explorers get, and to comfort him if he gets hurt or is in pain.

In this way he is not overprotected but helped to enjoy a sense of curiosity and risk whilst keeping reasonably safe.

These are some of the 'building blocks' of a child's personality that will enable him or her to function reasonably well in the relational world of which he, and all of us, are a part.

This capacity to get along with others is a fundamental and crucial aspect of human mental health. Human beings are the most social of creatures.

There is recent research evidence which strongly suggests that social isolation can adversely affect hormone levels. Nature 'rewards' real human contact (Sigman, 2009). Face-to-face human contact also seems to positively affect rates of disease and early death, a phenomenon which was first noticed on hospital wards which treated sufferers of tuberculosis. Patients seemed to improve if they were encouraged to join social groups. The Sigman research, above, indicates that 'social networking' sites such as Facebook may actually increase isolation by substituting a 'virtual' world for a real one.

ACTIVITY **2.2**

A young girl comes to talk to a youth worker because she is lonely. In the course of talking with the youth worker, she says tearfully that she has over a thousand 'friends' on Facebook, but no friends! She feels crippled by loneliness.

Are virtual 'internet' friends the same as relationships with real people?

Specifically, what are the differences between a Facebook interaction, and those in 'real life'?

Safety and control

Returning to Sam, significantly, he would feel that the primary areas of his life are under some *thoughtful and deliberate control* by people whom he feels are consistently there to protect and help him. The parents to whom he can feel safely attached are also able to offer him *empathic attunement* and real help in expressing his feelings and thoughts in words. He is helped to have adventurous contact and play with other children, and also to negotiate any difficult feelings evoked around the birth of a brother or sister.

Sam, an imaginary child in an imaginary family is only created as a brief sketch to illustrate a few significant points; there are many other angles on child development that could be explored. The features mentioned above are not exhaustive, but they do emphasise the importance of relational and social values, such as the centrality of the ability to communicate with, and the attempt to try to understand others. Sometimes – and perhaps increasingly in our current culture – values such as these which enhance well-being, conflict with the competitive, rivalrous environment and individualistic context in which we find ourselves, leading to distress and confusion.

Attachment theory helps us to understand secure attachment as a necessary feature of human development. Secure attachment in the context of family, economic and social security and physical safety helps facilitate the growth of empathy, curiosity and the ability to understand others. Secure attachment enables the sense of feeling understood and known to develop. We could add to this a sense of continuity, of a history and a future, reliability, consistency and a feeling of personal protective 'presence' rather than virtual relationships.

With distressed young people, the significant questions regarding attachment needs are:

- Does the child have at least one safe, consistent adult figure that the child feels, and is, protected by?

- Does the child have a safe, reliable and predictable environment where the adults are consistent figures and act consistently and reliably in the child's best interests?

Note the emphasis on **attachment, consistency and reliability** here. These are simple, but key concepts in working with distressed young people.

So the ability to be flexible, to look again and again at changing circumstances and adjust your focus, is a critical area in providing a secure and emotionally healthy environment.

Holding and containing: two key concepts

A baby is 'held' in its mother's arms, and the mother 'contains' the baby's unprocessed and inarticulate feelings in order that they can be given words and thought about. A growing child and young person need to be 'held' by supportive family and social structures so that feelings can be 'contained' and thought about.

Unless there is a 'holding environment' where the child feels safe and secure, feelings cannot be thought about with any degree of consistency and intelligent management. Children need help with understanding, thinking about, controlling and communicating feelings, especially strong emotions like anger and sexual feelings, and in order to do this they need to feel safely 'held' so that feelings can be sustained and thought about.

Holding refers to the child's experience of their environment, and the ways in which a child is enabled to feel safe and secure. This will include, if necessary, the firm assertion of boundaries, limits and behavioural norms in the settings in which the young person lives and grows. In other words, their physical and psychological safety, including safe attachments to trusted adults. It is fundamentally a psychological process; it does not imply physical contact or even a building.

Containing refers to the feelings, often inarticulate, that are experienced within the young person and which can only be thought about and reflected upon safely within the context of a reliable holding environment. Containment will very often require the presence of an adult who is able to attune empathically to the feelings of the young person and thereby help them to give words to the feelings themselves, and give them a 'place to put their thoughts'.

Holding comes first. It may be in the setting of a family home, a youth club or up a mountain. **Containing** is a process which can occur satisfactorily only if a holding environment is maintained.

Distressed children and young people need special thought and consideration in this regard, and we shall say more about this later in the book.

Holding for the youth worker

It must be remembered that youth workers working with young people also need to feel 'held', and to feel safe in a reliable and supportive working setting, otherwise their capacity to work with distressed young people will be severely impaired. Designing, creating and maintaining a 'holding environment' for staff is an essential management function, characterised by good staff support, supervision and care given to practical matters like reliable funding.

Problems stemming from lack of strong early attachments can easily be triggered by the uncertainty and challenges of adolescence. Fortunately, adolescence offers an opportunity to resolve earlier difficulties by providing safe attachment figures to assist the transition into adulthood.

Youth and community workers are one of the groups of professional youth workers who may find themselves in the position of becoming an important attachment figure to a distressed young person.

This is clearly a situation in which a youth worker can be in great danger of compounding problems by poor professional management of attachment issues. Access to continuing professional training, reflective practice groups and consultancy are vital to enable the youth worker to be 'held' in order to function safely and manage powerful feelings adequately.

ACTIVITY 2.3

Group discussion

Using your experience, can you add to the list of factors that go to make up a 'holding environment' for youth and community workers working with distressed young people? What do you need to enable you to function in a comfortable and reflective way?

Do you consider regular staff meetings and reflective practice groups to be an essential part of this?

More social factors

The Good Childhood Inquiry (2009) commissioned by the Children's Society concludes that children's lives in Britain have become 'more difficult than in the past', adding that 'more young people are anxious and troubled'.

According to the panel, 'excessive individualism' is to blame for many of the problems children face, and needs to be replaced by a value system where people seek satisfaction more from helping others than pursuing private advantage.

Strong feelings

Young people need help with understanding, thinking about, controlling and communicating feelings, especially strong emotions like anger and sexual feelings.

They also need to feel loved and appreciated, and to be a valued part of a family group which is itself related to a wider social network. Later, children need to feel able to be part of a supportive peer and friendship group. If a child lacks connection to a benign and supportive family group, they may well take a dysfunctional peer group, for instance the gang culture of anorexics or a delinquent 'gang', to be their social reference point, offering them an identity and a 'social role'.

Skilled, relevant and practical group work is one of the key areas in successful youth and community work interventions with distressed young people.

Groupwork which enables young people to become part of a group that has fun, is socially constructive, where they have a valued role and feel that they can contribute something to others and to the achievements of the group is of great benefit to young people who are struggling to find a place in the world. (This is the answer to the question about Jamie, in Chapter 1 on page 15.)

ACTIVITY 2.4

Are social networking sites the same as face-to-face interactions? Could you be alone in your room and still get human contact through a computer?

What does 'dissociation' mean? Think of an example with yourself or someone you know.

What does 'in denial' mean? Think of an example. Can you think of a time when someone you know is clearly not aware of something they are doing that is self-destructive or damaging in some way? This could apply to you as well.

What do we mean by social values?

Think back to when you were a child. What values were most prevalent in your family, your school and your peer group?

Is it true that helping others makes us more happy than helping ourselves?

It is central to some political philosophy that society should ideally consist of self-interested individuals in competition with each other. This seems to run counter to the view that 'excessive individualism' causes difficulties for children. What do you think of this apparent contradiction?

C H A P T E R   R E V I E W

In this chapter, we looked at some of the optimal conditions necessary for healthy child development.

In particular, the fundamental concepts of holding and containing were outlined and emphasised as essential aspects of optimal psychological child development.

FURTHER READING

Bowlby, J (1973) *Attachment and Loss.* London: Hogarth Press.

This is an absolute classic and is quite accessible.

Children's Society, The (2009) *The Good Childhood Inquiry.* London: The Children's Society.

An interesting report that touches on many of the themes in this chapter.

Gerhardt, S (2004) *Why Love Matters.* London: Routledge.

An in-depth, accessible account of the importance of empathy and attunement in the early years.

Lasch, C (1986) *The Culture of Narcissism.* New York: Norton.

A groundbreaking work published in the 1980s that picked up, very early, the themes of individualism and 'selfishness' that are common currency today.

USEFUL WEBSITES

www.guardian.co.uk/science/2010/mar19/evolution-darwin-natural-selection-genes-wrong

www.thecrimson.com/article/2006/12/14/alarm-over-antidepressants-antidepressants-may-cause/

http://changingminds.org/disciplines/psychoanalysis/concepts/true_false_self.htm

Chapter 3

Young people who are disturbed, distressed and difficult

CHAPTER OBJECTIVES

By the end of this chapter you will have:

- explored the often perplexing and problematic ways in which young people communicate their distress;
- explored attachment responses and learning theory;
- examined the concept of projective identification;
- explored basic assumption groups.

In this chapter, we will explore some of the often perplexing and problematic ways in which young people communicate their distress. The descriptions of specific behaviours is by no means exhaustive, as distress is communicated in ways that are very specific to circumstances, and that are heavily dependent on the culture and time that the child grows up in. To give you a rough example, a young person today may say that they feel depressed, whereas a few hundred years ago they may have said that they felt possessed by an evil spirit.

Distress and difficult behaviour is usually an attempt to communicate something that the young person finds hard to put into words. We shall be looking at *concepts* that help us to understand distressed behaviour to frame and think about helpful structures and interventions, and to explore some ways of thinking about young people who apparently reject help.

The case studies and short case studies in this section, as in the other parts of the book, are based in real events with details changed to preserve anonymity.

CASE STUDY

A broken bicycle

Simon, a 13-year-old boy in a children's home, has had a very long history of disrupted attachments (see the section on safe attachments in Chapter 1). His mother is a heavy drug user and was unable to give him much in the way of empathic, attuned care when he was an infant. He never knew his father, although he knew of his father's existence. His mother's serial boyfriends paid him little attention and were frequently openly hostile to him.

CASE STUDY *continued*

Due to his mother's further decline, Simon was fostered at the age of two, already past the optimal time for healthy early empathic development (Schore), and already at that young age showing difficult and disturbed behaviour, throwing frequent tantrums and expressing inconsolable tearful rage. He drove several well-meaning foster parents to the edge of distraction, leading to rejection, the breakdown of placements, further disruptions and more breaking of Simon's very delicate 'affectional bonds'. He frequently induced and evoked feelings of rage and helplessness – and rejection – in carers. His behaviour made him unbearable in groups of other children and resulted in his exclusion from school.

Eventually, at 13, he found himself in an exceptionally well-run children's home. It was comfortable and safe. The staff were well trained and reliable; there was a low staff turnover, and they met regularly together to think about the feelings that the children induced in them.

One Christmas, two of the therapeutic workers involved with Simon and touched by his long history of neglect and deprivation, clubbed together and bought him a bicycle, as they knew he would dearly like one. They joyfully presented it to him. As soon as he was left alone with the bike, he took it to pieces and threw the bits around all over the lawn.

The workers were distraught; their loving and thoughtful gesture had been destroyed and they felt angry, hopeless and rejected. They also felt deeply disappointed, denigrated, and treated with contempt.

It would have been easy to react with anger and punishment. But the staff thought about it. They had regular meetings together as a staff team at the beginning and end of each day, and regular meetings with an external consultant who could help them see events more objectively and to think conceptually. They came to understand that, without his being aware of it, Simon was forcing his feelings of anger, rejection and disappointment into them in an unconscious attempt to communicate his broken inner world. **This is an attempt to seek out empathy and attunement.**

Simon had also re-enacted a situation where a loving gesture had been treated with contempt, this time with him in the driving seat, so to speak.

Paradoxically, and confusingly, it is often when a young person experiences reliable 'holding and containment' that all the previous horrors of their broken attachments and traumas re-emerge with force. It is as if this happens when it is safe to do so.

Another difficult problem which arises when working with distressed young people is that when testing behaviour has diminished, the storm is apparently over, and the young person experiences safe and reliable holding and containment and settles down, it can be imagined that problems are over and that all will be well. However, this can be wishful thinking; it takes a very long time for seriously distressed young people to build up a safe 'inner world', and for the most damaged it may be almost an impossible task.

The safe inner world is built up by repeated, safely held and contained experiences of:

- attachment;

- separation;

- reattachment.

This is an incremental process and may need to continue for a very long time; it is not a cognitively learned process; it is internalised by repeated experience.

Another confusing dynamic that can occur is that when an attachment is re-made, a young person may not respond with gratitude, but with *protest*. A youth worker may be ignored, or treated with disdain. The young person may be responding with distress and reacting to the *separation* rather than the reunion.

Wishful thinking?

It is a crucial point to bear in mind that a young person may be more settled because they feel safe, and protected, but that if the reliable and psychologically attuned 'holding environment' is changed or withdrawn too soon they may well be pitched straight back into the psychological state they were in before, leading to a chronic and demoralising 'revolving door' situation.

Feeling safer and more secure, after a while, the young person settles down, becomes more able to think about feelings and communicate them, becomes better able to get along with others and manage relationships with authority. Social interaction becomes better and the situation looks brighter.

Adults, who want to believe that integrated change has happened for once and for all, may withdraw or alter services available to the young person, and may not be aware that it is the actual provision of the services themselves and the development of healthier relationships that are enabling the young person to function better. Change in the young person may be only superficial alterations in the young person's behavioural responses which are actually the result of their feeling safer and better understood. With very damaged young people, the process of helping them to build a safe inner world is incremental and can take a very long time indeed.

Attachment responses and learning theory: a fundamental and essential difference

There is a crucial distinction here that it is essential to understand; otherwise much practical work will go to waste.

Distressed, reactive behaviours due to attachment disturbances are not amenable to being solved by teaching a young person better behaviour.

It is a fundamental error to think otherwise. As John Bowlby puts it, unless you understand this important distinction, your efforts to teach better behaviour are likely to be experienced as disapproving and irrelevant (Bowlby, 1973, p375).

Learning theory does not help us much in cases of disturbed attachments. The distressed young person cannot 'learn' or be taught better behaviour, except in the most superficial sense, and may even develop a convincing 'coping' or compliant 'false self' as a result (see Chapter 1 for definitions of false self). She is, in fact, at the mercy of her powerful and overwhelming feelings of fright and anxiety, and will express these fears usually by some sort of disturbing behaviour that forces adults to become preoccupied with her, such as a severe eating disorder (a perverse form of attachment), or by withdrawal. It is actually the underlying difficulties of achieving a safe, empathic, attuned attachment with a protective adult that need to be addressed.

Attachment disorders, by definition, almost always involve the early absence or loss of a reliable empathic relationship with an adult felt to be safe and protective; therefore the capacity to think about feelings and empathise with others may be impaired. Because of this difficulty in symbolising feelings by putting them into words, communication of distress due to disturbed attachments is frequently by means of projective identification.

Projective identification is a vital and extremely important concept and is well worth taking some time to understand.

Projective identification

The mode of *communicating by inducing strong feelings in others* is called *projective identification*. It is as if the young person *puts these feelings into others* in an attempt to gain empathic understanding (remember Jamie and his putting his 'impossible dilemma' into the police?). This process, which may seem odd and difficult to understand at first, seems to occur mainly by means of induction.

The template for this process is the way in which a baby, before it is able to speak, induces feelings in the parent as a means of communication. Incidentally, most arts, especially drama and music, operate at a similar level of inducing feelings and mental states in the audience.

Projective identification is a very important concept in work with distressed and disturbed young people. It might seem like rather a strange idea to start with, but if you see it as a way of a young person attempting to communicate distress when they are unable to express emotions and feelings in words, then you are half way there.

Can't think straight?

Of special note is the fact that if you are on the receiving end of projective identification, you will find it very difficult to think about what is going on. By definition, feelings and emotions that are communicated in this way are hard to process and think about because your mind is being affected by the mind of another person. Feelings and mental states projected *into* you will, by definition, make it difficult to maintain your usual thought processes.

Expert supervision has a vital place to play here, and we shall discuss this essential aspect of work with distressed young people later in the book.

If you are finding it 'difficult to think straight' when relating to a young person, you could well be experiencing the effects of projective identification.

Rage and repetition

Rage at rejections and disappointments, although often powerfully overwhelming feelings in themselves, may emerge most strongly when there is something 'good' to measure them up against. It is then that the sense of loss is at its greatest, and one often apparently incomprehensible 'solution' for the young person is to destroy the current 'good' and helpful relationship to avoid feeling the intense loss and pain of what has been missed out on. This can appear as a very contradictory series of events, often extremely perplexing and confusing for the surrounding adults, especially those in helping roles. The young person appears to destroy the help that is on offer, to act destructively towards that which they most need.

Also, once a safe and reliable relationship is found, *the terror of losing something that is so desperately needed* is so profound that the relationship may not be accepted with gratitude for fear of losing it, or having it taken away, as has happened in the past. In the mind of the child, this fear may not be consciously linked to the earlier losses, which makes thinking about the current situation doubly difficult. Even if the current situation for the young person is actually safe and reliable, in their mind it may well be fraught with terrible dangers of impending catastrophic loss.

Children and young people who have experienced separation trauma and perhaps multiple bond-breaking frequently exhibit testing behaviour. In order to feel safe they may test adults to the limits to try to reduce their severe anxieties about being rejected and abandoned. The tragedy is that these behaviours can be so extreme that the young person actually *is* rejected, thereby repeating and confirming their expectations. Children who have been serially traumatised by separation and rejection may repeat the trauma by serially traumatising their caretakers and others around them, thus compounding and multiplying the problem. This is a tragic and desperate situation that needs careful thought and management by well trained, well supported and resilient workers.

Overdetermined

Distressing and disturbing behaviour usually has a number of determining causes. A technical shorthand word for this is to say that distressing behaviour is *overdetermined*, in other words, it has several causes operating at once.

Many distressed young people have experienced multiple traumas in the course of their developmental cascade. They may well be affected by a number of interrelated negative influences on their development acting all at the same time and all influencing each other.

CASE STUDY

Roy

Roy's mother suffered from severe post-natal depression, and was an intermittent heavy drinker and drug user, both of which impaired her ability to relate in an empathic and attuned way to her child. She would sometimes disappear for a few days leaving Roy in the care of a young relative.

Roy's father was absent for long periods, and when he was home, he and Roy's mother fought, sometimes physically. He would attack Roy verbally, and sometimes slap him if he showed any signs of distress or dissent. Roy spent much of his early years in states of fear, and developed nervous tics and a stammer.

Due to the lack of empathic attunement, he found thinking about his emotions very diffi-cult; parental models of dealing with conflict and strong emotions were poor and this led to problematic relations with other children. His trust in parental and authority figures was understandably impaired, creating difficulties with teachers and other helpful adults. He felt himself to be hateful as his father hurt and rejected him.

It is very rare to find only one 'causative factor' when trying to understand distressed young people. Roy's experiences constitute multiple developmental trauma and tend towards dissociation as a way of coping.

CASE STUDY

Jane

Jane is an attractive and superficially confident girl of sixteen, apparently with lots of friends and acquaintances. She is quite sporty, and an accomplished violinist. Her parents are comfortably off and they live a relaxed and somewhat bohemian lifestyle with maxi-mum freedom for the three children, of whom Jane is the eldest. Her mother is a psychologist who believes that children should explore life and make their own decisions from an early age. Father is busy, friendly but distant. Jane is expected to go to a 'good' university, like her parents.

Jane, however, is secretly starving herself, bingeing and vomiting. She is totally preoccu-pied in her mind with achieving and maintaining what she believes to be her 'perfect weight', often weighing herself over thirty times a day. She becomes preoccupied with how she is measuring up to other girls, always finding that someone is thinner than she is, and having, therefore, to become thinner than them.

If she cannot compete, or becomes envious of another girl's thinness, Jane copes with the painful feelings by cutting herself, gaining some relief from the pain by locating the painful feelings in her body and 'controlling' them there. She is also preoccupied with 'germs' and 'cleanliness'.

After a period of intense depression when she seriously considers suicide, she eventually talks to a youth worker about what is going on. She begins to think about the desperate confusion that has arisen in her mind from having to make her own mind up about 'everything' from a very young age, without guidance.

She has also recently and secretly become involved in a sexual affair with a married friend of her father's, and has intensely ambivalent feelings about this. She feels 'special' but at the same time feels that she is doing something very wrong. Her parents encourage her 'freedom', but she knows they would actually be horrified if they knew what she was really doing.

CASE STUDY *continued*

In reality, Jane feels extremely angry with her parents for not protecting her and for being blind to what is going on; at the same time she blames herself for having sexual feelings, being secretive and for getting involved, which has caused her to feel guilty and 'grubby and stained' as she put it.

She feels profoundly out of control, and in desperation displaces these feelings into obsessive control of her body weight, controlling painful feelings by preoccupation with binging, starving and self-harm. When she cuts herself, she feels that this pain is under her control, whereas the painful feelings of guilt and loneliness are not. She counteracts her feelings of being 'grubby and stained' by her preoccupation with germs and cleanliness.

Do be clear that there is not a direct 'cause and effect' between specific emotional difficulties and specific problems and behaviours. The emergence of *any* strong emotion or feeling can be deflected or controlled by preoccupation and obsession with the body (or something else) and any unbearable feelings may be induced in the other and felt to be got rid of by means of projective identification.

Having said that, however, difficulties in coping with sexual feelings, feeling fearful and unprotected, anger, and competitive jealously frequently play a very strong part in the causation of distress in young people.

As if family and developmental problems were not enough, there is another factor to be added to the mix when attempting to help. What follows may have special relevance when a young person experiences themselves as inadequate, damaged or diminished in some way.

Envy and re-enactment

It is one of the most soul-destroying of experiences to have one's attempts to understand and help rejected or ruined by the person you are trying to help. It may feel strange to consider that this contradictory reaction can be due to envy.

Envy is a deeply problematic process, but it can account for the paradoxical appearance of destructiveness when help is at hand. It can be a very difficult concept to grasp, but can also be very useful in understanding negative reactions to attempts to help. Envy is often *unconscious*, or 'out of awareness' of the young person, which is an added complication, requiring careful thought. It is also a concept that is very easy to mis-apply, so it is worthwhile spending some time trying to understand it.

Put quite simply, if you have something that I think I need, and I feel deprived of it, this may induce in me feelings of deprivation or inadequacy. If you offer me something, with generosity, it reminds me, maybe even 'rubs it in' that I do not possess what you have, thereby heightening my feelings of inadequacy and envy of what you have. Your generosity may also arouse my envy of your capacity to give generously. I may deal with this by destroying or 'rubbishing' what you are offering, thereby gaining a feeling of control and perhaps superiority, and so diminishing my feelings of inadequacy. This is the destructive aspect of envy – quite deservedly one of the 'seven deadly sins' (see Epstein, 2003).

This is a difficult concept, as envy operates 'invisibly' and it requires careful thought to understand and apply properly. It is one of the concepts that may help us to understand Simon's relationship to the bicycle gift, and his relationship to the two generous youth workers. The two youth workers had both the means and the generosity of spirit to make a loving gift. Simon did not have the means or the generosity to receive it, due to his earlier deprivations.

This paradox seems to fly against common sense: one might expect *gratitude* when presented with something, especially a relationship that gives you something that you have never had, or have felt deprived of.

But gratitude, it seems, can only be experienced fully when the receiver has minimal feelings of envy of the giver. Envy, like jealousy, is an extremely difficult feeling to articulate; so difficult that it is often rationalised and kept out of awareness, or *dissociated* (see Chapter 2). In other words, separated off from the conscious mind.

Fortunately, in Simon's case, the staff persevered with good results, painstakingly helping him to put the bike back together, talking with him about his feelings, and to some extent helping him to begin to build a more constructive inner and relational world than his distress and rage was in danger of destroying.

Let us not forget that originally it is the *child's loving feelings* that are rejected, destroyed and broken when attachments are disrupted or when he is brought up in an abusive environment. If he is not 'held' and his feelings 'contained' and given words, he is likely to feel rejected and humiliated by the experience. He may then re-enact this situation with caretaking adults on the receiving end, unconsciously communicating his distress by evoking feelings of rejection and humiliation in the adults. This is a wordless, but powerful form of communication.

In Simon's case, the rejection of the workers' 'loving feelings' could be thought of, or conceptualised as a re-enactment of a rejection. When a child is traumatised by rejection, and this is out of awareness, the trauma may be re-enacted with the child as the rejecter, thus communicating the feelings of rejection by evoking them in the caregiver, but tragically destroying what is so desperately needed.

Another frequently encountered re-enactment is when the child or young person puts the adult in an impossible situation. As we have seen, distressed and particularly abused children often experience themselves as being in impossible situations, for instance, as having to choose between two warring parents, or being trapped in an abusive relationship with an adult whom they also depend on.

A paradoxical injunction

It has been noted that disturbed mothers may show a high level of communication by 'paradoxical injunction', that is, telling their children to do the impossible. For instance, in the case of Jane, above, she was told to 'be free' but Jane also knew that her mother would condemn the choices she actually made. The paradoxical injunction was 'be free and do what you like, but only in the ways that I find acceptable'. An example that is often given of a paradoxical injunction is to give an order . . . 'be spontaneous . . . NOW!'

This creates a 'double bind' situation where following a request or conforming to an expectation will lead to its negation or its opposite.

These sorts of communications, usually made unwittingly, can literally drive you mad.

ACTIVITY 3.1

A 15-year-old girl persistently walks out of a classroom in the middle of a lesson, sauntering seductively past the young male teacher on her way to the door. The teacher cannot touch her for fear of reprisals or a complaint. Neither can he just let her go. In that moment, he feels paralysed, ashamed and powerless to act. Later, it transpired that a relative was sexually abusing the girl.

  Is the teacher caught in a 'double bind'?

  Is this also an example of projective identification?

  How do you think you might have dealt with this situation?

Young people are programmed to reach out to make attachments and seek empathic attunement and approval in a trusting and loving way from the adults who look after them. This originally includes parents and other caretakers in the child's world, and later on from other children and adults and people in authority.

If this reaching out is met with neglect, hostility or other forms of rejection and abuse, then great damage is caused to the child's inner sense of trust and safety. They may well re-enact traumatic situations, push unbearable feelings back into themselves, project their feelings into others and otherwise test out the capacity of adults and their peers to tolerate and contain them. Shattered inner worlds can often only be healed with painstaking effort and immense tolerance.

But . . . this tolerance does not include accepting physically abusive or dangerous behaviour, which has to be limited and 'boundaried' to keep a safe 'holding' environment. Adults and other children must never become 'punchbags' for aggressive or violent behaviour.

Ordinary social norms must apply at all times with regard to physically damaging or violent behaviour, especially if directed towards persons. Emotionally and physically damaging behaviour, such as bullying, also requires active intervention.

> ### CASE STUDY
>
> ### *Shazia*
>
> *15-year-old Shazia comes to a youth worker saying that her friend and class mate Kalina is cutting herself on her arms. Shazia thinks that Kalina is also drinking vodka and has talked about wanting to kill herself. Kalina refuses outright to get help, saying that everyone will think that she is mad and that her parents would kill her if they found out that she was talking about family matters outside of the family.*
>
> *Shazia is terrified and worried about her friend. It is as if Kalina has pushed her feelings into Shazia, but Shazia has a good sense to talk the situation over with the youth worker to sort out what she can do, what she can't do and to decide upon the limits of her responsibility.*

> ### ACTIVITY 3.2
>
> *As the youth worker, what would you do? How would you manage the situation?*

Paradoxically many behaviours, such as self-harm and eating disorders, for instance, or delinquency, *force* adults to be preoccupied with the young person whilst the young person can remain in denial or unaware of their need for connection to adults. Their dependency needs may be so strong as to be *dissociated*. Some severe anorexics, for example, who need constant care to keep them alive, will at the same time assert that they are quite alright and only need to be left alone to get better (thus placing adults in an impossible situation, as outlined above; if the adult takes the wishes of the young person at face value, the result will be the death of the young person). As in the case of the young driver in Chapter 1, the young person may force adults to take notice of them by means of some activity that grabs the adults' attention, and maybe even has the quality of 'invading' the mind of the adult.

This can be very dangerous for adults working with distressed children, and the main reason why adequate staff meetings and 'case discussion' are essential for adults working in these areas (see Chapter 6).

> *We should remember that what the distressed child actually does, is not as important psychologically as the feelings that the child evokes in those closest to them. Adults need to be able to **think** about the feelings that are **evoked** in them, and to wonder if these feelings are an attempt at communication by the child of their internal state. But do bear in mind the paragraphs above. Thinking about what is going on also means that ordinary behavioural **boundaries** must be kept.*

Now for the easier, more logical and less paradoxical part of our conceptual journey. This process of *evoking feelings in others* is analogous to what goes on in the **empathic**

relationship between a parent and a young child that is described in the previous chapter. When things go well, the parent is able to *empathically attune* to the feelings of the child, and the child **gradually becomes enabled to think about feelings and communicate feelings in words.** This is a difficult process at the best of times, and is usually only partially achieved, even in the most favourable of circumstances.

However, when things go badly wrong, the results can be disastrous. The child may well be left with all sorts of terrifying feelings that they desperately try to communicate to others, but be ill-equipped to do so. If the child lacks **an empathically attuned relationship in the context of a reliable attachment**, they will be severely impaired in their capacity to put feelings into words and to communicate feelings to others. With no access to words to describe feelings, a frightened young person may well *communicate fear by evoking fear in others.* This is a *primitive form of attempting an empathic connection.* A terrified child may evoke terror in others. A confused child may evoke confusion. A child who has experienced multiple traumas may evoke the experience of multiple traumas in others, a child who has been put in impossible situations with no way out or apparent solution may also evoke in others feelings of being in an impossible situation with no apparent solution; helpless and hopeless.

Violent and aggressive behaviour may well be a distorted attempt to evoke deep feelings of fear and terror in others as a form of communication.

A recent perpetrator of a knife crime had a background of severe neglect, physically threatening abuse, and abandonment. This fearful and terrified teenager evoked fear and terror in all around him, eventually resulting in a murder. Again, this is mentioned not in any way to excuse any form of violent behaviour, but to further a conceptual understanding of a very damaging process that may well end in tragedy for the young person and others around them.

Once a neglected, psychologically damaged child has reached adolescence, change can be a very difficult and arduous process. A detailed discussion of therapy would be out of place in this current book; these concepts are intended to be helpful in gaining some ways of thinking about distressing and disturbing behaviour and the underlying processes.

It is important to recognise that, to some extent, human life is full of problems and dilemmas, and that we each resolve – constantly – the difficulties of human existence on a daily basis. All of us have to deal with issues of attachment, connection and disconnection throughout our lives, and manage these difficult problems for better or for worse. Deep problems, like the ones described here in the case of Simon, are *exaggerations and amplifications* of issues that we all face in one form or another, from birth through to the final separation of death.

Resolution

The good news, however, is that whilst there is no way of magically turning the clock back and making traumatic separations and abuses 'un-happen' as it were, there is a way forward.

The way through is by creating situations in which the young person can:

- feel safe in terms of a good *enough holding environment.* A good holding environment has the qualities of consistency and reliability;

- feel that the *attempt* is being made to understand them in terms of empathic attunement. This eventually enables the containment of strong feelings.

This does not mean that we have to make smart 'therapeutic' interpretations about the past and so on, although at the right time some linking of current problems with past experiences may be of some help.

The key is to find ways of creating *holding environments* where a young person can feel that genuine attempts are being made to understand them.

It is useful to remember that it is the *attempt to understand* that is most important. We do not have to be able to fully understand: it is the genuine attempt that is crucial.

CASE STUDY

Informal free-group discussion

A youth club boys' soccer team is taken on a training run by a youth worker acting as football coach. The team is well established, has more or less the same players week in week out and meets at regular times in the week for matches and training. However, several of the boys have been exhibiting quite distressed behaviour of late. In particular, one of the boys, Vince, has been getting into a lot of fights and has been bullying younger, smaller boys. Their training run takes them up a steep hill overlooking the town where the boys live, and they collapse exhausted at the top. The boys look down over the town below and begin to pick out their houses and the houses of their friends. Vince says 'that's where I live, there'. Then, pointing some distance away, he says, angrily 'and that's where my Dad lives . . . the f*****g ba***rd. I want to kill him'. The youth worker and the other boys are taken aback by the forcefulness of Vince's outburst, but nobody says anything. A silence ensues, and nobody moves. The youth leader experiences a mixture of emotions: shock, anxiety, confusion . . . he thinks about the feelings evoked in him and wonders if Vince is feeling something similar. After a while, the youth leader comments gently: 'so, your parents are separated, and that must be really tough?' There is a general murmur in the group. It turns out that almost everyone's parents are separated. A discussion ensues about what it is like to have separated parents, and the boys' different experiences of family breakup. Some of them talk about missing their dads. At one point, Vince says, 'My dad used to hit my mum, that's why he had to go. He used to hit me too . . . still does, if he can get hold of me'.

The youth leader remembers stopping Vince chasing and whacking a frightened smaller boy with a corner flag, but doesn't say anything.

The discussion about parents continues for some time until it is too dark and cold to go on. The youth leader quietly tunes into the emotions and feelings in the group. His ability to stay with the feelings in the group without influencing or 'getting in the way' enable the group to feel safe about expressing painful thoughts and feelings that it would have been difficult to communicate otherwise. The presence of a safe adult who is able to tolerate difficult and disturbing feelings enables the group to communicate with each other, each feeling a little more understood and a little less alone as a result.

This is an example of informal free-group discussion which can take place spontaneously if the conditions are favourable. The football coach had not intended this discussion to happen, but was aware enough to realise that the boys felt safe and 'held' enough by the situation – the football group was reliable and consistent – to allow something further to happen, in this case, emotional communication and the attempt to understand each other in a deeper way. If the situation had not felt safe and 'holding' enough, then it would have been better for the youth worker not to make his initial comment in case the emotions were not able to be 'contained' by the setting.

Afterwards, the youth worker began to wonder if Vince's bullying was an attempt **to induce in others** the feelings that he experienced in his relationship with his father. Again, this does not excuse anything, and bullying should of course be intervened in and, where possible, stopped, but the youth worker's thoughts, and the attempt to understand and empathise with Vince began a process of exploring with him how his experiences with his father tended to shape his own relationships with smaller children. In turn, this helped Vince to start to empathise with the effects his behaviour was having on others weaker than himself instead of re-enacting the trauma.

It is clear that this process of developing empathy is extremely important. Sadly, the all too frequent news stories of child abuse that evoke the response 'how could someone do that to a child' refer to perpetrators who have never developed the capacity for empathy with their victims.

The type of informal group discussion described above can be extremely productive and can lead on to further more intensive work. Discussions begun in this form can be extended into more formal groupwork, if so wished. Young people often respond surprisingly well to an invitation to form discussion groups. This will be explored more fully later, but the key concepts are safety, management of setting, reliability, consistency, empathy, and attunement, holding and containment.

Basic Assumption Groups

When thinking about the way in which disturbances and distress are manifested and communicated in group behaviour, Bion's (1962) concepts of Basic Assumptions are very useful. Bion postulated that when anxiety is high in a group, the group will tend to respond in three basic ways. These are:

1 Fight/flight;

2 Dependency on a 'leader';

3 Pairing.

> ### *Learning outcomes*
> *Two (detached) youth workers take a group of 15 young people aged between 16 and 18 on a weekend trip to a well-appointed, comfortable residential centre in the countryside. The young people come from deprived and violent backgrounds in an inner city area and*

many have first-hand experience of domestic violence and street crime, one girl witnessing the gang murder of her older brother. The group is composed of both boys and girls. The youth workers know most of them quite well, and have developed reasonably good relationships with them.

The weekend, from a practical point of view, is an unmitigated disaster. From almost wrecking the minibus on the outward trip to trashing the residential centre and refusing to go out on any of the planned activities, the group persistently refuses to co-operate, fighting amongst themselves, running amok generally and for several hours disappearing dangerously into the night. The youth workers find themselves confused, anxious and frightened and at a loss as to how to cope.

In talking with each other about what was going on, the youth workers formed the hypothesis that perhaps these apparently streetwise young people were themselves confused, anxious and frightened by this sudden switch to a new environment. Many of them, although superficially arrogant and brash, had actually never been away from home before. Somehow, just before the time came to leave, and as the group gathered for their lift home, the youth workers with great effort managed to persuade the young people to sit down for a moment and to think about what had happened on their weekend. The group began a series of somewhat odd accusations and counter accusations. 'Sharon was scared of the dark . . . Chris only eats egg yolks, his mum only feeds him egg yolks . . . Darren was scared of ghosts . . . Mags thought people were going to come and get her . . . The level of fear and anxiety was palpable. Very largely, the disturbances and mayhem were a result of fear and anxiety about coping with a new and unfamiliar environment. The group exhibited somewhat classic 'fight/flight' behaviour, in Bion's terms.

In the bus on the way home, the mood was somewhat quieter, mainly due to exhaustion. Some of the group expressed concern and regret about what had happened and the youth workers suggested that the group meet at the youth workers' office later on in the week to talk about it. It surprised them that most of the group turned up and were keen to discuss their experience. The group wanted to continue their discussions, so the youth workers set a regular time and the group continued. The group continued to meet for over a year, discussing a whole range of matters important to them, and which worried them a great deal, including sex and their peer and family relationships.

In the example above, a true story with only some details changed to protect anonymity, it was the youth workers' ability to 'tune in' to their own feelings which gave them the clue as to what was actually going on in the group at an emotional level. In being able to conceptualise the group behaviour as 'fight/flight' they were able to conceive the behaviour as driven by fright and anxiety rather than random destructiveness or plain badness. The group adopted a mode of fighting or running away (flight) as a means of coping with anxieties about safety and emotional containment. It was the exploration of the anxieties in the group which enabled the youth workers to make a better connection with the group and to offer them a space in which to explore the problematic issues in their lives in more depth.

C H A P T E R   R E V I E W

This chapter has described some of the ways in which young people express their distress. We note causative factors of distress, such as attachment and separation issues, and look at some of the ways in which attempts to help may be disrupted. These disruptions may be due to fears of yet another loss, and also due to difficult and destructive feelings that are out of awareness, such as envy. Projective identification is discussed as a primitive form of an attempt to gain empathic understanding and communication. Lastly, using Bion's concept of Basic Assumption groups, we consider how distress and anxiety can become manifest in group situations, and how an understanding of these processes can lead to a creative resolution.

FURTHER READING

Bion, W (1962) *Experiences in Groups*. London: Tavistock Publications.

Written by Bion himself, this is a very readable (although in slightly old-fashioned language) and sometimes amusing account of some of the early days of experiential groupwork showing how his theories were arrived at.

Symington, J and Symington, N (1996) *The Clinical Thinking of Wilfred Bion*. London: Routledge.

An excellent outline of Bion's major theories. Highly recommended to anyone seeking more in depth understanding.

USEFUL WEBSITES

www.groupanalysis.org

Part Two

Practical help

Chapter 4
When things go wrong, how can we help?

CHAPTER OBJECTIVES

By the end of this chapter you will have:

- considered common problems and manifestations of distress in young people;
- examined support structures;
- explored crucial elements of staff support, supervision and training;
- considered the issue of confidentiality.

This chapter contains a description and discussion of some common problems and manifestations of distress in young people, with notes on eating disorders and depression. We will consider some helpful interventions and the circumstances in which they might be applied.

We will examine the support structures that are needed to sustain and maintain work with distressed young people, to help them to begin to deal with the fundamental tasks of dependency, independence and autonomy.

This discussion emphasises the crucial elements of staff support, supervision and training.

Key ideas: Dynamic administration, group leading, co-working, staff support, supervision and training.

Introduction

The capacity of staff members to contain, understand and work with very difficult feelings is an essential part of an environment designed to help young people in distress. The attitudes, training, continuing professional development and supervision of staff members is of the most fundamental importance.

I will make the essential point here that the term 'supervision' in the context of working with distressed young people does *not* mean line management! Unfortunately, especially in British culture, the term 'supervisor' carries with it connotations of a management function, and a 'supervisor' is someone 'official' probably with a pencil and a clipboard, who keeps an eye on a team of workers to make sure that they do their work and do not slack.

However, supervision in the context of therapeutic working with distressed young people means a person who is expert, experienced and qualified in guiding and helping others to think about the deeper *psychological* aspects of their work. Working with distressed young people requires expert help in understanding the powerful feelings and often intense emotions that are evoked in the youth worker in the course of this work. These feelings are frequently evoked on an interpersonal level; that is, *between* the youth worker and the young person. Often, feelings that are evoked in this way are so strong that the youth worker becomes unable to think clearly about what is going on and so needs external help to think about what is happening on an emotional level.

Sadly, the reality is that almost daily in the news media we learn about the most shocking abuses that adults inflict upon children and young people. We learn again and again that the young people involved have been known, sometimes for years, to social services and other professionals.

I would certainly not wish to scaremonger, or give the false impression that there are (or that I personally know of) infallible ways of spotting abused young people. Abusers, and their victims, are extremely adept at covering up what is going on; adults through manipulation and deceptions, and children and young people by developing 'false selves'. It is a mistake to think that there are certain signs of 'abuse' as there are no 'signs and symptoms' that are completely reliable indicators. However, you can make efforts to get to know a young person who is in obvious distress and has been over a period of time, and to begin, preferably helped by expert supervision, to build up a picture of what may be going on.

Spaces and structures

One of the most important aspects of working with distressed young people is the construction and maintenance of psychological 'spaces' and 'structures' that *hold and contain distressing feelings and emotions.*

These spaces are not so different in their essentials from those we normally use in every day life to structure and contain our work and our social and leisure experiences; most of the time we do not give them a second thought. However, when working with distressed young people, especially if we want to work with them in a group, which is most often the option of choice, we have to give these spaces special consideration or we will most likely fail in our attempts to help. This will be true no matter how well meaning we are, and no matter how interesting and innovative our ideas may be. The spaces needed to hold and contain strong feelings and emotions will need to be more resilient and reliable than usual, if they are to withstand the great pressure that distressed young people will place on them and the staff who work in them.

This is a good place to mention that groupwork is often *the* intervention of choice with young people, not just a way of working cost effectively with more than one person at a time. Young people need to learn how to function effectively in groups as part of the process of growing up into adults capable of being in families, work groups and teams, and social groups.

It is very significant that distressed young people are almost always impaired in their capacity to function effectively and communicate at a constructive level in groups. Remember that a person can operate apparently adequately in a social or group setting, but may be presenting an entirely false self by simply imitating the behaviour of others. Gangs may offer opportunities for such a loose form of attachment and a tenuous sense of safety and identity, but also tend to fall into 'Basic Assumption Group' patterns (Bion), as briefly described earlier.

Individuals, instead of being helped to develop by the group, are prevented from growing and maturing by a need to merge with the gang; to become the same as the others. Autonomy and individuality is not fostered; it is inhibited.

The following case study is another true story; it is somewhat extreme, but is included to show what can happen if a destructive group, based in 'basic assumption' dynamics, especially fight/flight, and dependency (on a 'leader') are allowed free rein.

CASE STUDY

The limits of fair play

A group of young people calling themselves 'Hell's Angels' approach a centre-based youth worker and ask to use one of the rooms at the centre for their 'club meetings'. The youth worker is caught somewhat off-guard by this unexpected approach. The gang leader produces a convincing argument and points out that other young people's clubs and associations are able to use the centre's rooms for meetings, so why shouldn't they be able to? The gang leader, an arrogant and articulate young man, pushes forward and insists that the Hell's Angels group is a special interest motorcycle group, just like any other special interest group. He points out that his parents live locally and pay Council Tax. There is already a badminton club on a Tuesday, a Young Women's Group meets for discussions and talks on a Wednesday; there is a music group, boys' and girls' football teams and so on. Why shouldn't his group have some space?

Reluctantly, and feeling uncomfortable, the youth worker agrees, out of a somewhat optimistic sense of 'fair play for all' and thinking that she might at least find some ways of working with these young people. She explains the club rules and is clear about her expectations. The gang starts to use a room once a week. Very quickly, however, the room becomes 'their' room, they stop talking to, and ignore, the youth worker and her colleagues. She finds herself shut out of communication with the gang and gang members drift in and out of the centre, more or less when they feel like it, finding ways to avoid paying their subs, letting each other in through fire doors and toilet windows.

The sense of order and safety at the club quickly begins to break down. The usual youth club members become frightened to use the room, or even go near it. Members are threatened if they wear denim – a method the gang use to establish control and identity – and jackets are ripped but no-one will say who did it. An atmosphere of fear rapidly develops. Rumours begin to circulate about what is going on in 'their' room.

Matters come to a head when the centre is attacked by bottle throwing members of a rival gang. The police are called and a shotgun is found hidden in the boot of a car.

It took many months to regain a sense of safety at the centre, although, surprisingly there was not the mass exodus of members that one might expect. The youth worker did manage to regain a sense of safety and security, partly through the use of groups with members where they could talk about and think about what had happened.

Although the situation was very difficult, and it could be argued that some fundamental errors were made at the outset, the youth worker never gave up trying to understand, think about and manage what was going on. This was felt as 'holding' by the members in general, and the centre was able to recover and resume as usual.

Gang culture, as mentioned earlier, is not a group culture. Gangs tend to be based on fight/flight principles and dependency on 'leader' figures, neither of which create the conditions for interaction, interdependency and autonomy amongst members of the gang and healthy, communicative relationships with the surrounding social matrix.

The discussion groups that the youth worker organised provided a safe space where feelings could be aired and ideas shared. The youth worker concentrated on providing a space where the club members could talk openly with each other about what had happened.

Boundaries, expectations, trust, adult care and control

This example shows what can happen when ordinary boundaries, expectations, and adult care and control begin to erode.

When working with groups of young people where local 'gang cultures' exert a strong influence, it is essential for the adult presence to maintain a strong sense of authority, leadership and control. This authority needs to be flexible and resilient and self-confident, as it may well be confronted by the gang culture.

Gang culture is, to some extent, a response on a group level to a social environment where parental and adult authority is not present enough to provide young people with an adult world that they wish to join and emulate.

Gang culture

An inner city detached youth work project operated for several years with groups and gangs of young people who were not in contact with any form of 'statutory' provision. Most were school refusers, some were homeless, and all were 'unclubbable' in the traditional sense. The only 'adult' organisation that they had any time for whatsoever was the local professional football club, and they defined themselves and their identity by various 'gang based' delinquent and criminal acts, which included burglary, stealing cars and fighting young people from other areas of the city.

The project had the use of a large caravan, which had a small kitchen with coffee making facilities in it. The caravan was towed around to various street sites, establishing a reliable pattern of turning up at the same place every week. At first, young people would literally come in out of the cold.

A very high proportion of the young people who were made contact with in this way were estranged from their families and had little or nothing in the way of adult help and guidance. Many were disturbed and distressed but found some connection and comfort in their gangs.

The team of detached youth workers managed to successfully engage these difficult young people in alternative activities partly by insisting on more ordinary behavioural norms when they were in contact with the project and by rigorously applying a house rule of 'natural consequences'. For instance, if someone stole the coffee money, there would be no coffee. There were remarkably few incidents of difficult behaviour. And in the main the project was welcomed with curiosity, which became gratitude and respect. As well as coffee, the project provided 'advice and information' which helped give a starting point to making contact with the young people.

It is very important to emphasise that the staff team of one full-time and 12 part-time and voluntary youth workers was extremely well trained and supervised, and therefore firmly 'held' by the context of the local youth service provision. Before the project began, the team spent many weeks working together in training situations, so that they all knew exactly what they were trying to do. All staff were trained in basic counselling and group-work practice. The team worked in groups of three or four each evening. The youth service line management in the area had instigated the project and was totally supportive. The team of youth workers also had access to psychologically informed training and supervision. The project was well funded and well linked into other Local Authority support services, right down to the people who maintained the caravan.

Adults leading the work with difficult and distressed young people must know exactly what is tolerable and what is not; in other words there must be clear expectations and limits to behaviour. The adults must be consistent with each other in their approaches. When boundaries, limits and expectations are challenged or broken, as they inevitably will be, there must be ways of re-engaging with young people and re-defining ordinary social and behavioural norms and expectations.

In this project, preliminary and ongoing training helped immensely to ensure the reliable containment of a very challenging client group in a difficult working environment.

Dependence, independence and autonomy

Human beings are creatures of habit; we seek safety in dependability, repetition and reliability. Feeling safe and protected is one of our primary needs. Remember our *attachment* needs outlined in Chapter 1?

All young people need safe attachment to reliable and trustworthy adults. Young people need the experience of being able to get close to and maintain a relationship with an adult that they can trust.

Crucially important in our early years of extreme dependency, these needs stay with us in modified forms throughout life. Early attachment issues frequently get stirred up again in the turbulence of adolescence. Although safety and protection needs are originally probably best met by a secure attachment to one other person by whom we feel safe and protected, as time goes on we can also gain a similar sense of safety, security and protection by attachment to a group.

In fact, this progression from a dependency within mother–baby pairing to *interdependency* within a group is an essential aspect of human development. We never quite lose this desire for pair-bonding. Throughout adult life, most people maintain a sense of being attached to one significant other by forming a couple or partnership of some kind, within which there is a sense of mutual care-taking and interdependency as well as connections to groups of various kinds external to the couple or pair.

Young people need a safe base to come home to, from which to experiment with independence and growing autonomy. You can see this progress toward independence in action on any sunny day at a park near you. As soon as little children can walk, they take great delight in running off and making mum or dad chase them and keep them safe. Many disturbed and distressed young people, for various reasons, are not able to make the transition from a pair bonded mother/child type relationship to one of functional interdependency in a group.

CASE STUDY

False self and a double bind

Sixteen-year-old Mary is becoming noticeably thin. She manages to present a carefully constructed and apparently coping exterior that covers a very confused and troubled inner world (this, again, is another example of a false self type of 'solution' (Winnicott, 1971). Despite this, she has been able to form a connection with a perceptive youth worker, James, who notices that something is wrong, and is able to 'tune in' to the distress behind Mary's somewhat 'perfect' self-presentation. Mary has experienced James as a reliable figure at the youth club and feels that he might be a safe person to talk to. She decides to talk to him about something that is bothering her. (We shall discuss issues to do with 'making contact' in a later chapter.)

In the course of several informal conversations with Mary, James learns that Mary's mother phones and texts her sometimes more than 20 times a day to 'see how she is' and to tell Mary of all the latest problems and difficulties in her own life. At the same time, Mary's mother verbally encourages her daughter to be 'independent'. Mary actually feels both highly dependent on her mother as her mother's clinginess has prevented her own movement towards independence and she also feels responsible for her mother's dependency on her.

Her mother's anxieties persistently spill over into her relationship with her daughter, and Mary feels that she has to somehow 'sort her mother out' as well as deal with her own adolescent dilemmas and problems.

Mary feels caught in an impossible paradoxical situation; the more she actually becomes independent from her mother, the more her mother becomes alarmed at losing her daughter's support, and the more her mother becomes alarmed, the more Mary becomes frightened at losing her mother as a helpful adult that she can rely on. This becomes a vicious circle. It is sometimes described as a 'double bind' (Bateson et al., 1956). Mary is being told to be independent but then subtly punished and made to feel guilty when she 'abandons' her mother. This is a complex interaction, as dependency issues between mothers and daughters can be difficult at the best of times. It is not as simple as two contradictory instructions being given; there are intricate, long-term family relationships involved.

In addition, because this situation has been going on for some years, Mary has not interacted with other children in a confident way. Due to her mother's own unmet needs, her mother has unwittingly kept her tied to her apron strings. She would tell Mary to go and play with other children, but then criticise her choice of friends. Mary also shows signs of serious problems in her ability to empathise and communicate with others, which may stem from a much earlier lack of an empathic, attuned attachment relationship with her mother. Because of her difficulties in empathising and understanding others she is significantly impaired in her capacity to use adolescent peer groups for attachment and support.

She withdraws into bulimia (bingeing and vomiting) as a way of gaining some control of her emotionally chaotic life by desperately controlling what goes on in her body. Sadly, she tells the youth worker that 'bulimia is my only real friend'. She also confides in the youth worker that she has secretly been cutting herself as it relieves her painful feelings. Mary appears worried and frightened by her disclosure and insists that the youth worker must never, ever, tell anything she has said to anyone else. She tries to control James, as she herself feels controlled by her mother.

The youth worker experiences feelings of shock, despair, helplessness and great responsibility. In addition, he has been subjected to a confusing 'double bind' himself, having been given some worrying information and then emphatically told not to tell anyone about it. He is a professional youth worker, has discovered a young person in distress, doesn't know what to do and been told by the 'client' not to do anything about it. He feels very disturbed by this, but stops to think about it, and considers the possibility that he is being induced to feel something of Mary's inner confusion and turmoil and sense of responsibility.

Having been trained to think beyond the 'presenting problem', and to reflect upon the feelings that are stirred up in him, James begins to feel some hope and optimism that help can be offered. He resolves to break his double bind and decides to get some help himself, to talk confidentially with his colleagues about this encounter, and the feelings induced in him. He can then think together with others about how best to manage this situation. In this way he is breaking the cycle of isolation and 'false self' presentation.

Mary's relationship with her mother is still 'merged' and over involved. That James can think and act independently from Mary's attempt to control him is a step in the right direction and helps him to start to disentangle a merged, controlling relationship.

A note on safety and confidentiality

It hardly needs saying that in extreme cases where health and, possibly, life is at risk you should *always* get assistance from your manager, or from a professional consultation, *no matter what a young person has required – or demanded – of you in terms of confidentiality*. In all cases where there may be imminent danger you should inform your line manager immediately.

And of course (hopefully rarely), you should act personally, immediately and as appropriate in any instance should the police or other emergency services be needed. If life or safety is genuinely at risk, don't think, act!

Even if a young person has insisted that any information remain confidential, you are still firmly recommended to get some consultation with an experienced practitioner. You may choose not to use anyone's real name if this feels more comfortable for you; but what is extremely important is that you do not feel burdened with impossible dilemmas, secrets or problems and feel unable to talk about them. Otherwise the dynamics of the relationship, including any 'double bind' situation that a young person is bringing to you is simply repeated, only this time it is the youth worker in the firing line, so to speak.

This must never be allowed to happen.

In cases of abuse, either physical, sexual or by neglect, the youth worker may be induced, told or feel obliged to 'keep a secret'. This is unfortunately a frequent occurrence when working with cases of abuse, and may be a *repetition* or *enactment* of one of the dynamics of the abuse, although this time in the context of the relationship with the youth worker. If you are in any doubt, discuss what is going on with a trusted colleague or an independent professional from outside of the immediate situation.

We will discuss these types of problematic dynamics later in the section on Supervision, which is a special way of helping us to work effectively with distressed young people.

Stress

Stress is essentially due to the perception that the situations we are facing are greater than the resources we have to deal with them.

Know your limits, and don't be afraid to get help if something is worrying you. This is your professional responsibility.

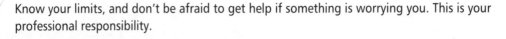

> ### ACTIVITY 4.1
>
> *It is well established that babies and young children need reliable, protective parents who are able to offer secure, emotionally attuned attachment figures to the growing person.*
>
> *Why do children need this? What tends to happen if they do not get it?*

Modern family patterns, often with both parents working, and absent grandparents, can make the achievement of close attuned bonding with children very problematic.

Mothers who stay at home may feel that their previous successes, or identity, in the social world have been significantly and painfully diminished. Our culture tends towards atomisation and social isolation, and may offer little in the way of rich *social* experiences of parenting.

Fathers may feel 'duty bound' to supply high levels of material comfort to the mother and children and, in an uncertain and unstable job market, can become obsessed with earning money, keeping a job and scaling the career ladder (in Japan, these men are known as 'ghost fathers').

Children may be shunted from childminder to playgroup to DVD to computer game with little opportunity for affect-regulating social experiences. ('Mummy told me if I was naughty she would take away my virtual world'.) They are subject to aggressive marketing and mind-deadening 'children's TV'.

Human beings are naturally social animals. Many humans find these conditions isolating, depressing and distressing. Our civilisation is apparently creating a good deal of discontent and stress.

ACTIVITY 4.2

Can you think of an example from your experience in working with young people where goal driven thinking and the 'consumer culture' has 'muscled out' taking time with relationships, and where a young person is clearly suffering as a result?

Can you think of someone you know who is still trying to get from a parent, or a parent figure, what they feel they failed to get when they were a child? How does this manifest itself?

There are a vast range of youth work interventions and activities that can be used in work with young people in order to help them develop healthy relations with others, to develop their interpersonal relationships, and to help them develop in the areas of empathy, attunement and intersubjectivity. Such activities will also enrich their lives generally. We are limited only by our imaginations.

Similarly, the manifestations, and signs of distress are as varied as one can imagine.

ACTIVITY 4.3

What are the signs of distress in young people? How many can you think of? Are some more serious than others?

As mentioned earlier in the book, depression is a very serious problem for young people and those who work with them. This short section gives a brief introductory guide to the salient points. It is not conclusive, and is intended to encourage you to read and study further.

Depression

Research in neuroscience implies that we are able to think and use our cognitive capacities more effectively when we are in conditions of safe, secure attachments, emotional connectedness, and when we are in the presence of others who are empathic and attuned to our emotional states.

This partly explains why working with distressed young people can be a demanding and 'draining' occupation, as youth workers are very likely to spend a great deal of time in close contact with persons who require high levels of empathy and attunement but are unlikely to be able to reciprocate.

ACTIVITY 4.4

Spend 10 minutes with a partner. The topic: How are you at the moment?

Listen carefully, but with an open mind. See if you can tune in to your partner's emotional and feeling state.

How do you do this?

After five minutes change roles and repeat.

Discuss the experience.

Pay attention to your partner's tone of voice, and any feelings that are evoked in you.

What else do you notice?

Modern neuroscience strongly indicates that babies come into the world with a need for social interaction to help develop and organise their brains. If they don't get enough empathic, attuned attention – in other words if they don't have a parent who is interested in them and who is reacting positively to them – then important parts of their brain will simply not develop as well as they might. Babies need, in Winnicott's terms, 'primary maternal preoccupation', or a state of 'reverie' (Symington, 1996, p168).

Depressed people easily feel that they are ineffective and unwanted. People vulnerable to depression tend to feel that ruptures in relationships and self-esteem are irreparable. They cannot stop thinking about their unmet emotional needs, and in serious cases, lack the resilience to 'try again' in the face of the inevitable setbacks that life brings. Depression in young people is often triggered by a rejection or a relationship that doesn't work out or by feelings of loneliness and exclusion by the young person's peer group. 'Bullying' is a major problem in this regard, and can have tragic consequences.

The difficulty in recovering from psychological blows can be thought of as a problem in 'self affect regulation', which is short hand for the ability to think about and manage your emotions. A crucial aspect of depression is that it involves the feeling that there is no way of recovering 'lost love', be it from an individual or social group and that there is no way of mending the damage.

Schore (2003) calls this the 'disruption and repair cycle'. A healthy child – or adult – will either give up and try something else when a situation becomes hopeless, or address the situation and change it. A depressed person tends to assume that the relationship with an individual, family or social group is ruined for all time and that there is no way back, or forward, and that this is true for all relationships at all times. Failure may be taken to be a mark of inherent 'badness'.

It is crucial to learn that positive relationships can be restored.

This process of restoration is at the heart of the relationship between firmly and positively attached parents and children. In all relationships, things can, and will, go wrong, but feelings and hurts can be thought about and understood, both parties can struggle with understanding the other's feelings, and perhaps an even firmer bond and attachment can follow.

The child of a persistently depressed mother, or primary care giving parent, will not gain the deeply important experience of things going wrong in relationships yet having the potential for being mended.

Studies have shown that such children tend to adopt a 'fight/flight' mode of operation; they either become avoidant or aggressive. Significantly, this is a high cortisol producing affective state; children left in these conditions by misattuned parents, left unsoothed and without the adequate psychological equipment to deal with the fear inducing circumstances, will be less able to deal with their own feelings and the feelings of others partly due to the biochemical action of high cortisol levels caused by psychological stress.

These young people will be convinced that feelings cannot be managed jointly and in co-operation with other people and the child will fear being denigrated, shamed and belittled. Sadly, this condition tends to be cumulative; the longer this goes on, the more difficult it becomes to recover. For a very well written and poignant account of this process, see Wurtzel, 1994.

And for some slightly disturbing light relief, you might like to try Jeremy Clarkson's (2008) account of a woman who deliberately leaves her baby to cry on a transatlantic flight. Clarkson is very sympathetic to the baby, as well as aware of the feelings induced in him by the baby's distress. His account shows how behaviour that is potentially actually damaging to developing children can be accepted and even socially condoned. Clarkson's book is aptly sub-titled, 'For crying out loud'.

ACTIVITY 4.5

Using your everyday experience, what do you see around you, and what can you think of, that seems to condone disconnected, unempathic, misattuned parenting?

Young people need attuned adults around them who can help them to deal with problems bit by bit. They need adults who are emotionally resilient enough to cope with and tolerate what can feel like a humiliating battering of hopelessness and negativity and who can contain and think about the grief-stricken mental states often 'pushed into' them by means of projective identification. In work with very distressed young people, youth workers must be able to retain realistic optimism, and a willingness to give up and start again in the face of apparently insoluble impasses; and be willing to use help for themselves!

However, an empathic and attuned relationship with another person may offer the young person a new way of dealing with emotions that enables them to engage with their own inner worlds more constructively. The downside is that this is not a one-off psychoeducational learning process, and may not be very stable over time, as the patient's damaged emotional 'processing equipment' itself may not develop a great deal. The young person may need continued access to the 'auxiliary ego function' of a 'therapeutic environment' or a psychotherapist. The mind is 'plastic' and can change, but this can be a very slow process.

The process of repeatedly making and breaking the affective connection in the course of therapeutic work may enable the young person, in time, to gain the confidence to ask for and expect emotional and practical support in times of distress, which is a huge gain in terms of helping to stabilise and improve otherwise chronic and often chaotic conditions.

Involving young people in groups

Although the signs of distress are many, it is something of a relief to learn that most problems have much the same roots, that is, in the complexities of family and social relationships. These are problems that originated in a group-based environment, and a group-based approach to helping can be very useful. Well constructed groups in the youth work context can go a long way towards helping to alleviate distress.

However, young people who find it difficult to be in groups are of course likely to find group-based approaches challenging. We shall concentrate on the ways in which distressed young people exert special pressures on group work efforts in particular, no matter what the 'content' of the work is.

Children and young people who have problems such as those described in earlier chapters have great difficulties in forming safe attachments to groups due to problems in identifying and communicating their own emotions and in establishing empathically attuned relationships with others. Children who have not developed the capacity to identify, think about and communicate their emotions *in words* will be reduced to communicating their feelings *by impact*, that is, by the means of *projective identification*, as described previously. Feelings will be *evoked in others* instead of communicated in words.

This is a very important concept, and is also helpful in understanding how emotional states are induced in relationships in and between groups, as well as between individuals.

This idea also helps us to understand difficult and disturbing processes like bullying and scapegoating. For instance, a gang of hopeless, fearful young people may attack another group or individual maybe using race, colour, geographical location, culture, sexuality, body shape, political views or some other distinguishing feature as a 'reason' for inducing these feelings elsewhere.

When someone else, or even a whole group, is made to feel helpless or frightened it is then as if these feelings exist outside of the gang and become located within the other group. This enables the gang to gain a temporary sense of relief and triumph. It is short term, though, as when the other group is 'defeated' then the feelings will return very quickly.

Remember that this is a natural process, and a primitive attempt to gain an empathic connection. It is not a bad thing in itself, it just 'is' although the process may be very unpleasant for all concerned. *Do not forget that it is important to stop or limit abusive and violent behaviour and to request – or demand – that whatever is going on stops and is talked about.*

Construction and maintenance of reflective spaces

But how to *construct and maintain* situations in which we – and young people – might begin to be able to think about and understand what is going on needs careful thought, and is the subject of the rest of this chapter.

These concepts apply to more ordinary situations as well, so to illustrate the point, I shall start with a somewhat unusual example drawn from recent experience. This example does not have much to do with distressed young people as such, but is chosen to illustrate how unwittingly we can perpetuate problems – and even create them – by not paying enough attention to 'structural' issues, that is, the way in which we construct the settings in which we work with distressed young people.

CASE STUDY

How not to involve young people in politics

At a recent event organised by a major political party at the House of Commons, the central theme was about how to involve more young people in politics. The meeting was held in a Committee Room which somewhat resembled a courtroom, with the speakers at the front on a large wooden stage behind lecterns. There were a few young people in the audience, which consisted of about 150 people altogether. There were several presenters, mainly people in late middle age, who spoke for over an hour, leaving less than half an hour for discussion. When the speakers finished, and the 'discussion' began, ironically it was dominated by the older, somewhat noisier members of the audience who long-windedly took up most of the time, allowing little space for contributions from those whom the meeting was supposedly about. Although the meeting was themed on the problem of greater political participation, especially amongst young people, the 'adults' took up virtually all the space and time complaining about young people's lack of involvement.

This example highlights how problems can be caused or perpetuated by the very structures that are created to solve the perceived problems. One 'solution' would have been very simple; meet in a room where the group could all see each other and where there was a minimum of seating hierarchy, and conduct the meeting in a way in which all felt that they had an opportunity to contribute. This apparent simplicity is not as easy as it sounds, though. First, rooms of this nature are hard to come by; they would ideally allow people to sit in circular forms rather than in rows, and the skills needed to conduct such a group so that all feel able to contribute, again, are by no means easy to acquire. Although it may appear to be a simple skill, it is by no means as easy as it seems.

Simply sitting in circles does not, of course, guarantee equality of contribution, although the setting and seating arrangements are very important and carry a good deal of meaning. And a meeting held in the plush setting of the House of Commons clearly carries a different meaning than one held in a well-worn community centre.

The manner in which groups are put together, prepared, conducted and led, organised and administrated, and the setting and context in which they are conducted have a great bearing on their success or failure.

In a term borrowed from group analysis, the sum total of all these things is called dynamic administration.

This is a very important concept so we shall spend some time learning exactly what this means.

Group management

A group which exists in a safe and secure setting, where the administrative aspects are sound, where staff feel well trained and supported by line management, and which is, therefore, a 'holding' environment, is far better able to process and think about emotional content.

The sum total of all we do to create and maintain groups is sometimes called 'dynamic administration', because the *way* in which groups are set up and run profoundly affects their effectiveness, resilience and their ability to withstand the testing and challenging behaviour of distressed young people.

A group that is well set up has a far greater potential for creating the reciprocal free-flowing communication of thoughts and feelings. These are the conditions for the development of communication and empathy, which is the capacity to enter into the feeling states of others, and an essential aspect of a young person's capacity to be with others in a constructive way. The ability to connect with, think about and communicate one's own inner world is also of the greatest importance.

Distressed young people who have been traumatised by their experiences may well have great difficulties in identifying *internally* their own feelings and emotions. It is as if very deep and painful experiences are separated off by the mind because they are too painful to bear. Dissociation is one of the most problematic features of working with traumatised young people.

There is a vast range of different types of planned group activity that can be helpful to young people, which help them to gain a sense of connection, identity and purpose, and which help with *socialisation* and general social education and personal development. These range from sports and outdoor activities, including 'adventure' trips and travel, special interest groups of various kinds, music, art and dance, theatre and performing arts, committees and political groups, themed discussion groups, educational opportunities, therapeutic groups and so on. A fuller list is given in Chapter 5.

However, distressed young people who have problems in relating to others very often need special help, and have difficulties in integrating into the ordinary groups of their peers.

CASE STUDY

Anorexia on the Orient Express

A youth worker is co-leading a group of young people on an International Exchange trip to Russia. Half way through a three-day train journey, somewhere in the middle of Russia, it was reported to one of the group leaders that one of the young women on the trip, Satinder, hadn't eaten for three days and had 'fainted and wouldn't wake up'. This caused a considerable impact in the group, and quite a problem for the group leaders.

As a group leader, using some of the ideas discussed so far, how would you have understood and managed the situation above?

We all respond to, and connect to, certain types of activities in different ways. In working with distressed young people, there are certain *aspects* of activities that are fundamental, and which are of the greatest importance to them.

The factors that are of greatest importance are the ones that we have identified earlier as being central to the creation of a safe holding environment. The central features are:

- safe attachment and protection;

- reliability and consistency;

- attempts to understand;

- empathic attunement;

- safe limits and boundaries.

ACTIVITY 4.6

With a partner, separately, take ten minutes to draw up a quick list of all the groups you have been involved in as a participant. Go back as far as you can remember. (This is more of a 'brainstorm' than any attempt to get a complete list.)

Share the results. Which ones stand out as 'good experiences' for you? Why?

Which ones stand out as 'bad experiences'? Why?

In the short case study above, half way through the trip, Satinder felt lost and disconnected in a strange country with a group and leaders that she hardly knew. Her 'eating disorder', which had been going on for several years, as it turned out, made her very quickly the centre of protective attention, although not in a very constructive way. Incidentally, she, and the group as a whole, responded well to some firm adult control; and the trip was concluded without further problems.

Dynamic administration

The sum total of all we do practically to create and maintain groups is called 'dynamic administration' (see the section on group management on page 68).

It is called 'dynamic administration' because it refers to the way in which the group relates to and interacts with the environment that 'holds' it. This is a dynamic – that is, an active and changing interaction. It is about the management of the *setting* of the group. This may seem at first glance to be the dullest part of running a group, but it is actually one of the most important and can be a very interesting process when the dynamic aspects are explored. Unless attention is paid to this aspect of groupwork, the group will lack the 'tensile strength' to work with distressed young people.

We are trying to create the optimal conditions for the group itself to become the agent of change and for each member to play a part in this work.

Dynamic administration, and other aspects of practical groupwork will be discussed in more detail in the next chapter.

ACTIVITY 4.7

What aspects of a setting might you have to manage in order to make sure that it is comfortable and reliable?

Who might you need to liaise with to ensure that the group space feels safe and protected?

In the next chapter you will find 'A short course in groupwork' where these and other ideas are discussed more fully.

Training is essential if you want to be able to run groups effectively.

Training

It should go without saying that training is a vitally important part of a youth and community worker's professional life.

Alongside the professional supervision of *process*, as distinguished from line management supervision, training has a special place to play if a worker wishes to focus on helping distressed young people.

Youth workers working with distressed young people are exposed to very complex and difficult interpersonal processes, some of which have been described above. Projective identification and the powerful emotional fields created by envy and jealousy, for instance, can be very difficult to manage and may even affect the physical and mental health of adults engaged in this work.

The development of our conceptual thinking through training is one way in which adults can help themselves to remain engaged and connected but also maintain enough professional objectivity to be able to think about what is going on. It is very easy, and all too common for youth workers to get caught up in the powerful emotional currents that are an inseparable aspect of working with emotional disturbance.

Training helps us to use supervision more effectively. Supervision and training are essential elements in the construction and maintenance of a professional environment that supports, enhances and sustains good and effective work with distressed young people.

C H A P T E R   R E V I E W

This chapter has looked at some of the common problems and manifestations of distress in young people. We have explored support structures, dynamic administration and examined elements of staff supervision and training. The issue of emotional safety and confidentiality are issues that need to be given full attention.

FURTHER READING

Phillips, A (2007) *Winnicott.* Harmondsworth: Penguin.

An easy to read and very pertinent account of Winnicott's major theories and approaches to practice.

Wurtzel, E (1994) *Prozac Nation: Young and Depressed in America.* Boston MA: Houghton Mifflin.

An engaging and sometimes harrowing account of a young woman's struggle with depression.

USEFUL WEBSITES

http://en.wikipedia.org/wiki/Double_bind

Chapter 5

What's in a group? Working with distressed and disturbed young people in groups

CHAPTER OBJECTIVES

By the end of this chapter you will have:

- considered group processes and group dynamics;
- examined the concepts of thinking about work with distressed young people;
- considered the manifestations of distress, delinquency and perversion.

This chapter contains a look at the fundamentals of the following approaches in practice: youth and community work in action; the relationship between socialisation and psychological approaches; sexuality and cultural issues.

Included is 'A short course in groupwork', a look at the impact of working with distressed young people on professional staff, and working with extreme distress.

We will examine how the concepts outlined earlier help in thinking about work with distressed young people, and we will also consider the more 'extreme' manifestations of distress: delinquency and perversion.

We will look first at the broad range of youth and community work provision, and in more detail at how effective groupwork approaches may be constructed.

Even if you are not especially interested in working with troubled young people, sooner or later you will be called upon to do so. The later part of the chapter will explore further issues to do with working with extremes and severe distress. We will look at special aspects of working with chronic difficulties, personality disorder and severe and enduring problems, with advice on how to identify and manage extreme situations.

The broader context

To give us a broader context, on page 74 you will see listed a common range of youth work programmes in English local authorities as of March 2010. The list is extensive, but may not be complete.

Some of the programmes listed are specifically targeted at work with distressed young people, and some are not. However, even in the context of the most general, everyday types of provision we may come across very disturbed and distressed young people. First, a note on socialisation.

Socialisation

At its best, youth and community work is an excellent and valuable way of helping in the socialisation of young people. Socialisation is about becoming aware of society, social and group norms and learning how to behave with others. It is a key developmental domain.

Young people do not, of course, wake up in the morning and decide to go out and get socialised. It is a natural human desire to want to belong, and they will seek out groups of others in order to join in with larger groupings outside of the family where they can find friends and potential sexual partners.

However, young people who are impaired in their capacity to relate to others due to attachment based problems in developing a capacity for empathy and attunement, have great difficulties in joining in the opportunities for socialisation that are available, and therefore can become isolated, or develop unhealthy ways of creating connections and attachments to others.

As we have seen, severe anorexia or delinquency are instances where the young person forces adult 'attachment behaviour' and attention upon themselves thereby requiring adults to establish a relationship of power and control over them. At the same time they can reject help and pretend to be self-sufficient. Adults can neither ignore them nor relate to them normally, as the perverse (forced) 'attachment' is manipulated through self-starvation or persistent rule breaking and controlled by the young person. The anorexic or serial delinquent has thus achieved power over the adults and is inducing feelings in them of failure and helplessness, thereby feeling better about himself by triumphing over them and gaining displaced revenge over disappointing or neglectful parental figures.

Youth and community work provides an excellent opportunity to offer sustained and creative ways for young people to engage socially with each other and with adults who care about them and achieve a sense of power and independence in ways that are socially and personally useful, creative and developmental.

However, if the psychological problems associated with early relational issues as outlined here are not addressed, distressed young people will simply not be able to make use of even the best efforts of creative and dedicated youth workers and the resources available.

Remember that distress is expressed in a wide variety of ways, including depression, self-harming, delinquent and anti-social behaviour of various kinds that disturbs other people; in other words, behaviour that induces or 'pushes' distressing and disturbing feelings into others. The case study of Jamie in Chapter 1 describes a young person who communicates his painful feelings in this way. Remember, too, that a young person may not look unhappy or disturbed; they may well appear untroubled and even triumphant in their demeanour.

A common range of youth work programmes in English local authorities (March 2010)

Positive activities that are universal

1. Positive activities (sports, arts, etc. – usually with accreditation)

2. Youth clubs – council run

3. Youth clubs – voluntary sector

4. Uniformed bodies – scouts, guides, air corps, etc.

5. Summer University (all holiday period and some term time) of tutored classes (arts, sports, enterprise, health) with accreditation

6. Volunteering programmes (many types; demand far out-strips supply).

Targeted youth support – 'TYS'

1. Detached work

2. Key worker support – for targeted young people to access positive activities

3. Targeted youth support – one to one or group referrals in response to vulnerability

4. Multi-agency teams: in locality offices providing targeted interventions with young people who are, or could become, vulnerable (including detached youth worker, youth club workers, health visitors, drugs workers, crime diversion workers, Connexions PAs, etc., often applying a lead professional case management function and the Common Assessment Framework)

5. Groupwork for vulnerable targeted work – young mothers' projects, asylum seekers

6. Online – many youth workers relate to young people at non-social hours through Facebook, text, e-mail, etc.

7. Youth counselling and emotional well-being: youth counselling projects; referrals to mental health services (CAMHS, Young Mind, etc.)

8. Looked After Young People Centres – social relaxation, lounge, activities, groups, etc.

9. Youth Crime diversion and prevention programmes – reparation (saying 'sorry' face-to-face), YISP – Youth Inclusion Support Projects – a panel for pre/ASBO young people to agree their programme of positive activities – highly effected diversionary programmes, Positive Activities for Young People – usually estate-based diversion such as sports and so on (usually targeted at young people or for whom LA has a statutory responsibility through Family Courts, corporate parenting or youth justice).

ACTIVITY 5.1

This list is extensive, but may not be complete. Can you add to it from your experience and knowledge?

Youth work is groupwork

The above list is, quite rightly, heavily biased towards working with young people in groups.

Groupwork is not just a way of working with many people at once, or chosen as an intervention because young people tend to hang around in groups. A well-run group can not only be a remarkable force for change, but also be a very rewarding and satisfying activity for a professional youth worker to engage in.

Young people need experiences in groups to help them on their way to becoming functional adults, able to join in with work and social groups, families and teams.

In a very rapidly changing world in which the ability to be geographically mobile is increasingly becoming an essential requirement, the ability to constructively join, participate in and leave groups is a very useful social skill. Even if people remain relatively static themselves, they are still likely to have to deal with shifting, transient and changing group environments around them.

ACTIVITY 5.2

Take a few minutes to jot down as many different sorts of groups that you can think of.

How do these groups deal with people joining and leaving them? For example, in a family, joining and leaving would be by birth and death.

Like anything with an inherent power, groups can also be damaging and destructive. If you are to create groups, or use naturally occurring groups in your work with young people, it is essential that you are familiar with and understand the basic concepts.

An ability to run groups, and a knowledge of groupwork, is an essential youth work attribute. Before moving on to look at specific issues that arise in working with distressed young people in groups, let's take a look at basic groupwork practice.

Below is 'A short course in groupwork' that outlines the basics that you will need to consider in your practical work.

A short course in groupwork

Key concepts

The group in mind, the setting, dynamic administration, recruitment, boundaries, behavioural limits, 'closed' or 'open'? Leadership styles, interventions, co-leading, the 'wisdom' of the group, thinking about the matrix of relationships of which the group is a part, 'trusting the group'. Group dynamics: scapegoating, monopolising, subgrouping, dependency, fight/flight, pairing, managing conflict, managing powerful feelings, projection and projective identification, authority, status and dominance, dramatisation and enactment.

The following is a short step-by-step framework, which can be adapted into different environments and used for groups with different purposes. It will help you think about how to set up and run an exciting and creative group.

It will also help you to *sustain* the work. Remember, distressed young people will almost certainly find groups difficult to manage, and may gravitate towards gangs and masses that are anti-social in nature rather than socially constructive.

Distressed young people may also *avoid* groups and become isolated and cut off from social contact, which can become extremely problematic for them in both the short and the long term.

Groupwork with distressed young people could be thought of as 'groupwork with people who find it difficult to be in groups'. By definition, it will often be difficult and challenging work, and requires careful thought and attention.

Groupwork is not about working one-to-one with a number of individuals at the same time. Remember that the *group itself* will be the medium that helps the individuals who participate in the group.

Your job as a group-worker is to create the optimum conditions for the group to become a place where communication, dialogue, connection and safe attachment can develop, and where new thoughts and experiences can emerge.

However, you are responsible for organising and maintaining the relationship with the setting within which the group will 'live'.

And don't forget that the most important part of the group, especially at the beginning, is you and your imagination. You need to be able to imagine, and keep, a 'group in mind'.

Imagination is not only the uniquely human capacity to envision that which is not, and therefore the fount of all invention and innovation. In its arguably most transformative and revelatory capacity, it is the power that enables us to empathise with humans whose experiences we have never shared.

JK Rowling. Address to Harvard University students. *Harvard Gazette* 5 June, 2010

Key questions

What might emerge from the group? How will the group expand the experiences of the group members? What are the group processes that will be of most help to group members?

What special understanding and attention might distressed young people need? Distressed young people might not only communicate in words. How else do they communicate?

How can you tell the difference between disturbed attachment responses and learning needs?

The group in mind

Before you start, what sort of group do you have in mind? What will it 'look' like in action? Visualise it. What will it feel like to be a member of this group? What will it be like to run the group? Will someone run the group with you, or will you go it alone?

The task and work of the group

Let your imagination play for a while, but eventually be as specific as possible about the sort of group that you want to create. Discuss it with colleagues. If it is a football team, what sort of football team? How might it play? If it is a free-discussion group, or a theme centred group, how might it communicate? Would you share dreams? What is the primary task, or work of the group? What is it for? Are you looking for specific outcomes or are you prepared to work with what emerges from the group process?

Who 'owns' the group? Who is responsible for it?

The setting

Where will the group meet? If it will meet in an institution of some kind, what is the nature of the institution? Will you need a room? What sort of room? Does it need to be a quiet space? Chairs? Cushions? Tables? What are the basic practical requirements? Is the room too warm? Too cold? A cold room usually kills off discussion groups, or a yoga group, but is great for anything energetic.

For example, if you want to run a discussion group, do you have enough chairs of equal size and type to form a circle so that the group feels equal at the outset? (nothing is more annoying than someone bagging the only armchair, or the sofa . . .)

Dynamic administration

What practically do you need to do in order for the group to function? Who do you need to liaise with? Managers? Colleagues? Administrators? Secretaries? Receptionists? Caretakers? How can you minimise interruptions? Who do you need to inform? Do you need to book the room? Who will take messages if someone can't make it? Do you need resources; materials or equipment of any kind – any expenses?

Recruitment

How will you let potential group members know about it? How will you spread the word? Will you approach people personally?

Boundaries

What are the times group meetings begin and end? What is the duration of the group? Four weeks? Six months? Open-ended until it ends naturally? How large can the group get? How small?

Have you made sure that other people will not wander in and out, thereby disrupting your group? Might your group disturb anyone else? Check to see that your dynamic administration has created a reasonably well-protected space.

Closed or open?

Will it be a 'closed group' with a fixed membership for the duration of the group? Or will it be 'open' to new members? How will people join and leave? Who will be in it? Who will not be in it? Is it a 'drop-in', available to whoever turns up on the day? Can people join and leave by arrangement (this is sometimes called a 'slow–open' group) and who decides? What happens to latecomers?

'Boundary issues' may seem to be simple and innocuous, but in fact are an integral part of the development and feeling of safety in the group.

Creating a protected, reliable space is frequently much more problematic than it might appear at first. Intrusions of various kinds can manifest as if by magic: rooms can get double-booked, other activities may be organised by other staff members at the same time as your group thus drawing away your group members; chairs disappear; suddenly your room is completely filled with jumble for the junior club jumble sale on Saturday . . .

All these things have to be thought about and managed by the group-worker. It is the group-worker's responsibility to take care of the setting of the group.

Behavioural limits

What is considered to be acceptable behaviour? What are the ordinary group or 'social norms' expected in this group? Who decides? How might any transgressive behaviour be managed?

How to manage boundaries and limits

The management of boundaries, like the management of behavioural limits, is not in the nature of 'once and for all' decisions.

Youth workers are often faced with questions like: How do I decide what the boundaries and limits are? When are boundaries 'holding' and when are they rigidly oppressive and controlling? When are they too loose and therefore ineffective, tending to make people feel unsafe?

The answer is that you have to think boundaries out yourself, work boundaries out with other staff members and with the young people themselves. How much 'power' you allow young people is, of course, a matter of judgment and depends on the young people's specific capacities for self-management.

There are no hard and fast rules here, although some guidance is offered below; some boundaries and limits have to be set by adults, or by an individual in authority, some can be thought about in group discussions. The establishment of the right sort of boundaries for a particular group is as much art as science, but always the final say remains with you as the group conductor.

If boundaries are too rigid, we may get lifeless, legalistic structures that kill off a sense of liveliness and creativity. If boundaries are too loose, we get a soggy mess where nothing gets done and we risk an organisational decline into collapsed states.

We need to find a balance between rigidity and chaos.

You can think of group boundaries as being like cell walls in biology. Cell walls need to be permeable and flexible to some extent. If they become too rigid or too permeable, then the cell will not function efficiently.

Abusive families are often characterised by *rigid* boundaries, rigid control, resist any change, are notoriously closed to outsiders and can be very difficult to penetrate. Abusive families are also frequently characterised by *collapsed* boundaries, especially in terms of intergenerational roles. For instance, in abusive families, children may take on adult or 'parental' roles, and adults may abdicate responsibility to children. Children may feel – or actually be responsible for the emotional or psychological welfare of the adults.

In organisations and groups, rigidity, legalistic forms of control, role diffusion and collapse are problematic, and may be indicative of deeper problems.

The best attitude is probably one of clear and safe benignly authoritative control with a slightly fuzzy edge of permissiveness and tolerance.

CASE STUDY

Role diffusion and blurring of authority in a youth centre

A youth worker, Jasmine, takes over a club at a large community centre. The previous youth worker left under something of a cloud, and there has been a leadership vacuum for several months. Although the centre is huge and well resourced, it is almost deserted, and membership is very low. Jasmine works hard to publicise the centre locally, and potential new members soon arrive, but very quickly leave without making any real contact. Jasmine is both worried and curious about the reasons for this. She notices that there are a small group of members who know each other very well and who have been connected to the centre for several years. They are at the centre most evenings.

Jasmine observes that this 'in' group has been giving new members the 'cold shoulder' and making it uncomfortable for new young people to join. She decides to discuss this with them. The 'in' group is quite amenable to thinking about the problem as they can see that the current situation is untenable. One of them, Frank, says, 'well, I can see your point, but Eric says we should keep the club the way it is as it is our club'. Jasmine is perplexed by this and asks Frank to explain. He tells her that Eric, the caretaker and cleaner, is telling them to keep the newcomers out as the centre belongs to the current users. Eric had been left 'in charge' during the time when there was no designated youth worker in post, and had picked up somewhere along the way that the centre 'belongs to the centre users'.

Eric tells them that the centre doesn't need all these new people coming in, misusing the facilities and making a mess. Eric often sits with the 'in' group drinking tea in the coffee bar area and has become indistinguishable from the youth workers and members.

Jasmine realises that Eric has taken on an influential role, beyond that of caretaker and cleaner. She suddenly realises that if the centre develops, the caretaker will have far more duties regarding opening and closing, cleaning, maintenance and so on. She decides to discuss the matter with her supervisor to think about ways of tackling the situation of role blurring and confusion, as it cannot be allowed to continue.

Leadership styles, roles and authority

As a group-worker, you will often want to conceptualise your efforts as working with the 'group as a whole'. A useful term for a youth worker who adopts this leadership style is 'group conductor'. This is a term that describes the way in which the group-worker enables each group member to join in and contribute to the group in their own way in much the same way that an orchestral conductor enables a group of musicians to play together.

The conductor may well pay attention to individuals and sub-groups of musicians, but he is largely concerned with how the 'group-as-a-whole' performs. If the group as a whole performs well, then each individual is likely to feel that they are fulfilling their potential, and feel connected, engaged and productive.

ACTIVITY **5.3**

Think of a group that you are running, or one that you have in mind. Is the group process 'conducted', or led in an 'authoritarian' way, 'democratically' or in a 'laissez-faire' style? How much real power and control will the young people have? How might you work with the 'group as a whole'?

Co-leading

Will the group be led by one, two or more youth workers? What are the reasons for this?

The best reasons for co-working are to give each other help and support in understanding what is going on. The worst reasons are to 'cover' in case of absence or sickness. Remember that reliability and consistency of adult leadership are very important due to *attachment issues*. What arrangements will co-leaders need to make to ensure that they meet together to discuss their work? (See also 'Supervision', below.) Will the co-workers meet together before the group and afterwards to 'de-brief? What exactly are the co-workers expectations of each other in this respect? How best can they work as a team?

Interventions and trusting the group

How far can the group be trusted to develop its own constructive group culture? How much control might the group-workers need to take?

What sort of interventions might the group leaders need to make? Why?

Using the 'wisdom of the group'

Will the youth workers themselves make the most of the input into the group, or will they focus on bringing out the awareness and knowledge of group members? Perhaps the group-workers will decide to do both. Is it possible to tell beforehand what the balance might be? Will the group be 'theme centred' or 'free-floating discussion'?

The matrix of which the group is a part

What do you know about the wider relational context that the group is a part of? How are group members connected to wider social and group networks, local community and others?

Group processes and group dynamics

Group-workers may need to pay attention to the following group process and group dynamic issues.

- Scapegoating;

- Monopolising;

- Absences and avoidance;

- Subgrouping or 'ganging up';

- The development of Basic Assumption groups; fight/flight, dependency, pairing (Bion). Basic Assumption groups interfere with the task and 'work' of the group;

- Managing conflict;

- Managing powerful emotions, for instance anger, jealousy, envy, anxiety, shame and guilt;

- Managing powerful psychological processes, especially projection and projective identification;

- Managing and thinking about dramatisation and enactment in the group;

- Issues of roles, status and dominance;

- Relationship of the group to other groups in the setting (see 'Boundaries', above).

Group process and group dynamics are very complex and a detailed exploration is beyond the scope of this book, but with good supervision and support and a willingness to learn much can be achieved even by relative newcomers to working in groups.

Supervision and support

Who will you discuss the group with? What help will you need from managers and colleagues?

Please note that youth workers will need specialist consultancy and perhaps even psychologically expert psychodynamic 'clinical' supervision when working with very disturbed and distressed young people.

The impact of a disturbed individual

Occasionally, even in the most innocuous of circumstances, a disturbed individual will make an impact on a group. The case study below is a somewhat complex situation, but is based on a real case with details changed for reasons of confidentiality.

CASE STUDY

A case of multiple identities

Maggie is a centre-based youth worker at a large community centre. She decides to run a discussion group about 'Relationships' for a mixed gender group of young people at the centre. She has a sense that such a group would be welcome and has had some positive interest already from a number of young people with whom she has developed friendly and basically trusting relationships over time. She organises a time and meeting place and the group begins to meet.

After the third session, one of the girls, Lizzy, approaches her and tells her in confidence that a young man in the group, Peter, whom she has known for some time and considers to be a friend, has been contacting her on a social networking site. Unbeknown to Lizzy, on the site Peter has adopted the character of a girl called 'Nikki'. Peter has been masquerading on the site as 'Nikki' with quite a fully developed female identity for over a year using photos, links and messages to create 'Nikki's' personality.

Lizzy felt that she had been developing an intimate friendship with 'Nikki' and has exchanged some very personal details with 'her'. Lizzy has since found out that Peter has been using no less than twelve other identities that he has created, mainly female, which she has believed to be real, and some of which he has been using in contacts with other friends of hers. Some of these friends are in the discussion group at the youth centre.

Lizzy is both shocked and appalled by this discovery. She feels that her friendship and trust with Peter has been ruined. In addition, she is extremely confused by Peter's behaviour and does not know what to make of it. She feels angry, but also strangely unable to express her feelings. Lizzy has become preoccupied by this sequence of events, and says that she cannot sleep for thinking about it. She asks Maggie whether or not she should remain friends with Peter. Maggie is not so sure it is that simple.

Lizzy also insists that none of this is mentioned in the group in case people think she is 'a bad person' for 'causing trouble'.

Maggie is also shocked and disturbed by what has happened. She feels angry and helpless; very unsure about how to proceed. Should she bring this strange situation up in the discussion group? The group theme is 'Relationships', and if this isn't about relationships, then what is? If she brings it up, is she betraying confidences? If she doesn't do anything, then will Peter carry on his disturbing behaviour? Does it matter if he does? She, too, finds that it preys on her mind and loses sleep over it.

ACTIVITY 5.4

If you were Maggie, how would you manage this? What are the issues involved?

Discussion

The case above is an example of **perverse dynamics** enacted in a group.

The central characteristics of perverse dynamics are twofold.

- The primary aim of the activity is to gain *power* over others.

- There is also a motive of *revenge* that is usually covert or displaced. This means that the hateful revenge is not aimed at the original person (which is usually a parent) but at a substitute.

Perverse in this sense means the opposite of 'loving'.

> One moves from victim to victor, from passive object of others' hostility and power to the director, ruler; one's tormentors in turn will be one's victims. With this mechanism, the child imagines himself parent, the impotent (has become) potent. One no longer fears . . . conscience or the outside world.
>
> (Stoller, 1975)

These dynamics may appear confusing, and they frequently are, but they are not too difficult to understand.

These human psychological forces have always fascinated storytellers, artists and writers, and are the stuff of legends and fairy tales. Myths and legends often include a character who has been rejected and humiliated, and who then attempts to turn the tables on those whom he feels has wronged him. He may want to gain power over the whole world . . . There is a strong theme in Norse legends, for instance, of such a person being a 'shape shifter' and being able to take on different forms . . .

Effective work with distressed young people who are beginning to adopt perverse solutions to their feelings of powerlessness, helplessness and guilt is of the most profound importance. If these young people are not worked with effectively, and safe attachment experiences are not offered early enough, there is a real danger that perverse solutions will persist into later life. Sometimes this is called 'anti social personality disorder'. In other words, if safe and loving attachments are not available, then perverse and hateful dynamics with the aim of gaining power and revenge may be adopted and, over time, become deeply ingrained and built into the developing personality.

Thus, the perverse rewards of power and destructive potency, covert revenge and freedom from feelings of guilt and helplessness can be structured into the personality *as it is growing* and become therefore extremely difficult to shift or change. This is because perversion becomes the primary way of operating of the personality *as a whole* rather than being simply one or two odd or inconvenient behaviours.

Consider for a moment that exercising power or revenge over someone – or everyone – might take many forms, and this will help in understanding the plasticity of these dynamics.

This is why, in these cases, treating or attempting to change specific behaviours by reward and punishment is almost always a failure strategy. In the case of perverse dynamics that have hardened into the personality, the behaviours themselves are only a means to the end of exercising power and gaining revenge. If you try to control one behaviour with the threat of punishment or coercion another one will pop up in its place to maintain the position of power, revenge and freedom from helplessness and guilt.

Depersonalisation

The main problem with perverse relationships is that they are always destructive. Even in cases where no-one appears to be harmed or damaged in any way, persons on the 'wrong end' of perverse relationships are always depersonalised as they are only a part of the fantasy of the one exercising the power. Depersonalisation is the opposite of warm intersubjective communication, where two or more people gradually get to know each other's minds, experiences, thoughts and feelings in a spirit of enjoyable and confident curiosity.

It is always deeply disturbing to experience depersonalisation. Being treated simply as an object for the use of another person in order to exert power, or in order to enact misplaced revenge is a violation of one's identity and individuality. This is so even if the relationship is apparently entered into willingly.

Professional youth workers with distressed young people are often in just such a position. By virtue of a desire to help, youth workers may well find themselves on the wrong end of perverse dynamics, and feel confused and hurt, like Maggie in the case study above.

Again, expert supervision is required to help youth workers stay as thoughtful and reflective as possible in their attempts to understand what is going on. This is not a 'policing' issue in order to exercise adult control, although there are obviously times when an adult has to step in to manage dangerous behaviours, sometimes using sanctions. However, this is a situation where it is essential to try to understand the process. Punishing the behaviour will only push the young person into finding some other form of power or covert revenge.

In the case study above, what is it exactly that Peter is doing to the others? What feelings is he evoking in them and in Maggie? What clues does this give us about Peter's mental state? Is he confused and hurting? He seems to be communicating difficulties with sexual identity? Might this be an issue for him? He seems to be evoking shock in others. Might he be struggling with experiences that are shocking, overwhelming and difficult to think about?

These are all *tentative hypotheses* that youth workers can reflect upon to see if there is any evidence for any of these thoughts. Reflecting in a professional and thoughtful way about what is going on helps to change the situation from one that is reactive or punitive into one that looks for meaning and ways to help the communication of, for instance, confusion and hurt in more socially acceptable ways. Discovering that you have been tricked is humiliating . . . might Peter have been humiliated?

It must be emphasised again that any actively destructive behaviour, physical or psychological must be stopped first and then thought about afterwards. This approach does not condone destructive or perverse activity, and in fact is a means to better identify it, and distinguish it from 'ordinary' behaviour (remember the Army mothers making their toddlers fight in Chapter 2).

Some commonly accepted ways of 'disciplining' children are, in fact, designed to punish, frighten, humiliate and thereby exert power over them. I'm thinking here of TV pundit inspired 'naughty steps' and similar bizarre responses to troubled children.

Young people do need firm boundaries and 'external' adult control to help keep them safe. They do not need punishment and humiliation. They need friendly adults around who they can get to know and rely upon, who can get to know them, and with whom they can make safe attachments.

Young people need to be able to get close to and feel protected by adults they can trust.

C H A P T E R   R E V I E W

This chapter has outlined some of the things that you will need to take into account when thinking about engaging in groupwork with distressed young people. Socialisation is discussed and is highlighted as a key developmental domain that can be targeted, although it must be borne in mind that earlier problems caused by unempathic and misattuned parenting may make this task difficult. Some 'perverse' solutions to the difficulties of problematic attachments are described.

FURTHER READING

Horne, A (2007) Brief Communications from the Edge: Psychotherapy with Challenging Adolescents, in Morgan, D and Ruszczynski, S (eds) *Lectures on Violence, Perversion, and Delinquency.* London: Karnac.

Has chapters with interesting titles like: 'Trans-sexuality: the Emperor's New Clothes'. You will need some familiarity with psychoanalytic terminology, but it is not too hard going. Chapters on internet pornography, risk assessment and aggression and violence as perverse solutions.

See also the film 'The Piano Teacher' by Michael Haneke.

This is a brilliant but disturbing exposition of perverse dynamics. Not for the faint-hearted!

Chapter 6

Getting started and keeping on going

This brings me to communication. In its origin, communication is effected by realistic projective identification. It may develop into a capacity for toleration by the self of its own psychic qualities and so pave the way for normal thought. But it also does develop as part of the social capacity of the individual. This is of great importance in group dynamics. Its absence would make communication impossible.

Yet its presence may arouse feelings of persecution in the receptors of the communication.

(Bion, 1967, p118; amended)

Here is a request from a youth worker with very disturbed young people whose work team was asked for suggestions regarding themes for an upcoming training day. The youth worker wrote: 'I would suggest something about shame and guilt, which seem to be very hard for the clients to think about and move on from, and also suggest something about invasiveness of feelings from the client to the youth worker'.

The youth worker has not only noticed that shame and guilt are frequently emotions that distressed young people find it difficult to tolerate, but she has also has realised – and probably experienced – that work with distressed young people can be emotionally 'invasive' to youth workers; in other words, emotions communicated or induced by means of projective identification may well arouse feelings of persecution in the receptors of the communication: the staff members.

The youth worker here has herself noticed the very same things that Bion has written about; that feelings get induced or pushed into you by means of projective identification.

However, communication with others is also one of the surest ways of alleviating emotional distress.

In this chapter we will look at how to plan and sustain projects that will help you to facilitate communication with young people who are experiencing emotional distress. This will have groupwork as its primary focus, as groups can be a very effective medium in this form of intervention.

First we will look further at the practical steps that are essential in creating an effective groupwork environment, how to maximise the essential features of groupwork that makes it effective, followed by an account of common problems that arise and some tips on how to deal with them.

Some of these points have been raised in the earlier section containing the 'Short course in groupwork', so only the most significant aspects will be mentioned again.

But first, a case study.

CASE STUDY

Group dynamics

A discussion group is organised for young people who have interpersonal and emotional problems. These problems range from difficulties with managing emotions such as anger, experiencing serious family problems, depression, isolation and severe social anxiety. The group is destined to run for a calendar year. The group meets for an hour and a half each week and is well attended with very few absences. Christo, however, is always at least half an hour late for every session. The group facilitator is very tolerant of this to begin with, hoping that Christo will settle down, but apart from only one occasion, he is persistently late, which often causes disruption to whatever is going on in the group.

At a session beyond the half-way stage of the group, one of the girls is describing a delicate situation with her family that is causing her a great deal of worry and concern. Christo bursts in, half an hour late as usual, and disrupts the girl's fragile connection with the group.

The group facilitator feels a welling up of anger, and makes a flash decision to say how annoyed he is at Christo's persistent lateness, pointing out the disruption he causes. Christo says, 'Right! Now I am going to say nothing. I have many things to say and now I feel I cannot. This group will end soon and it will end before I have properly begun'. The group is rather surprised by this uncharacteristic lack of tolerance on the part of the group facilitator, and one or two members comment on it.

This whole incident, including the group facilitator's unusual behaviour, is discussed in the group. After a while, one of the other young men gently asks Christo what he would like to say but feels he now cannot. Christo hesitantly talks about not liking girls as other men do. After a short, thoughtful and respectful silence, Christo tells the group that he is gay and has quite an active sex life but feels forced to hide this from his family, especially his father, and everyone else, including the group. He fears anger, intolerance and abandonment if he is open about himself, and feels very unsafe about being close to anyone,

---

including the group, for fear of losing the friendships and contacts that he has. As he speaks, he becomes increasingly angry at the way in which he feels obliged to hide himself.

Christo's anger gradually subsides into a calmer assertion of his wish to be known for who he is, rather than maintain the pretend self that he feels he has had to present to the world, and which was becoming increasingly hard to maintain.

In his lateness, it seems that Christo had been adjusting his level of intimacy and connection to others in the group to a level that he could manage and where he felt safe that he would not have to reveal himself. However, the group shows great interest and understanding of Christo's predicament. The group relaxes considerably, and each individual is able to move on to a deeper level of exploration of their current experiences in the group, their everyday lives outside of the group and of family relationships in particular.

The group facilitator notices that angry feelings were induced in him, by projective identification, and, although he feels that he could have managed the angry feelings better, is pleased at the way the group handled things.

On this occasion, even if the group facilitator had acted a little hastily, the group had been expert in helping Christo to express himself more fully.

This is 'therapy *in* the group *of* the group *including the conductor*' (Foulkes, 1990).

Many groupwork concepts are adapted from group psychotherapy, and can be very useful in conceptualising about social groupwork generally, and of course specifically in work with distressed young people.

The group as the agent of change

This is a good example of *the group itself acting as the agent or medium of change.*

For a group to work 'as a group' and to optimise our aim of maximising communication amongst group members, we need to shift our thinking away from groups that have a 'leader' to groups that have a 'facilitator' or a 'conductor'.

Some types of group – think of a sailing skipper in an off-shore race, or if you are leading a group in a 'risk environment' of some kind – need a very firm or even dictatorial leader, and sometimes this is true of 'facilitated' groups as well. But in the main we are trying to design situations where the group members can take as much responsibility for themselves in the group and the group-as-a-whole as possible.

This involvement and responsibility can dramatically increase the sense of self-esteem and self-worth of group members, and greatly improve young people's capacity to empathise and communicate with others, which in turn enhances social functioning and further improves self-esteem.

This improvement in the ability to relate in groups is a vital aspect of maturational development and has many knock-on effects in other aspects of the lives of individuals in family life, education and work. There is clear research evidence for this. (See the discussion of 'developmental cascades' in Chapter 1.)

Initial project planning

To recap some of the points in the previous chapter in the 'Short course in groupwork', the group facilitator is responsible for:

- Knowing clearly what are the *aims and objectives* of the group and keeping these in mind from inception to the ending of the project;

- Creating and maintaining the physical *setting* of the group: getting a room, chairs or whatever else the group needs for its basic functioning. Who else needs to be informed or brought into the group's basic supporting network? What other relationships need to be fostered?

- Attending to the aspects of the setting that must be attended to in order for the group to function comfortably?

- Establishing the group *boundaries*: time, place, membership, behavioural expectations;

- Establishing the boundaries of the group that must be respected by group members and conductor that contribute towards a feeling of consistency, safety and reliability in the group?

- Deciding what *staffing levels* are needed, and what training, supervision and support is necessary?

Who do you want to work with you? What do they need to know and do?

Practicalities

These may seem like very simple requirements, and in many respects they are. But they are often ignored or forgotten about, leading to problems in getting started and sustaining the work.

Even in the most helpful and facilitating environment, it is surprising how much effort has to go into creating and maintaining physical and psychological 'spaces' where 'groupwork that facilitates communication' can occur.

The basic functions outlined above have to be adapted into whatever environment the group will be run in. Again, this adaptation is the responsibility of the group worker. For instance, in the 'detached' caravan-based youth work project mentioned earlier in Chapter 4, in terms of the *setting*, the youth workers running the project:

- organised parking places and negotiated local authority parking restrictions;

- dealt with the people who loaned the Land Rover that towed the caravan;

- notified and met with the police and explained what the project was doing;

- met with local residents to explain what was going on and involve them if possible;
- made sure the gas bottles on the caravan were topped up.

Initial project planning will take as much of the above into account as possible. Careful planning and clear thinking will go a long way towards helping your group get off the ground. And you will, of course, need to adapt to changing conditions, deal with things you didn't plan for, or forgot about, and be flexible if necessary.

Making contact with distressed young people

In the youth work context, the work of *making contact* depends largely on simply and naturally being available, approachable and helpful. Consistency and reliability are key themes in gaining the trust of young people who are seeking adults with whom they can feel safe and protected. Showing a genuine interest and concern for those around you and being professionally dependable and reliable will go a long way in creating basic trust. Then, the chances are that those seeking help will naturally gravitate towards you.

There are no magic bullets when it comes to being able to make contact with distressed people of any age, but people who have been emotionally hurt or damaged do need some special considerations.

- They may feel especially wary of anyone who they feel is going to *do* anything to them, or put them in a situation in which they feel out of control;
- They may well feel extremely sensitive to loss, abandonment or rejection and show this by being rejecting and abandoning of people who are trying to help;
- They may be denigrating or contemptuous of helpers, or idealising of some people and denigrating of others;
- They may appear abnormally normal (false self) or draw attention to themselves in some way that is bizarre (not ordinary adolescent excess);
- They may be bullies or be serially bullied;
- They may suffer extreme jealousy and envy;
- They may self-harm in some way or threaten suicide or harm or threaten to harm others;
- They may be isolated and depressed or seek constant excitement, perhaps with dangerous activities of some kind or substance misuse.

ACTIVITY **6.1**

This list is not exhaustive by any means as there are many ways to express distress . . . can you add to it?

In all cases above, a youth worker just being natural, interested without being intrusive, realistically concerned where necessary and not trying to 'do' anything to the young person except try to understand them is usually the most fruitful attitude. Most people, more than anything, want to be heard and understood.

Let them get used to you first before offering anything; maybe then offer a place to talk? Bear in mind that disturbed young people may communicate primarily by means of projective identification; by inducing strong feelings in you and others around them. Their strong feelings may be disguised or hidden in some way; jealousy, for instance, can be particularly acute amongst very emotionally deprived young people, and can be expressed by behaviour that disrupts any relationship where someone gets attention.

And don't forget that young people need to be able to get close to and feel protected by adults they can trust.

It goes without saying that if there is a genuine cause for real concern over someone's safety, you should act in whatever way is appropriate and seek help immediately. If you are worried and do not know what to do, ask a senior youth worker or colleague as soon as possible.

Remember that people with attachment difficulties, including very strong needs for attachment, may well respond with 'protest'; that is, anger or detachment, to the return of a person they are attached to after a separation. If the child has given up hope and is in despair (dis-pair) they may express this in various ways that includes very arrogant, grandiose and controlling 'narcissistic' behaviours that induce despair in youth workers. This can be very confusing. Commonsense might expect gratitude at gaining the attention so desperately desired, but a more frequent response is anger and denigration following an experience that feels, to the young person, like abandonment. Despair, in particular, is a very hard emotion to cope with!

As in the case of Simon, the 'bicycle boy' in Chapter 3, it is important to consider that distressed young people may react with behaviours that are paradoxical and apparently inconsistent, illogical and contradictory.

All of the above reminds us that in work with distressed young people, we need to attend to structural and process aspects of the work in more detail than is usual. Although your efforts to work with distressed young people may seem not so different in overt appearance from more ordinary activities, the structures you create will need to have more 'tensile strength'. We can expect boundaries to be pushed, limits to be tested and patience to be tried.

Dynamic administration, especially where relationships with colleagues are concerned, will need to be carefully thought through so that boundaries and limits can be maintained firmly but flexibly. The youth worker will frequently be faced with working with the 'group' or network of adults who are involved with the young person, so you may well spend a considerable amount of time liaising with other professionals.

You may well be faced with repeated breakdowns of your work and have to mend and re-mend relationships, re-pair and re-mind yourself of what you are doing and why you are doing it.

Remember that our key concepts are empathic attunement in the context of a reliable relationship that the young person experiences as protective. A well functioning group can provide these elements.

Working with distressed young people will remind us again and again of the need to be able to tune in to the feeling states that are induced in us by means of projective identification, which is a form of proto-communication.

This is a theme and an activity in itself that needs to be persistently re-worked. The main reason for this is that the process of projective identification communicates a potentially infinite array of feelings, emotions and mental states. In much the same way that a good actor creates feelings and emotions in his audience, projective identification is always in the process of shifting its shape and form, so to speak. And, when feelings of helplessness and despair are induced, this can be especially difficult for a youth worker to manage and tolerate.

The good news is that, although the process is complex, and the feelings involved frequently 'invasive' and somewhat unpleasant, even persecutory, the accuracy of the communication is often stunningly and even satisfyingly accurate. Understanding this process and working with it can even enhance job satisfaction in what can be uncomfortable and thankless work. If handled well, understanding this process can lead to a considerable advancement in the level of communication with a young person.

Remember that you do not have to understand a young person fully, or at all; it is the genuine attempt to understand that is of greatest importance, not that you 'get it right'. If you can tune in accurately and help someone to articulate a hitherto incommunicable thought or feeling, then that is a bonus. Feelings and emotions are constantly changing, and in a state of flow.

It is the effort to try to understand that remains a constant, not the understanding itself.

After all, the main aim of our work with distressed young people is to increase their capacity to tolerate and communicate difficult thoughts, feelings and emotions in words and to be able to empathise with and understand other people and themselves.

Working with distressed young people: dealing with your emotions and feelings

One of the themes of this book has been to alert you to the feelings that can be induced in you by means of projective identification. This psychological 'field effect' was first noticed and described by workers in the field of psychotherapy, but as Bion remarks in the quote at the head of this chapter, projective identification

> . . . *develops as part of the social capacity of the individual. This is of great importance in group dynamics. Without it, communication would be impossible.*

> (Bion, 1967, p118; amended)

It is an ordinary part of everyday life. However, distressed individuals will tend to communicate by inducing feelings in the other rather more so than most people. So if you work with distressed young people, you are more at risk than in normal everyday life.

Why is this?

The reason is that the feelings induced in projective identification **are experienced as if they are your own.** This is the meaning of the 'identification' part of the term. The feelings are 'projected' into you and you 'identify' with them. More specifically, you identify with feelings and emotional states without being aware of it. It is an unconscious process.

How can I tell if a feeling is a projective identification, or if it is simply my own feelings?

When you are with a client, allow yourself to have a completely clear mind, receptive, but with nothing much in it. (This in itself is a difficult state of mind to achieve . . . almost meditative . . . without memory or desire.)

Notice what your own feelings are.

Now, what feelings and state of mind does the client induce in you?

It is difficult, but you will get better at it in time with practice. You will benefit greatly from help from an experienced psychodynamic practitioner who can help you to disentangle the client's projections from what is going on in your own mind. Then you can experience and think about the projection you receive from the client as a communication.

This process will help you to sort out what is being projected into you from the client from your own thoughts and feelings, and thereby lessen the impact of intrusive emotions and thoughts.

This is a difficult process to understand and work with, but can be an extraordinarily precise way of understanding communications that otherwise would be incomprehensible.

Projective identification, separateness and dependence

There is simply not the space, and this is not the place to go into this fascinating process more fully. If you would like a more detailed exposition, see Joseph (1988).

She writes about projective identification:

> *Thus the infant, or adult who goes on using such mechanisms powerfully, can avoid any awareness of separateness, dependence or admiration or of the concomitant sense of loss, envy, anger etc.*

(Joseph, 1988, pp. 65–6)

You can see from our previous case studies and discussions how feelings of separateness, dependence, admiration, loss, envy and anger are very much related to distress in adolescence. Projective identification may be used unconsciously to defend against experiencing these painful feelings.

As professional youth workers, the way to manage these feelings, and indeed to use them to good effect, is through the process of supervision and staff support.

Supervision, training and staff support

Clinical supervision

Supervision, in this context, refers to the way in which feelings induced in you are managed and thought about with the help of a senior practitioner, who should be trained and experienced in psychodynamic work. This will then be thought about in terms of what is going on for you and your clients in your work together.

This is different from 'line management supervision', which is basically about how you do your job and are 'managed' in line with the aims of the organisation that you work for.

To differentiate the two types of supervision, discussions with a psychodynamically trained professional are sometimes termed 'clinical supervision'.

A fundamental aspect of clinical supervision that differentiates it from line management supervision is the emphasis on the emotions that are induced in the worker. It is very important to be able to talk about difficult feelings like hopelessness and despair, or perhaps feelings of failure or rage without having to do anything about them and without being criticised for having the feelings. Only if the feelings are first accepted as valid can the meaning be explored to see if the process tells us anything about what is going on within the worker/client relationship and particularly feelings and emotions that the young person is struggling with.

This process assumes that the worker's practice is reasonably sound, that they have been well-trained and are being adequately line managed.

Training

You may wish to develop your groupwork skills further, and move towards becoming a skilled therapeutic practitioner, in which case specific training is a good idea. There are reputable organisations that run training courses in therapeutic groupwork. Details are given at the end of the book.

Staff support groups

Many organisations also now provide 'staff support groups' where staff come together to discuss their work as a team. This is also helpful in thinking together about what is going on with the young people that the agency is working with, helps reduce isolation and the tendency for individuals to feel overly responsible, which is a risk especially with neglected and deprived client groups.

If you are working in an agency with a high proportion of disturbed and distressed young people, it is actually dangerous to your own mental health not to have proper clinical supervision. Otherwise, you may find yourself experiencing high levels of distress yourself, or finding ways to 'switch off' from or avoid real contact with clients.

Where these processes get out of hand, agencies and organisations can suffer high levels of staff sickness, absenteeism, high staff turnover, and individuals may suffer from sleeplessness, depression or unaccountable angry outbursts.

The total environment

Remember Eric, the caretaker and cleaner who thought that he ran the youth centre? Keep an eye on the total environment. Sometimes the secretary or another worker who is not part of the youth work team will be picked out by young people as safe people to talk to; they and the organisation may benefit from their being a part of the staff support system.

ACTIVITY 6.2

Run a discussion group

In a youth project that you know, how would you go about creating the optimal conditions for a discussion group to meet? What planning requirements are there?

How would you go about recruiting people for your group?

Would you need any support to help you run your group? What support would you need?

Making contact

ACTIVITY 6.3

This is a group activity. Take 2 hours to do this.

Go out and make contact with some young people.

Find out who they are and what they feel are the major concerns in their lives. You will need to do some preparatory planning before you go.

How do you make initial contact? How do you explain what you are doing. What happened? What sort of response did you get?

Report back to your study group and share experiences.

Make sure that you feel safe and comfortable about doing this exercise.

C H A P T E R   R E V I E W

In this chapter, we looked at some of the ways in which working with distressed young people can put the worker under a great deal of pressure by evoking strong feelings in them. We explored aspects of group dynamics and looked at the need for adequate staff support, 'clinical' supervision and training. The process of making and sustaining contact with distressed young people was discussed, and aspects of the total environment and dynamic administration were considered.

FURTHER READING

Behr, H and Hearst, L (2005) *Group Analytic Psychotherapy*. London: Whurr

An excellent introduction to therapeutic group work, with informative chapters on dynamic administration and common problems in running groups.

Nitsun, M (1996) *The Anti-group: Destructive Forces in the Group and their Creative Potential.* London: Routledge

A very good account of difficult and problematic processes in groups and how to resolve them. Quite complex, but within the range of a reasonably well-read student.

Chapter 7
Summary and concluding remarks

Introduction

This chapter brings together the main ideas in this book. We review how the social context permeates the lives of young people, and has a deep effect on the conditions that shape the child-rearing practices that in turn affect the developmental trajectories of individuals. We remind ourselves that it is the capacity to form empathic and attuned relationships and the capacity to regulate, think about and communicate our emotions that forms the basis of our ability to relate in groups that are not dominated by 'basic assumptions' of 'fight/flight' and dependency or perverse ways of gaining attachment.

We remember that the development of the capacity for empathy and attunement occurs in the context of a reliably attached relationship within which the child feels protected, and that this relationship works best in a setting where the safely attached relationship is itself safely held so that emotions and feelings can be effectively contained.

Young people need to be able to be close to adults they can trust. These adults, parents and professionals, also need to know when and how to 'let go' so that the young person can enter the social world equipped to get along with others as well as have the capacity to be alone. We conclude that mental health is not dependent on material acquisitions but in the effort to know ourselves and to fully express our individual potentials whilst remaining in constructive relationships with others.

This book was intended to be written for, and used by, ordinary youth workers who happen to find themselves working with distressed young people. If you are engaged in regular and committed youth work practice it is likely at some point that this will be the case. It is noteworthy, and regrettable, that there are more emotionally disturbed and distressed young people, certainly in the UK, than ever before. There is evidence to support this.

The proportion of 15 to 16 year olds experiencing significant emotional difficulties rose a lot between 1974 and 1999, since when it has remained roughly stable. In addition, more young people have behavioural problems.

(Layard and Dunn, 2009, p. 2)

It may seem strange that in a period of relative affluence, where most people have a roof over their heads, enough to eat, comprehensive education and healthcare, that unhappiness and distress amongst the young has more or less doubled in the past 25 years. There are many reasons for this; the most notable single element probably being the high incidence of family discord and breakup and the psychological effect on parents, and therefore children, that this creates. Parental discord is a known cause of distress amongst children. The culture of individualism and consumerism is also thought to play an important role.

Much of the content of this book deals with the way in which distressed young people *communicate* their feelings and emotions. In the main, young people (or older ones for that matter) do not come for help in a calm frame of mind with a well worked out, neatly defined 'problem' that they want you to 'solve' (sometimes this happens, but it is frequently the 'wrong' problem that is presented, see the case study about Shadira, below). More often than not, they will present with some difficult, awkward or confusing behaviour that calls attention to their state of mind. They may well provoke painful and unpleasant feelings in peers and in the adults who are in helping roles, and test their resilience to the full.

One of the most helpful qualities that an adult can bring to a relationship with a distressed young person is the ability to *keep on trying to understand*, and not give up in the face of repeated rejections that may well be the young person repeating his own rejections within the current relationship with the youth worker.

The chapters and sections on projective identification show us ways in which incomprehensible behaviours may be better understood by means of exploring the feelings that are induced in others, meaning ourselves in this context. These concepts are drawn from psychotherapeutic practice, where they originated, but can very usefully be adapted into social groupwork and other forms of work with young people in order to inform practice and to help us to understand what is going on.

Being ordinary

Remember that ordinary social behavioural conventions should mostly be adhered to. I say 'mostly' because work with young people goes best with a certain amount of permissiveness, but adult intervention will be needed to establish safe limits when necessary. With certain young people there will be considerable slippage from this, and ordinary social behaviour may need to be repeatedly re-established. Remember, though, that there is never any reason for a youth worker – or a young person – to be treated as a 'punchbag', literally or metaphorically.

None of the above is an invitation to 'play at being a therapist'. Some of the information and guidance given here may be helpful if you are not experienced in this type of work, but the best way forward is to get some further training and consultation and supervision from an experienced psychodynamic practitioner.

The sections on 'holding' and 'containing' are vital in this regard. If your work is not adequately 'framed', there is very little chance that you will be able to create the conditions in which you can devote the time and effort needed to understand emotionally distressed young people. They may well need to repeat their efforts to get you to understand over and over again, and if there is not adequate 'holding and containing', these efforts will almost certainly dissipate into hopelessness.

A culture of 'individualism' and a preoccupation with money, competition, status and objects (which is certainly not confined to the UK and is spreading rapidly worldwide, especially in the Far East) does not help in this regard, and is actively damaging. Conversely, a healthy group life with friends and fun social activities is of huge benefit in living happily and in dealing with the inevitable setbacks and difficulties in day-to-day living.

That some young people are impaired in their capacity to relate empathically and attune to other people is a massive drawback in their ability to relate to others in groups. The reasons for this are outlined in the book in the earlier chapters.

If this specific problem of impaired empathic connection is not taken into account, then all the great social groupwork opportunities in the world will not make any real difference to the affected individuals. They need a more focused, group therapy approach where attention to this specific issue can be maximised and addressed in the context of the group process. Some group therapeutic approaches can be integrated into ordinary groupwork, for instance, the example of the football coach in Chapter 3 who enabled a 'free group discussion' but this needs to be done with as much thought as possible and awareness of what you are doing so that issues of 'holding and containing' are taken care of.

Using yourself and your own emotions as a 'receptor' for the feelings of others that they are unable to communicate in other ways is a skill that needs to be exercised in a thoughtful and reflective way.

Good and bad

An issue that was glossed over somewhat in an earlier chapter is the issue of good and bad, and right and wrong. This is self-evidently an important matter; unless we have some way of thinking about it, we will at some point find ourselves stumbling around in the dark, so to speak.

Working with distressed young people will inevitably confront us, sooner or later, with whatever it is that is disturbing or distressing them. So it is worth spending some time looking at how we judge the issues involved.

What is good and what is bad? How do we decide? Are some things always wrong? Or right? When we make an 'intervention' in the lives of young people, what are we trying to change for the better?

The problem of relativism

Are we trying to make distressed young people happier, and if so, what should we concentrate on? Are there absolute values and absolute truths that can guide us and influence the ways in which we can decide to live? If so, what does this mean in terms of the way in which we raise children and young people and the values that we instil in them deliberately or by unconscious inference? Should we direct our lives in order to achieve 'worthy goals' in terms of socially accepted status and acquisitions, or are there other 'human' values of 'self-actualisation' that ought to take precedence?

Perhaps it would be better to give up ideas altogether of what we 'ought' or 'should' do, and simply live according to our natures, like a fish or a giraffe? If our natures include lying, stealing, killing and torturing other people and animals, or creating social and economic conditions that effectively enslave and exploit others, isn't this just our nature? Perhaps some aspects of human 'nature' are intrinsically better than others; maybe the creation of art and music, thoughtful reflections on the causes of pain and distress, and developing love and concern for ourselves and others that enables us to refine our natural skills and fulfil our potentials?

These questions are difficult and have taxed the minds of great thinkers since human beings developed the capacity to think about and consider the consequences of their actions.

To some extent, each human generation has to revisit these issues over again, and it is part of the pleasures of working with young people to be constantly a part of this process of re-examining the values by which we live our lives.

But to continue the discussion, isn't it a fact, though, that each of us has our own viewpoint about things, and we are all equally entitled to hold a viewpoint or a view of the truth, so therefore each of our viewpoints is equally true and valid because each of our different viewpoints are true for each of us?

'Relativism', that is to say the idea that all viewpoints have the same value and therefore everything is just a matter of opinion, is a way of avoiding the work of deeper enquiry into the nature of things and the nature of differences between things. Hanging on to simple 'absolute truths' is another way of avoiding complexity. 'Absolute truth' may take the form of a 'leader' or a religion, or a political party of some kind, or in a belief or explanation that is clung to as deeper understanding is too difficult to think about. This might be due to emotional or intellectual naiveté, or the effects of trauma that has caused the suppression of more complex feelings. An example of this is the belief that all my problems are caused by the 'fact' that I smell bad, or that socialism would cure all social ills, or that a free-market economy is the only way to allow people to express themselves fully, or that a breast enhancement would solve my relationship problems, or that if I had more money everything would be ok . . .

It is a sad fact of modern life that the full force of psychological manipulation has been aimed directly at young people in particular, deliberately to enhance feelings of inadequacy so that products can be sold to make us feel better. A perverse misuse of the 'deep' insights of psychoanalysis linked to the advertising world of Madison Avenue was directly involved in the genesis of this trend. It has led directly to a massive level of social and personal insecurity (Curtis, 2010).

A similar confrontational debate is going on currently between the simplistic and repetitive 'cognitive' approaches to 'counselling' and the deeper explorations of psychodynamically informed psychotherapy. (To read more about the topic of relativism, see Terry Eagleton (2004) *After Theory*, London: Penguin and especially Paul O'Grady (2002) *Relativism (Central Problems of Philosophy)*, Montreal: McGill-Queen's University Press.)

Measuring up: status anxiety

It is a fact that our current society is riddled with status anxiety. Children from a very early age are becoming obsessed with 'performance' and 'results' to an extent that many who feel that they cannot achieve and compete give up altogether and become depressed and withdrawn, although they often find other ways of making their presence felt in the world. A sense of failure and humiliation may well lead to someone finding 'perverse' (hateful) ways of gaining power.

Experiencing oneself as a failure and inferior in relation to others, defeated and humiliated, are very frequently precursors of depression and a feeling that who we are and what we have is not enough. This has been known about for centuries. In art and literature, such persons are often depicted as cripples, dwarfs or marginalised malignant gnomes, like Alberich in *Das Rheingold* (**www.metoperafamily.org/metopera/history/stories/ synopsis.aspx?id=78**).

Another example is *Rumpelstiltskin* (see the following link for a brilliant telling of the tale by Rik Mayall, at: **www.youtube.com/watch?v=xRi-v_7cJ_U**). The story of *Rumpelstiltskin* in the Grimm's folk tale begins with a man, a miller, feeling hopeless and inadequate in relation to a king and trying to deal with his feelings of inadequacy by making an impossible claim that endangers the life of his daughter. Many more folk tales and myths, dramas and religious stories deal with these themes of thwarted ambition, jealousy, envy and rivalry amongst peers and brothers and sisters. It was also a favourite theme in Shakespeare's tragedies, notably Macbeth's 'vaulting ambition' that got out of hand, and Othello's susceptibility to the jealous and envious Iago.

Another often-quoted example is the fact that Hitler was a failure at almost everything, notably as a painter and a beaten soldier, until he discovered a talent for public speaking that was used initially in the political wing of the defeated and humiliated German army. A less pernicious example is that of the massively gifted footballer, George Best who, as his powers declined on the field to that of a merely ordinary player, drowned his sorrows in a sea of denial, alcohol and sex, leading to an early death from liver failure after many years of humiliating public decline. A hotel worker, entering George's room and finding him drinking champagne in bed with Miss World, is said to have remarked: 'George, where did it all go wrong'. Best used to tell this story as a humorous example of his continued success, unaware of the bitter irony and denial that it also intimated.

There are many excellent books that include discussions of status anxiety, including Alain de Botton (2004) *Status Anxiety*, London: Hamish Hamilton and Oliver James (2007) *Affluenza*, London: Vermilion. It is worth mentioning that competition for status affects all levels of society; depression, which is a huge and growing problem in many areas of the world, is directly related to feelings of failure, bitter rivalry and inadequacy when one feels that others are more successful or socially esteemed than oneself. Feelings of worthlessness and inadequacy are by no means reserved for those who appear most obviously at the bottom end of society; in fact these feelings can be most acute amongst people, like George Best, who appear to be amongst the most successful.

At first sight, it may appear paradoxical that individuals in societies that have the appearance of a meritocracy experience the greatest levels of distress caused by feelings of inadequacy. Individuals in societies and groups that have clear 'rankings' of class, caste or status (such as rank in the Army, Church or Police Force) are relatively free from such dissatisfactions. In other words, if you 'know your place', have no obvious chance of becoming 'upwardly mobile' and assume that others who are higher ranked have an entitlement to be there, you are actually *less* likely to suffer from envy and feelings of failure than if you feel that you *might* have achieved more but have failed.

However, currently, most Western countries, and increasingly countries globally, have constructed societies where there are apparent opportunities for social mobility, but in fact the actual levels of social mobility are very poor. This leads to vast pools of frustration in the populations as expectations are not met, and depression and feelings of failure are commonplace. For instance, at the time of writing (2010), it is not uncommon for students with top class degrees from renowned universities to be taking unpaid work as a means of getting into the job market. This leaves many students with a massive challenge to overcome feelings of failure by becoming creative in some way; the alternative may be to lapse into depression.

Unfortunately, the compensatory need to triumph over others when someone feels defeated and marginalised may be greater than their ability to rectify the situation in a more constructive way. For instance, in the Grimms' story, Rumpelstiltskin could have used his unusual entrepreneurial talent more productively; instead he used his abilities to try to take the life of a newborn rather than try to re-invent himself in some way and start anew. He is 'perversely' hatefully destructive rather than creatively constructive in his efforts.

Incidentally, the Kaufmann Foundation, which is devoted to the values of entrepreneurism, suggests 'creative destruction' as an antidote to despair and hopelessness in modern market economies in which, like it or not, we all live.

Kaufmann also suggests that you:

- treat others as you want to be treated;
- share life's rewards with those who make them possible;
- give back to society.

Separation from mother: what can go wrong?

We know that an essential part of early development that affects the child's later capacity to form healthy peer group relationships, and healthy relationships with authority, is bonding and an attachment to an adult with whom the child feels safely protected and attuned and where the child can learn to experience, think about and express its own feelings and empathise with those of others. This is an integral building block of the young person's 'developmental cascade' and will become a part of who they are in relation to others (remember the man who said 'I am now all the ages I have ever been'?)

This attached and attuned relationship implies that the parent (for argument's sake, I shall use the term parent to include other caregivers who are involved long-term in the life of the child and with whom the child has formed an attachment) can also 'let go' at an appropriate point and enable the child to make their own way in the world whilst still remaining a helpful and supportive figure in the background.

This is the phase of life during which a youth worker is likely to be involved with a young person who is trying to deal with separating out from parents or a parental figure.

There is some evidence that, partly driven by economic circumstances, this natural process of separation is taking longer and longer

---

CASE STUDY

Paradoxical injunction/double bind – separation anxiety

Maureen is an Irish girl who has come to London to study. Her mother, back home in Ireland, telephones and texts her at least eight times a day, and sometimes more. Mother also goes to mass almost every day, and makes sure that she rings Maureen to tell her that she is praying for her. Mother goes on a pilgrimage every year and walks up a stony mountain barefoot, telling Maureen that she is doing this penance for her. She often tells Maureen how lonely she is, and implores her to come back to visit, often getting Maureen's father to buy her the plane tickets without asking if she wants to come home or not.

Maureen comes for help after collapsing into a deep depression having taken to her bed for several weeks. She has, over the years, become very obese, bingeing on chocolate and biscuits. She has no idea what she wants or what her own needs are, and feels that the only option is to go home and go to bed and be looked after by her mother.

She feels terribly guilty that she is unable to make her mother's life better, and feels that she alone is responsible for trying to make her mother happier. Her mother also persistently tells Maureen that Maureen is not doing as well as she could do, that she is wasting her time studying, that she is not a good student as her sister is the clever one in the family and that no man will ever want her because of her size. Maureen feels completely miserable and dejected, but also dependent on her mother for approbation. She feels that it must be her fault that her mother is so dissatisfied with her, and tries desperately to make her mother love her.

Mother frequently says to Maureen 'I only want the best for you and to help you make your own way in the world'. And then follows this up with a demand that Maureen come home immediately as mother is so lonely without her; a 'paradoxical injunction' leading to a 'double bind' situation. This has the known effect of making the subject, Maureen in this case, feel that either and both of the options presented will lead to the wrong choice being made. This then rapidly makes the subject lose confidence in their ability to make choices resulting in further dependency, confusion and loss of self-direction.

The vicious circle is completed because Maureen is to some extent genuinely poorly equipped to exist on her own, and part of her believes that she needs the permanent 'nursing' attention of her mother in order to survive. They are enmeshed in a rigid system of dependency on each other. Maureen feels so guilty and dependent that she feels that she cannot let her mother go through the loneliness that might eventually lead to mother finding a life of her own, and her mother cannot let go of Maureen because she fears losing her for ever as a friend and companion.

Variations on this theme are actually much more common than one would like to think and are often linked to serious eating disorders, because the 'child' never learns to gain a sense of what their own needs actually are as they have yet to experience themselves as a separate person. In fact, the 'child', Maureen in this case, is in reality 'mothering the mother' by trying to deal with the mother's anxieties about being left alone. When she finally plucked up the courage to speak to someone, she said, poignantly: 'I have never felt that I own my own life'.

ACTIVITY **7.1**

It could be argued that the mother in this case study is actively disabling her child because of the mother's own unmet needs and dependency. Is this a case where the mother's attitude is absolutely wrong and should be stopped or changed? Or should we adopt a 'non-judgemental' attitude and accept that she has a right to be whatever way she chooses?

If you were working with Maureen, would you give her any advice or make any recommendations? Or would you talk through her feelings with her and let her make her own mind up?

You might be somewhat relieved to know that in the real case that this is drawn from, when Maureen started to become a little more assertive about her needs she found some surprise support from her father, who gently encouraged her and helped reassure the mother. This was quite an unexpected and welcome development, but unfortunately is a somewhat rare outcome.

Transitions and rituals

Separating from parents is a universal human developmental task, and, as with any growth and change, there is usually emotional pain involved. Many cultures have ritualised this transition with ceremonies and rituals of various kinds.

Some of these rituals include demonstrations of the ability to suffer pain. It is accepted in many cultures that becoming an adult requires the ability to contain painful feelings and still be able to function, and treat this ability as something to be valued and celebrated.

This is in stark contrast to current trends to reach for the antidepressants and medications as a way of attempting to get rid of painful or difficult feelings, and trying to live up to the even more stupid imperatives that we are supposed to be happy, think positively or even worse, 'bubbly' at all times. This is actually a form of socially reinforced 'double bind' that many young people find impossible to negotiate. 'You will be constantly happy and think positively at all times' is an impossible expectation as there will inevitably be disappointment, loss and difficulty in life. It is how we manage pain and distress that is important, not that we should never experience them.

In some African tribal initiation rituals, girls are ritually scarred as part of their transition to adulthood. Anthropologists were horrified by this practice, seeing it at first through Western eyes as a way of male tribal elders exerting power over the females.

When the anthropologists thought to ask the girls what they made of it, the girls said that it meant that they could now take part of the life of the group as adults and change their social identity from that of children to that of adult women who could bear pain, most obviously the physical pains of childbirth but also the eventual deaths of their parents and other troubles in life. The ceremony marked a transition from one phase of life to another. The scarring was an acknowledgement of their life achievements, their strength and identity – not of their subservience, and also created a powerful bond amongst them and the older women in the group. For boys, scarring and other forms of bearing pain marked life transitions into being men, and hunters and warriors, and identity with the group.

Some governments have tried to put a stop to these practices, but they live on as a testimony to the power of the meaning that these rituals have in the group.

It goes without saying that current trends in piercing and tattooing amongst young people can have similar forms of social meaning, although the meaning may be lost and obscured in the context of current urban life (see **www.i-c-r.org.uk/publications/ Monographarchive/Monograph37.pdf**).

Holding and containing by the staff team

Some young people are so disturbed that they need additional holding by an institution, as they cannot function by themselves or in the context of their family environment.

Holding and containing in an institutional setting

The following case study illustrates the ways in which an institution experiences difficulties in maintaining a 'holding environment' that can 'contain', understand and think about the emotions of seriously distressed young people; and also, crucially, give the young person an *experience* of being 'held'. The example below is chosen because it illustrates problems that are frequently encountered in this sort of work. Work with disturbed young people is inherently difficult, but this study shows how a failure in the holding environment, in a well-run unit, exacerbates an already problematic situation.

Don't forget that failure is inevitable. It happens sometimes when we try to do things, especially creative things that are new for us. Nobody is perfect and mistakes happen. It is how we deal with a problem that is important. The experience of things being handled constructively and calmly when they go wrong is also a good education for young people in how to deal with life generally.

For professional workers, working with and thinking about severe pathologies is a great way of learning about how mental distress manifests in different people. Like most illnesses, serious mental distress is an exaggeration or amplification of processes that are found in 'health'. For instance, projective identification is a cornerstone of communication generally, and is the main drive in artistic productions, but *excessive* projective identification is a feature of psychosis and other serious psychological problems, analogous to the way in which *excessive* mucous production is a feature of a cold or flu.

Remember that problem behaviour is usually the young person's attempt at communicating something (usually fear or anxiety of some sort) and is also their best attempt at a *solution* to their difficulties. Joining a gang, isolating themselves, developing some odd behaviour or an apparently incomprehensible 'symptom', may well be a young person's solution to difficulties in relating to others and the often messy business of separating from parents and becoming more independent and autonomous.

CASE STUDY

The staff of a residential centre that specialises in working with very disturbed young people aged between 16 and 24 decide to take them on a day trip to the seaside. Two staff members will accompany four girls and three boys on the trip. (I'll occasionally use the terms 'boys' and 'girls' for brevity and to avoid the more impersonal terms of males and females or 'young men and young women'.) Attendance at the centre is voluntary and it is not custodial.

The day of the trip has arrived, and the staff meet to do a 'handover' before the party leaves to catch the train. The two staff members taking the trip have both been on compassionate leave due to bereavement and family illness and are looking forward to the trip as a way of reconnecting with the residents.

The handover usually consists of the staff team getting together and sharing information about the young people and anything else that might be of relevance or of help to whoever is coming on to the shift. This is an important part of the 'holding' environment; how the care of the young people is passed over from one shift to the next (think of the way in which a baby might be passed from one person to another to look after, carefully without dropping it . . .) and the staff team is usually very thoughtful about this aspect of their work.

One of the staff members, who is key worker to one of the girls, has some important information about her client and is preparing to share it with the two workers leading the trip, both of whom are somewhat out of touch with what is going on in the centre, having been away for a while.

Just as the staff team are about to meet, two of the boys suddenly start to rush around the building setting off the fire extinguishers. The staff meeting is abandoned as workers deal with the mayhem and mess. Two of the girls then refuse to leave the house and say they are not going out after all. One of them refuses to move at all and, strangely, looks as if she is stuck to the wall in a corridor, giving every impression that she would have to be peeled off. Eventually, however, everyone gathers together and they head off to the train station.

The trip is to a seaside town where one of the girls on the trip (the one who appeared stuck to the wall) had made a serious suicide attempt the year before coming to the centre. She had been talking about this with the other young people, including the two boys who had made the mess, and had rather dramatically indicated that she might make another attempt. This information is known by the girl's key worker, and would have been discussed in the staff team had it not been for the disruption.

It is information that is known by everyone except the two workers leading the trip.

> *CASE STUDY continued*
>
> *The party arrives at the train station and boards a train without too much fuss. However, when the time comes to change trains, after an altercation with the staff, two of the boys run off and disappear, saying they are going home. They are of an age where they can be expected to look after themselves, so reluctantly the group continues to the seaside, where two of the girls immediately do the same as the boys and disappear. The trip is rapidly disintegrating.*
>
> *After a troublesome day (the details of the trials and tribulations are far too extensive to go into here) everyone is gathered together again and back at the unit, except one of the boys who ran off. He eventually returns extremely drunk and collapses in a somewhat theatrical manner in front of everyone, causing such anxiety amongst the staff that an ambulance is called; the boy then refuses treatment from the paramedics, resulting in yet more fuss and confusion. Eventually he settles down and allows himself to be 'nursed'.*

What is going on?

As mentioned earlier, most problems of this nature are determined by more than one cause, however, on this occasion, and again for the sake of brevity, we will stay simple and just look at a couple of aspects of the holding environment that were experienced as fragile on this occasion.

All the young people at the unit were very sensitive to anything that felt unsafe in the sense of feeling unprotected or separate from protective figures, and especially where they may have to deal with anything unexpected. Their capacity to handle anxiety was very poor and they very quickly went into states of panic. They tended to make what is sometimes called 'adhesive identifications' (Bick, 1968). The girl 'stuck' to the wall makes us think of this. Their capacity to talk about their feelings and anxieties was extremely impaired. Because of their extreme problems in managing relationships with attuned caregivers, the young people had learned ways of forcing adult attention that they could then feel in control of. The group-as-a-whole easily flips into 'fight/flight' mode, rapidly alternating with actions that create adult attention and preoccupation in 'dependency' mode (Bion, 1962).

The idea of going out on a trip in itself was enough to raise anxieties in these young people, most of whom had very enmeshed relationships with their mothers to the point where they had never had to experience themselves as separate individuals. The experience of separation was frightening, and this was re-enacted in relation to the building and setting of the centre.

Add to this a feeling of dread and terror that the 'suicidal' girl was evoking in the group, and the fact that there was a breakdown in communication in the staff team – important information was not transmitted – and you have an incendiary mix. It may seem as if the precipitating factors are minimal, but let us not forget that survival anxiety is very fright-ening in itself. The two boys who set of the fire extinguishers were, in a sense, raising the alarm and testing the capacity of the staff team to deal with a psychological emergency. How were the staff going to deal with a challenge to their primary task of maintaining a holding environment? Could they be trusted to give full attention to the needs of the young people by completing a proper 'handover' in the face of a distraction?

The two staff members taking the trip were both, themselves, still recovering from their own personal experiences; they had both been on compassionate leave due to family issues and were not, as individuals, as 'containing' as usual.

In hindsight, it would have been better for the staff to have their handover meeting and share information. That the staff group could be deflected from their primary task of keeping their handover space – a time to think about and reflect upon what is hap-pening in the residents' group – would have been felt by the young people as unsafe and as if the adults could not manage the anxiety that was projected into them by the 'emergency'.

The day ended with the 'collapse' of the holding environment being symbolised by the 'collapsed' boy being physically nursed by the ever-calm and anxiety-containing para-medics.

Repetition and repair

The above might sound like a criticism of the staff team. *It is not.*

Distressed young people usually need repeated experiences of re-enacting the trauma of a failure of holding which then, if the situation is managed in a 'good-enough' way by the adults around, will gradually become internalised through repetition. This helps incremen-tally to repair the damaged and fragile inner world of the child.

The situation described above would not have happened with more 'ordinary' young people. Disturbed young people will unerringly, and without being aware of it, seek out any 'cracks' in the holding environment as a way of testing its resilience and safety. The team and the unit in the case study actually had very good internal systems of staff sup-port, supervision, training and well established groupwork programmes with the young people.

We are reminded constantly in working with distressed young people of the process of repetition and repair; the holes in our best efforts will be found out and we will be reminded again and again that there is no perfect solution or structures that will avoid or prevent distress.

It is actually these cracks in the system that are most instructive and that we can learn most from; we deepen our knowledge of what it is that distresses young people – and learn more about just how fragile we all are.

Shadira

Shadira comes for help because she is having great difficulties at school. She is a very able student, but has always felt unconfident in relation to her classmates and just recently has developed a real fear of speaking in class. She feels that all the others are much better than she is and becomes paralysed by fear in case she makes a mistake or says something that will make her appear incompetent or silly or mark her out as different.

She has discussed these fears and realises that they are probably irrational, but her level of anxiety is so great that it makes it impossible for her to think about changing her behaviour.

She talks about her family.

Her father is from Pakistan and her mother is white Anglo-Saxon English. It is her mother's second marriage and there are four much older children from her first marriage. These siblings stick together and have a special relationship with mother; they are quite dismissive of Shadira and use her as a messenger to tell her mother when they are all going on holiday together. Shadira feels that they are 'rubbing it in', that they are a 'little club' and she is out of it. Mother and father's relationship is not good at the moment and appears to be falling apart. Mother refers to Shadira and father as 'you two' and 'your lot' referring to their colour and racial similarity.

The parents' relationship is being affected adversely by the fact that the family business is failing and shortly to go into receivership. Father has also recently been diagnosed with a malignant cancer that may be life-threatening. Shadira's Middle Eastern boyfriend has recently gone back to Egypt with his family and at any rate, his father was against the relationship because Shadira is not a Muslim. She has also fallen out with a best friend over a planned trip abroad that went wrong.

It is not difficult to see that Shadira's experience of being marginalised is being trans-ferred onto the other groups of which she is a part. She is in a very 'unheld' situation: her relationship with mother has never felt close and is certainly not empathic; her mother's response to her daughter's problems with classmates being 'well, leave school then'. Shadira is frightened of losing her father, as he is the only family member she feels close to. Her boyfriend has gone and she has fallen out with her other close friend, whom she describes as 'like the sister I never had'. Her parents are at war and the family are having to sell up and move to a smaller house in a cheaper location.

Shadira's network of support is very tenuous; although a pleasant and intelligent girl, she is emotionally somewhat naive and has difficulty in empathising with and understanding other people (her mother has not helped much in this respect). She imagines that every-one else has no anxieties except her; she has not grasped that some anxiety is normal in a classroom situation when you may be called upon to answer a question. She does not have a holding environment that would enable her to take on the challenge of trying her-self out more in a group and of developing the resilience that she needs to enter more fully into group life.

> ### CASE STUDY *continued*
>
> *Although she is quite capable of intellectually understanding her position and what she might do about it, she needs the experience of being in a group to enable her to overcome her fears and gain ego-support whilst she gets to understand the emotional lives of herself and others better. A good group in this respect will offer 'ego training in action', that is, a real experience of being with others in a group so that problems in relating can be overcome in a supportive and helpful setting where there are no real 'consequences' to making mistakes whilst you learn.*
>
> *Most importantly, however, a well-run therapeutic group will offer a first rate experience of emotional processing in a way that is analogous to an empathic and attuned 'other'. Gradually, the group's ability to experience and think about emotions and intersubjective relationships will be internalised by the group members and will enable them in turn to have better relationships both within groups and in relation to themselves and others generally.*

A word on assessment, 'symptoms' and trying to understand

Here is a process which may help you in the work of building up a psychological picture of a young person you are working with.

Remember that symptoms themselves are in the nature of imaginative solutions to problems brought about by deep issues such as abandonment, enmeshment and engulfment, separation, dependence/independence, loss, jealousy, envy, love, hate and other powerful feelings and emotions.

A sequence might look like this:

Look at and observe what is happening with the young person.

What is happening between us; what are our reactions?

What feelings are induced in us?

Build up a tentative hypothesis about what might be going on in the young person's inner world; what might the young person be struggling with and what may they be trying to communicate? Free-associate and see what comes to mind.

Discuss your thoughts with others, informally or in a supervision group with a senior practitioner.

Are there any ideas, thoughts or theories that may help us? For instance, does attachment theory throw any light on things? How about projection and projective identification? Bion's Basic Assumption groups, perhaps?

Look again at what is going on. Observe. Gather more evidence. Formulate hypotheses, discuss with others, especially experienced practitioners.

- Remember that we are not trying to 'prove' anything; it is a search for understanding.

- Gradually try to understand what is happening in the internal world of the young person.

It is a scientific method: we gather information using our thoughts, senses, attuned empathy, intellect and imaginations, then we formulate hypotheses and see if these help us in our attempts to understand.

We accept and keep in mind the fact that we are fallible and may often be wrong, but when this happens we try again to correct and improve our understanding.

How to be wrong when you are right

Remember, too, to choose your time and place in work with distressed young people so that the setting – the holding environment – is able to help hold and contain any difficult feelings that may emerge.

Do bear in mind that exploratory or any 'depth' work may well be experienced as an impingement or frighteningly intrusive and even threatening by a young person. Psychological defences are there for a very good reason; namely, because the young person is not able yet to deal with the feelings that are defended against.

Do not go crashing through into areas that a young person is not yet ready to deal with. But do not be too hesitant and 'walk on eggshells' either.

If you make an accurate observation about a young person's feelings or inner world and they are not ready for it, your correct but intrusive words may be experienced as an attack or even abusive. The young person may well clam up even more, and become even more defensive or avoid help altogether.

If you make an accurate observation or interpretation of what is going on and a young person is not ready for it, you may be right . . . but you'd be wrong. This would be a failure of attunement on your part.

So how do you tell when is the right moment to talk about a delicate matter, confront something, or address powerful feelings?

You have to learn by experience and practice, and each person is different. This is part of the 'art' of working with distressed young people.

CASE STUDY

Kareena

Kareena was born in the Far East. She arrived in the world two months prematurely, and spent some time in an incubator after birth. Her mother was ill for most of Kareena's first year.

It is usual in Kareena's culture for grandparents to look after the children, and this is what happened in her case; however, both grandparents were very old, and not very interested in playing with and relating to a young girl, although she was well looked after physically. Both parents worked a considerable distance away and hardly saw their little daughter for the first four years of her life. Kareena was an only child and had very little contact with other children until she went to school when she was six. She lived a long way from school and didn't get to play much with other children.

Again, for reasons of parents' work and family matters, Kareena went to a boarding school when she was 11 until the age of 16. She describes these years as very happy, and she thoroughly enjoyed sharing her room, playing and learning with the other girls whom she got to know very well. Quite suddenly, at 16, she was sent on an 'Exchange Year' abroad to America.

Although a very intelligent girl, Kareena struggled with the new language. More significantly, she had enormous problems with the young people in the school that she joined. Kareena had the distinct disadvantage of being not only extremely able academically, but she was also very pretty and somewhat exotic in the small town in the Mid-West where she was staying. She got considerable attention from the boys, but felt completely out of her depth in this area, so politely refused and avoided any advances and any real contact.

A group of influential girls – the 'in' group at the school – immediately began making life very hard for Kareena, and she wasn't very well equipped to deal with it. She quickly became ostracised and marginalised. Kareena became confused and infused with anxiety which made it even less possible for her to think about and understand what was going on. Why was she being treated in this way? It didn't make any sense. She was used to a close group of girls in her boarding school that she had known for years, and she had felt warmly and securely attached to them. She was a long way away from home and even when speaking to her parents on the phone, felt that she had to pretend that everything was alright to avoid worrying them.

Kareena couldn't make any sense of this situation. She had been taught to be polite and smile and be 'nice' to people, so no-one knew how depressed and isolated she was feeling inside. She was also not very good at thinking about and describing her feelings in words so it never occurred to her to talk with the school counsellor. She began to think that there must be something wrong with her, although she had no idea what it was.

One day, when she was feeling especially unhappy and isolated, she decided to make another effort to be friendly with the other girls. She approached them with a smile, but one girl turned around to her and said 'Get lost will you . . . you smell!'

Kareena felt hurt and ashamed. Was it true? Did she really smell? Was this the reason that nobody seemed to like her? Maybe this explained why the other girls gave her such a hard time. Nobody else was treated in this way. So it must be true.

Quite rapidly, Kareena's belief that people avoided her because she smelled became a very fixed idea in her mind. She got into the habit of avoiding most form of human contact as a result, which made matters progressively worse. She arranged many doctors' and hospital appointments to try to find the cause of the non-existent smell, which she now firmly believed to the source of all her problems.

Bullying

Girls who feel insecure or inadequate and have their status in the group threatened may well bully another in order to make her feel defeated and depressed, and in order to get rid of their feelings into her by means of projective identification. Bullying is a major problem and can leave deep emotional scars on those unfortunate enough to be targets. With the advent of mass electronic communication and 'cyber bullying' the problem has probably become worse.

Many young people are bullied and the problem is worse in groups that are riddled with status anxiety.

Young people who stand out for some reason are particularly susceptible. Gay and lesbian young people are especially at risk of being picked out as 'different'.

Bullying deserves deeper and more extensive consideration than is possible here in this context, but it should be emphasised that adult intervention is necessary whenever bullying is known to be occurring.

Eventually, Kareena approached an adult for help; someone whom she felt she might be able to trust.

Each attempt to help should be in the manner of research, where you might have some general ideas and develop some tentative hypotheses, and then begin to gather evidence and test them out. For instance, the worker began to think about the rather odd 'symptom', and then the context in which it arose. In this case it was Kareena's estrangement from her parents and her problems in relating to others outside of the family home. The worker also thought about her premature birth and period in an incubator, the known separation from her mother at an early age due to her mother's 'illness' (possibly depression) separation from grandparents and difficulties in bonding with her parents, especially her father, at a later stage. This might have left her with a tendency to have problems in thinking about and managing her emotions; in other words, in 'affect regulation'. Kareena had also experienced a very sheltered upbringing that left her with a lack of confidence in dealing with the social world outside her home, and further major disruption at age 16.

Cultural issues to do with food and changes of social and cultural expectations had also added to the mix. And this was also in the context of the fact of already being an unwittingly threatening 'foreigner' and a threat to the status and power relations in an unstable group of insecure and somewhat aggressive adolescent girls.

You can see that this is a situation of some complexity that we trying to understand.

Summing up

This book is largely concerned with the period in life known as adolescence; the time between being considered to be a child and being considered to be an adult. In its original form, the word 'adolescence' meant 'to grow up' and was usually taken to mean the period between puberty and legal adulthood; the part of life spanning the ages of about 13 to 20 years. Due to the way in which our global culture is developing, and due to the effect of economic circumstances in particular, this period seems to be extending. Adolescence was originally linked to the 'teenage years' and especially to the rapid development of physical sexual maturity. Childhood was considered to be a time of 'innocence' and dependency, and 'adulthood' to the growth of 'experience', 'independence' and autonomy.

However, in practical terms, the developmental tasks at both 'ends' of adolescence have become increasingly blurred; very young children are frequently worried about things such as physical appearance and school grades, and legally adult young people well into their twenties and beyond are unable to get paid work and leave home as they cannot support themselves economically in a way that meets their material expectations.

Our current culture of compliance, fake and fallacious notions of quick and easy perfectibility, fast cures and celebrity feeds directly into the constructions of 'false selves'; and, also in Winnicott's terms, the young person longs for someone to bring understanding. Rebellious, delinquent and destructive behaviour may be a desperate – or perversely and revengefully hurtful – bid to get someone to understand just how much an individual's belief and trust in their environment has been shattered. Remember that damaging behaviour will need adult intervention to stop it going too far.

Sometimes, however, behaviour that tests you to the limit will stretch your resilience to breaking point. You are not in the work to be abused or hurt; get some help from an experienced colleague to sort out what is going on so that you can work the situation through differently.

Remember that many young people live in home environments that are impossible for them to manage; children cannot deal with depressed or addicted parents, or those that are at war with each other. As a consequence, they may well create 'impossible' situations for those who work with them. This is then chaos that the young person *is* in control of – rather than the alternatives of false compliance or depressive withdrawal.

Growing up has never been easy, but it could be argued that being a young person in the context of modern, early twenty-first-century culture is more difficult than at other times in history when social roles were more defined and expectations were more easily met. At any rate, there is a considerable weight of opinion and research that tends toward the view that the high levels of distress amongst young people is related to the social and economic contexts in which we live, and is also linked to current attitudes and practices related to child rearing.

The development and 'creation' of an individual is a highly complex matter and is the result of many subtle influences that interact with and influence each other to form a unique person. This process is made more elaborate and intricate by the fact of infinite possibilities arising from the social, group and family contexts in which the child develops and the adult person arises.

This is a *dynamic* process in the sense that it is subject to influences and unpredictable events that may be glaringly obvious, like a messy and acrimonious parental divorce, or subtly imperceptible, like the failures in 'holding' described earlier in this chapter.

However, in this book we have been able to trace some of the major themes in the way in which a child develops into a young person who can cope reasonably well with the challenges of becoming an adult. Fortunately, these themes aren't too difficult to outline, and give us some very good clues as to how we can understand and help young people who become distressed.

To begin at the beginning, first a baby needs a reliable sense of being 'held' in an environment that is safe, secure and where he feels protected. His feelings and emotions need to be able to be received, understood and tolerated by those around him, and he needs not to be troubled too much, at least at first, by the requirement to understand the minds of the people who are looking after him – that can come later. Gradually, the very young child builds up a capacity to start to understand his own inner world and that of others. He begins to take a curious interest in others and to be able to join in their games. In time he feels able to be more separate from his mother and to enjoy a different relationship with his father and other adults who look after him and play with him.

Going to playgroup, and then on to school, he can be in groups with other children and just join in without too much anxiety, and is confident enough in himself to enjoy the rough and tumble of group life; winning and losing. Feeling generally OK about himself, safe at home and able to get along with others at school and in other groups, he is able to learn comfortably and deal with schoolwork and with the job of learning new skills in other activities, trying himself out and seeing what he can do, and finding out what he likes best.

This sets the scene for the more testing challenges of sexual development, and the teenage years generally, but if things have gone well earlier, and if there is continued support from parents who remain a united co-operative couple, the accelerated physical and emotional growth period of adolescence can be traversed successfully with gains of knowledge and useful experience.

We said earlier in the book that:

> All young people need safe attachment to reliable and trustworthy adults. Young people need the experience of being able to get close to and maintain a relationship with an adult that they can trust.

A youth worker may provide a crucially helpful, reliable and trustworthy presence if a young person feels distressed and overwhelmed by problems in growing up.

However, if the young person has a disastrous background with little or no connection to adults who try to understand her, she may feel overwhelmed by terrifying 'survival anxiety' like an infant who depends on a 'receptive other' for her very survival. Don't forget that, in our inner world we are 'all the ages we have ever been'.

Even in the best of circumstances, and if it hardly merits the term 'distress', we all have problems to face up to, and having some skilled, aware, thoughtful and reflective help from someone outside the family can be a great help in the natural process of gaining some healthy separation and autonomy.

But, sadly, as outlined in many of the case studies in this book, things often go badly wrong, and need more considered, professional approaches to first understand what is causing the distress, and then to reflect upon and think about ways of dealing with young people who are miserable, anxious and unhappy.

Many unpleasant things in life cannot be 'dealt with' and many causes of distress cannot be altered, but talking about our thoughts and feelings, and in the process of dialogue with each other in groups, we can go some way towards gaining greater understanding of our selves and our relationships.

Some of the concepts in this book have been adapted from theories and practices that are known to be useful in the field of psychotherapy which is a specialised way of treating emotional distress, pain and suffering. However, this is not a book that is intended to pre-pare you to become a psychotherapist or even a counsellor; you need special training for that. And do not forget that attempts to understand, even the best intended, can some-times be experienced as an impingement or even a violation. It is wisest to never make any comments or 'interpretations' that are not asked for or wanted.

But if you take on board the concepts outlined here and adapt them into your working environments to make them as holding and containing as possible without being intrusive or controlling, then you will have gone a long way to providing and creating places that distressed young people can use to help themselves, and maybe have started a process of further learning and development in yourself. It is a life's work to understand ourselves in relation to others.

Adults who create reliable and consistent environments where young people can be related to attentively in an attuned and empathic way, who try intelligently and in depth to understand the inner worlds of young people in their social, relational and cultural con-texts and who do not impinge upon or control a young person's growing sense of autonomy will be offering a major – and long-term – service to our somewhat troubled and confused communities.

As Philip Larkin put it, unless we are careful, 'Man hands on misery to Man' (Larkin, 2001). I hope that this book has helped you to think about this process, and encouraged you to learn and practise further in the important work of working with distressed young people.

References

Bateson, G, Jackson, DD, Haley, J and Weakland, J (1956) Toward a theory of schizophrenia. *Behavioral Science*, 1: 254–64. **http://en.wikipedia.org/wiki/Double_bind**

Behr, H and Hearst, L (2005) *Group Analytic Psychotherapy*. London: Whurr.

Bick, E (1968) The experience of the skin in early object relations. *International Journal of Psychoanalysis*, 49: 484–6.

Bion, W (1962) *Experiences in Groups*. London: Tavistock Publications.

Bion, W (1967) *Second Thoughts*. London: William Heinemann.

Bowlby, J (1973) *Attachment and Loss*. London: Hogarth Press.

Children's Society, The (2009) *The Good Childhood Inquiry*. London: The Children's Society.

Clarkson, J (2008) *For Crying Out Loud: The World According to Clarkson*, Vol. 3. London: Michael Joseph.

Epstein, J (2003) *Envy*. Oxford: OUP.

Foulkes, S (1990) *Selected Papers: Psychoanalysis and Group Analysis*. London: Karnac Books.

Gerhardt, S (2004) *Why Love Matters*. London: Routledge.

Grant, R (2002) *Wah-Wah*. A film by Richard E. Grant.

Grant, R (2006) *The Wah-Wah Diaries: The Making of a Film*. London: Pan Macmillan.

Harris, B (2007) Inpatient groups: Working with staff, patients and the whole community: Personal reflections of a group analyst. *Groupwork*, 17(1): 45–56.

James, O (2007) *Affluenza*. London: Vermilion.

Jensen, E (2009) *Teaching with Poverty in Mind: What Being Poor Does to Kids' Brains and What Schools Can Do about it*. Alexandria VA: ASCD.

Joseph, B (1988) Projection and projective identification: Developmental and clinical aspects, in Sandler, J (ed) *Projection, Identification, Projective Identification*. London: Karnac Books.

Kohlberg, L, Lacrosse, J and Ricks, D (1972) The predictability of adult mental health from childhood behaviour, in Wolman, B (ed) *Manual of Child Psychopathology*. New York: McGraw-Hill.

Kouros, C, Cummings, E and Davies, P (2010) Early trajectories of interparental conflict and externalising problems as predictors of social competence in preadolescence. *Development and Psychopathology*, 22: 527–37.

Larkin, P (2001) *'This Be the Verse' from Collected Poems*. New York: Farrar, Straus and Giroux.

Lasch, C (1986) *The Culture of Narcissism*. New York: Norton.

Layard, R and Dunn, J (2009) *A Good Childhood: Searching for Values in a Competitive Age.* London: The Children's Society/Penguin.

Leach, P (2010) *The Essential First Year: What Babies Need Parents to Know.* New York: Dorling Kindersley.

Long, G (trans) (1862) *The Thoughts of the Emperor Marcus Aurelius Antoninus.* London: Bell & Daldy.

Margo, J, Dixon, M, Pearce, N and Reed, H (2006) *Freedom's Orphans: Raising Youth in a Changing World.* London: Institute for Public Policy Research.

Masten, A and Cicchetti, D (2010) Developmental cascades. *Development and Psychopathology,* 22: 491–5.

Morgan, D and Ruszczynski, S (eds) (2007) *Lectures on Violence, Perversion, and Delinquency.* London: Karnac.

Palmer, S (2006) *Toxic Childhood.* London: Orion.

Resnik, S (2005) *Glacial Times: A Journey Through the World of Madness.* Translated by David Alcorn. Hove/London: Routledge/Institute of Psychoanalysis.

Rifkin, J (2010) *The Empathic Civilisation.* Cambridge: Polity.

Rowling, J (2010) The fringe benefits of failure, and the importance of imagination. From the *Harvard Gazette,* **http://news.harvard.edu/gazette/story/2008/06/text-of-j-k-rowling-speech/**

Schore, A (1994) *Affect Regulation and the Origin of the Self.* Mahwah NJ: Lawrence Erlbaum Associates.

Schore, A (2003) *Affect Regulation and the Repair of the Self.* New York: Norton.

Sigman, A (2009) *Well Connected? The Biological Implications of 'Social Networking',* Vol. 56 No. 1. pp 14–20. London: Journal of the Institute of Biology.

Stoller, R (1975) *Perversion: The Erotic Form of Hatred.* London: Karnac.

Symington, J and Symington, N (1996) *The Clinical Thinking of Wilfred Bion.* London: Routledge.

Winnicott, D (1960, 1965) *The Maturational Processes and the Facilitating Environment.* London: Hogarth.

Winnicott, D (1971) *Playing and Reality.* London: Tavistock.

Wurtzel, E (1994) *Prozac Nation: Young and Depressed in America.* Boston MA: Houghton Mifflin.

Index

Counselling, Psychotherapy and the Law

Second Edition

Peter Jenkins

Los Angeles | London | New Delhi
Singapore | Washington DC

First published 1997
Reprinted 2012

SAGE Publications Ltd
1 Oliver's Yard
55 City Road
London EC1Y 1SP

SAGE Publications Inc.
2455 Teller Road
Thousand Oaks, California 91320

SAGE Publications India Pvt Ltd
B 1/I 1 Mohan Cooperative Industrial Area
Mathura Road
New Delhi 110 044

SAGE Publications Asia-Pacific Pte Ltd
3 Church Street
10-04 Samsung Hub
Singapore 049483

Library of Congress Control Number: 2006940401

British Library Cataloguing in Publication data

A catalogue record for this book is available from
the British Library

ISBN 978-1-4129-0005-8
ISBN 978-1-4129-0006-5 (pbk)

Typeset by C&M Digitals (P) Ltd., Chennai, India
Printed and bound by CPI Group (UI) Ltd, Croydon, CR0 4YY
Printed on paper from sustainable resources

Counselling, Psychotherapy and the Law

Second Edition

The *Professional Skills for Counsellors* series, edited by Colin Feltham, covers the practical, technical and professional skills and knowledge which trainee and practising counsellors need to improve their competence in key areas of therapeutic practice.

Titles in the series include:

Contents

Foreword

When I began to read this book I was struck by the notion that we, as psychotherapists and counsellors, are in a struggle. Our struggle is how to be in and of the world but to hold a space that is unique. This uniqueness is based on the relationship between the client/patient and a world that the therapist creates through individual or group work. *Counselling, Psychotherapy and the Law* presents a way of viewing that relationship in a contemporary context where there is a demand to bring the practice of our profession into a system of accountability that can seem counter intuitive to the intimacy of being alone with another in the consulting room. Regardless of the regulation of the profession, we are subject to the same laws as our colleagues and clients/patients. This book takes us through the specialised considerations in the work we undertake.

We are all subject to the same rules of social organisation but are constantly seeking a way of being an individual in society. I am reminded of Robert Bellah's statement,

> We are hesitant to articulate our sense that we need one another as much as we need to stand alone, for fear that if we did we should lose our independence altogether. The tensions of our lives would be even greater if we did not, in fact, engage in practices that constantly limit the effects of an isolating individualism, even though we cannot articulate those practices as well as we can the quest for autonomy. (Robert N. Bellah et al., Habits of the Heart).

As a psychotherapist or counsellor we are often the subject of 'isolating individualism' and perhaps it is the law that reminds us that we need each other and that to meet that need we have to sacrifice some of our independence.

Our ability to create a space where we can explore relationship and independence requires a process of learning not only about theory, but about ourselves through a therapy that is congruent with our chosen way of practising the art and science of psychotherapy. It is our own therapy that gives us a sense of the journey being made alone and its requirement for a protected space. This is the point at which theory can become dogma and lead us to believe we have a right to protect ourselves rather than focusing on protecting the space we create.

It is true that the protected space needed by counselling and psychotherapy requires co-operation from our social systems as well as the individuals who engage in the provision and use of it. We also have a right to know that we are engaging in a most intimate and powerful relationship that is safe. I say we because most counsellors/psychotherapists are or have been and continue to be users of counselling and/or psychotherapy as our continued growth, as well as the providers of these services. There is an inherent risk of exploitation in an intimate situation in which one party has a primacy of thought. In life safety is never guaranteed, but we can manage the risk by making sure the rules are known or knowable for all those involved in a process.

One of the accusations made against the resistance of the professions to state regulation is the notion of protectionism – that we have a vested interest in protecting our own regardless of what wrongs are done. This has been impacted by several high profile cases that are based in the world of medical ethics which tend to dominate the government's perception of most relationships that involve healing and the power of the practitioner.

Whatever the perception, the reality is that there is a system in which we operate in which there has to be a client/patient, a counsellor/psychotherapist and an overarching system that governs the expectations in the relationship. At the outer edge of this system is the law. We are all subject to the laws that govern our behaviour, especially in a professional context where we have the power to influence and change the perceptions and behaviour of our clients/patients.

The journey in this book begins by developing the connection between what we do and the ethical landscape on which we base our 'moral authority'. We are given ways of understanding our foundation in the modern context of the law and how it has operated in cases that we can encounter in our practice.

Throughout this book we are given real world situations in which we operate as counsellors and psychotherapists where the judgments of the courts have been exercised. The chapter headings raise situations and concerns that we often avoid due to the level of anxiety they produce. We are then taken in to the world of the legal system and given case studies that show where the starkness of the law is contrasted with the outcomes that give the added dimension of how we are likely to be treated should our work come under scrutiny.

The book concludes with the topic on the 'Statutory Regulation of Therapists' which is a very lively topic that connects with the publication in February 2007 of the Department of Health's White Paper, *Trust, Assurance and Safety – The Regulation of Health Professionals in the 21st Century*. I would commend that this final chapter be read by anyone that wishes to understand the history and issues to do with Statutory Regulation.

James Antrican
Chair, UKCP

Acknowledgements

Many people have helped me in various ways to produce this book. I would like to acknowledge, in particular, support, advice and information from James Antrican, Professor Tim Bond, Roger Casemore, Jill Collins, Karen Cromarty, Debbie Daniels, Lynne Gabriel, Barry Gower, Nicky Hart, Dr Anne Hayman, Rick Hughes, Michael Jacobs, Vincent Keter, Andrew Kinder, Susan McGinnis, Janette Newton, Sue Parkes, Maggie Pettifer, Dr Filiz Polat, Philip Pollecoff, Val Potter, Pat Siddons, James Sinclair-Taylor, Julie Stone, Gudrun Stummer, Keith Tudor, Professor Sue Wheeler, Tim Woodhouse and Ray Woolfe.

My current colleagues in the Directorate of Counselling and Psychotherapy, at the University of Salford, including Liz Coldridge, Andy Hill, Vee Howard-Jones, Parveen Marrington-Mir and Jane Hunt, are also thanked for their interest and support. Staff at Sage Publications have been consistently helpful and supportive throughout, including Alison Poyner, Claire Reeve and Louise Wise, as has the series editor, Colin Feltham. Finally, my thanks are due to my family, near and far, but especially Jane, Lisa, Rachel and Xavier.

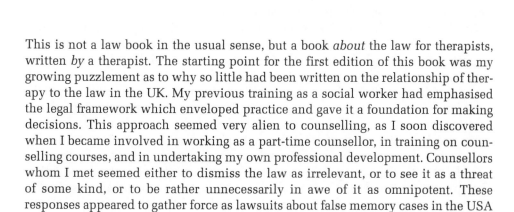

Introduction

This is not a law book in the usual sense, but a book *about* the law for therapists, written *by* a therapist. The starting point for the first edition of this book was my growing puzzlement as to why so little had been written on the relationship of therapy to the law in the UK. My previous training as a social worker had emphasised the legal framework which enveloped practice and gave it a foundation for making decisions. This approach seemed very alien to counselling, as I soon discovered when I became involved in working as a part-time counsellor, in training on counselling courses, and in undertaking my own professional development. Counsellors whom I met seemed either to dismiss the law as irrelevant, or to see it as a threat of some kind, or to be rather unnecessarily in awe of it as omnipotent. These responses appeared to gather force as lawsuits about false memory cases in the USA started to surface, and a more general concern about therapists' vulnerability to legal action seemed to take root.

In a sense, the book is a response to a speaker at one conference on therapy and the law, who expressed the view that 'there is no case law on counselling in the UK'. This may be true in a strict sense, but this book is an attempt to describe the case law concerning counselling as far as it can be divined by looking at a broad range of related fields, such as medicine. Based on the example of medical case law, this is an attempt to read the main characteristics of the law as applied to therapy, in the absence, so far, of extensive case law. Hopefully, therapists may be able to avoid actually featuring in future case law by following some of the suggested guidelines included here.

If any lawyers read this book, they may be somewhat frustrated that it does not follow the format of a conventional law book. In addition, general statements are made about the application of the law which a trained legal eye will recognise as often containing exceptions which are hinted at, rather than fully explored. For every general legal principle, there seems to be an exception. The existence of exceptions to almost every general rule in law provides one of the reasons why this book cannot be taken as a definitive guide to the law, but is, rather, a general outline of the terrain. Advice to therapists is, in most cases, to stick to established paths. Therapists needing more detailed guidance on specific cases should seek legal advice, as the law is frequently changing, and no coverage of the law can be comprehensive in every respect.

Whilst on the topic of advice, therapists are often asked by clients what they should do, to which the classic response is for the therapist to turn the question round for the client to find their own preferred solution. However, when it comes to legal questions, it often seems that therapists become frustrated with the lack of certainty in the face of complicated and difficult legal issues. Responding to questions about what a therapist *may* do, or *may not do* or *must do* or *must not do* frequently depends upon the *context* in which they work, the nature of the *client group* and the *type of issue of concern*. This is especially true of therapists working with children and young people, for example. Therapists may prefer certainty in the form of a straight answer, but often the legal position provides less than absolute certainty, and simply sets out the parameters within which decisions can be made. The paradox seems to be that, as therapists, we encourage our clients to learn to work with ambiguity and uncertainty in their own lives, but we seem to prefer absolute certainty for ourselves, when encountering complex and difficult legal issues.

On the issue of therapists seeking an element of clarity about legal issues, it is perhaps worth pointing out the differences between *liability* and *risk*. Any lawyer is trained to identify liability in any transaction or responsibility. However, liability and risk may not necessarily belong to the same family of concepts. The liability of people being struck by lightning in the UK may be evenly spread across the population, but the actual *risk* incurred may be much more narrowly focused on a small proportion of people. In theory, therapists may be liable for a whole range of activities. In reality, the risks that they actually run in doing their work may be quite small. Few therapists are currently sued, and even fewer are successfully sued by clients. This may well change in the future, but the present culture both of therapy and the law would have to change to make this a more likely possibility.

There is, it seems, a fairly widespread perception of the law as a vague external threat to therapists, either in the form of unknown requirements concerning breaches of confidentiality, or for compliance with court-ordered demands for access to client information, along with the ever-present spectre of being sued by angry clients. This seems to have given way more recently to another, more optimistic construction of the relationship of therapy to the law. In some spheres of counselling and psychotherapy, the perception is emerging and gaining strength that therapy's relationship with the law is an opportunity to be grasped and explored in full. The recognition linked to this point is that therapists need to be better informed of their rights and responsibilities under the law as a starting point.

In recent years therapists have developed a major preoccupation as a profession with ethical issues related to their therapeutic work. This is exemplified by the production of the BACP *Ethical Framework for Good Practice in Counselling and Psychotherapy* in 2001, and by the successive conferences on ethics held by the UKCP. This book explores the crucial relationship between ethics and the law at a number of different levels, first, by illustrating the diversity of ethical models which influence legal decision-making. Secondly, it suggests the ways in which ethical principles, such as autonomy, find clear recognition and expression in legal concepts, such as informed consent and contract. My own view is that *ethics*, rather than *the law*, should drive therapeutic practice. However, therapists also need to take an active part in the developing dialogue on ethical principles and legal duties, in order to be fully informed about the options open to them and to their clients.

A note on how to use this book

In writing this book, I have tried to combine a theoretical discussion of the law affecting therapy with more practical information for therapists facing legal issues involving their work. Thus the general outline of the law includes detailed reference to original sources, and to the relevant case law. Hopefully, these references will be useful for readers wanting to check original and more detailed sources, and will not break the 'flow' of the book for other readers. Frequent case studies, taken from therapy or from case law, are included, to illustrate some of the key issues being explored in each chapter. Legal references are written in a style which is probably unfamiliar to non-lawyers, so this style is briefly described at the beginning of the Table of Cases at the end of the book. The same section also contains an index of case law for the USA and UK, and Acts of Parliament referred to in the text, again for readers with a more specialist interest. The Glossary contains professional terms for which lawyers, therapists or clients may want brief definition or explanation.

For practitioners who may simply want to check the legal situation regarding a topic, such as defamation, or contract, for example, key points are displayed in summary boxes, together with sets of guidelines for professional practice for quick reference. Part of the therapist's role may be in passing on information to clients, or in gaining access to recent public documents, publications or legal advice. The Resources section at the end of the book contains a comprehensive list of organisations which can be contacted for further information by therapists or clients. For trainers and students, suggested questions are included at the end of each chapter, which identify key points for discussion.

In terms of its structure, the book begins with an outline of key terms relating to the law, and a survey of the relationship between ethics and the law, noting the perhaps surprising diversity of ethical approaches to be found at work within the law. The following chapter provides a broad overview of the law, its content and structure, with particular reference to civil law. The chapter on the courts describes the structure of the courts system, provides information for therapists facing involvement in legal proceedings, and explores issues of compensation, particularly regarding psychological damages.

Concerns about professional negligence are then explored in the fourth chapter, which looks at the closely related fields of medical and psychiatric case law. In the next chapter, the limits to confidentiality are identified, with the focus on the therapist's role as custodian of sensitive client information. This is distinguished from the legal pressures to grant access to this information to outside agencies, such as the courts, which is the subject of the following chapter, together with an outline of data protection requirements. In the following chapter, therapy with children and young people is examined as a specialist area in its own right, albeit one with implications for other therapists as well. The final chapter describes the development of statutory recognition of therapy, in terms of adoption counselling and infertility counselling. This is followed by a brief history of moves towards the statutory regulation of therapy in the UK.

The overall theme of this book is that the law is dynamic, fluid and rapidly changing, rather than being fixed for all time. Therapists need to be alert to all issues which have an impact on a broad spectrum of their work with clients. Hopefully, this book will be of assistance in this process.

Therapy, Ethics and the Law

1

Therapy and the law enjoy, at best, an uneasy relationship. They inhabit different spheres of emotion and logic. They employ contrasting languages of feeling and evidence. Each operates in a space that is either essentially personal and private, or is, by definition, highly formalised and public. The points of intersection between therapeutic practice and the law are often obscure, highly specialised and subject to nervous speculation by therapists. The areas of overlap tend to be seen as uncharted territory, full of hazards and pitfalls for unwary therapists, unschooled in the harsh world of litigation. All too often in this area, discussion by therapists is premised on an underlying, and frequently unrealistic, fear of being sued, as a result of imperfect knowledge of the law or of inadvertent negligence.

The starting point for an exploration of therapy and the law is to look at the basic building blocks of any discussion of the topic – law, ethics and therapy. The growing interest in the role of ethics within therapeutic work is linked to ways in which different models of ethics permeate the law. The law may be strongly influenced by a utilitarian, or outcomes-based, approach to ethics, but there are also other, divergent, strands within the law, which emphasise other approaches, such as the concept of individual rights to privacy and confidentiality.

Law

The term 'law', as used here, includes all systems of civil and criminal law, including statute, common and case law. As the legal systems of Scotland and Northern Ireland have their own characteristics, the focus here will mainly be on the law relating to counselling in England and Wales. However, basic legal principles will often be fundamentally similar within each of these jurisdictions. The legal system is based on a mixture of statute, or laws passed by Parliament, such as the Data Protection Act 1998 or the Children Act 2004, and common law. The latter embodies long-established principles, regarding confidentiality or contract, which are not necessarily expressed in one single piece of law. Case law is the interpretation of the law made by judges on individual cases, often with far-reaching implications. The *Gillick* case in 1986, for example, gave legal backing to the provision of confidential contraceptive advice by doctors to young persons under the age of 16. The hierarchy of the courts system, described in Chapter 3, means that decisions taken at one level of the legal system can be overturned by a decision in a higher court, such as the Court of Appeal or the House of Lords. This decision then becomes a point of reference and sets a legal precedent for deciding similar cases appearing before the lower courts.

Ethics

'Ethics' is 'a generic term for various ways of understanding and examining the moral life' (Beauchamp and Childress, 2001: 1). The study of ethics provides 'normative standards of conduct or actions', by exploring what is 'right' or 'correct' as a moral course of action (Austin et al., 1990: 242). Ethical principles and frameworks can therefore provide assistance in framing decisions about what is morally right or wrong. The main ethical framework relating to therapy is based on the concepts of autonomy, fidelity, justice, beneficence, non-maleficence and self-interest (Daniluk and Haverkamp, 1993; Bond, 2000: 58). These ethical values seek to promote the well-being and self-determination of the client, to avoid harming the client or others, and to maintain the competence of the therapist. They underpin the published codes of ethics and practice, such as those of the British Association for Counselling and Psychotherapy (BACP), the British Psychological Society (BPS), and the United Kingdom Council for Psychotherapy (UKCP). At certain points, key ethical principles, perhaps those regarding client autonomy and avoiding harm, may be in conflict. This may happen with regard to the issue of preventing suicide, or avoiding harm intended by a client towards third parties. In addition, a therapist may be bound by legal duties which conflict with deeply held ethical principles. As Bond has suggested, 'What is ethical may not be legal. What is legal may not be ethical' (2002: 124).

Therapy

The terms 'counsellor', 'therapist' and 'psychotherapist' are self-defined occupational terms, with, as yet, no legal restrictions on their current use. Only the titles of 'registered medical practitioner', 'chartered psychologist', and 'registered nurse' are protected. Anyone can call themselves a doctor, psychologist, nurse, counsellor, social worker, psychotherapist, sexual or marital therapist, or any other therapeutic title, providing they do not mislead patients by falsely claiming to have certain qualifications (Jehu et al., 1994: 191). Statutory regulation of counsellors and psychotherapists has been actively pursued since the 1970s, via the *Foster Report* (1971), *Sieghart Report* (1978) and the unsuccessful Psychotherapy Bill (2001). Statutory regulation would introduce restrictions, enforceable by law, on either the use of occupational terms such as 'counsellor' or 'psychotherapist', or the formal practice of counselling and psychotherapy. The generic terms 'counselling' and 'therapy' are used here to include a wide variety of forms of therapeutic exploration and resolution, of emotional distress and behavioural problems, using psychological methods, within a dyad, triad or group. The terms 'counsellor', 'psychotherapist' and 'therapist' are used interchangeably here to denote persons carrying out these activities. The distinction between counselling and psychotherapy is one which is widely debated in therapeutic circles, but carries no legal weight outside these narrow confines, and the distinction is unlikely to interest or impress a court of law.

Therapy and the law

Therapy and the law operate within distinctly different discourses. Whereas therapeutic practice prizes the raw, subjective nature of individual experience, and works with ambiguity and metaphor rather than literal truth, the law is concerned with establishing objective, verifiable facts. Therapists, for the most part, take a co-operative, if challenging, approach to work with clients, in trying to co-construct felt meanings and experiences. Much of the law is based on adversarial proceedings, where one side wins and the other loses, through a robust process of proving, or disproving, contested statements by parties and witnesses. While therapists are at pains to present themselves as being accepting and non-judgmental of client behaviour, however much the latter may be at odds with their own moral standards, the law works towards a final judgment of proven or not proven, guilty or not guilty. Some of the main differences between the respective cultures of therapy and law, perceived from a US perspective, are set out by Rowley and MacDonald, in Box 1.1.

Box 1.1   Relative differences in culture between counselling and the law

Counselling	Law
Systemic and linear reasoning	Linear reasoning
Artistic, subjective–objective understandings	Objective, fairness understandings
Growth, therapeutic priorities	Order, protection priorities
Individual or small group focus	Societal focus
Priority on change	Priority on stability
Relativity, contextual understanding	Normative dichotomies understanding
Co-operative, relational emphasis	Adversarial, fact-finding emphasis
Recommendation, consultation emphases	Legal sanctions and guidance emphases
Ethical, experiential, education bases	Legal reasoning basis
Deterministic worldview or unknowns, or both, accepted	Deterministic worldview

Source: Rowley and MacDonald, 2001: 424

The authors highlight a key difference between lawyers and therapists. 'Attorneys conceptualize, strategize and represent a case for their clients. They generally speak for their clients. Counselors, on the other hand, typically encourage clients to speak for themselves' (2001: 426). Of course, the differences between these two professional groups may be overstated. The law has increasingly accommodated itself to the value of therapeutic activity, such as pre-trial counselling for victims of abuse, and counselling as a pre-condition for some sensitive processes, such as seeking adoption records or undergoing fertility treatment (see Chapter 8). Many therapists choose to work closely with the law, by writing court reports or by acting as an expert witness. Bruner's work suggests that narrative theory is the closest area of parallel and overlap between therapy and the law, in that both activities are based on a form of purposeful story-telling. Given the premise that stories provide 'models of the world' (Bruner, 2002: 31), it follows that 'a legal story is a story told before a court of law' (2002: 37). While both client and plaintiff may tell a story in their own terms, the latter does so in a public, highly formalised arena, with serious personal and social consequences.

> To sum up, law stories are narrative in structure, adversarial in spirit, inherently rhetorical in aim, and justifiably open to suspicion. They are modelled on past cases whose verdicts were favorable to them. And, finally, they are really consequential, since the parties involved must have standing and must be directly affected by their outcome. (Bruner, 2002: 41)

Therapists may need to recognise more fully the value to some clients of 'having their day in court', and of having their story vindicated in front of a judge and jury. For their part, lawyers might also need to accept that 'in pleading cases, they create drama, indeed, are sometimes carried away by it' (Bruner, 2002: 48). This aspect of a narrative approach to the workings of the law is emphasised by Burnett, when reflecting on his fictional account of jury service in the US.

> a 'story' hangs together, is treated whole. But once you tell your story into the law, it becomes the object of a precise, semantic dissection. The whole of the story is of no interest; instead, patient surgeons of language wait and watch, snip and assay, looking for certain phrases, certain words. Particular locutions trip particular legal switches and set a heavy machine in motion. (2002: 50)

Therapists, highly skilled in detecting affect and meaning in their clients' words, in the privacy of the counselling setting, thus enter into a very different paradigm in the courtroom. This kind of close, adversarial attention to language in a public setting can be unsettling and de-skilling for many therapists, who may be keen to preserve the integrity of the client's original story from this kind of scrutiny. There are, however, limits to a narrative approach as a means to understanding legal processes. Some critics would point to the role of enduring structures of authority, deeply inscribed by factors such as gender, class and power, which a narrative approach is in danger of understating (Foucault, 1991; Lees, 1997).

Therapists and the law

Whatever their misgivings and uncertainties, therapists are ultimately bound by the law. However, the BACP *Ethical Framework for Good Practice in Counselling and Psychotherapy* does not require practitioners to obey the law as such. Instead, there is a broader and looser requirement that 'Practitioners should be aware of and understand any legal requirements concerning their work, consider these conscientiously and be legally accountable for their practice' (2002: 6). This represents a significant change from the earlier BAC *Code of Ethics and Practice for*

Counsellors, which clearly stated that 'Counsellors should work within the law' (BAC, 1992: para. B.2.6.1).

This shift appears to recognise that therapists may well have difficult choices to make, for example concerning the disclosure of sensitive client information about past criminal offences, or of current suspected child abuse. It is not necessarily helpful to perceive the law as a monolithic structure which will always dictate a clear and obvious course of action. Quite often, legal principles will be in direct conflict, so that a therapist may decide to *maintain* client confidentiality, which would be a position strongly supported by common law and statute. Alternatively, the therapist may decide to *break* confidentiality in the public interest, a completely contrary position, but one that is also strongly supported by common law and statute. The key point is that therapists remain accountable for their decisions, both in an ethical sense and in terms of the law.

Therapists need to develop a basic, working knowledge of the law in order to work safely and competently within their ethical code or framework. The relationship of the law to therapy is, however, fairly complex. It is mediated by three main factors:

- by the *context or setting* in which the practitioner practises, e.g. whether working in a statutory agency, voluntary organisation, or in private practice;
- by the nature of the specific *client group* the practitioner is working with, e.g. children, or clients with significant and enduring mental health problems;
- by the practitioner's *employment status*, i.e. whether the therapist is employed or self-employed.

Thus a therapist working with young people in a secondary school would need to have a good grasp of child protection requirements, whereas another, working as a private practitioner, would benefit from having a working knowledge of the basic principles of contract law. A therapist in primary care, working with clients recovering from severe mental health problems, will need a basic understanding of the Mental Health Act 1983. A self-employed supervisor might want to be clear about the differences between personal and vicarious liability, both for herself and for her supervisees.

Ethical principles and the law

None of the previous statements should be taken as suggesting that the law should be a primary focus for therapists, or, indeed, that the law should drive the priorities of therapeutic work with clients. If anything, it needs to be ethical principles that inform and energise therapeutic practice, but in the context of an awareness of what the law may require of both client and therapist. Changes in the professional regulation of therapists have shifted away from prescriptive and ever-lengthening codes of ethics, towards more demanding, but flexible, sets of ethical principles, which make allowances for therapists' differing work settings and client groups. The BACP *Ethical Framework*, for example, adopts many aspects of the broader, relativistic framework of biomedical ethics (Beauchamp and Childress, 2001). In addition to principles, it includes *values*, such as increasing personal effectiveness, and *virtues*, such as integrity and wisdom, to produce a complex and multi-faceted system for ethical decision-making. In doing so, it has decisively moved away from the position adopted by the earlier BAC *Code of Ethics*, where one key principle, that of respect for client autonomy, was clearly 'the ethical priority' (Bond, 2000: 58).

Ethical principles

Therapists will be familiar with the key principles set out in the BACP *Ethical Framework* (2002). These are:

- Fidelity
- Autonomy
- Beneficence
- Non-maleficence
- Justice
- Self-respect

Fidelity requires the therapist to be trustworthy in their dealings with the client, and to maintain confidentiality. Autonomy relates to respect for the client as a self-determining agent, freely capable of making choices and decisions. Beneficence, or, more simply, welfare, involves the therapist in promoting the best interests of the client, via achieving positive outcomes, wherever possible. Non-maleficence ensures that harm to the client caused by the therapist, via exploitation or incompetence, is avoided. The principle of justice emphasises fair treatment for all clients, based on a commitment to equal opportunities. Finally self-respect encourages the therapist to develop self-knowledge and self-care, through supervision and personal development activities, in order to be able to work safely and competently with clients. In Box 1.2, these key ethical principles are translated into corresponding legal concepts.

Box 1.2   Relationship of ethical principles to legal concepts

Ethical principles (BACP)	Legal concepts
Fidelity (Trust)	Duty of confidence Fiduciary duty
Autonomy	Informed consent Contract
Beneficence (Welfare)	Duty of care
Non-maleficence (Avoiding harm)	Standard of care Duty to warn?
Justice	Non-discrimination
Self-respect	Pre-conditions necessary to fulfil duty to apply 'reasonable care and skill'

Fidelity

The ethical principle of fidelity, or keeping trust with the client, is closely linked to the legal concept of the therapist's duty of confidence, or confidentiality. This duty of confidentiality is set out both by common, or judge-made, law and further strengthened by statute, such as the Data Protection Act 1998. The therapist has also been held by independent legal opinion, to possess a 'fiduciary duty', maintaining ultimate trust and responsibility, towards the client. The law provides strong support for the therapist's ethical duty to hold and maintain client confidences. A client could take legal action against a therapist for breach of confidence, where, for example, an identifiable and damaging case study was published without the client's consent.

Autonomy

In legal terms, the principle of autonomy is exercised through the concept of informed consent. Therapy is a voluntary activity, and the client is normally able to make a free choice as to whether or not they take part in it, or to work with a particular agency or therapist. The developing doctrine of informed consent is perhaps stronger in policy terms in some settings, such as the NHS, than it is in actual law. Nevertheless, it requires that the client is capable of understanding the nature of therapy, can consider information about the relative advantages and disadvantages of taking part, and can make a free choice. Similarly with contract: the client and therapist are free in law to choose whether or not to work together, and to negotiate the terms of the agreement. In practice, many therapists use the term 'contract' fairly loosely, as an umbrella term for a working document or agreement. Without certain conditions being met, principally the exchange of money or consideration for the counselling being provided, the agreement will not necessarily qualify as a legally binding contract. An aggrieved client could take action against a therapist, or vice versa, for breach of contract, if the required conditions were held to apply. Action for failure to acquire the client's informed consent to therapy is probably more of a theoretical than a practical possibility at present, given the state of current case law.

Beneficence

The therapist has an ethical duty to promote the client's welfare. In legal terms, this translates as 'a duty of care' towards the client. The therapist has a duty to work to the relevant standards set for the profession, whether by law, guidance or codes of ethics. This might require the therapist to carry out a competent assessment, or to make a referral to another agency or practitioner for more specialised work, if necessary. The therapist needs to be sufficiently trained, qualified and skilled, in order to practise safely and to provide the appropriate level of care to the client. The law in the UK tends to frame the duty of care quite narrowly, so that it refers to the immediate client, rather than to third parties, such as the client's partner or family. Legal action against a therapist for breach of duty of care would be taken under professional negligence or personal injury law. The client would need to establish that, given the duty of care, the therapist had caused foreseeable damage, in the form of a physical or psychological injury.

Non-maleficence

As well as the duty to promote the client's positive well-being, there is a corresponding duty to avoid causing damage to the client. In medical terms, the duty is, under the Hippocratic Oath: 'never do any harm to anyone' (Mason and Laurie, 2006: 741). The legal test for establishing whether a therapist had negligently caused harm would be by assessing whether the therapist had fallen below the relevant standard of care for that profession. The standard of care, again deriving from medical case law, has been set by the *Bolam* test, namely a failure to act in accordance with the practice of 'competent respected professional opinion'. A court would refer to relevant codes of ethics, or to statutory guidance. It would also rely on the opinion of expert witnesses to help determine whether a therapist's practice was adequate, judged against the standard of his or her peers. The client would be seeking to establish that the therapist had fallen below this standard, or that the standard itself was, in some way, illogical or flawed.

Another aspect of avoiding harm is the question of whether the therapist owes 'a duty to warn' third parties of a risk posed by his or her client. The BACP *Ethical Framework* currently frames avoidance of harm as relating mainly to avoiding harm to the *immediate* client, rather than to third parties (2002: 3). Nevertheless, the threat of harm posed by a client may be to the wider society, as in a threat to carry out terrorist offences, or to a specific named individual. Thus, in working with a client in a domestic violence situation, the therapist may be concerned about credible threats of revenge against a former partner. The law in the UK currently has few mandatory reporting requirements on therapists, with terrorism as a clear statutory exception. Other reporting of risk, if breaking client confidentiality, would need to be justified 'in the public interest', referring to previous case law on this issue. Legal action against a therapist for failure in 'a duty to warn' (other than for terrorist offences) remains, again, more of a theoretical than a practical possibility at present under UK law.

Justice

Under this ethical principle, the therapist has a duty to promote fairness and equity for all clients. From a legal perspective, this requires, at a minimum, compliance with legislation prohibiting discrimination against clients on the grounds of gender, race, age, disability or sexual orientation, or other attributes. In employee counselling, therapists also need to be aware of injustice experienced by staff in the form of harassment and bullying, and to be informed of the steps which can be taken to challenge this within the organisation. Therapists need to take account of any factors which may limit client access to their services. These might include aspects such as cost, long waiting lists and limited physical accessibility, and the action the therapist must take to limit their impact. In some cases, it may be that policy and practice limit client access in ways that are potentially discriminatory. Access to a counselling service in health care might be limited to those aged 16 or over. School-based counselling services may require evidence of parental consent for pupils aged under 16. Both of these could constitute examples of unjustifiably discriminatory practice, which would be in conflict with case law, in the form of the *Gillick* principle, and of the Human Rights Act 1998.

Self-respect

Under this principle, therapists need to engage with all those activities which maintain their own well-being and competence as a practitioner, as entitlements for self. This will include recognising a need for personal self-care, whether in the form of personal therapy or by maintaining an appropriate workload and work–life balance, in order to avoid undue stress or eventual 'burn-out'. In professional terms, the therapist needs to work at maintaining their 'edge' as a practitioner, by keeping up to date with relevant literature and research, and by continuous updating. Supervision, support and access to consultation are all recognised ways in which therapists can engage in self-respect, contributing and benefiting from active participation in the wider professional community.

In narrowly legal terms, there is no exactly corresponding concept for this ethical principle. However, under the terms of consumer protection law, any professional providing services for payment, whether as a plumber or as a psychotherapist, is required to do so with a standard of 'reasonable care and skill', comparable to that of the profession as a whole. In order to work safely and competently as a therapist, and to provide such reasonable care and skill, the practitioner would need to be maintaining an appropriate level of self-respect. In other words, the therapist must work within accepted norms relating to expertise, supervision, workload and continuing professional development. This may be regarded as the weakest of these translations of ethical principles into legal concepts. It may be more helpful, from this perspective, to see the ethical principle of self-respect as an essential *precondition*, in order for the therapist to provide a necessary standard of reasonable care and skill to the client. In the event of a grievance relating to sub-standard therapy provided for payment, the client can take legal action against the therapist under the Supply of Goods and Services Act 1982.

Therapists will have their own personal moral standards, professional training and access to supervision as supports and guides when making complex decisions regarding their work with clients. However, they may be wary of 'ethics' as a more general topic for discussion, perhaps perceiving it to be rather abstract, academic and philosophical, rather than as being of any real benefit in approaching complex practice dilemmas in real life. It may help to have an understanding of how differing ethical stances inform aspects of legal decision-making. Any ethically informed viewpoint can be challenged by another, equally valid, but based on differing ethical principles. Box 1.3 presents a map of ethical positions, derived from the work of Meara et al. (1996).

Rule-following approaches to ethics

There has been a rapidly growing interest in the recent past in the topic of ethics as applied to therapeutic work (Bond, 2000; Clarkson, 2000; Dryden 1997; Jones et al., 2000). Approaches to ethical reasoning can be grouped broadly in terms of approaches based either on ethical *principles*, or on the concept of *virtues*. Principle ethics are based on the idea of obligations to others, and often provide the basis for professional codes of practice. Within principle ethics, deontological approaches emphasise the importance of following rules, derived from the concept of Kantian imperatives. A rule-following approach might, for example, require a

Box 1.3 Mapping ethical approaches to therapy and the law (derived from Meara et al., 1996)

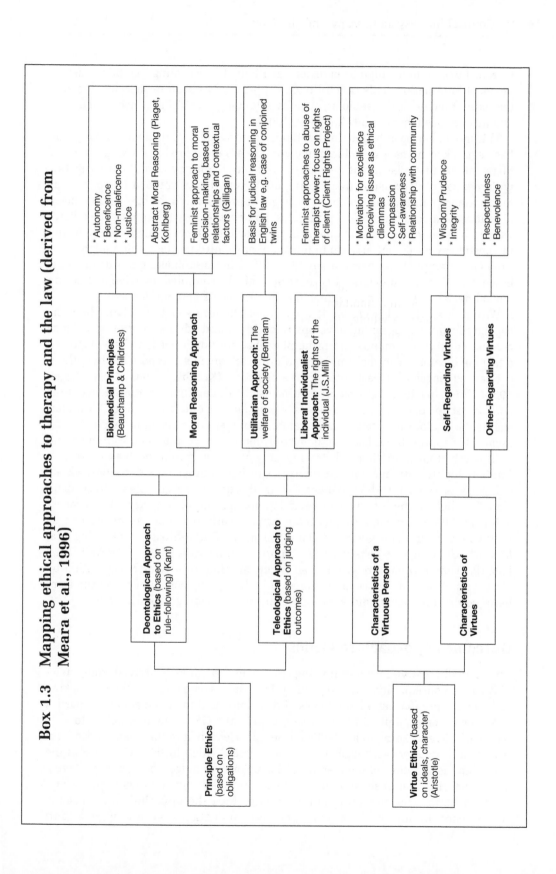

Principle Ethics (based on obligations)

Deontological Approach to Ethics (based on rule-following) (Kant)

Biomedical Principles (Beauchamp & Childress)
* Autonomy
* Beneficence
* Non-maleficence
* Justice

Moral Reasoning Approach

Abstract Moral Reasoning (Piaget, Kohlberg)

Feminist approach to moral decision-making, based on relationships and contextual factors (Gilligan)

Teleological Approach to Ethics (based on judging outcomes)

Utilitarian Approach: The welfare of society (Bentham)

Basis for judicial reasoning in English law e.g. case of conjoined twins

Liberal Individualist Approach: The rights of the individual (J.S.Mill)

Feminist approaches to abuse of therapist power; focus on rights of client (Client Rights Project)

Virtue Ethics (based on ideals, character) (Aristotle)

Characteristics of a Virtuous Person
* Motivation for excellence
* Perceiving issues as ethical dilemmas
* Compassion
* Self-awareness
* Relationship with community

Characteristics of Virtues

Self-Regarding Virtues
* Wisdom/Prudence
* Integrity

Other-Regarding Virtues
* Respectfulness
* Benevolence

therapist to maintain a high level of confidentiality by protecting a client's sensitive personal information. This rule-following approach has been further developed in the form of biomedical principles, such as autonomy, beneficence, non-maleficence and justice (Beauchamp and Childress, 2001).

This model has been hugely influential in framing medical decision-making, and has been taken up as a valuable framework by other professional groups, such as therapists. A therapist might respect the right to autonomy of a client struggling with feelings of depression, by deciding not to report a heightened risk of suicide to the client's employer or doctor. A different approach might be based on the need to follow countervailing ethical principles, namely the duty to promote the client's welfare by seeking appropriate medical help for the client. It might also consider the need to avoid potential harm to the client or to third parties, which might arise from any attempt at self-harm or suicide. Ethical decision-making in this model is based on using a framework of competing ethical principles to arrive at a sound ethical decision, which is accountable to clients, peers and employers.

Within this rule-following model, psychologists have sought to clarify how the capacity for moral reasoning develops in children and adults. In order to balance competing ethical demands and principles, the individual needs to have achieved a level of abstract or formal thinking, in order to consider the possible hypothetical consequences of a particular course of action (Kohlberg, 1981, 1984; Piaget, 1965). This capacity for abstract reasoning can be linked to the requirements of the *Gillick* test for determining whether a young person under the age of 16 understands the doctor's advice and is therefore competent to consent to medical treatment. This approach has been challenged by feminist research, on the grounds that it is overly rigid and linear, betraying an implicitly masculine bias towards a limited, highly rational and narrowly cognitive approach to decision-making. Gilligan's research into how women facing abortion make complex ethical decisions highlighted the influence of key relationships and of context on this process (Gilligan, 1993). Elements of this more empathically informed approach can be found in the rationale given by Dame Elizabeth Butler-Sloss, in deciding that Mrs B. had the right to have her life support machine switched off (*B v NHS Trust* [2002]). Dame Elizabeth referred to an article arguing for a greater recognition by the courts of patients' subjective values and felt experiences, rather than the standard judicial reliance on more objective, abstract reasoning (Atkins, 2000).

Outcomes approach to ethics

The main alternative to rule-following approaches to ethics is derived from a teleological, or consequentialist, perspective. This emphasises ethical decision-making in terms of anticipating the outcomes of decisions, and their impact on all parties concerned. For example, in the *Tarasoff* case in the US, a therapist failed to pass on an effective warning to a client's former girlfriend before the client carried out his threat to murder her. Judges in this case were divided in their views about the ethical and legal duties of the therapist. The majority of judges took a rule-following stance, i.e. that therapists should be under a clear legal duty to warn others of a threat of harm. The dissenting minority judge took the opposing view, that the consequence or outcome of breaching client confidentiality, even to warn a third person at risk, might itself have unintended harmful effects. Breaching confidentiality could destroy the patient's trust, or the wider reputation of therapy, on which the latter actually depends for its very effectiveness (Sim, 1996).

Within the outcome-based approach to ethics, the utilitarian approach has been very influential within the English legal system. Bentham's philosophy argued that the purpose of an ethical decision should be to achieve the greatest happiness of the greatest number of people. This is, therefore, a strongly welfare-based model. This approach is exemplified by current proposals to promote the existing level of human happiness in society through the wider use of positive psychology and cognitive behaviour therapy (Layard, 2006).

Utilitarian principles underpin a great deal of judicial reasoning in the legal system. This was evident in the rationale for authorising the separation of two conjoined twins, where both twins were likely to die without medical intervention, and one was likely to die if separated, but the separated twin would be likely to survive (Levy, 2003). It is also evident in judges' reasoning applied to the concept of 'the public interest', or the greater good of society as a whole. Thus judges decided it was against the public interest for the press to reveal the identity of two doctors who had contracted the HIV virus, because this would undermine public confidence in medical confidentiality. The greater public good was served by protecting medical confidentiality, rather than via the media publicising the perceived risk to a much smaller number of patients thought to be at risk of infection.

Another aspect of an outcomes approach to ethics is that based on a liberal individualist perspective. Based on the work of J.S. Mill, the individual is seen to have the right to pursue their own interests, but not at the cost of infringing the rights of others. The law then provides the necessary safeguards to prevent one person's right to self-expression becoming a licence to damage the reciprocal rights of others. For example, a parent might claim the right to know of a child's under-age pregnancy, as in the case brought by Sue Axon discussed in Chapter 7. However, if this right is exercised, that young person, and other young people, might be dissuaded from seeking appropriate confidential medical or contraceptive advice. From a public policy point of view, the outcome of a change in the law to permit parental knowledge of a young woman's pregnancy would have wider, and potentially damaging social consequences for young people as a whole, whatever the expected benefit to one particular individual.

Feminist approaches to rights have extended this line of argument and explored the abuse of power within the therapeutic relationship (Proctor, 2002). This takes its sharpest form in, but is not limited to, the sexual abuse of clients by therapists. This rights-based approach is evident in the work of the Client Rights Project in Canada (Beamish et al., 1998), and similar publications in the UK (Palmer and Szymanska, 2001). The view advanced here is that clients who are assertive and well informed about their rights within therapy are less vulnerable to abuse and exploitation, and better placed to benefit from therapeutic work.

Virtue approaches to ethics

The slightly old-fashioned term 'virtue' refers to the moral qualities of the individual in making ethical decisions, following the approach taken by Aristotle (Russell,

1969: 185–6). A decision, for example, to break confidentiality in order to report malpractice by a colleague is not taken in a social vacuum, but depends on a real person deciding to take a stand on an issue felt to be of crucial importance. Rather than focus on the *process* involved, whether rule-following or evaluating the likely *consequences* of a decision, this approach is much more personal. It tries to identify the necessary characteristics of a virtuous, or highly moral, person. These characteristics may include a facility for perceiving everyday practice issues as having a distinctly ethical component, rather than simply accommodating, say, to a new agency procedure on confidentiality or record-keeping. Virtues can be divided into those which are primarily observed in relation to the self, such as integrity, and those which relate more to interpersonal relationships with others, such as respectfulness.

Meara et al. (1996) develop a detailed critique of principle approaches to ethics, which, they argue, overemphasise principles, such as individual autonomy, at the expense of context and community. They present a spirited argument for a return to virtue ethics, where 'the focus is on the agent or actor rather than on the action or decision' (1996: 27). An ethical decision, for example to report malpractice, involves distinct moral qualities, such as courage, rather than simply an abstract interest in philosophy. Sharon Watkins, a whistleblower of the Enron accounting scandal in the US, has talked about how her childhood instilled in her a sense of optimism that her individual decisions *mattered* (BBC, 2006). Similarly, in the Hayman case in the UK, the therapist involved was prepared to accept the personal consequences of refusing to give evidence against a client, even at the potential cost of being sent to jail for contempt of court.

The BACP *Ethical Framework* embraces ethical *principles*, derived and extended from the biomedical model, the concept of *virtues*, described as personal moral qualities and the notion of *values*. A value is fundamental commitment to a certain way of behaving towards others, such as respecting human rights and dignity, which may, in turn, be linked to an underlying ethical principle, such as autonomy. The above attempt at mapping ethical approaches to therapy and the law is no more than a very approximate guide to what is a very complex field. It does not refer, for example, to the developing terrain of relational ethics, which is of increasing interest to therapists, but aims to illustrate some of the ways in which abstract ethical concepts, such as the rights of the client or the 'public interest', inform a legal discourse.

Mapping ethical approaches

The law does not present a single, monolithic approach to the use of ethical perspectives in its decision-making, whatever the strong influence of philosophical perspectives, such as utilitarianism. The table in Box 1.4 sets out some of the attributes and resources which may be seen as an integral part of developing an informed ethical stance. These include personal qualities, such as the intellectual ability to reason and to develop an awareness of the consequences of one's own actions on others. At an emotional level, perhaps of at least equal interest to therapists, ethical behaviour might require some understanding of self and an ability to empathise with others, and to have an awareness of the nature of relationships with others.

Frameworks for understanding and responding to ethical issues may be divided into those which focus primarily on one's own needs, rights and duties, leading to prioritising entitlement to one's *own* individual rights; and those which focus on an awareness of enduring responsibilities for the well-being of *others*. A highly developed sense of commitment to the needs, rights and duties of others may be reflected in the active use of principles or rules as a form of guidance in ethical decision-making. At the furthest edge, this heightened, rather abstract, concept of the need to act in the interests of others might be expressed in terms of a commitment to act in 'the public good', rather than out of any more immediate, or narrowly defined, self-interest.

Box 1.4 Mapping positions related to ethical behaviour			
Attributes & resources as the basis for ethical behaviour		**Applied towards self**	**Applied towards others**
Personal Qualities	**Cognitive Development**	Ability to reason	Awareness of social consequences
	Emotional Development	Understanding of self	Empathy/relational awareness
Frameworks for working with ethical dilemmas & challenges	**Primary focus on own needs, rights and duties**	Entitlement to individual rights	Awareness of obligations/ responsibilities/ duties towards others
	Primary focus on needs, rights and duties of others	Use of principles/rules as guidance for decision-making	Awareness of 'the public good'

Tracking ethical perspectives in the law

This diversity of ethical perspectives can be translated into a range of legal concepts, with specific examples, where an ethical approach has been integral to decision-making with regard to a particular case, or in drafting a certain statute. The ability to reason and consider alternatives, for example, is expressed in the legal concepts of capacity and consent (see Box 1.5, p. 20). This was central to deciding the *Bournewood* case, described below (see pp. 48–9), which hinged on whether psychiatric treatment without either consent or legal authority was unlawful and contrary to human rights principles. The exploration of the potential social consequences of one's actions is central to the *Gillick* case, which concerned access to contraceptive treatment by young people.

Utilitarian principles – of deciding cases on the basis of the greatest happiness of the greatest number – imply a rather abstract, objective and calculating approach to resolving ethical issues. This has been challenged by the ethical approach of applying empathic understanding, in this case to the right of *Ms B*, in seeking to have her ventilator turned off (see case study). The judge argued that proper acknowledgement of autonomy requires respect for difference and for lived individual experience, rather than the use of a more objective approach.

Rights-based approaches can be found in terms of the right to consent, to confidentiality and, more recently, the right to privacy, all expressed in recent court judgments. Duties towards others can be found in the rare mandatory requirement to report certain forms of threat of harm to others, such as terrorist offences, and the more generic obligation upon therapists to provide 'reasonable care and skill' under consumer law.

Ethical principles, such as beneficence and non-maleficence, find legal expression in concepts such as the therapist's duty of care to the client, and the detailing of the appropriate standard of care, to be found in relevant case law such as *Werner*, and the *Bolam* test. Finally, awareness of the greater 'public good' as an ethical goal is to be found in the judicial concept of the public interest as a deciding factor. Case law illustrates that the public interest can lie both in maintaining confidentiality, in the case of doctors with HIV, and, in certain situations, such as the *Egdell* case, in permitting confidentiality to be broken.

Of course, it also needs to be acknowledged that the idea of 'the public interest' is not itself an objective or neutral concept immune to the influence of class, gender or other social influences. For example, in the US, the public interest is held to embrace the concept of privilege for therapists, while the courts in the UK have decisively rejected this approach (*Jaffee v Redmond* (1996)).

There is, consequently, a wide diversity of ethical positions, which can be found as the rationale for judicial decision-making. Some of these, such as the empathic or relational approach, may still be fairly marginal to the utilitarian mainstream, but it still remains true that there is a wide range of ethical positions operating within the law. This provides an opportunity for therapists to engage with and critique the legal process from their own ethical position, rather than have to accept the process and outcome of legal decision-making as a given fact, beyond their understanding or influence.

Case study   The case of *Ms B*: Empathic understanding as an aid to judicial decision-making

Ms B was a 43-year-old woman from Jamaica, who had lived most of her life in the United Kingdom. She had worked as a qualified social worker and team manager. In 1999, Ms B suffered a haemorrhage of the spinal column in her neck. In 2001, Ms B began to suffer from general weakening on the left side of her body, and experienced greater numbness in her legs, and was admitted to the hospital, where she became tetraplegic, suffering complete paralysis from the neck down. She was transferred to the Intensive Care Unit (ICU) of the hospital. She experienced respiratory problems,

(Continued)

and became entirely dependent upon treatment by a ventilator. She informed the doctors involved in her care that she had a Living Will on file, and did not want to be ventilated. Medical staff did not accept this as authority to cease ventilation, on the grounds that the Living Will was not specific enough in relating to her present circumstances.

For the ensuing court case, Ms B's mental competence was assessed by Dr Sensky, a consultant psychiatrist.

He concluded she had the mental capacity to make decisions. In his overall judgment, Ms B was at the extreme end of competence, despite the limitations of her physical state and her environment in the ICU. She was likely to remain competent to make decisions for the foreseeable future ... He considered that she had a good understanding of her circumstances and had given a great deal of thought to her decision. She had gone to considerable lengths to find out the relevant information on her condition. She told him that she was a fighter by nature but said that

'I cannot accept myself as disabled and dependent – it's too big a leap to make. The totality of dependence is intolerable.'

Dame Elizabeth Butler-Sloss quoted from the article by Kim Atkins (Atkins, 2000), which Dr Sensky had used in presenting his argument in favour of Ms B's right to autonomy.

... our respect for each other's differences and autonomy embodies a respect for the particularity of each other's points of view.

However disturbing it is to see someone, especially one's loved one, on something like [a ventilator], it is essential that one tries to imagine what it is like to be that particular person on [a ventilator] if one is to attempt to act from respect for that person's autonomy. The difficulty here lies not in becoming more objective, but in being appropriately subjective ... I need to imagine not just what it would be like to me to be on [a ventilator], but what it would be like for [Ms B]. ... Insisting that a decision be made from a fully objective perspective can only produce a decision that is further from the patient's own point of view, not closer to it.

The Judge concluded that Ms B was competent to make all relevant decisions about her medical treatment, including the decision whether or not to seek to withdraw from artificial ventilation.

Source: Ms B v An NHS Hospital Trust [2002]

The case of *Ms B* presents a powerful example of a different ethical standpoint, rather than one based on utilitarian principles. Butler-Sloss places a value on empathic understanding of affective experience, which is, arguably, very close to the perspective which a therapist might be seeking to develop. For Atkins, empathy is a *pre-condition* here for respecting patient autonomy. 'When we are faced with the regrettable position of having to make dire decisions on behalf of another, the only way to act so as to respect that person's autonomy is to promote a consideration of that person's subjective experience' (Atkins, 2000: 78).

Box 1.5 Ethical attributes and their application in legal decision-making

Ethical attributes	Legal concepts	Examples from statute or case law	Page reference
Ability to reason	Capacity/consent	*Bournewood* case	48–9
Awareness of social consequences	'*Gillick* competence'/ 'Fraser guidelines'	*Gillick* and *Axon* cases	153; 162
Understanding of self/empathy/ relational awareness	Empathic respect for right to autonomy	*Ms B* case	18
Entitlement to individual rights	Right to • consent • confidentiality • privacy • access to records	*Diane Blood* case *Gillick* case *Naomi Campbell* case *Gaskin* case	183 153 111 140
Awareness of obligations, responsibilities, duties towards others	Duty to break confidentiality	Terrorism Act 2000 *Tarasoff* case (US)	115 121
	Obligation of 'reasonable care and skill'	Supply of Goods and Services Act 1982	30
Use of principles, rules as guidance for decision-making	Duty of care	*Werner* case	79–80
	Standard of care	*Bolam, Maynard* and *Bolitho* cases	78, 80
Awareness of the 'public good'	Public interest in: • *breaking* confidentiality • *maintaining* confidentiality • therapist privilege	*Egdell* case *X v Y* case *Jaffee* case (US)	108 110 103–4

The cases referred to in Box 1.5 are outlined and discussed in more detail in the following chapters. For example, the concepts of capacity and consent are related to the position of adults with learning disabilities in Chapter 3, and to that of young people in Chapter 7. The notion of a rule-based therapist duty of care is discussed more fully in Chapter 4, while the overall public interest in confidentiality is central to the material in Chapter 5.

Summary

Therapy enjoys an uneasy relationship with the law, given that its nature is private, personal and co-operative, rather than public, formalised and adversarial. Ethics have occupied an increasingly important role within therapy in the recent period, with a shift away from rule-following approaches and towards more flexible models which emphasise ethical principles, values and personal qualities. Distinct ethical models, such as utilitarianism, can be identified in legal decision-making approaches with regard to defining the public interest in key cases. However, there is a developing diversity of ethical perspectives to be found within the law, including rights-based models and the empathic valuing of individual experience. Clarifying the complex relationship of therapy to the law requires further exploration of the legal *context* in which therapists work, which will be outlined in the following chapter.

Discussion points

1 Where ethical principles and the law are in conflict, which should the therapist follow and why? Discuss a specific example from your own professional experience, relating to third party risk, child abuse or potential client suicide.
2 How can therapists develop their knowledge and use of ethical terms? How could ethical awareness be encouraged amongst therapists?
3 Do therapists really need a formal knowledge of different approaches to philosophy and ethics, such as utilitarianism, or can they simply rely upon their own innate sense of right and wrong?
4 Where might you locate yourself in relation to the 'map' of ethical positions outlined in this chapter? What were the key influences, or personal choices, which have contributed to the development of your current ethical stance?
5 Referring back to the case of *Ms B*, what alternative judicial stances might have been adopted? How might these be justified in *ethical* terms?

2

The Legal Context of Therapy

The legal system in the United Kingdom is complex and many-sided. The first part of this chapter will offer a brief guide to some of the content and structure of the law, or rather to the main areas likely to be of interest to therapists, such as tort, contract and the responsibilities of service providers. Issues of communicating information, such as data protection and defamation, are then explored. A final section looks at responsibilities relating to service provision and employment regarding employers' liability, criminal records checks and legislation concerning discrimination. The structure of the court system and more practical aspects of going to court or claiming damages are dealt with in Chapter 3.

Content and structure of the law

The language used by the law gives a strong clue to the origins of the legal system. Thus, 'law' itself is a Norse word, as in the Danelaw. The terms 'jury' and 'verdict' come from Latin (*iuro*: I swear; *vere dicere*: to speak truly). The term 'sheriff' comes from the Anglo-Saxon phrase 'shire reeve'. The word 'tort' comes from French, meaning simply a civil wrong. Each of these terms provides a clue to the historical combination of different systems of law – Roman, Anglo-Saxon and Norman – into the current system of law.

It needs to be said at the outset that there are different systems of law in the UK for Scotland, Northern Ireland, England and Wales. The main focus of this chapter is on the law relating to England and Wales, with some reference to specific features of the law in Scotland where this is relevant. There is also some passing reference to the law relating to therapy in the USA. This system has some similarities with law in the UK, being based on a mixture of statute and common law. However, US law possesses a very wide diversity of law at the level of the individual states, for example in terms of law regarding therapists' duty to warn third parties, the registration of therapists, and therapists' rights to privilege. Legal principles applying in some states in the USA are of interest to therapists in the UK, but often have no immediate relevance for law in England and Wales, except as a point of interest, for comparison and discussion.

Statute

The term 'statute' refers to pieces of primary legislation passed by Parliament, such as the Mental Health Act 1983, Children Act 2004, Consumer Protection Act 1987 and Data Protection Act 1998, all of which have a bearing on the work of therapists in different ways. In some cases, secondary legislation operates in the form of Statutory Instruments, authorised by the relevant Minister, as, for example, with data protection law. Certain pieces of legislation also have detailed operational guidelines, as with the *Mental Health Act 1983 Code of Practice* (DoH/WO, 1999), or the Guidance issued by the Department for Education and Skills, such as *Safeguarding Children in Education* (DfES, 2004). These are authoritative official documents requiring relevant agencies and staff to comply with their directions.

Common law

Common law is a term used in contrast to codes of law. Codes seek to regulate a wide variety of circumstances on the basis of set principles. The European system of law is based firstly on Roman, and then on Napoleonic, codes of law, which both express this centralising principle. Arguably the European Union (EU) now picks up this mantle, hence some of the tensions evident between EC Directives and UK law. The latter is based more on a combination of statute and common law. Common law is often described as law made by judges, based on their practice and experience. On this model, the law evolves on an empirical basis, adapting to new circumstances without necessarily requiring fresh legislation. Hence, 'in common law countries judges adapt the past to the present from actual experience of cases, with a measure of legislative interaction' (Fleming, 1994: 210). The relevance of this to therapists is that large and important areas of law are not codified in statute in England and Wales, but operate on the basis of established principles, which have evolved through common law. These areas include much of the law relating to key areas such as contract, confidentiality and tort. Scotland combines elements of both common law and codified law (Manson-Smith, 2004).

Case law

The concept of case law is important both in relation to the evolution of common law, and in terms of influencing future legislation. Principles, for example, concerning the rights of young people with 'sufficient understanding' to access confidential medical treatment were expressed in the *Gillick* case, which, in turn, later influenced the framing of the Children Act 1989. Another less well known instance, the *Gaskin* case, helped establish the rights of a wide range of service users to access their files, across the fields of health, education and social services. Statute will generally carry greater authority than case law, unless the case in question, such as *Gillick*, clarifies an important principle of law as a point of future reference.

Civil and criminal law

A useful starting point is the exploration of the fundamental differences between civil and criminal law, which are set out in Box 2.1. In Scotland, there are certain differences from this outline. Criminal cases are brought to the court by the Procurator Fiscal. The levels of the court system include District Courts at the local level, Sheriff's Court at regional level, and the High Court of Justiciary for appeals. In criminal trials, verdicts can include 'not proven' as well as guilty or not guilty.

Box 2.1　Comparison of features of civil and criminal law (England and Wales)

Civil law	Criminal law
Proceedings can be brought by private interest to secure a direct remedy	Prosecution normally brought by public agency, i.e. Crown Prosecution Service
Parties referred to as plaintiff and respondent or defendant	Parties referred to as prosecutor and the accused or defendant
Courts include tribunals, Magistrates', County and High Court, Court of Appeal, House of Lords	Courts include Magistrates', Crown and High Court, Court of Appeal, House of Lords
Case proven on 'balance of probabilities', i.e. it is more probable than not that this is true	Case proven to be 'beyond reasonable doubt', i.e. a more stringent criterion of proof
Leads to judgment or order for:	Leads to acquittal or sentence, i.e.
• unsuccessful party to pay damages • party to take action, e.g. comply with contract • party to stop activity, e.g. molesting another person	• fine, custody, etc. • criminal conviction

---

Civil law provides remedies for resolving disputes between parties, such as private individuals, on issues concerning property, child and family proceedings and the protection of the interests of individuals, such as privacy, personal reputation and confidentiality. The criminal law operates to punish breaches of the law within the wider community. Two key elements of criminal law are proof of the committing of a guilty act (*actus reus*), and of the possession of intent or of a guilty mind (*mens rea*). In rare cases, a person can be found not responsible for their actions by reason of insanity, under the McNaughten rules.

Tort law

The most likely area of relevance to therapists, generally speaking, will be proceedings under the civil law, rather than the criminal law. In civil law, the question of tort, or delict in Scotland, is a key area. The term 'tort' derives from the word for 'wrong' in French. In legal terms, it refers to a civil wrong inflicted upon another person, such as a neighbour, who wishes to correct this or to seek compensation. Thus 'the general gist is damage or injury arising to one person from unfair, careless or unreasonable action (or inaction) by another' (Fleming, 1994: 165). In England and Wales, the parties involved in tort cases are referred to as the plaintiff and defendant. In Scotland, the parties are known as the defender and the pursuer. This chapter will give a brief outline of the concept of tort, which will be explored more thoroughly with regard to professional negligence in Chapter 4, with specific reference to therapists.

Negligence law

Within tort law, the concept of negligence derives from the landmark case of *Donoghue v Stevenson* [1932], where the plaintiff found a decomposed snail in a bottle of ginger beer, and accordingly sued the manufacturer for damages. The case confirmed what is known as the 'neighbour' principle, namely that one should take care not to cause harm to one's neighbour through any positive act or omission. Proving a case based on tort requires the fulfilment of three conditions:

- existence of a duty of care
- breach of that duty
- resultant foreseeable harm as a consequence of the breach

Professional negligence relates to the specific application of this general principle to those working in a special, professional relationship, and the duty that follows from this to act with care regarding the client. The application of these principles to therapeutic work is discussed in more detail in Chapter 4.

Assault, battery and harassment

Therapists using physical or tactile methods of therapy may need to consider issues of trespass on the person, assault and battery, to avoid unnecessary complications arising later on. Trespass to the person may consist of assault and battery, or false imprisonment, namely holding someone captive against their will without due authority.

Assault can include a threat, or a reasonable fear and apprehension of immediate violence or battery. **Battery** must include some application of actual force. It involves the unlawful application of force to another, such as touching someone without their consent or making an uninvited sexual advance, even when the other person may be unaware of this, because of being asleep or drugged. Battery does not include the normal, unavoidable touching which is part of everyday life. Reasonable force, or what is seen to be necessary and proportionate, can be used by a person to defend themselves against unlawful violence.

Recourse to the criminal law will apply where a therapist carries out a physical or sexual assault on a client. In 2001, two therapists in the US were sentenced to 16 years for 'reckless child abuse' leading to the death of Candace Newmaker, a 10-year-old girl. Candace, diagnosed as having reactive attachment disorder, had been subjected to a three-hour re-birthing procedure, where she was wrapped in blankets and sat on by four adults. During this physically arduous procedure, she lost consciousness and died.

Criminal proceedings may also be necessary where a client seeks to assault or harass a therapist in the course of his or her work. Assaults by clients on therapists may be rarely reported, but do sometimes occur. Ruth Hunt was murdered in 1996 by an ex-client, a released prisoner, while working as a volunteer counsellor with the probation service. In psychiatric care, nurses and doctors may be the subject of attack, as with social workers and probation officers going about their work. Therapists working in private practice may also be at risk. Bob Cooke, a psychotherapist, was subjected to an unprovoked attack at his clinic by the aggrieved partner of a client. The client's partner felt that the therapy was breaking up the couple's relationship. The man attacked Bob Cooke with a spanner, badly bruising the therapist's head and shoulders, while accusing him of 'brainwashing' his client. The client's partner was later jailed for 14 weeks for this attack.

Harassment of therapists may also take other, less physically damaging but equally threatening forms. In very rare cases, it may be that the client or patient is suffering from delusions about a fantasised romantic relationship with the therapist. This is defined as De Clerambault's syndrome, and it leads the client to pursue and harass the therapist without due cause. In cases where a therapist is harassed by a current or former client, a civil procedure, such as obtaining a court injunction, will provide some degree of protection. The Medical Protection Society has developed substantial experience in advising practitioners on how to protect themselves from this situation. Sumerling (1996) indicates that police protection is unlikely to be provided unless there is an actual occurrence of violence against the therapist. Some of the possible defensive measures to be taken could include:

- civil injunction, breach of which can be dealt with by the court;
- prosecution for assault or battery, which needs to be initiated within six months of an attack;
- action for nuisance such as 'watching and besetting', i.e. lying in wait for the therapist;
- action for obscene, annoying or offensive phone calls under Telecommunications Act 1984 and Criminal Justice Act 1991;
- action for sending indecent, grossly offensive, threatening or false information under the Malicious Communications Act 1988;
- action for using abusive or threatening words or behaviour under s. 4, Public Order Act 1986;
- action against 'stalking' under the Protection from Harassment Act 1997.

Under the Protection from Harassment Act 1997, there are both civil and criminal sanctions for repeated harassment or unwanted intrusive behaviour. Robert Fine, a university lecturer, was the first person to be awarded damages as a victim of a stalker, following his experiences of repeated harassment by a former student (Fine, 1997). Therapists may be particularly at risk of being harassed by current or former clients, if the emotional intensity of the therapeutic relationship is misconstrued by the client (Holmes et al., 2000; Kamphuis and Emmelkamp, 2000). Chris Jones, a counsellor at Lewes Tertiary College, experienced harassment from a colleague after ending her counselling sessions. He received hundreds of unwanted phone calls from her, and was followed by her both inside and outside work. He then brought a successful legal action against her, under the Protection from Harassment Act 1997, to bring a stop to this unwanted contact.

This kind of response will not be necessary in the vast majority of cases, but it is important that therapists know of the possible defences available to them under the law, to help protect their privacy and security in the face of an unreasonable and threatening client. Personal security for therapists is often not taken seriously enough. It is worth considering advice from specialist organisations with expertise in the field, such as the Suzy Lamplugh Trust (see Resources section for address).

Gathering evidence of harassment may be an important step, either in convincing an employer of the threat, persuading the client to desist, or in preparing for possible legal action. Sumerling (1996) provides some useful suggestions, such as:

- Keep any evidence, such as poison pen letters, messages left on answer machines.
- Carefully record events and incidents after they occur.
- Respond to threatening clients in a calm, professional manner.
- Seek expert professional advice without delay.
- Do not minimise or underestimate the personal risks involved.

Using contracts

Many therapists are more likely to deal with verbal rather than written contracts. Still, contract represents one of the key areas of law that therapists need to understand. Contracts not only set out the respective obligations of therapist and client, but are increasingly used by voluntary organisations providing counselling and other services.

Requirements of contract

Contract is one of the areas covered largely by common law, rather than solely by statute. Contracts for the sale of goods have been regulated since the Sale of Goods Act 1893, a consolidating piece of legislation which tied together earlier legal enactments. There are four conditions required for a contract to exist:

- legal capacity of persons involved
- firm offer and unequivocal acceptance
- clear intention of parties to create a legally binding agreement
- consideration, i.e. an exchange of goods or services for payment

The persons involved must have legal capacity, so that they are not mentally disordered, drunk, or aged under 18 years. There must be a firm offer and unequivocal acceptance. The acceptance must be oral, written or implied by the contract. A contract must be supported by consideration: in other words, each party must give something or do something to or for the other. The considerations provided do not necessarily have to be equal in value. It must be clear from the terms of the agreement that the parties intended to create a legally binding agreement. Where the intention is unclear, a court will decide. Informal agreements for purely social or domestic arrangements are excluded. A contract between businesses is intended to be binding, unless expressly agreed otherwise. The doctrine of 'privity of contract' means that those who are not actual parties to a contract have no right to sue on it. A third party affected by a contract, for example the parents or partner of a client in therapy, cannot sue the therapist over contractual issues, but would have to find other means, perhaps via action in tort (see discussion on third party actions in Chapter 4).

Box 2.2   Using contracts with clients

- Valid contract requires:

  — legal capacity of parties
  — offer and acceptance
  — intention to make agreement
  — an exchange or consideration.

- Contract includes both express (explicit) and implied terms.
- 'Privity' prevents third parties from suing for breach of contract.

Therapists' use of contracts

Therapists often use the term 'contract', when it would be more accurate to use a term such as 'therapeutic agreement' or 'working charter' (Jenkins, 2006). If no money, or other form of consideration, is exchanged by therapist and client, then the document does not meet the conditions required for a legally binding contract. Therapists working in the NHS, for example, do not normally provide services to clients on a contractual basis (Pattenden, 2003: 100).

Contracts are particularly relevant, therefore, to therapists who work in private practice and who charge a sessional fee for their work with clients or supervisees. For these practitioners, there are a number of practical points to consider in drawing up and using contracts (Cristofoli, 2002). The same fundamental points will apply whether this is a contract between an individual therapist and client, or between a counselling agency and another organisation. The fact that terms appear on a contract does not mean that they are legally part of the said contract. Terms need to be incorporated into the contract. This is usually done by each party signing the document, which sets out the terms to be included. Presenting the other party with the terms after the contract is signed does not make for an enforceable agreement. Terms need to be made clear before agreement and signing takes place (see Box 2.2).

The terms of a contract, such as one between a therapist and client, would include express terms, or those specifically included, such as frequency of contact, length and cost of therapy sessions. The contract will also include implied terms, whether specifically mentioned or not, such as the maintenance of confidentiality. Implied terms are those terms implied by law, or which are held to be customary in the trade, such as the exercise of 'reasonable care and skill' by the provider of the service. Thus under s. 13 of the Supply of Goods and Services Act 1982, the supplier must carry out the service with 'reasonable care and skill'. This is relevant to therapists because in s.18, 'business' is held to include a profession, and the activities of any government department or local or public authority.

The professional person has to exercise the ordinary skill of an ordinary competent person exercising that particular art or skill. However, as common sense would suggest, there is no implied guarantee that the service will necessarily achieve the desired result. Lord Denning expressed this with characteristic bluntness. 'The surgeon does not warrant that he will save the patient. Nor does the solicitor warrant that he will win the case' (*Greaves and Co. v Baynham Meikle* [1975]). Nor, it could be added, does the therapist necessarily guarantee a positive outcome to the therapy.

Stuart Sutherland, a highly dissatisfied consumer of therapy and psychiatry, recounts one example where he considered taking legal action for breach of contract.

Case study   Proposed action for breach of contract in therapy

My condition continued to deteriorate, but the decision about terminating analysis was for the time being taken out of my hands, since my second analyst announced that he was going on holiday. I never saw him again, although I had not yet quite escaped the lure of psychoanalysis. I was so annoyed with him for what I regarded as very unhelpful treatment that I did not pay his bill. When many months later I received a peremptory letter from his solicitors, I took legal advice myself and wrote to him saying that I had no intention of paying. I contested the claim on the grounds that his treatment had been incompetent. In the state of desperate anxiety in which I then was, his threatening remarks had only increased my problems: to accept such observations as that at some level of the unconscious mind one has homosexual proclivities, that one's virtues stem from weakness, or that one has missed out on the best things of life, it is necessary to be in a much more robust state of mental health than I then was. I also alleged that he himself felt threatened by my own knowledge of the subject and my doubts about the efficacy of psychoanalysis, and consciously or unconsciously he had been attempting to punish me. Finally, I wrote that he had claimed to be able to make me feel much better within six months of commencing therapy, that this claim was fraudulent and that I had entered therapy only through false pretences on his part. Such was my fury that I think I would have been prepared to contest a legal action, but it never arose. (Sutherland, 1977: 22)

It is a moot point as to who would have won if the case had actually gone to court, not least over whether the therapy was consistent with reasonable standards of care and skill in the practice of psychoanalysis. For his part, Sutherland appears to have been in breach of contract by not paying as required by the terms of the contract, if contract there was. His complaints about the therapist's sudden disappearance on holiday, and the therapist's alleged claim to guarantee a positive result within six months could have assisted the client in winning a potential case that the contract was unfulfilled. At best, the example illustrates the dangers of therapists making exaggerated claims for the effectiveness of their work, claims which may well come back to haunt them in the form of complaints or litigation by dissatisfied clients. (Action by therapist or client for alleged breach of contract is discussed in Chapter 3.)

Reasons for using contracts

The use of contracts is widely seen as an integral and essential part of therapeutic practice. For example, Szasz claims that 'the concepts of autonomy and contract are crucial to psychoanalysis' (1974: 190). Bond also promotes the use of contracts by therapists as a means of ensuring ethical practice and promoting the autonomy of the client (Bond, 2000: 88–90). At a minimum, it may reduce the likelihood of later misunderstanding, complaint or litigation by the client. The use of contracts has also been advised for organisations providing training in therapy, in order for students and tutors to be clear about their respective obligations in case of later confusion or dispute. A contract for fee-based therapy could usefully include the elements listed in Box 2.3.

Box 2.3   Elements of a model contract for fee-based therapy

- cost of sessions
- duration and frequency of sessions
- arrangements and charges (if relevant) for cancellation or holiday periods
- main characteristics of therapy to be provided
- total number of sessions, and arrangements for review
- limits to confidentiality
- arrangements for termination of therapy
- cover or substitution of therapist in case of illness
- date and signatures of both parties

The use of contracts can be linked to the issue of obtaining the client's informed consent to therapy, which is discussed in more detail in Chapter 4. A more contentious issue, perhaps, concerns the extension of the therapist's duty to the client after the therapist's death. In an agency or organisation, continuity of care would be considered the responsibility of the organisation. In the case of private practice, it has been suggested that therapists write a therapeutic will, indicating the steps to be taken to conclude or transfer therapy with clients, destroy confidential client records and wind up the affairs of the practice (Traynor and Clarkson, 2000).

The Supply of Goods and Services Act 1982 regulates contracts for the supply of services. Under s. 14 (2) there is an implied condition that the goods supplied under the contract are of merchantable quality, unless otherwise indicated. The term 'merchantable' here means 'saleable' or 'marketable'. Hence, any goods that a therapist supplies, such as relaxation tapes, electronic stress level monitors, aromatherapy oils, candles, meditation mats or whatever, need to be of a reasonable quality, again as common sense would no doubt suggest. Under s. 2, Consumer Protection Act 1987, the producer of goods which cause damage produced wholly or partly via a defect in the product carries strict liability. This means that the affected consumer does not then have to prove negligence on the producer's part to succeed in a legal action for redress.

Communicating information

Therapists are inescapably involved in the business of handling and communicating sensitive personal information, from the very moment a client is referred. This section explores some of the legal issues concerning data protection and defamation.

Data protection

The use of personal data in computerised and manual form is governed by the Data Protection Act 1998. Personal data is defined as data which relates to an identifiable living individual (Information Commissioner, 2001). It includes opinions about, and intentions towards, an individual. The intended scope of data processing, described by the Information Commissioner as a 'compendious definition', is designed to capture electronic data as well as manually recorded information. Many therapists use computers for keeping records of their work, and will therefore need to be aware of the principles of data processing and the rights of subject access, which are contained in the Act (Jenkins, 2002a). The use of personal data in computerised form, or of manual data kept in 'relevant filing systems', requires notification to the Information Commissioner. The latter is an independent officer appointed by Her Majesty the Queen, reporting directly to Parliament. Under the Data Protection Act 1998, it is an offence to process data on an individual without undertaking notification with the Information Commissioner. However, where a therapist or agency hold its records only in manual and not in computerised form, then notification is not required. The current notification fee is £35 for a one-year period (see Chapter 6 for a more detailed outline of data protection and client access to therapeutic records).

Defamation, libel and slander

Another area of potential interest to therapists is defamation, covered by the Defamation Act 1996. This may be relevant in relation to making or challenging statements, whether as client or as therapist, about professional work, training establishments or in making allegations of malpractice. It has been suggested that fear of being sued for slander or libel may be an inhibiting factor for some clients and professionals, making them reluctant to report alleged malpractice, for example, such as another therapist's sexual relationships with current clients, or unsafe and unethical practice (Russell, 1993: 26).

Defamation is defined as a statement which injures the reputation of the plaintiff by tending to lower them in the thinking of right-minded members of society, or by causing the latter to shun or avoid them, or by bringing them into 'hatred, ridicule or contempt'. This does not include what goes under the label of an insult or general abuse, for example calling someone a scoundrel. The statement must not only be untrue, but must be damaging as well. Taking legal action over defamation is a risky and expensive business, which should be carefully thought through before being embarked upon, given both the legal costs involved and the appreciable risk of failure.

Libel and slander

There are two main forms of defamation: libel and slander. The difference is often assumed to be that existing between written and spoken forms of defamation, but the real difference is between permanent and temporary forms of defamation, so that libel can include words spoken in recorded form such as on TV, radio or video. Libel may also be considered as criminal libel if seditious or obscene. Community Legal Service Funding, or what was previously known as Legal Aid, is not generally available for libel actions, which may well inhibit an individual from taking action. Action for defamation may be undertaken on a conditional fee basis. In Scotland, it should be noted that the terms 'libel' and 'slander' are used somewhat differently, and almost interchangeably on occasion. Slander, for instance, is seen as a verbal injury.

Defences against defamation can include:

- The statement is true (an absolute defence).
- It can be jüstified as 'fair comment'.
- The consent of the person concerned was obtained.
- An apology and compensation were offered.
- Privilege is claimed.

There have been a number of cases involving therapists and the media, where legal proceedings for defamation have been taken.

- Katalin Blanc accepted damages of £10,000, following an interview with her former husband, the chef Raymond Blanc in the *Observer*, which was held to have made a number of statements damaging to her reputation as a psychotherapist (*Guardian*, 26 April 1997).
- Richard Wilmot-Smith, QC, and his wife, Jenny, a psychic healer, were awarded £350,000 damages against the *Daily Telegraph*, after an article in 1995, 'The dark side of the New Age', about a 'case of alternative therapy that left a happy family in tatters' (*Guardian*, 19 March 1997).
- Paul McKenna, a hypnotist, won a libel case against the *Daily Mirror*, for an article alleging that his first Ph.D., from an American university, was worthless (*Guardian*, 29 July 2006).
- Former psychoanalyst, Jeffrey Masson, brought a libel case in 1994 for $11 million against a journalist, Janet Malcolm, for an interview in the *New Yorker*,

in which she used the term 'an intellectual gigolo'. Malcolm's supporting evidence of the interview was in the form of a typed transcript of her notes, which had gone missing. The original notebook was found by her two-year-old grand-daughter, 10 months after the case had been successfully concluded in her favour (Malcolm, 1997).

Qualified privilege as defence against defamation

The use of the defence of 'qualified privilege' is likely to be of particular interest to therapists, as a defence against potential defamation charges in reporting alleged malpractice by a colleague. The crucial elements for claiming a defence of qualified privilege are:

- a moral or social duty on the part of the person giving the information, or making the statement;
- a corresponding duty on the part of the person receiving the information.

This reciprocity is essential in legal terms in order to claim this defence (Pannett, 1992: 242; *Adam v Ward* [1917]). While a professional person may not possess privilege, there is acceptance that, in some situations, this protection is needed for persons giving information of social value. This is described as qualified privilege. 'Qualified privilege provides that where the retailer of the information has a duty or interest in passing it on, and the person to whom he gives it also has a duty or interest in receiving it, then provided it was not done with malice there is no liability' (Pearce, 1988: 4). This would cover stating a professional opinion, as when taking part in a child protection case conference. Qualified privilege has also been taken to include the process of giving references. There is a degree of protection under qualified privilege for professionals who bring complaints against others for unprofessional conduct. In the past, professionals, therapists included, may often have been reluctant to disclose information about a colleague's incompetence or abuse of clients, for fear of counter-action for libel or slander. However, the use of qualified privilege does not provide an automatically successful legal defence against defamation, as the Shieldfield case illustrates.

Case study   Defamation and malice

Two nursery nurses, Dawn Reed and Christopher Lillie, brought libel charges, following the publication of a report on alleged sexual abuse of pre-school children, who were formerly under their care at Shieldfield nursery, Newcastle. Parents made allegations of sexual abuse against the pair in 1993, following the discovery of suspected abuse by a male nursery nurse at another nursery in the city. However, at the criminal trial in 1994, the judge dismissed the videotaped evidence given by the children, on the grounds that the interviews had been improperly carried out. Reed and Lillie were acquitted of the charges against them, on the direction of the judge, but were dismissed from their jobs by the council.

(Continued)

(Continued)

The council then set up an inquiry into the alleged abuse, staffed by a number of senior practitioners. Their report, produced in 1998, repeated the original allegations against Reed and Lillie. The latter then brought a case for libel against the authors of the report and against Newcastle City Council. They were each awarded damages of £200,000 in 2002. Unusually, the court rejected the plea of qualified privilege, which was used by the report's authors as a defence against the defamation charges. The court found evidence of malice on the part of the authors, but not the council, in the content and publication of the report, which was described as a 'specious and disreputable document'. The report had included 'a number of fundamental claims which they must have known to be untrue and which cannot be explained on the basis of incompetence or mere carelessness' (at 276).

Source: Lillie and Reed v Newcastle City Council [2002]

In everyday terms, malice refers to an attitude of spite or ill will. From a legal perspective, malice carries a very specific meaning, referring to an intentional act carried out without due cause. It is relatively rare for a court to make finding of malice with regard to a statement or publication made under qualified privilege.

Telecommunications and therapy

Therapy may be described as the 'talking cure', but it is increasingly affected in various ways by the new technologies. The Samaritans, for example, provide a counselling service by e-mail, which meets a previously unrecognised demand. Each advance in technology raises new questions about ethics and the law in relation to communicating sensitive personal information. There is provision under the law to limit or prevent some abuses of therapists' privacy and confidentiality:

- 'Hacking' into computer data is an offence under the Computer Misuse Act 1990.
- Unauthorised interception or recording of phone conversations is an offence under s. 45 of the Telecommunications Act 1984.
- The Home Office can stop programmes endangering the privacy of persons in vulnerable positions, under the Broadcasting Act 1990.
- UK websites have liability for any material posted which is libellous, under the Defamation Act 1996.

On-line counselling presents a number of challenges from a legal perspective. E-mails constitute personal data and therefore come within the scope of the Data Protection Act 1998. Individuals or agencies setting up on-line therapeutic services need to take account of key legal issues, such as the nature of the contract with clients, respecting and protecting copyright of material used on websites, and the impact of international law regarding liability and data transfer outside the UK (O'Dowd, 2001).

Law relating to service provision and employment

Understanding the law in terms of a wider set of responsibilities, such as those relating to employment and the provision of a counselling or psychotherapy service, is also important for many therapists. This section will cover the nature of employers' liability for staff, duty of care related to workplace stress, and criminal records checks. Finally, issues of discrimination, at the core of much therapeutic work, also are at the forefront of employment law, and require consideration by therapists and agencies alike.

Liability of employers

Employers have what is known as vicarious liability for acts carried out by employees, or by others who carry out activities without necessarily being formally employed. To illustrate the former point, in medical cases, for example, action for negligence can be brought against an individual doctor. If the doctor is employed by the NHS, then the claim is more likely to be brought against the relevant health authority or NHS Trust, from whom damages or compensation can be sought. This process is shown in the case of *Cassidy v Ministry of Health* [1951]. In this instance, a patient had an operation on his hand, which was placed in a splint to overcome the likely contraction of two fingers. However, on removal of the splint, it was found that the plaintiff's whole hand had become paralysed. Given that all the staff involved in his care were NHS employees, the court found against the staff's employer, the NHS.

Vicarious liability

The concept of vicarious liability is particularly relevant for therapists working in primary care, where issues of clinical accountability and legal liability can sometimes seem complex and confusing. In terms of liability, it is important to distinguish between staff who are employed by the practice and those who are self-employed. Employment relationships are a key factor in deciding where liability for negligence lies. Where a therapist is employed, or working as if employed, by the GP practice, then the practice would hold vicarious liability for any mistakes or poor practice. Where the therapist is self-employed, but simply using an interview room for counselling clients referred by the GP, then the therapist would be liable him or herself for any action brought by a dissatisfied client. The confusion arising here is that the issue is often presented in terms of the doctor's overall clinical responsibility for overseeing patient care. This is not necessarily the crucial element for the courts in determining legal liability, which rests much more on the *employment status* of the therapist or other member of staff, and their *employment relationship* with the practice concerned. The concept of vicarious liability also extends to cover students and trainees on placement at an agency. Vicarious liability does not remove the individual's liability as an employee, but extends it to the responsible employing organisation. In practice, lawsuits tend to be directed against an organisation, such as a hospital or NHS Trust, more often than against the individual practitioner concerned.

Employers' duties

In terms of negligence liability, employers have a common law duty regarding employees, deriving from the *Donoghue* [1932] case, in addition to certain statutory duties under Health and Safety law (see Box 2.4). These common law duties cover doing what is reasonably practicable regarding provision of safe equipment, a safe system of work, such as a duty not to put the employee at risk of attack (*Charlton v Forrest* [1980]), and provision of reasonably competent staff with whom the employee is required to work.

Box 2.4　Statutory duties of employer

Health and Safety at Work Act 1974:

s. 2　　　　to ensure the health, safety and welfare at work of employees
s. 2(2)(e)　to provide a working environment that is safe, without risks to health, and adequate for the welfare of employees

Management of Health and Safety at Work Regulations 1999 (SI 1999/3242):

3(1)　　　to make assessment of risks to the health and safety of employees and others at work
6　　　　　to ensure employees are provided with appropriate health surveillance

---

The growth of recorded stress levels at work has focused increasing interest on the issue of liability for stress-induced illness amongst employees. The case of *John Walker*, a social worker who successfully took legal action against his former employer, was hailed as a landmark decision in this respect. The judge's decision confirmed the employer's common law duty of care towards employees.

Case study　Employers' duty of care regarding stress-induced psychiatric illness

John Walker worked for Northumberland County Council as an Area Social Services Officer from 1970 to 1987. There was a high volume of work, often concerning problematic and stressful child protection cases. With no previous history of mental problems, Mr Walker suffered a nervous breakdown, namely mental exhaustion and stress

(Continued)

reactions, in 1986. This recurred in 1987, despite his employer having been alerted to the problems he was experiencing at work. In 1988, he was dismissed by his employers on the grounds of permanent ill-health.

John Walker then brought a successful legal case against his employers. The judge noted the expert evidence, which attested to the intrinsically stressful nature of much social work, but noted an additional factor, which was the structure and manning of the relevant social services department. In 1996, two years after winning the court case, Walker reached an out-of-court settlement with his former employer for a compensation payment of £175,000.

Source: Walker v Northumberland C.C. [1995]

The case needs to be read carefully to follow the main lessons to be drawn from it. The action against Northumberland was based both in tort law, for negligence, and in contract. The employers were found not liable for causing the first nervous breakdown, because it was not reasonably foreseeable that the pressures of work and the staffing and management arrangements would carry a material or significant risk of a nervous breakdown. However, on the plaintiff's return to work, it was held to be clearly foreseeable that a continuation of these conditions would cause this to happen all over again. Judge Colman held that the council 'provided no effective help. In so doing, it was, in my judgement, acting unreasonably and therefore in breach of its duty of care' (at 760).

Case study   Testing the employer's duty of care: The Hutton Inquiry

The Hutton Inquiry was held into the death of Dr David Kelly, a government expert on 'Weapons of Mass Destruction' in Iraq. In 2002, Dr Kelly committed suicide, following intense media interest in an anonymous interview he had given to the BBC Today programme. The Inquiry focused, in part, on the level of stress experienced by Dr Kelly, and the response by the Ministry of Defence (MOD), as his employer, in carrying out its duty of care towards him as an employee.

Mr Richard Hatfield, Personnel Director for MOD, examined by Mr Lloyd Jones, on 17 September 2003:

Q:	*Did Mr Kelly ever request legal assistance or welfare assistance?*
A:	*Certainly not from me.*
Lord Hutton:	*When did you tell him? At what interview did you tell him he would get departmental support?*

(Continued)

(Continued)

A: It came up on both the 4th and the 7th July ... And I specifically told him during one or both of my two final telephone conversations with him about the statement that he should now seek support through his line manager, in particular, but also particularly from the press office in relation to any contact with the media or any approaches from the media; and that was, I believe, put in hand.

Mr Richard Hatfield, Personnel Director for MOD, cross-examined by Mr Gompertz, Counsel for the Kelly family, 18 September 2003:

Q: Was there any counselling offered?
A: In relation to what?
Q: In relation to the stress which Dr Kelly was undergoing at the time?
A: On the basis of what we knew at the time, the only stress Dr Kelly was undergoing was the stress associated with appearances before the FAC and the ISC and the stress induced by what had come to be modern media behaviour. He was given advice in relation to all those things in the same way as anybody appearing before committees would be given, and support was offered.
Q: What I am asking you is did the MOD and you yourself, in particular, take any of these matters into account in order to assess whether Dr Kelly was likely to be suffering from severe stress?
A: The answer to your question is 'yes', and we believe, and on the basis of how he behaved during all this period, that he was not suffering any stress other than the sort of stress that we commonly expect from people going in front of committees in slightly difficult circumstances, and that we gave him the appropriate support.

Source: www.the-hutton-enquiry.org.uk/content/transcripts/hearing-trans36.htm

The *Walker* case firmly established the principle of employer liability for workplace stress, or more exactly, for breach of duty of care causing foreseeable psychological injury. Subsequent cases led to a number of employers, mainly in the public sector, accepting liability for such injury. The principle of employer liability for workplace stress can be seen at work, for example, in the Hutton Inquiry (above).

Media concern about the growth of a 'compensation culture' grew, and a key Court of Appeal ruling was made, concerning four conjoined cases (*Hatton v Sutherland* [2002]). Carefully read, this judgment restated the original *Walker* case, but in very clear terms, it spelled out the criteria for establishing future cases (see Box 2.5). The judge commented that no job was considered to be inherently stressful, and that, contrary to rising expectations of a stress bandwagon, 'some things are no one's fault' (at 10). Crucially, with regard to the future development of confidential counselling services, the judge concluded that 'an employer who does have a system along these lines is unlikely to be found in breach of his duty of care towards his employees' (at 11).

> **Box 2.5   Checklist for employer liability**
>
> - Is the individual subject to undue pressure of work which is:
>
>   - unreasonable by any standard?
>   - unreasonable judged in comparison with the workload of others in a similar job, or
>   - due to individual vulnerability, which is known to the employer?
>
> - Has the individual received an injury to health either physical or psychological, which is directly attributable to stress at work?
> - Was this injury reasonably foreseeable by the employer?
> - Is this injury directly and mainly attributable to the employer's breach of duty of care, in failing to reduce workplace stress (by providing confidential counselling, redistribution of duties, training, etc)?
>
> Adapted from: *Hatton v Sutherland* [2002]

The *Hatton* case sets a clear agenda for the courts in deciding future cases of workplace stress. Employers need to be aware of their responsibilities under both statute and common law. Counselling is now perceived as having a crucial protective function for employers, in limiting liability for claims for psychological injury. Employers also need to be aware that their liability is now seen to extend to the monitoring and prevention of harassment at work of members of staff by their colleagues, under the Protection from Harassment Act 1997.

Criminal convictions

The checking of prospective staff's backgrounds for criminal convictions is now standard procedure in both statutory areas such as health, education and social services, and the voluntary sector. Therapists' associations such as BACP and UKCP require members to inform them of any convictions. 'Relevant convictions' are considered by the Human Fertilisation and Embryology Authority when making appointments. According to an earlier version of its *Code*, 'relevant convictions will depend upon the particular post and the gravity of the particular offence, but may include any offence of violence or dishonesty, blackmail, sexual offences and offences against children, drugs offences and breaches of regulatory machinery' (HFEA, 1993: para. 1.18).

Provision for employers considering or setting aside past or 'spent' convictions is set out by the Rehabilitation of Offenders Act 1974. Under the Act, most types of previous criminal convictions become spent after a fixed period of time, in order to assist the re-entry of offenders into society (Harris, 1976). Apart from specified exceptions such as medical, nursing and other professional posts, previous convictions with a prison sentence of 30 months become spent after 10 years, and do not have to be disclosed to employers when seeking employment. There are wide exceptions to this, however, as set out below.

Police Act 1997

There are three types of access to past records under the Police Act 1997:

- *Criminal Conviction Certificates*: available to individuals only, listing unspent convictions, similar to a 'certificate of good conduct' (s. 100);
- *Full criminal records checks*: including spent convictions for those working with children under 18, elderly, sick and handicapped people (s. 101);
- *Enhanced criminal records checks*: for prospective employees, trainees and volunteers having regular, unsupervised contact with children and young persons under 18 or vulnerable adults. Enhanced checks include access to information known to the police, such as involvement in paedophile activity, which may need to be considered when making appointments for particularly sensitive posts (s. 102).

Some professions and activities are exempt from the protection against disclosure provided by the Rehabilitation of Offenders Act 1974. Agencies can apply to the Criminal Records Bureau to make criminal records checks of varying levels of scrutiny, regarding current or prospective staff or volunteers. For smaller agencies making less frequent checks, this can be done through a registered Umbrella Body, which acts as a consultant and gateway to this information. Criminal records checks can be carried out on individuals seeking to work with children in a wide range of settings, or with vulnerable adults. A vulnerable adult is defined as a person:

- over the age of 18, receiving care services in residential setting or at home
- with a physical or learning disability, or mental illness
- leading to dependency on others for basic physical functions, severe impairment in communication, or limited ability to protect him or herself from assault, abuse or neglect.

Persons who regularly care for vulnerable adults are subject to enhanced disclosure as described above, while those providing care services are subject to standard disclosure. Therapists as such are not included within the list of professions exempted from the provisions of the Rehabilitation of Offenders Act 1974, with the exception of chartered psychologists. Therapists will be required to undergo criminal records checks, depending upon the nature of their client group, such as children, or the context in which they practise, such as a school or hospital.

Unlawful discrimination

Experience of stigma and discrimination is at the heart of many clients' life stories. Therapists are often made aware of these issues through their practice and training, if not through their own life histories. There has been a significant expansion of legislation and of regulations designed to eliminate discrimination against people on the grounds of sex, race, disability, age, sexual orientation and gender reassignment. Recent legislation places a positive duty on public authorities to promote equality of opportunity in the areas of race relations and disability.

Discrimination on grounds of sex and race

The Sex Discrimination Acts (SDA) 1975 and 1986, incorporating the earlier Equal Pay Act 1970, make it unlawful for an employer to discriminate against men or women, either directly or indirectly, on grounds of sex or marital status. Case law has recognised for some time that sexual harassment actions can successfully be brought under the Sex Discrimination Act 1975. The SDA 1975 was amended by the Sex Discrimination (Gender Reassignment) Regulations 1999 (SI 1999/1102) to include transsexual men and women within its remit. Discrimination against people on the grounds of sexual orientation is unlawful, under the Employment Equality (Sexual Orientation) Regulations 2003 (SI 2003/1661).

The Race Relations Act 1976 similarly makes it unlawful for an employer to discriminate, either directly or indirectly, on the grounds of colour, race, nationality or ethnic or national origin. Following the publication of the Macpherson Report (1999) on police investigations into the murder of Stephen Lawrence, the Race Relations (Amendment) Act 2000 was passed. The Act covers all employers, large and small, and anyone providing goods, facilities or services to the public. It also places a new proactive duty on public authorities to eliminate unlawful discrimination and to promote equality of opportunity and good race relations.

Discrimination on grounds of disability, age and religious beliefs

In terms of disability, the Disability Discrimination Act (DDA) 2005 amends the earlier 1995 Act, which made it unlawful to discriminate directly, rather than indirectly, against a disabled person. Disability includes mental illness, and progressive conditions such as cancer, muscular dystrophy and HIV, according to Schedule 1 of the 1995 Act. The 2005 Act extends protection against discrimination to people diagnosed with cancer, HIV and multiple sclerosis but not yet showing signs of their illness. Also under the 2005 Act, mental illness no longer has to be 'clinically well recognised' in order to qualify as a disability. Discrimination is defined as unjustifiable less favourable treatment provided by an employer, such as dismissal, worse terms of employment, or fewer opportunities for training. The DDA 2005 also requires public authorities to promote equal opportunities for disabled people. With regard to education, the Special Educational Needs and Disability Act 2001 requires educational bodies to make 'reasonable adjustment' to meet the needs of students with disability, such as setting up accessible websites, and providing signers for deaf students.

The Employment Equality (Religion or Belief) Regulations 2003 outlaws discrimination on religious grounds, while the Employment Equality (Age) Regulations 2006 similarly prohibits age discrimination in terms of recruitment, promotion and training and bans unjustified retirement ages below 65.

Organisations may, however, discriminate lawfully in certain instances, for example by providing specific services, training or employment under ss. 7 and 48 of the Sex Discrimination Act 1975 and ss. 5 and 38 of the Race Relations Act 1976. The relevant sections could be used, for example, to recruit a black female counsellor to work in a hostel with young black adults.

In practice, therapists working with clients with disability, in the form of mental health problems, may experience a range of challenges, as the following case study from the US suggests.

Case study   College provision for a student who self-harms

At a college in the US, a student enrolled, indicating on her application form that she had experienced physical and emotional problems, including both in- and out-patient treatment for depression and sleep problems. At a session with the college's Director of Counselling Services she completed a form, indicating that her main concerns related to post-traumatic stress, depersonalisation, night trauma, nightmares and occasional insomnia. During the counselling session with the Director, the student explored further problematic behaviours, including anorexia, bulimia, repression, self-injury and social anxiety.

Shortly after this, the student experienced an episode of depersonalisation while in her dormitory at college and cut herself. Another student helped to take her to hospital for medical treatment for her cuts. The casualty department at the hospital informed the Director of Counselling about the incident, who passed this information on to the Dean. The student declined to attend for further counselling at the College Counselling Service, saying that she would rather look for another therapist. A further incident of the student cutting herself was passed on to the Director and Dean by college security, although this was not sufficiently serious to require medical treatment.

The Director of Counselling contacted the Dean several days later, and it was decided that the student should be withdrawn from her course on medical grounds, in part because another student had been upset by the cutting incident. The student had another episode of depersonalisation later that day and was admitted to hospital. Psychiatric staff agreed a treatment plan with her and decided that she was well enough to be discharged to resume her studies. However, on her return, the college informed her that she was being withdrawn from her studies on medical grounds, and would be required to leave the campus immediately.

The US Office for Civil Rights investigated the student's subsequent complaint, and identified a number of concerns:

- *whether the student's statements to the Director of Counselling constituted formal notice to the college of a disability, i.e. a mental health condition*
- *the nature of the college's response in making 'reasonable adjustment' to the student's mental health condition, both on admission to the college and on her discharge from hospital*
- *the level and severity of risk posed by the student to herself, to other students and to the college as an institution*
- *the lack of transparent and accountable due process for involuntarily withdrawing students from a course on medical grounds and setting conditions for later readmission*

Source: adapted from Pavela, 2006

The case study illustrates some of the pressures which therapists working in educational institutions might experience, in the form of working with very challenging behaviours from self-harming clients and responding to the pressure of anxiety conveyed by other students and senior staff. While the legal and policy framework may differ from that applying in the UK, there are some clear parallels, in terms of the overall operation of disability law. Educational institutions retain a duty to make reasonable adjustments upon formal notification of a disability, and need to follow due process in considering the decision to exclude a student on the grounds of disability and its effects on the institution.

Box 2.6   Guidelines for professional practice

Liability under tort and contract law:

- Review work practice for any potential areas of liability for therapists or students.
- Consider the use of clear contracts with fee-paying clients.
- Look at protection of staff from harassment or risk of harm.

Communicating personal information:

- Monitor compliance with data protection requirements, including electronic communication such as e-mail and on-line counselling provision.
- Be cautious about making unprofessional or potentially defamatory comments about other therapists, clients or agencies.

Employment and service provision:

- Clarify the standing of agency, staff and supervisors with regard to vicarious liability.
- Ensure that insurance cover adequately reflects such liability.
- Monitor health and safety requirements for staff.
- Monitor requirements for criminal record checks for those working with children and vulnerable adults.
- Review practices for possible unlawful discrimination on the basis of race, gender, disability, sexual orientation, gender reassignment or religious beliefs.

Summary

In the UK there are some differences between the legal systems of Scotland, Northern Ireland, and England and Wales. The legal tradition in England and Wales is based on a combination of statute and common law, with a crucial division between civil and criminal law. For therapists, tort and contract within civil law have the most direct bearing on their practice. Tort rests on the concept of the therapist's duty of care to clients, exercised according to the appropriate standard for the profession. Contracts with fee-paying clients contain safeguards for both parties. Problematic areas for practice include data protection, electronic communication systems and defamation.

There are important legal issues to consider with regard to employment or service provision, such as health and safety, and employer liability for workplace stress. Criminal record checks are standard practice for employers or service providers, for the protection of particular groups in society, such as children and vulnerable adults. Statute and regulations prohibit a wide range of discrimination on the grounds of sex, race, disability, age, sexual orientation, gender reassignment and religious beliefs.

Discussion points

1   What are the advantages and disadvantages of using formal contracts with fee-paying clients? At what stage should they be introduced?
2   Have you ever felt uneasy or threatened by a client? What steps are in place in your work setting or therapy practice to ensure your physical safety and to reduce risk of harm?
3   To what extent does your or your agency's practice conform to data protection principles? What changes would you consider need to be made in this area?
4   Should employers be held liable for stress-induced illness caused by work? Do therapists have a proactive role here, which goes beyond that of responding to stress or distress in the workplace?
5   Identify the main ethical and legal principles in conflict in the case study taken from Stuart Sutherland's book, *Breakdown* (see p. 29). How might this outcome have been better managed, or avoided altogether?

3 Therapists, Courts and the Legal System

There are a number of ways in which therapists may find a shift in perspective necessary to adapt to the world of the legal system. Fishwick has described some of these factors, which may amount to a culture shock for social workers and other caring professionals working in the courts (1988: 175–90). Slightly adapted, these factors are relevant to understanding possible misunderstandings between therapists and the court system. Some of the major contrasts relate to:

- a potential clash of values, perhaps regarding therapeutic confidentiality versus the concept of 'the public interest';
- precision in the use of language versus 'greyness' and ambiguity;
- public versus private practice: therapy is usually a private activity, whereas a court is a public arena;
- formal versus informal practice: the court's appearance and functioning are heavily bound by rules and tradition;
- an adversarial rather than co-operative approach to establishing the meaning of communication between parties.

The legal system in England and Wales is based on adversarial proceedings, unlike the French system, which operates via inquisitorial proceedings in criminal law. Under an adversarial system, the judge appears to play little active role during the proceedings. The case is heard as a contest between two versions of events, with the judge acting as an umpire, and with advocates playing a partisan role in marshalling witnesses and in presenting the case. The burden of proof rests with the party bringing the case, which needs to be proven beyond reasonable doubt in the case of criminal courts, or on the balance of probabilities in civil cases. A high value is placed on evidence given orally, particularly in criminal trials, and on the manner in which it is presented. 'Hearsay' or second-hand evidence not directly observed by a witness is normally excluded. Witnesses give evidence via a process of 'examination-in-chief', followed by cross examination by the advocates for the opposing side. The legal system is usually open to the public, except in the case of child care proceedings. Involvement of the public in the form of attendance on juries is an important aspect of the system of justice in England and Wales. Juries are widely used in hearing criminal cases, including fraud trials, but are less frequently used in civil cases, except for libel.

The system of justice in England and Wales is based on a fundamental division between criminal law, or offences against the rule of law, and civil law, where the courts are used to resolve disputes between individuals or corporate bodies. The legal system operates as a ladder of courts, extending from Magistrates' Courts at the local level, to the House of Lords at the highest level. Decisions made at the higher levels of the court system are then binding on courts deliberating at lower levels. In most cases, therapists are probably more likely to come into contact with the lower levels of the court hierarchy, such as:

- the Coroner's Court, if a former client has committed suicide;
- the Magistrates' Court, for example, by supporting a client bringing a court case against an alleged abusing parent;
- the County Court, in initiating or responding to litigation, or for action for breach of contract.

For many therapists, involvement with the courts may never extend beyond the mundane level of taking action over unpaid fees by a client. However, some therapists may be involved as a witness of fact, or possibly as an expert witness.

Faced with the different language, structure and values of the legal system, therapists without experience of legal proceedings may be tempted on the one hand to 'de-skill' themselves, or on the other hand to dismiss the legal system as unfeeling and archaic. It is important for therapists to avoid falling into either of these responses, and to find ways in which their expertise and professionalism will be of value to the courts when required. This chapter attempts to help therapists by focusing on key aspects of the court system. It provides a brief outline of the legal system, and explores areas of possible involvement by therapists, such as acting as a witness. It also considers some of the issues raised by the system of damages, particularly for psychiatric illness, which have a bearing on the concerns of therapists. Although much of this information is probably more detailed than most therapists will require for their day-to-day work, a basic knowledge of the court system may be helpful, should the need arise in the future concerning a particular case.

Reform of the civil law system

The Woolfe reforms instituted over the last decade have had a major impact on the systems and processes of civil law in England and Wales. These are designed to make the civil justice system more responsive and effective. In addition, the introduction of the Human Rights Act 1998 has firmly placed the issue of citizens' access to civil rights on the judicial and political agenda. Key changes include:

- reform of legal aid and funding for legal representation
- redesign of court systems to overcome delays
- use of alternative dispute resolution
- introduction of human rights legislation

Legal aid

The reforms have included a wholesale pruning of the former Legal Aid system. This is now referred to as public funding, via the Community Legal Service, which is managed by the Legal Services Commission. In addition, there has been the rapid growth of 'no win, no fee' schemes, or conditional fee arrangements for legal representation. Under this scheme, the lawyer takes on the case, and may take a 'success fee' if they win. Insurance is required to cover the other side's costs, plus expenses and disbursements in the event of losing the case.

Redesign of court systems

This includes:

- expansion of small claims procedures for claims up to £3,000;
- 'fast track' for straightforward claims of less than £10,000 with a fixed timetable of six months and fixed costs (for example, in defamation and negligence cases);
- a 'multi-track' system for larger cases over £10,000, with strict controls over costs, timetables and the volume of paperwork, and provision for the appointment of expert witnesses by the court.

Alternative dispute resolution

There are also measures designed to divert some forms of dispute resolution from the court system and into more appropriate areas of the judicial system or elsewhere. Alternatives to litigation include:

- *conciliation*: this can include referral to a counselling service, for example for couples undergoing relationship problems, as in the service provided by Relate and other agencies. Conciliation may help couples to resolve issues concerning contact and custody of children from the marriage.
- *mediation*: this service helps couples to sort out financial and property disputes while going through a divorce. Mediation is a voluntary process to which both parties must agree.
- *arbitration*: this involves an independent arbitrator, who may listen to both sides at a hearing, or consider relevant documents and then make a judgment which is binding on both parties.

Introduction of human rights legislation

The Human Rights Act 1998 is based on the application of the European Convention on Human Rights (1950), which was signed by the UK in 1953 (see Box 3.1). Under the Act, citizens of the UK have much more direct access to fundamental civil rights in the domestic courts, rather than having to take the arduous and lengthy process of applying to the European courts. However, there is widespread misunderstanding of the nature and purpose of the Act. According to Brazier, 'the 1998 Human Rights Act does not (whatever the media says) incorporate the Convention into English law. It renders the Convention enforceable against *public authorities*', which is a far narrower interpretation (2003: 18). Access to certain rights may be restricted, as, for example, with the UK suspending its obligations under Article 5, in order to detain suspected international terrorists, or where restriction is judged to be 'proportionate' and non-discriminatory.

Box 3.1   Human Rights Act 1998

Articles from the European Convention on Human Rights adopted by the Human Rights Act 1998:

Article 2:   Right to life
Article 3:   Prohibition of torture or inhuman or degrading treatment or punishment
Article 4:   Prohibition of slavery and forced labour
Article 5:   Liberty and security of person
Article 6:   Right to fair trial
Article 7:   Freedom from retrospective criminal offences and punishment
Article 8:   Right to respect for private and family life
Article 9:   Freedom of religion
Article 10: Freedom of expression
Article 11: Freedom of assembly and association
Article 12: Right to marry and found a family
Article 14: Prohibition of discrimination in enjoyment of Convention rights

---

A case has been made that the Human Rights Act (HRA) 1998 has significant implications for therapists, particularly those working for public authorities (Costigan, 2004). The major impact of the Act to date has been to make complaints procedures for therapists' professional associations more fair and transparent (Keter, 2002). Legal action under the HRA 1998 has also had major implications for policy and practice regarding the informal admission of psychiatric patients under the Mental Health Act 1983 (*HL v UK* (2004)). The latter, also known as the *Bournewood* case, is discussed below.

Case study   Taking action to defend the rights of psychiatric patients: The *Bournewood* case

Mr L was a 49-year-old man with autism, who was unable to speak and who was judged to have limited understanding. Psychiatrists assessed him as being incapable of either giving, or withholding, his consent to medical or psychiatric treatment. In 1997, Mr L was admitted as an in-patient at Bournewood Hospital in Surrey, after becoming very agitated at a day centre. He was not detained under the Mental Health Act 1983, but was accommodated under the common law doctrine of 'necessity'. It was made clear that, although he was not under a formal 'section', if he did attempt to leave the hospital, then he would be formally detained under the Mental Health Act 1983.

(Continued)

The following account is given by Mr L's carers, who took legal action on his behalf to achieve his release. In 2004, the European Court of Human Rights found against the UK government, in that detention on the grounds of 'necessity' was judged to be in conflict with Article 5 of the Human Rights Act 1998, i.e. the right not to be unlawfully detained. The court did not award Mr L damages, but ordered that the government pay €29,500 towards his legal costs. The case has major implications for revising the legal basis of the admission, treatment and aftercare of psychiatric patients with learning disabilities, under the Mental Health Act 1983.

As carers for the autistic man at the centre of the Bournewood case, we would like to clarify that we did not take legal action in order to seek compensation. We took the legal route in September 1997, in the form of judicial review and habeas corpus, in order to secure his release from his 'informal' detention.

It was the psychiatrist's sole decision to detain him; it was not at the request of social care staff. Contrary to the affidavit supplied by the psychiatrist, where she stated that he was compliant, hospital admission notes later revealed that this was not the case and he had in fact tried to leave. He was kept in a locked ward. The psychiatrist denied him contact from anyone he knew. His desperate efforts to show that he didn't want to be there were used by the psychiatrist as justification for keeping him.

Although we lost the first High Court action in October 1997, two weeks later the Appeal Court supported his case and ruled that his detention was unlawful. The Trust's reaction was to have HL sectioned straightaway 'to protect their legal position'.

After an independent assessment recommended his release, HL was discharged by the hospital managers, and after a three-year investigation the NHS Ombudsman found in HL's favour. In June 1998, at the House of Lords, the government successfully challenged the Appeal Court decision. This left HL and thousands like him with no safeguards at all. This is why we took the case to the European Court of Human Rights in December 1998. There was a public hearing of the case in May 2003 in Strasbourg, with the judgement on 5th October 2004. Although HL was not awarded damages, the judgement was certainly 'just satisfaction'. (Mr and Mrs E, 2004)

Structure of the court system

The structure of the legal system in England and Wales is briefly outlined in Box 3.2

Outline of the court system

Employment Tribunals: These deal with employment protection, equal pay cases, and discrimination on the grounds of sex, race or disability. They are described as being informal, but the growing complexity of case law and increasing use of legal representation mean that this appearance of informality may sometimes be misleading.

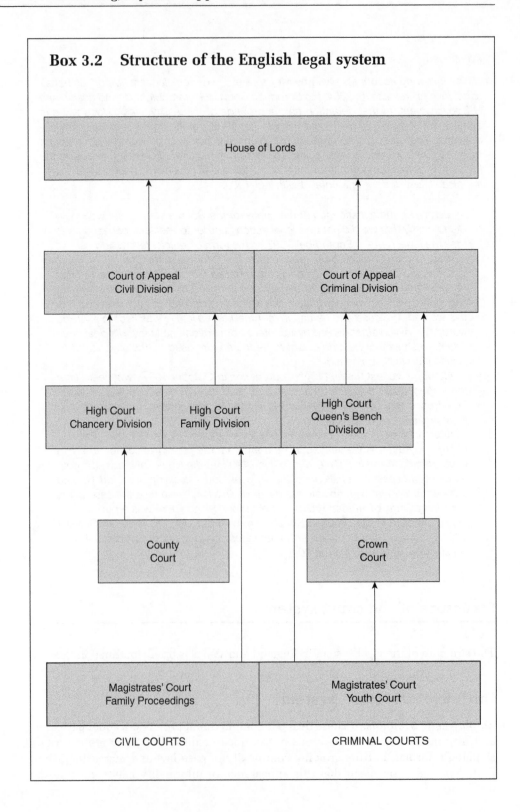

Box 3.2 Structure of the English legal system

House of Lords

Court of Appeal
Civil Division

Court of Appeal
Criminal Division

High Court
Chancery Division

High Court
Family Division

High Court
Queen's Bench
Division

County
Court

Crown
Court

Magistrates' Court
Family Proceedings

Magistrates' Court
Youth Court

CIVIL COURTS

CRIMINAL COURTS

Coroners' Courts: Inquests into sudden or suspicious deaths are held on an inquisitorial basis, where the coroner investigates the circumstances, sometimes with the assistance of a jury.

Magistrates' Courts: These deal with 98 per cent of all criminal cases, excepting those where the defendant opts for jury trial at Crown Court. It also deals with a wide range of civil matters, including child care proceedings in the role of the Family Proceedings Court.

Crown Courts: In Crown Court, criminal cases are heard by a jury, and by a judge from the High Court, or by a Circuit Judge, or Recorder. The rate of acquittals by juries is much higher in the Crown Court than in Magistrates' Courts for similar offences, as is the proportion of cases where the defendant changes their plea from not guilty to guilty at the trial.

County Courts: These deal with most civil cases, such as payment of money, debt, compensation, claims concerning matrimonial property, maintenance, domestic violence, custody, and undefended divorces. Most consumer cases will be dealt with by the County Court. Claims under £3,000 are dealt with in a less formal manner via the Small Claims Court.

High Courts and Court of Appeal: There is a complex system of appealing from lower courts to higher ones, in order to challenge verdicts. This can extend to the House of Lords, which only hears cases involving points of law of major public importance.

The law in England and Wales is increasingly affected by the decisions of European courts, a process accelerated by the introduction of the Human Rights Act 1998. The two main courts are:

Court of Justice of the European Communities, at Luxembourg: This is the main legislative body of the European Union (EU). The European Community became the European Union following the Treaty of Maastricht in 1993. European law consists of Treaties, which are primary legislation. In other words, they are directly enforceable in the UK, without any further need for legislation. Secondary legislation consists of Regulations made by Brussels, which have immediate effect, whereas Directives usually need to be incorporated into domestic legislation.

European Court of Human Rights, at Strasbourg: This deals with violations of the European Convention on Human Rights, as in the *Gaskin* and *Bournewood* cases. Claimants need to apply first to the European Commission on Human Rights (ECHR). Following the introduction of the Human Rights Act 1998, cases involving human rights will be heard initially within the UK legal courts, but can appeal on major points of law to the European Commission.

Therapists' involvement with the courts

Therapists will come into contact with the courts only in exceptional circumstances. Yet these may occur from time to time, and could include:

- taking legal action in the Small Claims Court over non-payment of fees by a client;
- attending Coroner's Court following the suicide of a client;
- supporting a client taking legal action against alleged abusers, either via a criminal prosecution or in a civil case for damages;
- providing pre-trial therapy for a vulnerable client;
- being called as a witness;
- acting as an expert witness;
- undertaking judicial review of a decision or policy;
- being sued in the County Court by a client for breach of contract or for professional negligence;
- being the subject of criminal prosecution for rape, assault, fraud or other serious offence.

(The latter two situations are not dealt with in detail here. Action against therapists for professional negligence is described in Chapter 4.)

Practical aspects of therapists' involvement with the courts

This section sets out the main practical aspects of initial involvement with the courts. This includes identifying sources of legal advice, key pointers in obtaining advice, taking action in the Small Claims Court, and giving evidence as a witness. This is then followed by an exploration of wider professional issues relating to therapists involved in the courts, such as the status of professional codes of ethics, the role of inquests, judicial review, providing reports for the court and acting as an expert witness.

Sources of legal advice

Difficulties faced by individuals in gaining access to information about the law or to legal representation have been identified as a major problem of the civil justice system at present. For therapists or clients seeking legal advice or representation, the following avenues should be considered. Legal advice can be obtained from a wide variety of organisations and sources:

- Citizens' Advice Bureaux may have a solicitor's surgery.
- Law Centres can advise on housing, employment, juvenile crime and child care cases.
- The Consumers' Association has a personal advice service, available by subscription only.

- Initial legal advice and information can be obtained from Employee Assistance Programmes.
- Trade unions, professional associations and pressure groups such as MIND (National Association for Mental Health) and the Children's Legal Centre have expertise in particular areas of the law. The Equal Opportunities Commission, Commission for Racial Equality and Disability Rights Commission can also give information on case law and legislation.
- Solicitors sometimes provide fixed fee advice, or offer a free first session. Under the Green Form scheme operated by the Law Society, legal advice is based on financial eligibility. There is a Regional Directory of Solicitors published by the Law Society, which includes panels of specialist lawyers, such as those in child care law and mental health.
- Professional indemnity insurance companies and professional protection societies usually provide telephone advice and legal representation for those insured. (See Resources for relevant addresses and telephone numbers.)
- Professional therapists' associations, such as BACP or UKCP, may be able to advise on legal issues. In the USA, most therapists obtain information about the law and get legal advice from their professional associations (Bowman and Mertz, 1996: 595).

First steps in obtaining legal advice

When looking for legal advice, it is worth trying to find a solicitor who specialises in the required area to deal with the case, whether this is to do with professional negligence, personal injury or child care law. On first meeting, assuming a decision to proceed with the case and with this representative, the following points need to be checked out verbally before finishing discussion, and then confirmed in writing afterwards. Consumers of legal services are advised to ask the following questions (DCA, 2006a).

- What will the legal adviser do for me?
- How much will this legal adviser cost me, compared with others?
- What do I get for my money?
- How often has the legal adviser handled this type of work?
- How long will it take for the transaction to be completed?
- What can I do if something goes wrong, or I am not satisfied with the service provided?
- Have I got a good deal?

(Addresses and phone numbers for complaints about legal representation are in the Resources section.)

Taking action via the Small Claims Court

The most common form of involvement by therapists in the courts is likely to be taking action to reclaim unpaid fees by clients (Cristofoli, 2002). Claims of this kind can be dealt with in a very straightforward way by using the Small Claims Court, which is a branch of the County Court. Representation by a solicitor is not usually necessary or to be recommended, as the purpose of the small claims procedure is to provide a quick and informal way of resolving civil disputes. Resolving the dispute may follow the sequence set out in Box 3.3 starting with a formal letter to the other person (Simons and Harmer, 2002).

Box 3.3 Professional guidelines

Taking action for breach of contract in the Small Claims Court
First stage: writing a letter to the client or company concerning the problem

- Set out the main facts at issue, presenting points to support your claim.
- Explain the steps already taken to resolve the dispute.
- Remember that the letter may later be used in court (heading the letter 'Without prejudice' can prevent this from happening).
- Remain polite, and avoid becoming aggressive in tone, as this may be counter-productive in the long run.
- Be cautious about offering to accept less than the full amount at issue, as this may count against you later in court.
- Indicate that you intend to start legal proceedings in the County Court within 14 days unless the matter is settled.

Second stage: taking legal action to recover a debt

- Contact the local Small Claims Court (this is a branch of the local County Court).
- Obtain and complete the relevant forms to start the action.
- Issue a 'default summons', using form N1 or N2, retaining a second copy for your records, and a third copy for the court.
- Claim proceeds automatically if the defendant does not respond within 21 days.

There are a number of practical guides to help plaintiffs considering taking legal action via the Small Claims Court but who are unused to the procedures or terms involved (Major, 2002; Whimster, 2000). Simons and Harmer (2002), for example, give detailed advice on completing the necessary forms. Further practical advice to consumers is available from Citizens' Advice Bureaux and the Office of Fair Trading.

The expansion of the small claims system is some indication of its success. However, a third of those winning their cases recover no money at all, and there are still weaknesses to be overcome with this approach. As with all legal action, there is no certainty of outcome, however apparently straightforward the procedures involved.

Appearing in court as a witness

Most material on the subject of appearing in court seems to be geared to the needs of professionals such as social workers or probation officers, who appear in court on a regular basis. There seems to be limited information published for other professionals who may also have to appear in court for similar reasons, although this is now changing with the publication of detailed guidance for therapists (Bond and Sandhu, 2005). This section offers some pointers for those unfamiliar with the procedures involved in attending court to give evidence for the first time (see Box 3.4).

Advice to witnesses has been described succinctly as: 'Dress up, stand up, speak up and shut up!' (Knight and Palmer, 1992: 14). The purpose of the witness appearing is to put their evidence before the court. This may be done by giving evidence verbally and/or via a written report or statement. It is a mistake to assume that the court already knows the details of the evidence to be given. Unless the evidence is given clearly and carefully, certain important facts may be 'lost' to the court.

Box 3.4   Professional guidelines for giving evidence in court

Preparation
Some points to consider before going to court:

- Dress, appearance and overall level of confidence will all have some impact on the overall impression made on the court.
- There may be a Witness Support Programme to explain the court layout and procedure beforehand, and a separate waiting room may be available.
- Know the evidence to be given. The solicitor or barrister will make contact briefly in court on the day to quickly go over the statement before the case starts.
- On arrival, witnesses need to give the usher their name and whereabouts while waiting to be called, which may take some time.

In court
Witnesses wait outside the court while the case is going on, until called. Taking the witness stand:

- Enter the witness box as directed by the usher.
- Stand up, take the oath on the Bible or affirm to tell the truth.
- State your name and occupation when asked.

Order of proceedings for witnesses giving evidence:

- confirmation of identity
- examination-in-chief by the lawyer calling you as a witness
- cross-examination by the solicitor for the opposing party
- re-examination by the first solicitor
- release from giving evidence by the court

Style of giving evidence

- Address answers to the judge(s), not to the solicitor who is actually asking the questions.
- Take your time and consider your responses carefully.

(Continued)

(*Continued*)

- Be clear and definite in your answers.
- If you don't know or can't remember, say so.
- Project your voice clearly so that you can be heard properly in the court.
- You can, with the court's permission, refer to notes made at the time of the events you are being asked about.
- Magistrates are addressed as 'Your Worship'; Crown Court judges as 'Your Honour'; High Court judges as 'My Lord' or 'My Lady'.
- When the court has finished with hearing your evidence, you may stay in court, as directed by the usher, to hear the rest of the case.

Expenses

Therapists will be able to claim for travelling expenses, meals and lost wages arising from a court appearance, by contacting the court or solicitor. Carson (1990) has devised self-assessment exercises for potential witnesses, and a training video for expert witnesses, which provide a greater level of detail about preparation for court work (BPS, 1995a).

Professional aspects of therapists' involvement with the courts

This section explores some of the wider professional issues relating to therapists who are involved in the courts, including the role of the appropriate adult, inquests, judicial review, giving evidence as a witness, the status of professional codes of ethics, providing reports for the court and acting as an expert witness.

Courts and clients

Therapists would not normally come into contact with the legal system unless overriding circumstances make this advisable or necessary. In some cases a client may request their involvement, as, for example, when a distressed client is brought into police custody. The client may then be seen by the police as a 'vulnerable adult', requiring the presence of an appropriate adult. This situation is briefly described below. In other situations, a client may be involved in legal processes where an understanding of the procedures will be helpful to the therapist working with them. In the case of clients who have experienced traumatic bereavement, acquiring fuller knowledge of the circumstances of the death via an inquest may have an important part to play in coming to terms with their loss. In the case of clients who allege that they have been abused in childhood, taking court proceedings, either criminal or civil in nature, can represent a search for justice and reparation. At another level, it may express needs for validation and acknowledgement, which are important for them in coming to terms with the abuse and in starting to build a new life. These situations are explored in more detail below, with reference to case examples.

Acting as an 'appropriate adult'

Under the Police and Criminal Evidence Act 1984, and the relevant *Code of Practice* (Home Office, 2004a), the police are required to identify 'vulnerable groups' of those brought into custody. This includes juveniles under 17, and persons perceived to be 'mentally vulnerable'. A detainee may be considered to be mentally vulnerable where, because of their mental state or capacity, they may not understand the significance of what is said, of questions, or of their replies. Mental disorder follows the definition from the Mental Health Act 1983, under s. 1(2), as 'mental illness, arrested or incomplete development of mind, psychopathic disorder and any other disorder or disorder of mind'.

In this situation, the police are required to inform an 'appropriate adult'. Often this will be a social worker, or other person, such as a volunteer with suitable preparation and training for this role. The role of the appropriate adult (HO, 2004a: 85) is to:

- *advise* the person concerned
- *observe* that the interview is conducted properly and fairly
- *facilitate* communication between that person and the police.

The role of the appropriate adult is, therefore, to safeguard the rights of the person concerned. Without proper experience and training, this is not a role that a therapist would normally wish to take on, but a client might request their attendance, without the therapist being fully aware of what was entailed in the role.

Coroner's Court

Therapists are more likely to come into contact with the courts at the lower levels of the system, for example by attending a Coroner's Court to establish the cause of death of a client. The main purpose of inquests, under s. 8 (1) of the Coroners Act 1988, is to establish the causes of sudden, violent or unnatural deaths, where there are no criminal proceedings or where a death occurs in police custody or in prison. In fact, 'the inquest is the only formal state tribunal whose exclusive concern is death' (Wells, 1994: 213). There are certain unusual features of the Coroner's Court, which can surprise and distress parties not used to the format of this court. It is informal and inquisitorial, rather than adversarial. This places more discretionary powers in the hands of the Coroner, regarding the procedures adopted in court, and in calling witnesses. Juries can be called, for example, where there is a concern for public health or safety, or concerning a death in prison or custody. Legal Aid, or public funding for representation, is not available, and there is no right to have advance disclosure of documents, as applies in other civil and criminal proceedings. The verdicts available to the court include death by natural causes; unlawful killing; accident; misadventure; suicide and an open verdict, where there is insufficient evidence to justify any definite verdict.

Coroners' courts have been subjected to growing criticism by the media and by groups of bereaved families and relatives in the last two decades. 'The Aberfan inquest was concluded in four minutes. There is now much more pressure on coroners to allow grief to be vented at inquests. The growth of support groups and the development of legal specialists in disaster can be noted too' (Wells, 1994: 197). The Coroner's Court is an archaic relic in legal terms, which is at odds with many of the features of the rest of the legal system in England and Wales. There is an enormous gulf between the emotional agenda of the bereaved, and the dry, formal routine of the court, which is not easily bridged, according to some critics.

> Whatever words of reassurance are spoken, whatever arrangements are made to accommodate the needs of the bereaved, the court and its procedure is a formal setting, conducted by those familiar with the environment, its rituals, language and deference. For ordinary people thrust into such a situation, already distressed and hurt, it is an alienating experience. (Scraton et al., 1995: 65)

Growing concern has been expressed at the unsatisfactory nature of the inquest system in dealing with the needs of families and relatives, in particular after the Bristol and Alder Hey Inquiries. For families and relatives, a primary need is often simply to establish the truth, rather than necessarily to make out a case for financial compensation.

Case study   One family's experience of the Coroner's Court

He was our son. He was dead. We were worried, anxious, angry and frustrated...the atmosphere of the court was alien to us. Why should the prison authorities be represented by barristers and solicitors if they were hiding nothing? We felt intimidated and contrite, cowed and oppressed. The coroner would not call our witnesses; we had to intercede in his summing up. What was the purpose of our son's inquest? To determine the cause of death, or to bury forever the flaws in the system that killed him? The system failed him, the system failed us. (Brinkley, 1993)

This experience is not intended to be representative of all families or relatives, but highlights some of the strong emotions which can be aroused by attending a Coroner's Court. A report by the campaign group Inquest described the Coroner's system as 'one of the most neglected areas of law', with many failings for the families involved (Coles and Shaw, 2002: 2). It identified:

- the system's failure to develop a rights-based awareness of the entitlement of bereaved families to information and legal representation;
- lack of information for bereaved families about the availability of mental health and counselling support services;
- lack of research into the impact of an inquest on the bereavement process;
- lack of specific training on the unique features of the Coroner's Court for lawyers, therapists and bereavement agencies.

Following the Shipman Inquiry (Smith, 2003), a Fundamental Review of Coroners' Services in England and Wales was announced. This found the Coroner system to be 'fragmented, non-accountable, variable in quality and consistency, ineffective in part, and very much dependent on the abilities of those working within it at present' (DCA, 2006b: 2). The government has responded to some of the main criticisms of the system, proposing legislation on this topic. There is to be a coroner's charter, detailing the service which bereaved people can expect. Bereaved people will have a right to contribute to coroners' investigations, and a body of full-time coroners will be established.

Taking legal action via judicial review

Therapists may tend to see the law largely in reactive terms, in that their role would be determined largely by demands made by the courts for disclosure of client records or that they attend as a witness. Therapists may also be involved in the courts on a more proactive basis, by seeking to take action in order to achieve a remedy for a wrong relating to clients' entitlement to human rights. In one instance, 'abortion centre counsellors acting with women wishing to receive advice successfully challenged Irish laws prohibiting dissemination of any information about abortion' (Brazier, 2003: 24).

This more proactive stance may involve taking action under judicial review. Judicial review is a legal procedure under public law, whereby the courts can be requested to review and overturn a decision which is illegal, unreasonable, or which has been improperly arrived at. It has been judged that therapists' associations are public bodies, on the grounds of their regulatory activities, and are therefore subject to judicial review procedures. Action has been successfully undertaken against the UKCP via judicial review, on the basis that its disciplinary procedures were in conflict with principles of natural justice (Clarkson and Keter, 2000). This legal action also produced its own case law, in establishing the rights of a litigant in person, i.e. the therapist bringing her own case, to have an informal advocate present in court (*Clarkson v Gilbert* (2000)).

In a second case, judicial review was sought against the decision of the British Psychological Society. The BPS had permitted Dr Peter Slade to retain his membership and fellowship despite his having admitted to having a relationship with a client who was suffering from an eating disorder. The client support group, POPAN, now called Witness, sought to bring a judicial review of this decision, on the grounds that it was perverse, but the action was unsuccessful (Keter, 2002).

Supporting clients in court

Therapists may well prefer to avoid taking part in legal processes unless there are strong reasons for becoming involved. In some cases the therapist may support a client in taking legal action, perhaps where there is no other source of support for the client. The therapist could take the role of an informal supporter, actually alongside the client in the courtroom as a litigation friend, or *McKenzie*. This latter term was first used where a party in a divorce case was assisted informally by a barrister as an aid and supporter. According to this principle, 'any person, whether he be a professional man or not, may attend as a friend of either party, may take notes, may quietly make suggestions, and give advice; but no one can demand to take part in the proceedings as an advocate' (*McKenzie v McKenzie* [1970]).

For most therapists, their activity will probably be much more limited, and will consist of providing emotional support rather than active advice and encouragement. In the following case, one therapist worked with her female client for a lengthy period in exploring the context and effects of the sexual abuse she had experienced in her childhood from a number of male family members. Ultimately, the client decided to confront them and inform the police, with the result that the alleged perpetrators were prosecuted. The therapist provided support for the client throughout the court case, which extended to accompanying her to court. For legal reasons, the client's giving evidence in court became very complex and involved, and became part of a lengthy and drawn-out legal process lasting two and a half years. One defendant was eventually found guilty on one of the more minor charges. The other cases were still continuing at the time of the interview.

Case study   A therapist's experience of supporting a client in court

The therapist summed up her experience in court as:

An incredible feeling of helplessness. Initially, I thought it was brilliant that this could happen, because I've often wanted to say to her 'but all this is all being paid for, somebody's behind you, somebody believes you. The police have pushed it, the Crown Prosecution have taken it on board. They wouldn't do all this if there wasn't enough evidence.' But because the legal system took over, and the explanation for what happened wasn't really sound, there is a frustration and a feeling of...You have it taken away from you, when you were being offered something that was really good, and it's just been snatched away from you.

What would have been more helpful to therapist and client?

Somebody to explain how it all works. [Witness Support] did try to look after us. I guess knowing more about the system and not being very naïve in not [realising] what was going to happen. There's a sense when you go to court, it will all just go through. It's a whole other world. I was just naïve about all that. My overriding feeling now is that I've got another client, she can't take it to court, because her family won't support her, and my sense is, you're not really missing much, because, who knows? Who knows? It's a whole other set of issues that it brings up, on top of the ones you've already got, and sometimes it might work, and you might get a good...It might go well, and other times it can be just as damaging. That's the key thing, without me, I don't know how she would have survived.

If I had to go to court again, I would be able to be much clearer with her about [how] this is going to be a very difficult procedure, and you have to understand that it isn't just you standing up and saying what you want to say, because there are other people working in there that can take it out of your hands, and you have to be very, very clear that that is what you want to do. Now I know that it can be long, gruelling, complicated, and you won't necessarily get the result that you want, even though it's quite clear that you should.

Source: Interview with author

The legal process introduced a new and unfamiliar set of technical procedures into what had started out as the resolution of a therapeutic activity, that is, of achieving justice for the abuse experienced by the client. The process had included delays both within and before the court hearing, adjournments, a change of judges and major reversals of direction in the way in which the case would be heard. The police and the Witness Support Programme provided support to the client in what was otherwise felt to be an intimidating and unfamiliar environment.

In the court situation, the client's previous mental health history was available to the defence. There was concern that her history of receiving therapy and even the presence of the therapist weakened her credibility in giving evidence. The therapist, as the client's supporter in court, was not acting in any formal sense as a *McKenzie* as such, but was still unprepared for the professional and personal demands being made on her.

The therapeutic principle of the abused client seeking acknowledgement for her experiences is one that is strongly voiced by feminist schools of therapy and by the abuse survivors' self-help movement (Bass and Davis, 1991: 307–10). The impact of seeking redress for abuse through the law can be double-edged, however, according to Brown, writing of a US context. 'While litigation *can* be empowering to some survivors in some circumstances, and can be the experience that transforms their life in a positive way, for others it is equally likely to be profoundly disorganising and distressing' (1995: 350).

According to the therapist concerned in the above case, 'the overriding feeling when you're in court is that you're at their mercy. You feel so helpless.' Ultimately, the therapist reached the point where she was no longer able to continue attending court, given the amount of time it was taking, and the demands of the rest of her workload. She saw her role primarily as support for the client, 'so that she knew there was somebody in court that was there for her'. The therapist had no prior experience of this process, and had previously seen the law as a neutral or even benign force. 'The issue in taking it to court is that you want the world to hear in some sort of forum what really happened. It isn't that important what happens afterwards.' The therapist described her client as feeling angry and upset, because she had not been able to say her piece in the way that she felt she needed to. The client had to conform to the restrictions imposed by a court of law, and the principles concerning the admissibility of evidence. This client's experience tallies with the research carried out by Lees on women involved in rape and sexual assault cases: 'The majority of women found their experiences in court humiliating and distressing. A common complaint was that they were not allowed to explain fully what had happened to them or how they *felt* during the rape' (Lees, 1997: 31).

Achieving Best Evidence

Public concern over the treatment of women by the legal system and lawyers' aggressive questioning of female complainants' past sexual history has led to significant changes in the ways that courts hear evidence. A series of safeguards have also been introduced to protect the position of children and vulnerable witnesses in legal proceedings, codified in *Achieving Best Evidence* (HO et al., 2002b: 5). This defines 'vulnerable witness' as being a person:

- under 17 years
- with a mental disorder as defined in s. 1(2) Mental Health Act 1983
- with a learning disability, and thus significantly impaired in relation to intelligence and social functioning
- with a physical disability
- experiencing intimidation, i.e. suffering from fear and distress in relation to testifying in the case.

Practitioners may be involved in providing pre-trial therapy to a client in these circumstances. Guidance issued by the Home Office has clarified that counselling and psychotherapy can be provided for children and vulnerable adults prior to a criminal trial. However, this needs to be done in ways consistent both with the best interests of the client, and the particular requirements of the criminal trial process. The guidance expresses concern about certain forms of therapy, which may be likely to undermine the value of the client as a credible witness. These problematic therapeutic approaches include interpretive psychotherapy, hypnotherapy, psychodrama, regression and unstructured groups (HO et al., 2002a: 23).

Therapists agreeing to take on pre-trial therapy with a vulnerable witness need to take account of a number of factors:

- the legal context of the therapy being provided, i.e. relevant mental health law, court practice, rules of evidence;
- tensions between the best interests of the client, and the public interest in prosecuting alleged offenders;
- forms of recording appropriate to this work, i.e. recording which is factual, accurate and contextual (referring to date, times and names of persons present);
- potential limits on confidentiality arising from:

  - liaison with the police and Crown Prosecution Service (CPS)
  - the disclosure process, involving access to therapeutic records by both prosecution and defence solicitors;

- the implications of the type of approach used, and the focus of the therapy, on the viability of the client's evidence in court, via

  - the need to avoid the rehearsal of the client's evidence
  - the eliciting of allegations of further, previously undisclosed offences
  - the therapist attempting to distinguish fact from fantasy;

- willingness to work as a member of a multi-disciplinary team, with consequent limits to client confidentiality;
- specific obligations to an employer or to an agency where therapy is provided under contract, i.e. via an agreement to provide reports to the CPS on the process and outcome of therapy.

Standard of evidence in court

An important consideration here is that therapists are not normally formally trained or prepared for attendance in court as a part of their role, unlike comparable professionals such as social workers. A therapist's involvement in court proceedings could take the form of supporting a client, as in the above case, or acting as a *McKenzie* or informal supporter in court. Other forms of involvement may be via giving evidence, or acting as an expert witness. Whilst these activities are probably rare or exceptional occurrences for most therapists, they may arise in some circumstances, and will be described more fully below.

Evidence obtained by drugs or hypnosis

It is worth noting that certain forms of therapeutic technique, such as the use of hypnosis or drugs, may invalidate the testimony of therapists or clients. Barbiturate drugs, such as sodium amytal, have been used with varying degrees of effectiveness and popularity since the time of Freud, to assist the process of abreaction and aid the cathartic release of traumatic memories (Bazire, 1995: 63). This technique has tended to wane in popularity during peacetime, to be revived by the military as an effective short-term measure in wartime. This occurred, for example, during the Second World War, in the post-Vietnam period, and in Israel during periods of conflict with neighbouring Arab states (Perry and Jacobs, 1982). It has also been used historically to assist in the recovery of memories of childhood sexual abuse, for example in the *Ramona* (1994) case in the US, or to help in the retrieval of other unconscious material (Brown and Pedder, 1979: 73–5). However, while abreaction may be useful as a therapeutic measure, its value in producing convincing evidence for a court of law is much more doubtful. According to Putnam, 'therapists should be cautious about initiating legal allegations based solely on memories recovered during abreactive therapy' because 'abreaction is as likely to contaminate the process as it is to reveal the truth' (1992: 62). Neither the vivid nature of the memories retrieved, nor the force of the emotions released, provides a guarantee of the accuracy of the memory for evidential purposes in a court of law.

The therapeutic use of hypnosis has similarly gone through changes in the way that it is perceived in legal circles as a valid tool for producing evidence. Cases in the USA have emphasised the unreliability of memories retrieved under hypnosis, and limited the value of the witnesses' testimony as a result (Memon et al., 2003). Hammond, writing in a US context, cautions that 'material evoked through hypnotic exploration may include accurate information, partially accurate information and confabulation' (1995: 107). Confabulation refers to the process of incorporating inaccurate material into otherwise authentic memories. Under s. 76 of the Police and Criminal Evidence Act 1984, the court is unable to accept evidence that may have been obtained via an unreliable method. Under s. 78, the court has discretion to exclude evidence unfairly obtained, since hypnotically obtained evidence cannot be properly cross-examined.

Many therapists might respond that they would never use drugs in their therapeutic work with clients, and do not use hypnosis in any formal sense with clients. However, it has been pointed out that the dividing line between hypnosis and therapeutic techniques, such as regression, visualisation and guided imagery, may be a difficult one to draw with certainty. Client material retrieved in these ways will be more useful for therapeutic purposes than as evidence in a court of law.

The therapist's role as witness of fact

There are two types of witness in a court of law. First, a therapist may be called simply as a witness to facts, on the grounds that any person can give evidence about something that they have directly witnessed. Evidence of fact must be limited to the facts, and must not include inference or opinion. Thus, 'witnesses should give as much factual evidence as is possible and pay particular attention to its quality, credibility, authority and presentation' (Carson, 1990: 18). There is a danger in witnesses assuming that the court has some prior knowledge or understanding of the facts they are about to deliver. In fact, the outcome of the case may depend crucially on their evidence. The clear and confident manner in which it is delivered can be a crucial factor in its acceptance. 'The goal for the witness should be to describe and explain his or her evidence in a way which will be clear, memorable and authoritative to the judge and any jury' (Carson, 1990: 28).

The therapist's role as expert witness

The second kind of witness role that a therapist might assume is that of an expert witness. Only expert witnesses can give evidence of fact and *opinion*. 'The courts decide who they will recognise as an expert. It does not depend upon having special professional qualifications. Extensive practical experience could suffice. The distinguishing feature of an expert witness is the right to give opinion in court' (Carson, 1990: 2). Expert witnesses are experts in their particular field and, it should be stressed, need to be more than just an enthusiastic amateur (Nijboer, 1995). Some of the qualities required of an expert witness are outlined in Box 3.5.

Box 3.5   Qualities of an expert witness

- working to a higher standard of care than the average practitioner;
- an ability to analyse and make reasoned judgments;
- skills in research and concise reporting;
- personal qualities: patience, tact, ability to stay calm under pressure, negotiating skills;
- relevant experience and professional credibility;
- thorough knowledge of the subject in hand, including recognition of the merits of alternative approaches.

Adapted from Reynolds and King, 1989: 22–3

Psychologists and therapists, using both terms in a broad sense, have been involved in contributing their expertise to the courts since the time of Freud (1906/1971; 1931/1971). The use of psychologists and psychiatrists has been more marked in the USA, but has been increasing in the UK courts as well. This opens up an opportunity for therapists to develop a role in widening the courts' understanding of the extremes of human emotions and behaviour, a field in which they have some expertise through their clinical practice. The real value of therapists in giving expert evidence is precisely in order to challenge common-sense perceptions of what is normal or predictable behaviour. For instance, the concept of post-traumatic stress disorder was accepted by the courts, following testimony given by a psychiatrist at hearings about the Zeebrugge ferry disaster (Pugh and Trimble, 1993). Brodsky suggests that therapists need to be confident about their own specialist knowledge and experience. 'Psychotherapists should be able to admit to themselves, and to the court if the occasion arises, all of the limitations and conflicts they may experience in testifying. Yet psychotherapists should equally value their special expertise and information, and speak to those strengths as well' (1998: 162).

The presentation of evidence by an expert goes through a number of stages:

- preparation of the preliminary report, which is privileged in a legal sense
- presentation of the report to court
- examination and cross-examination in court

To improve access to appropriate experts, the Law Society has now produced its own *Directory of Expert Witnesses*. Guidelines for good practice by expert witnesses in civil cases were suggested by the Honourable Mr Justice Cresswell following a complex insurance case (*The Ikarian Reefer* [1993]) (see Box 3.6).

Box 3.6   Role of the expert witness

An expert witness should:

- be independent and not influenced by the requirements of litigation;
- provide independent, unbiased opinion in relation to matters within their area of expertise, and should not assume the role of advocate;
- state the facts or assumptions on which the opinion is based, without omitting material facts which contradict this view;
- make it clear when a particular question or issue falls outside his or her expertise;
- state where necessary that the opinion is no more than a provisional one, requiring further research;
- promptly acknowledge to the court any change in opinion following an exchange of reports;
- share relevant documentation with other parties.

The Ikarian Reefer [1993] at 69

The contrasting characteristics of the respective roles of expert witness and lawyer are set out in Box 3.7. This emphasises that the expert witness is *not* partisan and is *not* to play the role of a 'hired gun'. In recent cases involving senior paediatricians in cases of alleged child abuse, there has been concern that expert evidence may not be based on sound scientific reasoning or research. Following the *Bolitho* case in medical negligence, the court requires that the practitioner's standard of care be justifiable in objective and rational terms (see Chapter 4). The Academy of Medical Royal Colleges has proposed a number of criteria for the courts in assessing the quality of proposed medical experts (AMRC, 2005).

A therapist approached to take on the role of expert witness needs to be sure that he or she has sufficient specialist experience in the field and a working knowledge of the law, in order to be able to carry out the role competently.

Box 3.7   Differences between an expert witness and a lawyer

Expert	Lawyer
Independent	Partisan
Neutral	Puts client's case
Knows about field, not law	Knows about law, not field
Witness	Advocate
Gives evidence	Represents the client
Never argues	Argues
Assists the judge	Persuades the judge
Not a hired gun	Paid by the client

Source: Bond et al., 1999: 62

Status of professional Codes of Practice

A key issue for therapists appearing in court as a witness may well be establishing a professional rationale for their actions. It is easy for a therapist to assume that the correctness of a particular course of action can be established simply by referring to their professional Code of Practice as justification for making certain decisions, or for having acted in a certain way with their client. However, professional Codes of Practice do not necessarily carry authority in a court of law. Bond (1991) gives a telling example from a Coroner's Court. In this case, a counsellor working for a college's student services appeared in the Coroner's Court following the suicide of her client.

Case study   Status of professional codes of ethics in legal proceedings

The counsellor referred to the then existing BAC Code of Ethics and Practice for Counsellors, in order to justify her work. 'After some discussion it was established that professional codes do not have any legal standing' (1991: 285).

> *...one lawyer started to consider other provisions in the code to explore whether these had been implemented with equal vigour. He turned his attention to, 'Counsellors must take account of the limitations of their competence and make an appropriate referral when necessary'...After the section was read out to the court, the counsellor was cross-examined about her training in the assessment and treatment of suicidal clients, to determine whether she was working within her competence. The clear implication of this line of questioning was that if she had not been adequately trained, she was therefore working outside her level of competence, then she ought to have sought specialist help for her client. (Bond, 1991: 285)*

This line of questioning was not successful in discrediting the counsellor involved here, but underlines the importance of recognising the direction that a certain line of questioning is likely to take, and preparing oneself adequately in advance to meet it if possible. Simply basing one's professional stance on a Code of Practice does not meet all possible objections to be mounted by an opposing lawyer, but simply sets out the terrain on which the debate may take place. Any inconsistency between the therapist's practice and the Code, or between one section of the Code and another, will be used to undermine the overall value of the evidence given by that witness.

The Codes of Practice which do carry some weight in courts are those which have a statutory basis. Thus, in the *Egdell* case, discussed in Chapter 5, the judge referred to the General Medical Council's 'Blue Book' on fitness to practise in reaching his decision. He noted that the rules themselves do not have statutory authority, but that they were derived from the disciplinary function of the GMC under the Medical Act 1983 (*W v Egdell* [1990], at 843). Similarly, the Mental Health Act *Code of Practice* carries authority because of its statutory basis. 'The Mental Health Act 1983 does not impose a legal duty to comply with the Code but failure to do so could be referred to in evidence in legal proceedings' (DoH/WO, 1999: Introduction, para. 1). However, the courts are not bound to follow slavishly any existing guidelines in reaching a decision about the rightness of a course of action. Pattenden states that professional codes of ethics may offer guidance, but that this is 'not, of course, binding on the courts' (2003: 345). Guidelines or codes may be overruled by the court. In the case of 'W', an anorexic girl of 16, in 1992, Lord Donaldson indicated that the Department of Health *Guidelines for Ethics Committees* (1991) were not, in his view, consistent with the law on consent to treatment.

Cross-examination

Carson (1990) describes some of the more common techniques used by lawyers in carrying out cross-examination:

- 'pinning out': a sequence of apparently innocuous questions which actually fix the witness as if to a board, before the critical question is fired at them;
- 'leading witnesses up the garden path': inviting a witness to stretch their evidence by degrees to absurd or unlikely conclusions, based on their previous answers, which has the intended effect of discrediting their whole position.

Some of his suggested responses include:

- 'riding the bumps', i.e. remaining calm, seeking to clarify any possible misconceptions arising from the evidence or replies given;
- using opening comments to regain communication with the judge, and to correct or rephrase the information being given, e.g. 'With respect, neither term would be appropriate. It would be much more accurate to say...' (Carson, 1990: 47).

The sequence of the lawyer's questions and the answers they elicit effectively control the process of communication in court. A problem for therapists may be that the nuanced and sensitive language used to describe emotional processes and states of feeling or behaviour does not easily lend itself to the harsher, more dichotomous judgments required by the court (Carson, 1990: 62). To refer, for example, to a client as being 'borderline depressed', will probably prompt an inquiry from the cross-examining lawyer as to the medical qualifications possessed which can justify the making of such a diagnosis. This might then be followed up by inviting the therapist to make clear to the court whether, in the therapist's view, the client was clinically depressed or not.

Treading a path through the dangers of exceeding one's expertise, or overstating the case, is not easy for the witness. As a result, expert witnesses 'often feel that the questions misrepresent what they have to say or it does not give them an opportunity to isolate what they believe is important and want to communicate in court' (Carson, 1990: 64). One important failing is when a witness begins to weaken their case by becoming hesitant and doubtful about views that were previously stated with some conviction. This is 'an exasperating habit called by lawyers "failing to come up to proof"...' (Knight and Palmer, 1992: 13). Another technique used by lawyers to disorient witnesses is telling the witness they must answer 'yes or no' to their questions. Simeon Maskrey, QC, claims 'that witnesses are not bound to give such a concise reply. "Be firm and courteous but stick to the point", he says. "Tell the judge, 'I am not prepared to give a yes or no answer because it would not be complete"...'(Ward, 1995: 22). On the other hand, witnesses also need to avoid appearing unreasonable and inflexible in ways that seem to undermine the value of their evidence (Cohen, 1995: 105).

Providing reports on clients

Therapists may be approached to write reports on clients in a number of situations. This may include a request for a report from an organisation such as the Criminal Injuries Compensation Authority, or from an insurance company paying for therapy, or from a lawyer pursuing legal action on behalf of a client. Agreement to write a report can open the doors to a series of situations, each of which potentially impinges on client–therapist confidentiality. At the simplest level, a report may be requested to confirm the nature and extent of contact with a client. Assuming client agreement, then a brief factual report may be sufficient. In some instances, lawyers have requested reports from therapists seeking to substantiate a particular psychological condition, such as post-traumatic stress disorder, in order to support the client's legal case for damages. It is important here that the therapist does not presume to hold a level of training or expertise that may be more properly associated with that of a qualified doctor, psychiatrist or psychologist. It may even be that the solicitor is looking for a free opinion on their client from a therapist, when the advisable course of action would be to pay an expert medical witness for a formal psychiatric assessment.

Reports for the court need to be concise, relevant, and should distinguish between established facts and the writer's own professional opinions (Pollecoff, 2002). A frontsheet should set out the author's qualifications, experience and current post. The sources of information on which the report is based need to be described: for example via interview, a series of counselling sessions, or through the use of psychological tests (Academy of Experts, 2002). Professional jargon tends to undermine the impact of a report, unless it is essential to the point being made. Any expressions which are unclear or 'woolly' will be picked up in cross-examination, should the case come to court. The best rule is never to state facts or express opinions in a report that may later be regretted when they have to be defended in court.

A therapist may initially agree to prepare a report on a client in order to help him or her in some legal difficulty. The practitioner may be under the assumption that they are somehow required to do so on grounds of professional responsibility, perhaps after taking part in a child protection case conference. However, report-writing may have unintended consequences, as the report can become evidence in a wider legal arena, within which the therapist has effectively relinquished control over the document. *Authorship* of a report in this sense is not the same as *ownership or control*, once legal proceedings begin. If the therapist agrees to prepare a report, with the client's agreement, then this may be in the capacity of an expert witness. Reports of this kind are initially protected by legal privilege, but will then be requested by the legal representatives of the opposing party. Receipt of the report may then lead to a further request, for the original notes on which the report was based, which would presumably be the notes of the actual therapy sessions with the client. The original notes are not subject to privilege. The therapist may then be required to present a level of detail in court about their client, which was never their intention (Jakobi and Pratt, 2002).

Seeking damages via the courts

The main purpose in taking civil legal action under tort or for breach of contract is usually to claim damages, in order to compensate the injured party in monetary terms as far as possible. This is designed to put the claimant in the same position as he or she would have been if the contract had been duly performed, or if the tort had not been committed. There are a number of different time limits which apply to claims for damages, under the Limitation Act 1980, the Latent Damage Act 1986 and the Defamation Act 1996 (see Box 3.8).

The Law Commission accepts that the current law on limitation of actions is quite defective. It has proposed an initial limitation period of three years from the date the plaintiff discovered, or ought reasonably to discover, that he or she has a legal claim against the defendant. There would be a long-stop limitation period of 10 years, or of 30 years in personal injury cases, running from the date of the act or omission of the defendant giving rise to the plaintiff's claim. This would not be extendable except where the plaintiff was under a disability, i.e. lacking the capacity to make or communicate decisions, or was under 18.

For therapists, one of the main aspects of the current system of limitation periods is with regard to victims or survivors of past abuse. The Law Commission gives an example of the unfairness of the system in sexual abuse cases (such as *Stubbings v Webb* [1993], *S v W* [1995]).

Box 3.8   Time limits for bringing legal actions

Cause of action	Time limit
Libel	1 year from date of publication, extendable by courts
Negligently caused personal injury	3 years from date plaintiff discovered, or ought to have discovered, the injury (extendable to court's discretion)
Negligently caused property damage	3 years from date plaintiff discovered, or ought to have discovered, the injury; or 6 years from the date of the damage, with a long-stop limitation of 15 years from date of negligent conduct
Deliberately caused personal injury	6 years from date of injury
Breach of contract	6 years from the date of the breach

Source: adapted from Law Commission, 1998: 1–2

Case study   Limitation periods for civil action in cases of sexual abuse

Barbara was sexually abused by her uncle, Colin, from a young age until she was 14 years old. She is now 25 and suffers from a depressive illness and personality disorder. She has recently come to realise that her illness and disorder have been caused by Colin's abuse. Because different rules apply to actions seeking compensation for deliberately caused injury, and negligently caused injury, her action against Colin will be time-barred (the limitation period being six years after she was 18).

In contrast, an action against her mother for negligently failing to take reasonable steps to stop the abuse could be brought up to three years from the time Barbara learns that her illness is caused by the abuse, and the court could, at its discretion, allow her to bring an action outside that time limit.

Source: Law Commission, 1998: 2

The example neatly captures some of the illogicality and unfairness of the current system of limitations for civil action. As the Law Commission points out, it seems absurd that a victim or survivor could be better placed to sue a person who has *failed to prevent* the abuse, than to take action against the person who actually *carried out the abuse* in the first place.

Types of compensation

The purpose of damages is to provide compensation for loss or injury suffered (Simons and Harmer, 2002). Damages can be awarded for:

- loss of earnings
- other financial loss or expenses
- loss of amenity or enjoyment of life
- pain and suffering

Damages may be special, that is a precise sum estimated or calculated, or general, as a round sum, to be calculated by the judge. In personal injury cases, pecuniary damages refer to loss of earnings and the cost of medical expenses and of the care required. An individual can also be compensated for pain and distress and physical incapacity, or what is referred to as 'pain and suffering and loss of amenity'. The latter are usually lumped together by judges as a global figure. 'Pain' refers to the physical discomfort of medical treatment. 'Suffering' relates to mental or emotional distress. 'Amenity' means the capacity to do things previously enjoyed before the accident, or to participate in the normal activities of life. Loss of amenity can still apply, even though the plaintiff may not be conscious of the loss they have endured, for example as a result of incurring a brain injury. In Scotland, the relevant terms are 'solatium', referring to 'pain, suffering and amenity', while 'patrimonial' refers to pecuniary loss (Law Commission, 1995b).

Claims for damages could obviously be made against therapists for causing loss to a client. The *Ramona* case (1994) in the USA brought an award of third party damages totalling $475,000. Case law regarding successful claims against therapists in England and Wales is much more limited. In the *Landau* case (*Werner v Landau* (1961)), discussed in detail in Chapter 4, the judge commented on the difficulty of assessing damages to be awarded to the client. In the event, £6,000 was awarded to Miss Landau for personal injuries, including an attempted suicide, and for pecuniary loss, given that she had been unable to earn a living following her negligently handled therapy. This would amount to approximately £100,000 at current values.

Damages for psychological injury

The concept of damages payable for psychological injury is one of particular interest to therapists, given that this is, by definition, closely related to their area of work. However, this is undoubtedly a confusing aspect of law, with many inconsistencies remaining to be ironed out. As one authoritative legal survey of the topic states: 'Broken minds have always been greeted with a scepticism which contrasts sharply with the sympathy generated by broken bones' (Mullaney and Handford, 1993: 1).

The starting point for discussion is that under the law there are no damages payable for the normal human feelings of grief, anxiety and depression (Mullis and Oliphant, 1993: 23). This is as opposed to compensation, for example, for the death of a child, loss of an eye through assault, and so on, for which fixed rates are set. Damages may be payable for psychological injury where they follow on from physical injury, for example in the case of depression following amputation of a limb. However, the crucial point is that no damages are normally allowable for psychological injury, which falls short of being a recognised psychiatric illness (see Box 3.9). The more narrow legal view is framed by a number of factors, such as the problem of establishing proof of causation, where emotional states, feelings and distress are concerned. There is a greater degree of speculation in assessing psychiatric damages, due to:

- differing medical or expert opinions on the subject
- the fact that the effects of psychiatric illness vary from one individual to another
- the fact that psychiatric illness may be attributable to a wide range of factors which need to be separated out for the purpose of deciding damages. (Law Commission, 1995a: 36)

Box 3.9   Damages for non-physical injury

- Damages are available for pain and suffering, and loss of previous abilities.
- No damages are available solely for normal human emotions of grief, anxiety, distress.
- Damages for emotional distress require evidence of a positive psychiatric illness.
- Damages for psychiatric illness require plaintiff to be a direct victim of the event.
- Damages for psychiatric illness are not payable to persons less directly involved in the event, subject to narrow criteria.
- Damages for psychiatric illness are not available for professional rescuers.

Even defining a 'recognised psychiatric illness' can be somewhat problematic, as psychiatrists do not always agree on their diagnosis. There is also the 'floodgates argument', which is often invoked as a reason for not widening the criteria for claims for damages to include non-psychiatric emotional distress. The fear is that conceding a general principle capable of wide application to a massive number of situations will provoke a flood of litigation of American proportions, which would overwhelm and disable the court system. It could also be said that fear of opening the floodgates is a very effective argument for restricting the wider public's access to justice.

Nevertheless, psychiatric categories do adapt and change over time, as evidenced by the successive editions of the psychiatric diagnostic manuals such as the *Diagnostic and Statistical Manual* (APA, 1994), and *International Classification of Diseases* (WHO, 1992). The most obvious example of this has been in the addition of post-traumatic stress disorder (PTSD). The 1980 edition of the *DSM–III* introduced PTSD in terms of psychiatric symptoms and eligibility for compensation by the courts (Pugh and Trimble, 1993: 425). It was added to the legally accepted range of psychiatric illness following the cases of the *Herald of Free Enterprise* sinking at Zeebrugge, the fire at King's Cross underground station, and the death of 95 football fans at Hillsborough stadium.

Persons eligible for psychiatric damages

A further important factor is that there is a limited range of persons eligible for psychiatric damages. These are normally restricted to what are called 'primary victims', rather than to 'secondary victims', however badly affected the latter might be as a result of their trauma. Primary victims are those persons directly affected by the incident or event, via immediate, personal involvement. The claims of secondary victims such as bystanders or witnesses are subject to special scrutiny, along the lines of:

- a 'proximity test', in terms of eyesight, earshot, or immediate aftermath, i.e. within an 'hour or so' of the event
- or a 'relationship test', requiring closeness of relationship, such as a spouse, parent or child, or one of 'loving care and affection' with the victim

For example, most claims by relatives for damages after the Hillsborough disaster were rejected because they had witnessed the events on TV, which was not held to be sufficiently direct to meet the test required. Damages to professional helpers are normally limited to physical injury, rather than psychological injury. One review has highlighted the seemingly arbitrary nature of compensation in this regard: 'The law is plainly a lottery in which some bystanders are spattered with blood and others with money' (Pugh and Trimble, 1993: 429). Arguably, the increasingly complex judicial arguments applied to cases of psychiatric injury see tort law at its worst and most defensive. According to Conaghan and Mansell, these kinds of cases 'represent not a considered and logical extension to tortious rules of liability but rather an arbitrary and essentially non-logical extension to what we have argued is an illogical process' (1993: 28).

Scottish law on delictual liability, or negligently inflicted psychiatric illness, is broadly similar to English law in this field. A report by the Scottish Law Commission has commented that 'the courts have developed these rules of liability over the past hundred years or so on an almost ad hoc basis. As a result they are complex, productive of unjustifiable distinctions and ignore modern developments in the understanding of psychiatric injury' (2004: 21). The report proposed a radical break with the current system, and its replacement by a statutory obligation to make reparation.

Summary

Therapists are likely to have most contact with civil aspects of the legal system. The legal system is based on adversarial proceedings, and on a hierarchy of courts, extending from Employment Tribunals to the House of Lords. Recent changes in the civil legal system have seen the replacement of Legal Aid by limited public funding and conditional fee arrangements, and the development of alternative forms of dispute resolution.

Therapists have a range of sources of legal advice, and need to familiarise themselves with the protocols for giving evidence in court in the event of being called as a witness. Therapists may encounter a wide range of professional issues when involved in the courts, including the legal status of their codes of ethics, negotiating pre-trial therapy for vulnerable adults, supporting clients in legal proceedings, providing reports and acting as an expert witness. The legal system may be particularly problematic for bereaved clients involved in the Coroner's Court. It has become increasingly complex with regard to time limits for civil actions and compensation for psychiatric injury, and is now seen to be in urgent need of reform.

Discussion points

1 In what circumstances might a therapist become involved in legal action? How might therapists prepare themselves more effectively for such involvement?

2 What points of conflict or contrast can you identify concerning therapy and the law? What points of similarity and overlap are there? How might mutual understanding be promoted?

3 Is there a role for therapists in bringing their experience and expertise into the courts? What are the advantages and disadvantages of therapists taking on the role of expert witness with greater frequency?

4 Discuss the case history of the therapist involved in supporting her client taking legal proceedings for abuse (see pp. 60–1). Should therapists take on this active role, in the absence of other support systems for their clients? What effects, if any, might this have on the therapeutic relationship?

5 Should the legal system award damages for normal human emotions, such as grief, anxiety or distress, rather than simply for psychiatric illness? How might the current system of damages be made fairer from the point of view of clients and therapists?

4 Professional Negligence, Liability and Duty of Care

Therapists are perhaps less immediately anxious about being sued for professional negligence than in the past, as litigation in the UK has failed to develop on the scale experienced in the US. There is, however, intense and growing interest amongst therapists and their agencies about their 'duty of care' towards clients, and ways of defining, or even expanding, the range of their professional responsibilities towards clients, third parties, such as family members, and to society at large. The term 'duty of care' is often used in an aspirational sense regarding the kind of overarching ethical responsibilities that ideally therapists should take on, to avoid harm through their work with clients.

Thus it has been suggested that therapists are under a duty of care to report child abuse and to prevent clients from committing suicide, while agencies have a similar duty to provide supervision, and that supervisors have a duty of care towards clients. In a narrowly legal sense, these claims are incorrect, unless supported by either a clear statutory duty, or case law as precedent. In ethical, moral or professional terms, therapists may have wide and appropriate responsibilities to promote the welfare of clients and to avoid harm. In legal terms, their duties in law are very circumscribed, for the moment at least. Therapists and their employing agencies should be cautious about seeking to take on ever widening definitions of a duty of care, as where there is a duty of care, then there is also liability. If a supervisor does have a *legal*, and not just an *ethical*, duty of care towards a client, then the client can, in theory, sue the supervisor. Of course, it is the courts that will define the existence or otherwise of a duty of care, but it would be as well for therapists not to be pushing back the boundaries of their liability as a profession too enthusiastically.

Case law on therapist negligence is still limited in scope, so any detailed discussion of the exact nature of the therapist's duty of care is still quite hypothetical in nature. The nearest relative to case law on therapy in the UK is medical case law, and, within that, case law relating to psychiatry. There are obviously clear differences between therapy and psychiatry to be borne in mind, given that psychiatry comprises specific medical elements, such as diagnosis of illness and the use of medication, electro-convulsive therapy and even the use of surgical procedures. It is also part of a profession regulated by statute. However, the parallels between negligence by therapists and doctors or psychiatrists do indicate the form that the application of negligence principles to therapists would be likely to take. For this reason, this chapter explores some of the known features of medical negligence case law, particularly with regard to psychiatry. It moves on to examine some of the few, but significant, cases of therapist negligence case law, drawn both from the USA and the UK. Some of the main problematic areas, such as defining the therapist's duty of care, advice-giving and third party claims are explored, before the chapter ends with a discussion of the services offered by professional indemnity insurance schemes and professional protection societies.

Professional negligence

Professional negligence, or personal injury, cases are heard under a branch of civil law known as tort, derived from the French word for causing a 'wrong' or damage to others. Brazier suggests that 'one of the functions of the tort system is to make the defendant accountable for what he has done, and to deter negligent conduct' (2003: 244). It could be added that another is to compensate the plaintiff for the damage, such as loss of earnings, or the expense of having further therapeutic help to overcome the hurt which has been experienced.

Establishing a case for professional negligence or personal injury requires three conditions. These are:

- existence of a duty of care between the professional, or employing agency, and the client, or patient, concerned
- breach of that duty
- resultant foreseeable harm, caused by the breach of duty of care

Apart from any physical harm, the harm caused by the therapist needs to be 'a psychological injury', i.e. a psychiatric condition as diagnosed by reference to an accepted diagnostic manual, such as *ICD–10* or *DSM–IV*. The courts do not normally compensate for other feelings, such as annoyance, disappointment or distress, where this is the sole form of damage being claimed.

Media coverage of the alleged 'compensation culture' suggests that litigation for negligence is rapidly expanding, fuelled by 'no win, no fee' agreements. Reality is more complex. There has been a substantial rise in medical negligence claims against the NHS, which increased from £53 million in 1990 to £500 million in 2005. However, the NHS has set up a scheme for quick settlement of complaints worth up to £20,000, in order to limit the drain on resources taken up by costly legal cases (*Guardian*, 20 Feb. 2004; 14 Oct. 2005). There is, in fact, no real evidence yet of a medical 'malpractice crisis' in the UK, at least not on the scale of the US (see Box 4.1).

Box 4.1 Cases of therapist professional negligence in the USA

Anclote Manor Foundation v Wilkinson (1972): Husband sued after doctor encouraged his patient to divorce and marry him; she committed suicide one year after discharge/divorce.

Doe v Roe and Roe (1977): A therapist couple were sued for publishing a book describing the therapy of the plaintiff and her late husband; $20,000 compensatory damages awarded.

(Continued)

Hammer v Rosen (1959): Negligence via the use of 'direct analysis', regressing the patient to infancy and then 're-parenting', using violent methods.

Mazza v Huffaker (1983): Therapist had a relationship with the client's wife. Compensatory damages of $102,000 plus $500,000 punitive damages on grounds that he 'reacted improperly to transference or countertransference' to a third party, the client's wife.

Nicholson v Han (1968): Counsellor had affair with wife of couple in marital counselling with him.

Rowe v Bennett (1986): Client sued female therapist for negligent infliction of mental and emotional distress for continuing treatment after becoming involved with client's female partner.

Roy v Hartogs (1975): Counsellor had affair with client as part of her therapy, allegedly to help her overcome her lesbianism. Client awarded $153,000 damages, reduced to $25,000 on appeal.

Zipkin v Freeman (1969): Counsellor persuaded client to become involved in nude 'group swimming therapy', advised her to divorce husband and marry him, and lend him $14,000; client awarded $18,000 damages.

Sources: Feldman and Ward, 1979; Kermani, 1989; Otto and Schmidt, 1991

Litigation against psychiatrists

Within the field of medical negligence, it is the area of legal action against psychiatrists that most closely compares to the situation of therapists, although the crucial differences between the two groups must be acknowledged. In the UK, legal action against psychiatrists is rare, but the attendant costs in terms of time and expense are still high. 'Psychiatrists are among the greatest users of medico-legal advisory services of the medical defence organisations but they are not the heaviest users when it comes to claims. Some psychiatric claims are relatively expensive to settle, however' (Ingram and Roy, 1995: 620). One study of negligence cases brought against psychiatrists in the UK indicates that half of the cases relate to suicide or attempted suicide. These negligence claims can be 'very expensive to settle, particularly when a patient has suffered head or spinal injury following a suicidal attempt' (Bradley, 1989: 165).

Psychiatrists' duty of care

Bradley discusses a number of cases where negligence was alleged after hospitalised psychiatric patients caused themselves serious injury, such as hemiplegia, or partial paralysis, caused by attempting suicide. In one such case, a young man aged 16 was awarded £500,000 for spinal injuries, following such an attempt at suicide. The usual practice is that when psychiatric patients are admitted to hospital as potentially suicidal they are placed under 'special observation', or 'specialled', in nursing jargon. This means that nurses carry out continuous observation of them on the ward, to monitor the patient closely and prevent self-harm or suicide attempts. Bradley's study (1989) covered 50 cases dealt with by the Medical

Protection Society. However, it should be noted that none of these actually reached trial and, as with most tort cases, the majority were dropped or settled out of court.

In the USA, there seems to be a stronger duty on the part of psychiatrists to prevent harm to such patients by exercising reasonable care (Austin et al., 1990: 127–44). In the UK, the legal system seems to be much more protective towards psychiatrists, and inclined to give them the benefit of the doubt. In one case, Mr Justice Mustill declared that:

> the duty is not to prevent suicide but to take reasonable care to that end – and the word is 'reasonable', not 'perfect'. Thus there may well be cases in which the taking of no precautions is consistent with reasonable care. With hindsight such precautions can be seen to have been desirable, but there may have been nothing known at the time which would have led the doctors to suppose that precautions were needed. Moreover, precautions which were reasonable in all the circumstances might yet prove inadequate to forestall a really determined attempt. (Bradley, 1989: 166)

In a similar case in 1981, Lord Denning took the robust position that 'it should be the policy of the law to discourage such actions [against medical staff] whether the patient succeeds in his suicide or not' (Bradley, 1989: 167).

The problems involved in bringing successful cases against medical and other professionals are built into the very nature of tort law, which offers a system of peer defence against patients or relative claims for negligent treatment. The well-known case of *Bolam v Friern HMC* [1957] set the benchmark for deciding the standard of care in negligence cases. Here, the patient was given electro-convulsive therapy (ECT) without anaesthetic or relaxant drugs, and suffered a spinal fracture during the treatment. An expert witness testified in court that administering ECT without use of anaesthetic was accepted practice at the time. This provided a sufficient defence to clear the doctor concerned of negligence. Although medical practice has changed with regard to the use of anaesthetics during ECT, and, indeed, in the use of ECT overall, the prevailing standard at the time provided justification for the medical practice then adopted.

The dangers of overlooking relevant physiological symptoms are also illustrated in one case described by Bradley. Here, a patient with what was seen as psychogenic or undiagnosable backache was referred to a psychiatrist, who commented: 'He seemed to find it difficult to accept any psychological interpretation for his symptoms. Perhaps he is too naive to benefit from psychotherapy.' Two days later, the patient became paralysed from the waist down by an undetected spinal tumour (Bradley, 1989: 169).

Barriers to legal action against psychiatrists

An important point to consider is that the Mental Health Act 1983 has acted as a substantial barrier to litigation against psychiatrists in the UK. Bradley suggests two reasons for this. The first is the existence of mechanisms for the thorough monitoring of the Act's operations by hospital managers, Mental Health Review Tribunals and the Mental Health Act Commission. Secondly, there is the perhaps more significant role of s. 139 of the Act, which specifically restricts the use of civil or criminal proceedings against staff. Under this part of the 1983 Act, medical practitioners, social workers and other professionals are protected 'unless the act was done in bad faith or without reasonable care'. Legal action requires permission of the High Court in the case of civil proceedings, or the Crown Prosecution Service in the case of criminal proceedings.

Psychiatrists in the UK are therefore subject to protection from legal action via the very nature of tort law, which requires the plaintiff to prove that the damage experienced was caused by the negligence of the professional concerned. They are also specifically defended against legal action by statute, which aims to limit the use of the courts by patients seeking redress for decisions made, or treatment provided in the course of the exercise of professional judgment. A key question for therapists is whether they too will enjoy such a favourable position in the eyes of the law, assuming that their claim to professional status is fully recognised at some stage in the future.

Therapy case law

In the UK, the number of cases involving professional negligence by therapists is still small, with one key case recorded in detail at Appeal Court level, namely *Werner v Landau* (1961) (see below). There is a second relevant case, that of *Phelps v Hillingdon Borough*, which concerns the failure of an educational psychologist to carry out proper tests for dyslexia, in assessing a school pupil with educational difficulties, but this relates to a breach of statutory duty rather than breach of duty of care as a therapist (*Phelps v Hillingdon LBC* [2000]).

Case study   *Werner v Landau* (1961)

This was a case brought by Miss Alice Landau against Dr Theodor Werner, concerning 24 sessions of psychotherapy, which took place between March and August 1949 and during the resumption of treatment from March 1950 up until January 1951. In April 1951, Miss Landau attempted suicide. During therapy, she had developed a strong emotional attachment to Dr Werner, and there was a period of social contact between them after the first part of treatment was ended, which included letters, discussion about a weekend away together, and visits by Dr Werner to her flat. She brought a successful case against him for £6,000 damages for personal injuries and pecuniary loss sustained by her as a result of wilful misconduct and/or negligence by him as her medical attendant. This was upheld at Appeal.

The judge divided the case into three phases: the first covering the course of treatment, the second, when social contact occurred, and the third when an unsuccessful attempt was made to continue and resolve the treatment. His criticism was of the second stage. 'Dr Werner, with the best intentions in the world, made a most tragic mistake by introducing social contact...this was negligence on the part of Dr Werner' (Times Law Report, 8 March 1961). The social contact could not be justified as part of the treatment, and had the unintended effect of encouraging Miss Landau's affections for him. Dr Werner was defended by the Medical Protection Society.

(Continued)

(Continued)

His defence was that the social contact was justified in the exceptional circumstances of the case, where a strong emotional attachment had been formed towards him by the patient. 'He feared that she might if she was removed from his influence have a relapse and go into the state of anxiety neurosis in which she had been when she started the treatment' (TLR, 8 March 1961). While demonstrating that he was aware of the unorthodoxy of this approach, he argued that it was still necessary to protect the client's well-being and promote a positive outcome to the treatment, or at least min-imise the likelihood of a relapse.

Part of the plaintiff's case was that sexual impropriety had occurred on these social visits. Despite the evidence of the attachment in the form of letters, the court found the latter allegations unproven. The judge 'absolutely absolved Dr Werner of any such misconduct or any misconduct of any sexual kind to his patient' (TLR, 8 March 1961). The doctor's professional reputation was, to this extent, protected by this aspect of the judgment.

Source: Werner v Landau TLR 8/3/1961, 23/11/1961, Sol Jo (1961) 105, 1008

Therapist's duty of care

The main principle confirmed here is that of the breach of the therapist's (here the psychiatrist's) duty of care to the client or patient. Thus, 'it was the duty of a doctor to exercise ordinary skill and care according to the ordinary and reasonable standards of those who practised in the same field...The standard for the specialist was the standard of the specialists' (*TLR*, 23 November 1961). This standard essen-tially derives from medical precedent referred to elsewhere, such as the cases of *Bolam v Friern HMC* [1957], and *Maynard v West Midlands Regional Health Authority* [1985]. In the *Bolam* case, the judges set a standard for negligence as a failure to act 'in accordance with a practice of competent respected professional opinion' (at 121). The evidence heard in the *Werner* case was that to introduce social contact, for whatever therapeutic purpose, could not be sustained as a viable form of treatment. From the expert witnesses heard, it was deduced that 'the evi-dence of the doctors was all one way in condemning social contacts' (*TLR*, 23 November 1961).

Some variation of opinion here might have acted in favour of the defendant, as the later *Maynard* case has acknowledged that professional (here, medical) opinion is not necessarily unanimous in defining forms of treatment. Hence, in the *Maynard* case, 'it was not sufficient for the plaintiff to show there was a body of competent opinion which considered that the decision was wrong if there also existed a body of profes-sional opinion, equally competent, which supported the decision as being reasonable in the circumstances' (at 635). At a stage where psychoanalysis may have been the dominant paradigm for therapy, there were few other available competing schools of counselling to provide a contrary opinion to the view that social contact was likely to harm the client's well-being and future recovery.

The above action was brought under the scope of professional negligence law, which may possess two elements, that of action in tort (a civil wrong experienced by the plaintiff) or the separate grounds of breach of contract. Proving a case of negligence by establishing a tort is notoriously difficult to achieve, because of the difficulty in proving that the breach of the duty of care actually *caused* the injury suffered, rather than simply preceded it in time. This action via tort is distinct from an action brought for breach of contract, where the defendant may have failed to carry out specific undertakings set out in a contract, whether express or implied. One example of breaching express conditions of a contract might be a therapist failing to provide an agreed number of counselling sessions, which had been paid for in advance by the client.

Problems of proving causation

The client needs to prove, on the balance of probabilities, that the breach of the duty of care in therapy actually caused the damage alleged. In the case of *Werner v Landau*, the judges were satisfied that the long-term emotional damage that the client suffered was due to the doctor's negligent behaviour, rather than being the result of some pre-existing condition or of other external, intervening factors. This degree of certainty about the relationship of cause and effect will often be absent from cases involving therapy, where it can be, by its very nature, problematic to specify its intended or actual outcomes in individual cases with any degree of precision. The *Werner* case is also unusual in the amount of documentary evidence available, such as letters, which the plaintiff was able to produce in support of her case. Often, it seems this kind of evidence suggesting professional negligence is simply not available to the aggrieved client. The implication is that Dr Werner was working in private practice at this time, which determined his personal liability for damages. If he had been working as an employee of the National Health Service, then vicarious liability would have been borne by the relevant health authority, as established in the case of *Cassidy v Ministry of Health* [1951].

Transference and negligence

One of the most interesting aspects of the case is the weight given to a serious discussion of the concept of transference in a court of law. The reality of transference was accepted as a powerful and accepted part of analytic treatment. 'Describing the system of treatment known as "transference" his Lordship said that in the course of the process a great deal of past emotion became reactivated. A great deal of the emotion released could be attached or attracted to the doctor who had undertaken the treatment' (*TLR*, 8 March 1961). The court was critical, not of the adoption of transference as a method of working with the client, but of the doctor's failure to abide by accepted safeguards in its use. The necessary safeguards, as agreed by a wide body of informed professional opinion, included the avoidance of any planned social contact outside the consulting room (Gabbard, 1995). The allegations of sexual contact between the doctor and his client were dismissed by the court as erotic fantasy on her part, perhaps reflecting the conservative social mores of the time. Given more recent research into the widespread extent of sexual contact between therapists and clients, it seems possible that the client's case would perhaps be considered more sympathetically today, and not dismissed as easily as it appears to have been (Jehu et al., 1994; Masson, 1992; Russell, 1993: Rutter, 1991).

Feldman and Ward provide a detailed critique of this case along with other malpractice cases, the remainder occurring in the USA (for examples, see Box 4.1, pp. 76–7). They are critical of the court's decision with respect to the finding regarding misconduct. 'The case is wrongly worded and internally inconsistent. If the doctor is "absolved of all professional misconduct", upon what is the liability based?' (1979: 93). In their view, the court's perception of professional liability is unnecessarily narrow. Their argument is for a greater reliance upon cases brought under breach of contract, rather than via tort, which they claim unfairly disadvantages clients in any legal proceedings, for the reasons given above. Similarly, Cohen suggests that, following this case, 'we are unlikely to see a dramatic increase in such cases because of the uncertain state of our knowledge about counselling and psychotherapy, and because of the general obstacles placed by the law in the path of any plaintiff in any negligence action' (1992: 11). Other commentators argue, on the other hand, that therapy constitutes 'a ripe environment for litigation', where malpractice is unchallenged only because of legal obstacles inhibiting client challenges to the profession (Otto and Schmidt, 1991: 319).

To summarise, the principles involved here relate to the application of a standard concerning the therapist's duty of care, based by analogy on the medical profession. The case was brought by Alice Landau under the law relating to the tort of negligence, which is arguably more difficult to establish than simple breach of contract. The standard of care which applies is based on the requirements for safe and competent practice of the method adopted by the practitioner. Simply because the method is one used only by a minority of practitioners does not necessarily mean that the therapist is negligent as such. Hence the sympathetic discussion in *Werner v Landau* of the particular problems faced in working with transference issues. Finally, the values expressed by the court, in summarily dismissing the claim of sexual contact, are perhaps indicative of the unequal power relationships prevailing between male practitioners and female clients, and the way that the law approached issues of gender and power at that time.

Barriers to litigation via tort

The apparent uniqueness of the *Werner* case in UK case law perhaps illustrates some of the problems faced by clients in bringing actions for professional negligence against therapists under tort law. Various commentators have argued that this approach unduly favours the professional at the expense of the client. 'Establishing the causal link between the psychotherapist's breach and the injury is the most difficult burden of proof for the plaintiff' (Feldman and Ward, 1979: 68). They propose an alternative approach, where action for damages by a client would, instead, be based on breach of contract. 'In the contract approach the plaintiff need only show the existence of the contract, the breach of the fiduciary duty infused in the contract, and the injury' (1979: 80). By the 'fiduciary duty', they refer to the reposing of ultimate trust and confidence in the therapist. However, the weakness of this argument is that many therapists in the UK do not provide therapy on the basis of a legally binding contract, so action for breach of contract is not an option for these clients. It needs to be said that litigation against therapists is an onerous, expensive and often ineffective way of seeking recompense for a failed or damaging experience of therapy.

The legal notion of fault at work in tort law is an objective standard, based on what is perceived by judges to be reasonable behaviour, and which is therefore distinct from the personal qualities of the practitioner. In several cases, courts have decided that trainee practitioners have to provide the same duty of care as their more experienced or senior colleagues, on the 'learner-driver' principle (*Nettleship v Western* [1971]). In the case of *Wilsher* [1988], a junior doctor was still required to work to the standard of a reasonably competent practitioner, with no allowance being made for an evident lack of experience (Mason and Laurie. 2006: 323). Where a practitioner is represented as possessing specialist skills, they will be judged against the relevant higher standard to be expected of an expert in that field. 'The test is the standard of the ordinary skilled man exercising or professing to have special skill' (*Whitehouse v Jordan* [1981], quoted in Reynolds and King, 1989: 35).

Deciding on the standard of care for therapists

How are such standards to be set by the courts, which may be unfamiliar with many aspects of professional or therapeutic skill and practice? The answer is through hearing the testimony of expert witnesses, who can advise the court on the appropriate standards or procedures to be expected of the practitioner. However, simply calling one or more experts who can criticise the practice of another is not sufficient in itself to demonstrate that the first was negligent. The law recognises a degree of diversity in all forms of professional practice as healthy – to do otherwise would penalise new and innovative practice, which may, in turn, become the established benchmark of the future. Thus 'a doctor who departs from orthodox views is not automatically branded as negligent. But he will have to justify his course of action either by indicating features of the individual case which call for a different mode of treatment or by showing his novel method to be superior or at least equal to the general practice' (Brazier, 1992: 126). Lord Scarman put it more forcefully, as always, in the case of *Maynard v West Midlands RHA* [1985] (at 638):

> In the realm of diagnosis and treatment, negligence is not established by preferring one respectable body of professional opinion to another.

The weakness of this system is that it relies heavily on peer defence, and the evaluation of normative standards, namely the level of practice of reasonably competent practitioners at that particular time. However, this could mean that the standard, while constituting the norm for practice, is basically flawed, unsound or lacking in a convincing research or evidence base. The *Bolam* approach also put expert witnesses in a powerful position, in advising the court of standards of professional practice. This has changed following the *Bolitho* case, which restated the terms of the *Bolam* test, by requiring that professional standards be justified in objective terms, rather than the practitioner simply following the norms of the day (*Bolitho v City and Hackney Health Authority* [1997]). 'What *Bolitho* does is to require expert witnesses to justify and explain the basis of their judgements', in that 'responsible practice be demonstrably logical and defensible' (Brazier, 2003: 151, 153). Medical defence societies initially argued that *Bolitho* would have little effect on medical negligence cases, but others have seen it as a shift away from the power of professionals to determine their own standards, and a reassertion of judicial authority in such cases (see Box 4.2).

Box 4.2 Defining the standard of care in negligence cases

- The standard of care expected of a trainee is not lower than that of a reasonably competent practitioner (*Nettleship v Western* [1971]; *Wilsher v Essex AHA* [1988]).
- Criticism of one style of practice by an opposing approach is not sufficient in itself to brand the first as negligent (*Maynard v West Midland RHA* [1985]).
- The standard required for specialist practitioners is that to be expected from an expert, rather than from a less skilled practitioner (*Whitehouse v Jordan* [1981]).
- Expert witnesses must justify the rationale and evidence base for their assessment of competent practice (*Bolitho v City and Hackney HA* [1997]).

The elements listed in Box 4.3 could provide the basis for suggesting the elements of a duty of care as applied to therapists. Any statements, such as these, are, no doubt, immediately open to criticism and challenge as being well-meaning but rather vague. The list may also be incomplete, since it includes no reference to duties relating to recording, supervision or responsibilities towards third parties, for example. The reason for the choice of these particular aspects is to seek to define the boundaries of the therapist's duty of care more narrowly with regard to the immediate client, rather than to include all possible aspects of best professional practice. Ultimately, the precise set of standards for a therapist's duty of care has yet to be fully tested in the courts. Many of the above elements were involved in the *Werner* case discussed above. The full meaning of 'not engaging in exploitative or unethical conduct towards the client' will depend, in the final instance, on the decision of the court, assisted by the advice of expert witnesses. Until then, the above, or any established code of ethics for therapists, will orient therapists towards the standards they are likely to have to meet.

Box 4.3 Elements of a therapist's duty of care

- not engaging in exploitative or unethical conduct towards the client;
- obtaining informed consent, or negotiating a therapeutic agreement, for work with the client;
- acting within limits of own training, expertise and competence;
- providing selection and skilled use of methods appropriate to the client's situation;
- not harming the client as a result of physical or psychological methods employed;
- not giving inaccurate or damaging advice;
- clarifying and maintaining agreed or agency limits to confidentiality;
- making appropriate referral to another therapist or agency when required;
- ending therapy in a way consistent with client's best interests.

Negligent assessment and treatment

One element of professional negligence may relate to inadequate assessment and treatment. The very notion of diagnosis or assessment may itself be problematic to some schools of therapy, such as the person-centred approach, but it still remains a potential area where therapeutic mishap may occur. Non-medical therapists in the USA seem much more likely than their UK counterparts to be well versed and comfortable in using the diagnostic categories of manuals such as the *DSM-IV* or *ICD-10*, which are routinely used by psychiatrists in the US and UK. This may reflect US therapists' greater dependence upon health insurance funding as a source of income, as classification via *DSM-IV* is generally a crucial criterion for entitlement to therapy. One of the few cases in the UK relevant to the issue of negligent assessment is that of *Phelps v Hillingdon LBC*. In this case, an educational psychologist, employed by the Local Education Authority, was found to be in breach of her statutory duty, in failing to carry out a formal assessment for dyslexia of a pupil experiencing difficulties at school (*Phelps v Hillingdon LBC* [2000]).

The case of *Osheroff v Chestnut Lodge* in the USA, discussed below, raises a number of key questions, both about the use of psychiatric categories for assessment and treatment and about the vulnerable status of psychotherapy in treating certain forms of mental illness. As described above, both in the USA and the UK it is possible to defend against claims of negligence by establishing that the practice adopted was consistent with a body of informed opinion, even if it does not represent the current orthodoxy. In the USA, this is known as the 'respectable minority rule'. However, such a school 'must be grounded in sound scientific principles that are attested to by professional expert witnesses' (Packman et al., 1994: 178).

Case study   Case of *Osheroff v Chestnut Lodge* (1985)

In the USA, Dr Osheroff was hospitalised in 1979 for seven months at Chestnut Lodge, and was treated with individual psychotherapy four times a week. During this time, he lost 35 lb in weight, experienced severe insomnia, and had marked symptoms of physical agitation. This was evident in his incessant pacing, which was so extreme that his feet actually became swollen and blistered. He was discharged by his family, and then admitted to Silver Hill, where he was diagnosed as having a psychotic depressive reaction. Here he was treated with medication and started to improve within three weeks. He was discharged within three months, with a final diagnosis of manic-depressive illness, depressed type. He then sued the private psychiatric facility, Chestnut Lodge, for negligence, because the staff had incorrectly failed to prescribe medication and had instead treated him according to the psychodynamic model.

The case was settled out of court for an undisclosed amount, and therefore has no value in terms of setting a legal precedent. The conflict was in part over the making of the correct diagnosis, namely biological depression, versus narcissistic personality disorder. The suit against Chestnut Lodge pointed out that their diagnosis (narcissistic personality disorder) did not appear in the then current edition of DSM-II (1968

(Continued)

(Continued)

version), and that negligence arose from not using a commonly agreed system of diagnosis. It also alleged 'failure to treat appropriately', claiming that the law should regard the treatment of serious mental disorders through psychotherapy alone as negligence per se. The defence case rested on the argument that the real cause of the patient's behaviour at both hospitals was due to negative transference.

Source: Packman et al., 1994

While the case sets no legal precedent for the USA, it does raise concern about the relative status of drug-based and psychotherapeutic methods of treating clients. Packman concludes from his discussion that 'given the current legal climate, negligent psychotherapy, negligent treatment and misdiagnosis of psychiatric conditions are likely to constitute a ripe area for future lawsuits against psychotherapists. Psychodynamic psychotherapists may be particularly vulnerable to such lawsuits' (1994: 195). From another perspective, concern has been widely expressed that, in the shift towards evidence-based therapies in the NHS and elsewhere, therapies, other than cognitive behaviour therapy, will become marginalised, due to the effect of the National Institute for Clinical Excellence (NICE) guidelines.

The tort system presents a number of difficult hurdles for clients wishing to establish that their therapist has been guilty of professional negligence. The very lack of case law, particularly in the UK, is more likely to point to the problems involved in proving damage caused by a therapist's failure to observe a duty of care, rather than the simple absence of cause for complaint by aggrieved clients. The flowering of rival schools of therapy, now numbered at 450, may also mean that a variety of approaches now have to be seen as consistent with professional practice, rather than a single standard simply being adopted to judge all cases. The days of the *Werner* case in 1961, when the psychoanalytic school provided the dominant approach to therapy, have gone for good, and hundreds of competing schools now bloom. Without more case law, it is hard to say whether this will benefit therapist or client in defining the standard of care to apply in negligence cases.

Informed consent and contracting

One of the key issues concerned in the US *Osheroff* case was that of the alleged failure to obtain the client's informed consent to treatment. The implication was that the client would not have agreed to psychotherapy if the proven benefits of medication had been properly made known to him. 'Consent, to be effective, must stem from a knowledgeable decision based on adequate information about the therapy, the available alternatives, and the collateral risks' (Bray et al., 1985: 53). Law in the USA has moved away from a *relative* standard of disclosing risks of medical treatment, towards an *absolute* standard of disclosing *all* relevant information, even including a 1 per cent outside chance of permanent damage from surgery (Kermani, 1989: 9). The more restrictive UK medical model of informed consent is based on the more conservative model of the *Bolam* test, as applied in *Sidaway v Bethlem Royal Hospital Governors* [1985]. This emphasises the doctor's duty to release *appropriate* information, rather than the US model of the patient's *right* to be given *all* relevant information, however limited the risk. Part of the information needed for a client to give informed consent would be about the possible harmful effects of therapy, including, at least in the short term, deterioration of mood, worsening of behavioural symptoms and potential adverse effects on family and other significant relationships. Other well-established risks of therapy are described by a range of writers, including dissatisfied clients (Alexander, 1995; Grunebaum, 1986; Lambert et al., 1977; Masson, 1992; Sands, 2000; Striano, 1988). The effectiveness and relative benefits of different types of therapy obviously also need to be conveyed no less clearly to potential clients (DoH, 2001a; Hubble et al., 2002; Lambert and Ogles, 2004; Roth and Fonagy, 2006).

According to one view, 'consent is now a central issue in clinical practice' (Mayberry and Mayberry, 2003: 9). This is certainly true within the NHS, where there has been a significant policy shift towards clearly obtaining and documenting patient consent for a wide range of procedures and interventions (DoH, 2001b). However, the concept of informed consent raises a number of difficulties for non-medical therapists, not least that the outcomes of an interpersonal relationship cannot be specified in advance with any real precision, unlike the probable side-effects of medication or surgery. In addition, some aspects of the therapeutic relationship operate at other than a consciously understood level, for example transference in psychoanalysis and para-doxical injunction in family therapy (Holmes and Lindley, 1989). Holmes has argued that therapists in this situation cannot really offer their clients an informed choice between conscious and unconscious processes as alternatives, asking rhetorically 'can one give informed consent to transference?' (Holmes et al., 1994: 467).

Box 4.4   Consent

For consent to be valid the patient must:

- be able to understand in broad terms the nature and purpose of the procedure;
- be offered sufficient information to make an informed decision;
- believe the information and be able to weigh it in the balance to arrive at a decision;
- be acting voluntarily and free from pressure;
- be aware that he or she can refuse.

Source: BMAED, 2004: 72

One relevant factor here may be the concept of 'therapeutic paternalism' where the therapist balances the need for total disclosure with the need to preserve the client's well-being (Bray et al., 1985: 55). In medical terms, this is referred to in the *Sidaway* case in the UK as 'therapeutic privilege'. Here the doctor may decide not to disclose the full facts to a patient if it may cause the patient mental or physical harm or cause them to refuse necessary treatment. In medical terms, informed consent depends upon two factors on the client's part, namely capacity, or ability to comprehend information, and consent, or agreement to treatment (see Box 4.4). There are, however, definite limits to the usefulness of a medical analogy for informed consent. For therapists, informed consent will usually refer to a current or proposed therapeutic relationship, rather than a technical form of treatment. Bond argues the case that therapy depends on the active and conscious participation of clients in therapy, rather than passive acquiescence to clinical technique: 'consent is the absolute minimum standard of practice in counselling ... Most ethical guidelines for counsellors require a higher standard of actively engaging the client in the contracting process' (Bond, 2000: 88).

Some therapists, if using the informed consent approach, may tend to think of it as a one-off event, the signing of an agreement specifying the nature of the contact, and the risks and benefits involved. Packman argues against this approach, suggesting that informed consent really represents more of a process of dialogue, continuous updating and checking out with the client, rather than a once and for all event. 'Consent is an ongoing dialogue between the patient and mental health professional in which both parties exchange information, ask questions, and come to an agreement on the course of psychotherapy...Both parties must be active participants. A document cannot replace this important process. The emphasis is on communication, not the form' (Packman et al., 1994: 193).

Negotiating informed consent from clients, and revisiting this as necessary, is a hallmark of good professional practice in therapy. However, in narrowly legal terms, the doctrine of informed consent is still a developing and highly contentious area of law, where policy and practice in the NHS is probably in advance of any formal legal requirement.

Negligent advice

The benchmark for case law in terms of professionals offering negligent advice is that of *Hedley Byrne* [1964]. This concerned a faulty evaluation of a company's financial worth, but the basic principle will be held to apply to many fields well outside that of the commercial world. Professionals giving advice as a part of their activities need to be sure that the advice is accurate and well founded. While adding a disclaimer to advice can reduce liability, it does not remove it entirely. A client could seek damages for pecuniary or financial loss caused by a therapist's faulty advice, as perhaps in the hypothetical case of a client 'advised' by their stress counsellor to give up their highly demanding executive post.

Most therapists would claim that they do not give advice, because this approach runs directly counter to the ethical principle of promoting the client's right to autonomy. However, it may well be that the non-directive and highly nuanced style of therapy is unfamiliar to many clients. An invitation to reflect on conflicted feelings about a key relationship may be translated by the client in his or her mind as 'my therapist said I must end this relationship, because it is not meeting my needs'. Actually proving that a therapist gave advice of any kind may be somewhat difficult for the client to establish at a later stage. Two brief cases below illustrate some of the problematic issues involved in therapist advice-giving.

Case study   Stuart Sutherland, on confessing to his analyst his wishes to beat up his wife's lover

He was a genuinely kind and considerate man, and although he used some Freudian interpretations he also used his commonsense. I told him that I was thinking of going up to London and beating hell out of 'the lout', whom I felt like murdering. To my surprise, he said: 'That would be a much more sensible thing to do than what you are doing at the moment – you would be better to take it out of him than to go on taking it out of yourself.' I said: 'I never expected an analyst to advise me to indulge in physical violence', and he replied: 'You would of course have to make the violence commensurate with the crime and be careful not to inflict any long-term injury.' Sutherland, 1977: 17

No actual outcome is recorded to this therapeutic exchange. Assuming the accuracy of this account, the therapist is putting himself at risk here of encouraging his client to break the law.

Case study   Advice or paradoxical injunction?

I first obtained Marvin's agreement to help Phyllis overcome her phobia by promising to follow any suggestions I gave him. I instructed him to say to her, punctually every two hours, phoning her if he were at work, these words precisely: 'Phyllis, please don't leave the house. I need to know you are there at all times to take care of me and prevent me from being frightened.'...Phyllis, even though she knew Marvin was following my instructions, grew irritated with him for ordering her to stay at home. After a few days she went to the library alone, then shopping, and in the next few weeks ventured farther than she had for years. (Yalom, 1991: 267–8)

Paradoxical injunction is a powerful therapeutic technique where the therapist relays advice to the client to do something, not necessarily intending that they will comply. The 'advice' actually highlights underlying needs and drives which have been hitherto unexplored or unresolved. In Yalom's example the advice had the desired effect, and Phyllis, who was troubled by agoraphobia, quickly overcame it, perhaps as a consequence of this technique. If she had experienced a worsening of her condition, then she and her husband might have had legitimate cause for complaint or action against their therapist.

Liability of supervisors

Some observers suggest that supervisors owe a duty of care to their supervisee's *clients* (Harrison and Westergaard, 2006: 108). This will be true in *ethical and professional* terms, but if it applied in legal terms, this would mean that the supervisor is directly liable to the client and can therefore be sued for breach of duty of care. In the US, some supervisors are indeed liable to clients in law, as a condition of state registration. In one case, a client sued a supervisor on the grounds that the latter's supervisee had had a sexual relationship with that client (*Cosgrove v Lawrence* (1986)).

However, it seems unlikely that supervisors in the UK carry this kind of liability for the work of their supervisees. Supervision of therapists is a specialised form of professional consultation, which is distinct from both advice-giving and from direct line-management responsibility for an employee's work. The supervisor would have a duty of care to the supervisee, and would be personally liable to the supervisee for any breach causing damage. The supervisor might also be liable to the supervisee for any breach of contract, if a legal contract applied, as is often the case in therapeutic supervision. If the supervisor was employed by the same agency as the therapist in question, such as an NHS Trust, then both therapist and supervisor would be covered by vicarious liability, and the aggrieved client would need to sue the Trust.

There is no current case law to suggest that a supervisor would carry personal liability, or a direct duty of care to a third party, such as a client, or the client's family. The false memory litigation very clearly demonstrates that UK courts are traditionally cautious about extending the application of the concept of duty of care to ever-widening groups, unlike their counterparts in the US (Jenkins, 2001; Jenkins, in press). A contrary view of supervisor liability is offered by Griffin (2001), and Leonard and Beazley Richards (2001).

The table in Box 4.5 illustrates the different aspects of supervisory relationship, in terms of professional, organisational and legal responsibilities to the supervisee.

Box 4.5	**Professional, organisational and legal elements of the supervisory relationship**			
			Elements of the supervisory relationship	
			Professional responsibility	Legal liability
Employment context of		Individual (e.g. self-employed)	Personal accountability	Personal liability
professional practice		Organisational (e.g. employee status)	Personal and/or line management accountability	Vicarious liability
Source: adapted from Jenkins, 2001: 24				

Third party liability

Professional negligence by therapists may harm third parties, rather than just affect the client who is receiving the service. Third parties, such as the client's partner or parents, are unable to sue for breach of contract, not having been part of the original agreement, and would need to take action under tort law. Here, the principle of establishing a causal link between negligence and harm becomes even more tenuous and therefore difficult for clients to prove in court. However, a body of case law in the USA has been slowly growing which embodies this principle, extending the duty of care for therapists still wider in some exceptional cases (see Box 4.6 for examples).

Box 4.6   Third party legal action against therapists in the USA

Brady et al. v Hopper (1983): President Reagan's former Press Secretary, seriously injured in an assassination attempt, brought an unsuccessful case against the attacker's therapist for failure to diagnose, treat or warn.

Currie v US (1986): Victim's widow sued Veterans' Association for failure to admit their patient for psychiatric treatment, in view of his deteriorating mental condition.

Lipari v Sears (1980): Out of court settlement for $20,000 by Sears company and Veterans' Association (VA) over case of ex-VA patient who bought a gun from the former and fatally wounded the plaintiff's husband, six weeks after terminating psychiatric treatment.

McIntosh v Milano (1979): Victim's parents sued a psychiatrist for failure to warn of the actual danger posed to the victim by the patient receiving therapy.

Peck v Counseling Service of Addison County (1985): A child's parents sued the agency for failure to warn them of his realistic threat to burn down their barn made during therapy.

Petersen v Washington (1983): The plaintiff sued the hospital team which had authorised the release from psychiatric treatment of a drug addict, who drove through a red light and injured her in a car crash.

Tarasoff v Regents of the University of California (1974; 1976): Victim's parents successfully sued the University concerning staff who counselled the assailant, for failing to warn their daughter of a realistic threat to her life.

Source: Kermani, 1989

Third party liability for UK professionals

UK law is not as extensive in relation to third party liability for professionals as that of the US. For example, in a case which bears a similarity to some of the cases described above, Jayne Zito, widow of Jonathon Zito, was unable to sue the relevant health authority for breach of its statutory duty of care. Christopher Clunis, a patient discharged from a psychiatric hospital, fatally stabbed her husband on an Underground station platform. The health authority's duty of care, under s. 117 of the Mental Health Act 1983, was seen to extend only to the patient, and not to her as a third party. However, in another case, Christina Kopernik-Steckel was awarded £500,000 for a psychological injury, PTSD, caused by failures in psychiatric care. Her brother left hospital and stabbed his and Christina's mother to death and then committed suicide. This was the first reported case of an NHS Trust accepting the principle of liability, or breach of duty of care, towards a third party (*Guardian*, 8 November 2001).

Prior to the introduction of the Human Rights Act 1998, many professionals in the public sector, such as social workers and the police, were immune from legal action for breach of duty of care. This protection has now been removed. Social workers and their employing authorities have been sued for breach of duty of care towards children in residential care and for failing to warn prospective adoptive parents of the background and history of abused children placed for adoption.

Therapist liability for false memory

For therapists, the most dramatic and alarming development in terms of professional negligence law has been the growth of third party litigation in the USA over the promotion of allegedly false memories of sexual abuse. Allegations that therapists implanted, or encouraged, such memories of childhood sexual abuse received a great deal of media publicity. In legal terms, action against therapists in the USA can take the form of third party actions by aggrieved parents alleged to be the abusers. Another variant, again in the USA, is for clients to make allegations of abuse against parents, retract, and then sue the therapist for encouraging the false memories, via what is termed 'retractor action'. The basis for such litigation would be professional negligence. The best known case is that of *Ramona* (1994).

Case study   The *Ramona* case: third party action in the USA for false memory

Holly Ramona, 24, claimed to recover memories of early childhood sexual abuse by her father during therapy for depression and bulimia. As a result of the allegations, Gary Ramona's wife, Stephanie, divorced him, his three daughters refused to speak to him, and he was dismissed from his $500,000 job in a wine company. The therapists working with Holly were Marche Isabella, a licensed child, family and marriage counsellor, and Richard Rose, MD, a psychiatrist. In order to facilitate the recovery of her memories, the client had agreed to their suggestion that she take sodium amytal, a drug used to produce abreaction. Holly Ramona brought a lawsuit for $500,000 damages against her father, alleging abuse; he responded by bringing a case against Rose and Isabella for $8 million for malpractice, charging that they had implanted the abuse memories in his daughter. The case was unusual, in being the first time there had been a third party action in the USA against therapists on these specific grounds.

The plaintiff, Gary Ramona, was successful, winning the case in May 1994, although being awarded the significantly lower sum of $475,000 in damages. Holly Ramona's subsequent case against her father was dismissed by the court, the judge declaring that the earlier case had demonstrated that no abuse had taken place.

Source: Johnston, 1997

The *Ramona* case prefigured a wave of hostile litigation in the USA against therapists on the basis of accusations of false memories of abuse, including action by clients, as well as by third parties. Similar legal action has not taken place in the UK, although it seems to have been widely feared by therapists (Jenkins, 2002b).

The *Ramona* case undoubtedly received a large amount of media attention, but needs to be considered carefully. It did not necessarily demonstrate that therapist malpractice was widespread on the issue of encouraging unsound beliefs in sexual abuse. The question of malpractice may have been influenced by the therapists' use of sodium amytal, described as a 'truth serum' by the plaintiff, as it can produce images and memories which are not reliable evidence for legal purposes. The *Ramona* case raised many important questions about the techniques used by therapists to explore complex and sensitive areas, where a client's current problems of self-esteem, anorexia, self-harming or depression may originate in early unrecognised or unacknowledged childhood sexual abuse. The use of hypnosis, or related techniques, involving visualisation and regression, may lead to their clients' evidence being dismissed by courts both in the UK and USA, in subsequent actions against alleged abusers.

The reported litigation against therapists in the USA has raised concern amongst British practitioners that similar legal action may occur in the UK, and the need to establish boundaries of safe and competent practice. The probability of successful third party action in the UK against therapists for allegedly implanting false memories of abuse in clients' minds is currently limited. This is because tort law in England and Wales does not usually include third party action, as this is seen to be too remote from the original cause of action. The courts are also reluctant to keep progressively extending the boundaries of tort liability in an incremental fashion. By responding to each new cause for tort action, the courts would be in danger of creating whole new categories for civil action, with unintended consequences for the legal system and for society as a whole. There has been intense discussion about therapeutic practice and the development of allegedly false memories of abuse, which has clarified the merits of safe and competent practice methods for therapists (Brandon et al., 1997; BPS, 1995b: 25; Enns et al., 1995: 227–44). These are summarised in Box 4.7.

Box 4.7 Guidelines for professional practice in working with recovered memories of childhood sexual abuse

- Avoid using suggestion and leading questions.
- Be cautious about jumping to conclusions about abuse as necessarily being a causal factor, e.g. in eating disorders.
- Avoid discounting the possibility of abuse memories which are not conscious.
- Be aware of the danger of imposing views or information on the prevalence of childhood sexual abuse on the client.
- Work at the client's level: recovered memories may be actual truth, or part of a wider therapeutic narrative.
- Evidence required for legal proceedings is weakened or invalidated by use of drugs or hypnosis.
- Strict criteria are applied in deciding whether material from a client is admissible as evidence in a court of law.

Other forms of liability

Besides third party liability, there are some other forms of liability, which should be mentioned briefly. These include:

- *criminal liability*: where the degree of negligence amounts to a crime, as in the case of a doctor giving a fatal injection of sedative drugs for a routine operation;
- *strict liability*: under EU and UK consumer protection law, damage, death or injury caused by faulty products remains the responsibility of the producer or retailer;
- *public liability*: damage caused to a member of the public, for example injury to a client through tripping up on a carpet in the consulting room.

The tort system places clients and third parties at a severe disadvantage in trying to seek redress for damage caused by a therapist failing to exercise due care in their work. Litigation is expensive and uncertain of outcome. The tort system has been described as a 'lottery', in comparison with 'no-fault' compensation schemes, whose primary aim is to separate out the element of compensation from blame. The tort system requires both the establishment of fault, and resultant harm. Against this, professionals operate a system of peer defence, where the standard of care is set by current defensible norms of professional practice, rather than necessarily by best possible practice.

The Pearson Commission, reporting in 1978, was in favour of retaining the tort system as a check on medical malpractice, but the figures suggest that a strong series of filters operate to deflect most claims from ever reaching court. It recorded that 60 per cent of such claims were abandoned, and 34 per cent were settled out of court. Only 5 per cent actually went to court. Of these, 80 per cent were won by the defendants (Pearson Commission, 1978). Brazier describes litigation as 'capricious', of minimal value in achieving accountability of errant professionals and 'traumatic for both parties' (2003: 221). Some of the problems involved in taking legal action and making complaints are more fully explored in Chapter 3.

Indemnity insurance and professional protection societies

The increasing amount of litigation against professionals, from architects to doctors, and from veterinary surgeons to accountants, has pushed this issue to the forefront of current concerns of many therapists. Evidence of professional indemnity insurance is now required by professional associations, advertisers, and by some schemes for validating training courses. The therapist's fear of litigation may be greater than the actual risk, however. Box 4.8 outlines some of the action to be taken in the case of a potential complaint or litigation by a client. When the word 'sue' is mentioned, it is worth distinguishing between different levels of meaning. Suing may refer to:

- a dissatisfied client, who is considering action or complaint
- a similar client who has actually engaged a solicitor
- actual receipt of a writ, and the commencement of legal proceedings
- settling prior to, or out of, court

- legal proceedings in the Small Claims or County Court
- final resolution of the case, and decision of the court for or against the therapist or agency.

Box 4.8   Action to take in the case of potential complaint or litigation by a client

- Be alert to early signs of conflict, hostility or persistent misunderstanding with clients.
- Attempt to resolve these conflicts informally at an early stage wherever possible.
- Do not make admissions of liability which may invalidate your insurance cover or weaken a later court case.
- Keep detailed records of contact (letters, phone calls, conversations) for later reference.
- Contact your professional indemnity insurance company or professional protection society at an early stage for advice.

Only 5 per cent of cases successfully proceed to court, and of these, most are won by the practitioner. This is not to deny the considerable stress involved, for all parties, but to put litigation in its proper context. The spectre of medical litigation in the USA has had a number of effects, such as the adoption of defensive medicine via the use of often unnecessary tests, and the withdrawal of doctors from practice in vulnerable areas, such as obstetrics. One extreme response has even been that of 'going bare', or practising without insurance, on the basis that 'stones do not bleed'. All the practitioner's personal assets are at risk in this case, if he or she is successfully sued. It is also unfair to patients in cases of true liability, as no damages or compensation can be obtained, however valid the client's case (Hawkins, 1985: 251).

Critique of indemnity insurance

In the UK, the issue of therapists obtaining indemnity insurance cover seems to have become fused with the wider question of their acquiring fully professional status. The main counter-argument to the rush to insure has come from Mearns, writing from a person-centred perspective. His argument has a number of strands. First, he points out that there has been no significant claim by a client in Great Britain to date. Secondly, the risks to clients are overstated, as therapy does not rest on physically intrusive measures, nor on the supply of potentially dangerous products. Thirdly, promoting publicity about insurance actually increases the risk of claims by clients. Finally, the development of an insurance mentality in therapy erodes the autonomy of clients by emphasising their vulnerability and dependence. 'Indemnity insurance is a combatant defensive action to discourage possible challenge from clients' (Mearns, 1993: 164). How widespread or influential Mearns's critique is remains unclear.

The more mainstream position is that indemnity insurance is of benefit for therapists, and should be seriously considered by all practitioners (Johnson, 2006). The arguments are that insurance can fund the legal advice necessary to protect the therapist, can pay the damages ordered against them in a successful claim, and is necessary, on ethical grounds, to recompense the client for injury or damage caused by malpractice.

Forms of insurance cover and of liability

Some professional groups are covered against negligence claims via the nature of their employment; for example, doctors are partially covered by what is called NHS or 'Crown' Indemnity. In addition, within the medical field there are organisations, such as the Medical Protection Society and the Medical Defence Union, which offer additional support and legal advice on a wide range of issues, beyond that of NHS liability. Therapists may be covered in a similar way via the nature of their employment, on the principle of vicarious liability, whereby the employer must insure for acts carried out by employees in the course of their work. The principle of vicarious liability may extend to cover counselling students on placement and volunteer therapists working 'as if employed' by agencies, i.e. on terms and conditions which are fundamentally similar to employed staff.

Different types of insurance cover to be considered include:

- professional indemnity insurance
- domestic insurance cover for home and car (if used in connection with work)
- product liability
- public liability
- libel and slander
- employer's liability

A professional indemnity policy is 'essentially an insurance which provides resources and funds required to defend an allegation of negligence' (Flaxman, 1989: 19). It embraces both negligence in the form of errors and omissions, for example giving the wrong response, and malpractice, namely providing damaging forms of help. Although less than 5 per cent of claims actually go to court there can be a heavy cost of defending claims. An employee will be covered by his or her employer's insurance, under the principle of vicarious liability, but it is argued that it is still prudent to have independent access to legal advice and representation, as the interests of the employer and the therapist need not always coincide. The employer, for example, may have less interest in contesting a case in order to defend the practitioner's reputation. It may seek to settle out of court when the therapist wishes, for various reasons, the case to be heard and brought to a successful conclusion. Domestic insurance cover alone will not be sufficient for liability incurred while working at home; nor will it cover office equipment or other material used in such work. Working from home may also invalidate cover under contents or buildings policies.

Product liability covers the supply to clients of defective goods causing damage, for example aromatherapy oils, candles, relaxation tapes or biofeedback machines.

Public liability covers liability for death of or injury to persons other than employees or for damage to third party property, such as injury sustained by tripping over a loose carpet. Insurance should be obtained for libel and slander, covering, for example, comments made about clients or third parties in reports to agencies, or to the courts. Employer's liability insurance is necessary if the practitioner is employing others. If trading as a partnership or limited liability company, the company needs its own insurance cover, such as a 'firms' policy. Joint and several liability is a collective form of liability held by all partners for the actions or negligence of their partners in the firm. For example, with a legal partnership of therapists, a claim for damages could be made by a client against all partners in the firm for the negligent or abusive therapy practised by one partner.

Legal representation

One of the major elements of indemnity insurance relates to legal costs. Legal representation may be included for disciplinary proceedings such as the hearing of a complaint to the therapist's professional association. Legal costs are covered for the successful defence of an allegation of sexual impropriety with a client. An unsuccessful defence would not be covered, to avoid the problem of providing cover for a deliberate wrongful act by the therapist. The coverage is also reactive, rather than proactive, so that insurance companies will not normally undertake legal action to clear the therapist's good name. Companies will also usually provide a fully confidential legal helpline for those insured. When a claim is being made or is likely to be made, it is important to inform the insurers immediately. 'The policy contains clear instructions not to make any offers, promises, compromises, payments or admissions of liability' (Flaxman, 1989: 23).

The actual claim process is started when:

- the insured is served a writ, or
- the insured receives notice, either orally or in writing, of the intention of a third party to commence legal proceedings, or
- the insured becomes aware of circumstances which are likely to give rise to a claim.

'Circumstances' are usually undefined, but could be indicated by persistent unresolved problems, acrimonious correspondence, the withholding of fees, or poor personal relationships with clients (Flaxman, 1989: 118–19). Systematic and regular record-keeping may be one of the best ways for a practitioner to build a defence against a successful claim, according to one writer on indemnity insurance. 'In my insurance business we see many spurious claims simply disappear due to the rigorous attention to detail by the practitioner. Copious and detailed notes have been produced, while the client failed to produce solid evidence' (Balen, 1995: 15). Therapists deciding to keep minimal records need to bear in mind that insurance companies often recommend or require the keeping of detailed client records for defensive purposes (see Chapter 6).

Protection by insurance can be either on a 'claims made' basis, or 'losses occurring' basis, for the current period of insurance cover. Under the first type of cover, the practitioner is protected for claims made against them while the insurance is in force, but not after it has ceased. It is important in this case, therefore, to acquire 'run-off' protection to cover a past period of practice, as there may be a delay of some years before a claim is actually made. Under a 'losses occurring' approach, the insured is covered for the period to which the insurance relates, regardless of whether the claim is made at a much later date.

Professional protection societies

It is sometimes assumed, in the debate about malpractice protection, that the issue stops with a choice of professional indemnity insurance policy. It is worth remembering that there is another option; the medical defence bodies which act to protect medical practitioners. These are not insurance companies, but operate on a different basis. The key difference is that between a 'mutual non-profit-making defence association and commercial insurance' (Hawkins, 1985: 38). 'Such a policy, rather than being a legal contract of indemnity, is actually a discretionary promise to pay for support, advice, protection and, if necessary, legal and defence costs and any damages awarded by the court, without specific amounts, preconditions or exclusions defined' (Balen, 1995: 15). A professional protection society does not increase subscriptions on the basis of the number of claims made by an individual, whereas renewal of a therapist's insurance cover could conceivably be refused by an insurance company because of the high level of claim(s) made previously. It may also be the case that an insurance company may sometimes settle out of court for financial reasons, irrespective of the merits of the particular case. A protection society will, it is argued, build up a degree of specialist experience in defence work for therapists, which may be lacking in some commercial firms, which may not possess full sympathy with or understanding of the professional tasks involved.

The professional indemnity insurance model provides legal advice and representation via insurance policies. Organisations, such as the Psychologists' Protection Society, operate instead on a self-funding rather than an insured risk basis, similar to the medical protection societies mentioned above. The stated advantage here is that the access to legal assistance is more direct and immediate. Any therapist needs to remember the potential, however remote, for a conflict of interest developing between him or herself, and their insured legal representation, however provided. Instances of conflicts of interest may develop over professional issues. For example, from a professional point of view, there may be a need to appeal against a key court decision in a case of alleged false memory against a therapist in the UK, were one to occur. The commercial interest of the insurance companies may dictate otherwise, as appears to have happened in the USA, leaving the therapeutic community as a whole somewhat more vulnerable to future litigation. This is admittedly still a hypothetical situation in the UK, but therapists need, nevertheless, to consider their own position very carefully with regard to legal protection. Whatever the relative merits of taking out professional indemnity insurance, or of joining an appropriate professional protection society, therapists need to be aware of the changing face of professional negligence action (see Box 4.9). Some of the practicalities of responding to such legal action are covered in more detail in Chapter 3.

Box 4.9   Guidelines for professional practice concerning professional negligence litigation

Review your current practice in the light of the therapist's duty of care, with regard to:

- provision of a safe working environment for clients and staff;
- levels of your professional training and updating;
- working within the limits of your competence;
- appropriate selection and referral systems for clients;
- maintaining professional boundaries in therapy with clients;
- use of informed consent, therapeutic contracting and review with clients;
- avoidance of damaging forms of therapy, harmful 'advice', or risky 'homework' for clients;
- use of properly negotiated endings for therapeutic contact;
- compliance with an established code of ethics;
- use of informed and up-to-date assessment methods where appropriate;
- awareness of potential liability to third parties;
- maintenance of adequate levels of insurance cover for all purposes needed;
- membership of professional indemnity insurance scheme or professional protection society;
- access to expert professional consultation and informed legal advice.

Summary

The lack of extensive UK case law on negligent therapy can be fleshed out by looking at the parallels with medical negligence principles. Fears of a 'malpractice crisis' of US proportions in medicine and therapy may be overstated, given the significant differences between the UK and US health and legal systems. Therapeutic case law is much more in evidence in the USA, and includes third party actions against practitioners, as in alleged false memory cases. Therapeutic case law in England and Wales rests on the notion of the therapist's 'duty of care' to the client, as evaluated by expert witnesses in court. Therapists using a less mainstream approach are not necessarily more vulnerable to legal action than those using more conventional methods. Both minority and majority approaches need to demonstrate the maintenance of appropriate professional standards, and the discharge of their duty of care to the client. Safe and competent practice would include the use of informed consent, contracting and the avoidance of unethical or damaging ways of working with clients. In reality, the system of tort liability has not succeeded in putting therapists massively at risk from legal action by litigious clients intent on claiming damages. Nevertheless, sensible insurance cover and access to expert professional and legal advice are sound precautions for therapists to take against the threat of legal action.

Discussion points

1   Is it fair to therapists and to their clients that the standard of care expected of a trainee should be that of a reasonably competent practitioner? How can trainee therapists best work with this requirement, but lessen their apparent vulnerability to legal challenge?
2   In the case of *Osheroff* in the USA, can the attempt to treat the patient with psychodynamic methods be properly described as negligence, in your view? If so, where does this leave psychodynamic approaches in terms of their vulnerability to litigation?
3   Is the tort system a just and effective means of identifying poor professional practice and compensating clients, or is it simply a 'lottery'? What changes should be made to the system to overcome its main shortcomings?
4   Should third parties, such as a client's parents or partner, be able to take legal action against a therapist for damages? What circumstances might justify a charge of negligence against a therapist by a person who was not directly involved in the therapeutic relationship?
5   Should all therapists be required to take out professional indemnity insurance, or to join a professional protection society, as a condition of practice? What view do you take of the argument that such insurance is unnecessary, or even counter-productive for therapists?

5 Confidentiality, Privilege and the Public Interest

Confidentiality is one of the areas where therapy and the legal world may collide. Confidentiality is a central tenet of therapy, desirable both on pragmatic grounds, to enable the relationship of trust to develop, and on the ethical basis of promoting the client's autonomy and self-determination. From a legal perspective, confidentiality is subsumed under another set of concepts, those of privilege and the public interest. Therapists may focus their attention on the idea of privilege, but without necessarily stopping to consider the overriding principle of the public interest, which is of crucial significance in the world of the law.

This chapter explores the legal foundations of confidentiality, as an expectation or duty based on trust. The legal concept of privilege is defined. This provides a protected status for some forms of communication, albeit largely unavailable to therapists, except those working in marital counselling. The circumstances where therapists are obliged to break client confidentiality are described in detail. These can include breaking confidentiality under contractual obligation, or in the public interest to prevent harm to a third party, as in the cases of child abuse, potential suicide or suspected terrorism. Within these legal restrictions, some cautionary notes are finally added, covering the overall need to maintain confidentiality wherever possible, as an expression of the ethical value placed by therapists on promoting client autonomy and self-determination.

Confidentiality

The legal concept of confidentiality is based on the idea of equity, or fairness, in that a person who has received information in confidence should not take unfair advantage of it (*Seager v Copydex* [1967]). Every therapist will have some understanding of confidentiality, although it will not necessarily be one that other therapists would automatically accept. For many therapists, confidentiality is known to be limited, by reason of their professional code of practice or via their conditions of employment. Reporting suspected child abuse, for many, will be a requirement of their daily practice, so that their perception of confidentiality is already relative to the material that the client brings to sessions. Other therapists belong to schools of counselling where the concept of confidentiality is held to be absolute: what goes on in the therapy session is not revealed to the outside world (Langs, 1998: 191). However, many therapists are often not clear about the legal limits to confidentiality in therapy. When, if ever, do therapists have to break confidentiality? When, if ever, can they refuse to do so?

In answering these questions, this chapter will consider some of the key aspects of confidentiality, such as the legal version of confidentiality called privilege. The related concept of the public interest, which lies in maintaining confidentiality, but also in overriding it on occasion, is also explored. Situations where therapists can breach confidentiality *inadvertently*, for example through a lack of care in writing an article, are discussed. It is assumed that, before making any *intentional* breach of confidentiality, the therapist has taken every possible step to discuss the matter thoroughly with the client concerned, and has sought to obtain their permission to disclose the information in question. In some extreme cases, this may not be practicable, perhaps for reasons of urgency, or because of the immediate nature of the action required. This chapter is, therefore, based on the concept of the therapist as *custodian, choosing to contain or disclose* sensitive client information. This is distinct from a discussion of the powers of other external bodies to *enforce* such disclosure. The powers of other parties, such as clients, the courts or the police, to gain access to this confidential information provide the subject of a separate analysis in Chapter 6.

Confidentiality as duty and trust

Given the tension between legal and therapeutic perceptions on confidentiality, it is worth restating that the law takes a benign and supportive view of the need for confidences, as part of the everyday working of the worlds of business, of the professions and of personal relationships generally. According to Lord Goff:

> a duty of confidence arises when confidential information comes to the knowledge of a person (the confidant) in circumstances where he has notice, or is held to have agreed, that the information is confidential, with the effect that it would be just in all the circumstances that he should be precluded from disclosing the information to others. (*A-G v Guardian Newspapers (No. 2)* [1988] at 805)

Confidentiality and the public interest

The public interest, as defined by the courts, holds that confidences should be maintained and protected by law, rather than be broken without good cause (*A-G v Guardian Newspapers (No. 2)* [1988]). Confidences need to be kept where there is an expectation that the relationship is one of trust. However, there are exceptions to the duty to keep confidences (see Box 5.1). These are where information is trivial; where it is already in the public domain; or where the public interest in preserving confidentiality 'may be outweighed by some other countervailing public interest which favours disclosure' (*X v Y* [1988] at 807). According to Bond et al., 'while the basis of the law of confidentiality may differ to some extent in Scotland and England, the substance of the law in both countries is the same' (2001: 2).

> **Box 5.1   Confidentiality and the public interest**
>
> - The public interest requires that confidences be maintained.
> - Breaking confidence is possible if the information is
>
>   - trivial
>   - already in the public domain
>   - in the public interest (as defined by the courts).
>
> - Legal opinion has supported the principle of the counsellor's 'fiduciary duty' of confidentiality in student counselling.

Confidences arise due to the special nature of a relationship, where it would be reasonably expected that a trust would be kept. Therapy would qualify as one of these forms of relationship, along with others, such as a doctor–patient relationship, or even a friendship. If this is so, then surely confidentiality deserves some special form of protection? Such protection would prevent confidences being broken, and one party's interests perhaps being damaged as a result. However, the overall public interest in confidences being protected is not absolute; some confidential information is protected, but other confidences are not.

Privilege and confidentiality

The idea of privilege is perhaps an attractive one for certain therapists, as a way of seeking protection for client–therapist disclosures. In over half of the states in the USA, privilege is now held by a number of professional groups, such as psychiatrists, psychologists and social workers (Bollas and Sundelson, 1995: 11). Privileged information in these states is explicitly protected by law from action by the courts. For example, a US Supreme Court ruling protects client–psychotherapist confidentiality from disclosure in federal trials (*Jaffee v Redmond* (1996)).

> **Case study   *Jaffee v Redmond* (US): The public interest case for therapist privilege**
>
> *In this case, Mary Lu Redmond, a police officer, shot and killed a potential assailant, after being called to a domestic disturbance. Redmond then took part in counselling with a social worker. The family of the deceased man sued Redmond and her employers for excessive use of force, and sought disclosure of the therapy notes as evidence. The case was appealed and heard by the US Supreme Court, in order to decide the issue of disclosure. Fourteen professional associations, including the American Psychiatric Association, filed amicus curiae briefs, advising the court on the legal and professional arguments in favour of recognising therapeutic privilege.*
>
> *(Continued)*

(Continued)

The majority verdict accepted the case for therapist privilege, which was extended to include social workers, on the grounds that much psychotherapy was provided by the latter. The court concluded that there was a strong public interest in establishing therapeutic privilege, which would protect client records from enforced disclosure by a court, and which would also prevent therapists from being required to give evidence concerning their own clients. 'The psychotherapist privilege serves the public interest by facilitating the provision of appropriate treatment for individuals suffering the effects of a mental or emotional problem. The mental health of our citizenry ... is a public good of transcendent importance' (Jaffee v Redmond (1996)).

Justice Scalia submitted a dissenting opinion, arguing that the judgment created 'a privilege that is new, vast and ill defined'. In her view, the public interest argument for creating therapist privilege at federal level actually assumed what needed to be proven beyond dispute, namely that the contribution of psychotherapy to promoting mental health was so distinctive and of such importance that privilege could be justified.

The Jaffee principle establishing therapist privilege is significant, and has been used to defend therapist–client confidentiality in several prominent cases in the US (Pyles, 2003: 257–60). However, the overall impact of the case is limited. The case holds authority only at federal, rather than state, level, which is where most litigation concerning therapists actually occurs. It stands as a piece of federal case law, over and above a fragmented system of therapist privilege derived from statutes passed by a number of individual states. This structural weakness of the judgment in legal terms is emphasised by the dissenting opinion of Justice Scalia.
Source: Jenkins, 2005

In the UK, comments in Parliament are protected, but these forms of privilege are rare. The main example is that of communications between lawyers and clients for the purposes of preparing legal action, known as Legal Professional Privilege. The *client* holds the privilege, rather than the lawyer, and it is the client who, therefore, has the right to waive it. The rationale is that this form of professional privilege, termed communication 'without prejudice', is necessary for the law to function; without it, giving and receiving legal advice would become almost impossible (*Anderson v Bank of British Columbia* (1876)). Many other professional groups have an interest in similarly protecting their communication, whether with clients, patients or parishioners. However, the lines of privilege are tightly drawn (see Box 5.2). They do not extend to priests, to doctors or even to close friends. The legal professional privilege held by lawyers, however, is not absolute. It may be overridden by the courts in extreme circumstances, such as the court requiring disclosure of information where a child's welfare is at risk.

Box 5.2 Confidentiality and privilege

- Confidentiality arises where trust is reasonably expected in a relationship.
- Professional privilege (protection against compulsory disclosure of confidences) applies only to client–lawyer communications for legal advice.
- Marital negotiations for reconciliation or separation can be privileged from disclosure.

Privilege in matrimonial cases

On the one hand, the public interest lies in the protection of confidences. On the other, it also lies in overriding confidences when this is necessary for the wider social good. Areas where the law is reluctant to force such disclosure are rare. In matrimonial cases, there is a recognition that privilege should apply where the parties are seeking advice or guidance with a view to reconciliation or separation: this is known as 'conciliation privilege' (Pattenden, 2003: 538). In the case of *McTaggart v McTaggart* [1949], Lord Justice Denning stated that:

> negotiations which take place in the presence of the Probation Officer, with a view to reconciliation are on the understanding, in the ordinary way, by all concerned, that they are without prejudice to the rights of the parties ...The Probation Officer has no privilege of his own in respect of disclosure any more than a priest, or a medical man, or a banker. (at 97)

Another case further illustrates the principles at work here. This was a case of a probation officer giving evidence in court in support of the wife, based on what her husband had told the probation officer in a separate interview, regarding the cause of the break-up of the marriage. According to the probation officer, when giving evidence in court, the husband had made an admission of desertion, a so-called matrimonial crime at the time. According to Lord Merriman, the probation officer, working in his marriage guidance role at the time, 'certainly exceeded his authority in considering himself an agent to make vital admissions on the merits of the case' (at 806). The discussions with both parties were privileged from disclosure; it was not up to the probation officer to choose to break their confidences (*Smith v Smith* [1957]).

The reference to probation officers in both examples should not be taken to mean that somehow this form of privilege relates only to this particular role. It is simply that matrimonial work has long been an acknowledged area of the probation service's practice and expertise, as part of its work in conjunction with the civil courts. The privilege in matrimonial cases is actually held by the couples seeking advice or counselling with a view to reconciliation or separation – steps which clearly have legal implications. Because of this feature, it comes under the umbrella of quasi-legal discussion, and is therefore protected by the notion of privilege, according to these judgments (see Box 5.3).

Box 5.3   Privilege and couple counselling

- Couple counselling can be protected by privilege, if recognised as such by the court.
- Privilege, or protection from enforced disclosure, is held by the *parties*, such as husband and wife, and not by the therapist.
- This privilege can be waived or given up only by the permission of the parties involved, namely husband and wife.
- The counsellor does not have a right to waive this privilege, for example, to inform a court or a third party involved in legal proceedings of the content of the discussion or counselling, without the permission of both clients.

Courts may sometimes have an interest in gaining access to privileged marital communication, for example when one party has apparently made serious threats against the other, of wanting to harm or even to kill the other party. The experience of Relate, the relationship counselling agency, in this respect, has been to argue the need to preserve its policy of confidentiality. However, the privilege rule concerning matrimonial communication, while usually recognised by the courts, seems to need to be re-established with every new case that is taken to court. It does not seem to hold the position of being a binding precedent.

The limits of medical confidentiality

Medical confidentiality is often assumed to hold some sort of privileged or protected status, but this is far from being the truth. Doctors and medical personnel are required to maintain confidentiality, but they cannot claim exemption from a legal obligation to disclose information. In the case of *Hunter v Mann* [1974], a doctor was fined on this basis. He was ruled unable to withhold confidential information from police investigating a car accident. Under s. 172 of the Road Traffic Act 1988, any person must give information about alleged traffic offences, if required to do so by the police. However, there is no obligation to volunteer such information without a request from the police.

Another example is provided in the case where a psychiatrist was called to give evidence about consultations carried on with the wife and co-respondent in a divorce case. In the course of hearing a divorce suit, the husband subpoenaed the psychiatrist who had been consulted by the wife and the co-respondent. When examined-in-chief by the husband's counsel as to what the wife and the co-respondent had said to him, the psychiatrist protested against answering the questions, on the grounds of professional confidence. Judge Edgedale said that what a person said to a doctor in a professional consultation was not privileged, and the witness must either give the evidence or be committed to prison for contempt of court. The psychiatrist then gave the evidence (*Nuttall v Nuttall and Twyman* (1964) at 605).

What was different about this case, compared with the two earlier matrimonial cases, was that the discussions between the psychiatrist, the wife and the co-respondent were not principally about litigation; neither was a lawyer present. This contact was therefore a 'professional consultation' in the judge's opinion. It was not seen to be marital therapy for the purposes of reconciliation, separation or divorce. Medical confidentiality can thus be overridden by statute, or by the directions of the court, and the same applies to the confidentiality of the therapist. An often repeated legal saying in this context is that '... "confidentiality" is not a separate head of privilege' (*Alfred Crompton Amusement Machines v Customs and Excise* [1974] at 433). In other words, protection from disclosure is granted by the law as privilege. It cannot simply be *claimed* by a professional, on the basis of it being a confidential relationship. Where there is a conflict here, the courts will decide.

Public interest in requiring disclosure related to crime

In what circumstances does the public interest require disclosure? Broadly, it is accepted that there is a strong public interest in preventing crime. Another legal saying has it that 'there could be no confidence in iniquity', meaning serious crime (*Gartside v Outram* (1856)). Other judges have widened this principle to include 'antisocial' behaviour, however widely that might be defined (*Francome v Mirror Group* [1984]; *Fraser v Evans* [1969]).

Relating this to therapeutic practice at this point might seem somewhat abstract. However, the *Tarasoff* (1976) case in the USA (discussed below; see p. 120ff.) has brought this principle directly into the heart of practice in many states in that country. Case law in the UK is less extensive, but the above principles should make it clear that therapists could use the 'iniquity' or public interest defence to break confidentiality. Obviously, this justification would have to be carefully weighed against the potentially terminal damage to the therapist–client relationship, and the longer-term public reputation, both of the agency and of the individual therapist concerned. The most striking example of the use of a public interest defence to justify breach of confidentiality is that of the *Egdell* case.

Case study   Breaking medical confidentiality in the public interest

'W' was detained as a patient in a secure hospital without time limit as a potential danger to the public, after he had shot and killed five people and seriously wounded two more. In the belief that he was being persecuted by people living nearby, he had shot five neighbours, and drove off in his car, throwing home-made bombs as he drove away. (He had a longstanding interest and expertise in bomb-making, and reported that he always carried some made-up explosives in his car.) Later he shot two more people, unconnected with the first incident. He was diagnosed as suffering from schizophrenia.

After ten years, he applied to the Mental Health Review Tribunal to begin the process of seeking his discharge. His solicitors instructed a consultant psychiatrist to prepare a report in support of his application. Dr Egdell strongly opposed his transfer, drawing attention to W.'s longstanding interest in firearms and explosives, and indicating a need for further tests and treatment. Dr Egdell sent the report to the solicitors, and W. withdrew his application, but without the Tribunal or the hospital being sent copies. Dr Egdell, on his own authority, then contacted the hospital director, and copies were sent to the Tribunal and to the Secretary of State. W. brought a legal action against Dr Egdell for damages for breach of confidence owed to him as part of the doctor–patient relationship. In considering the case, the judge referred to the General Medical Council's 'Blue Book' regarding confidentiality, noting that the rules themselves do not have statutory authority, but that they were derived from the disciplinary function of the GMC under the Medical Act 1983.

Source: W v Egdell [1990]

The case hinged on the question of defining the public interest. 'There is one consideration which in my judgement, as in that of judge, weights the public interest decisively in favour of disclosure' (at 852). This was not simply the fact of the patient's prior history of violence, but the need for any decision to release someone who had a history of multiple killings to be based on informed judgment. This need entitled the doctor to communicate the relevant facts on a restricted basis to the necessary authorities, even if the facts were obtained in the course of a confidential relationship.

Breach of confidentiality: risk to third party

Initial discussions about confidentiality on training courses for therapists almost inevitably bring up the situation where the client is a potential or actual murderer as the acid test of the therapist's commitment to client confidentiality. Discussion may assume that this is a hypothetical situation, but this is not necessarily the case. Laing describes a case related to him by another psychotherapist, about his patient, a consultant anaesthetist.

> This patient had led him to suppose (had told him directly, in so many words) that he had killed three people in the last year, while he had been in therapy, by unobtrusively curtailing their oxygen in the course of long, complex, surgical operations. He kept his overall statistics normal, so that he had no more statistically significant anaesthetic deaths than the average for his sort of job. Anyway, he had had a good run for the last three months so was now about to kill the next victim. He would choose someone with a bad heart, poor lungs, or what not, so that their death would not raise any eyebrows. (Laing, 1985: 126)

The patient was not responding to therapy, and showed no indication of ceasing his murderous pastime. No decision or outcome is recorded in Laing's account.

As said above, there is a longstanding principle in law that there is no duty to maintain confidentiality about iniquity or serious crime, or even anti-social behaviour, which clearly has a much wider remit. Either of the therapists involved would have been justified in breaking confidentiality on the basis of the threat to a third party, on the basis of the public interest in the prevention of crime, assuming that their action was taken in good faith. Where the therapist is employed, then there is specific protection for making disclosures to an appropriate manager regarding serious crime, as in the case described above, under the Public Interest Disclosure Act 1998. This amended the Employment Rights Act 1996, to protect the position of employees who were involved in legitimate 'whistleblowing' activities in the public interest.

Of course, it can happen that a professional does decide to pass on highly sensitive information to colleagues, in order to avert a risk of harm, but no action is then taken. In the case of Jason Mitchell, a psychiatric in-patient, an occupational therapist reported to colleagues that her client had been experiencing homicidal fantasies, but this information was not acted upon by senior medical staff. Jason

Mitchell was released and later went on to murder an elderly couple, for which he was sentenced to life imprisonment (Blom-Cooper et al., 1996: 56–62).

In terms of the wider issue of confidentiality and crime, therapists in the UK are not under a legal obligation to report crime, except in the case of Northern Ireland (s. 5, Criminal Law Act (Northern Ireland) 1967). Therapists, as citizens, may report crime in the public interest, but with rare exceptions such as terrorism, discussed below, are not obliged to do so by law (see Box 5.4). For example, information may be passed on to the authorities, such as a Youth Offending Team, under s. 115, Crime and Disorder Act 1998, for the purposes of preventing crime.

Box 5.4   Legitimate breaches of confidentiality

- Therapists are required to pass on information on terrorist offences.
- Therapists may be required to report suspected child abuse by their contract of employment or professional code of practice.
- The child or young person's own views may be considered in deciding to report suspected child abuse, but may also be overridden.
- Therapists may break confidentiality in the public interest, in order to report serious crime.

In fact, there is far less legal compulsion on therapists in the UK to report crime and risk to third parties than in other countries, according to one international comparative survey (Garvey and Layton, 2005). In addition, there is no 'duty of rescue' under English civil law. Lord Keith has stated that a person who sees 'another about to walk over a cliff with his head in the air and forbears to shout a warning' is under no liability under negligence law to prevent the accident from happening (*Yuen Kun-Keu v Att-Gen of Hong Kong* [1988]; McKendrick, 2000: 258). In practice, therapists will want to act in an ethical and professionally responsible way to prevent harm to the client or to a third party, even if not actually required to do so by law.

Public interest in preventing disclosure

In other instances, conversely, the public interest may lie in the prevention of disclosure. In one case, the mother of a child aged 14 months brought a legal case to compel the NSPCC to reveal the identity of an informant. The latter had made unfounded allegations that the child was being maltreated. This had prompted a visit by a NSPCC (National Society for the Prevention of Cruelty to Children) inspector, causing her a great deal of psychological distress (*D v NSPCC* [1978]).

The appeal supported the NSPCC, in finding that the public interest was maintained by finding against disclosure in this case. The public interest here was in supporting the work of an agency which was critically dependent upon its confidential links with the public. Confidentiality *per se* would not debar the ordering of disclosure. 'The sole touchstone is the public interest...' (Lord Edmund-Davies, 246 B). But, in situations where there is doubt about disclosure, the courts should order disclosure.

Defining what is in the public interest is not always straightforward. It has been said that what is of interest to the public is not the same as what is in the public interest, as the case of Doctors *X v Y* illustrates. (See also *Lion Laboratories v Evans* [1984].) In 1987, confidential information was supplied to newspaper reporters concerning two doctors continuing in general practice despite having contracted AIDS. Despite a restraining order, an article entitled 'Scandal of docs with AIDS' was published. The doctors were to be identified in a planned second article. The court held that the public interest in preserving confidentiality of hospital records outweighed the public interest in the freedom of the press to publish this information. The public interest here was in avoiding the likelihood of AIDS victims being deterred from going to hospital for treatment (*X v Y* [1988]).

Statutory protection for confidentiality

There is some statutory protection for confidentiality in certain specific instances. Examples include:

- Contempt of Court Act 1981: journalists' sources
- Consumer Credit Act 1974: creditworthiness
- Data Protection Act 1998: data processing
- Human Rights Act 1998: respect for right to privacy
- Rehabilitation of Offenders Act 1974: criminal offences

Protection of privacy

The UK lacks a substantive law protecting privacy comparable to that applying in the US, although Article 8 of the Human Rights Act 1998 affords the right to *respect* for privacy, if not a right to privacy as such. However, some steps have been taken by the courts to protect privacy, often involving the commercial interests or reputation of public figures. Naomi Campbell successfully brought a case for damages against the press for revealing her attendance at a confidential group therapy session run by Narcotics Anonymous (*Campbell v MGN Ltd* [2002]). It has been noted that, although the award was later set aside on appeal, the principle of compensation being payable for emotional distress remained intact (Pattenden, 2003: 283).

Pattenden has distinguished between *privacy*, which is about holding information within a relationship, either by oneself or with another person, as part of a dyad, and *confidentiality*, which concerns the disclosure of personal information to a third person, as part of a triad (2003: 6). Privacy has a number of differing dimensions from a legal perspective, many of which have uncertain degrees of protection under current law. These are explored in Box 5.5.

Box 5.5 Dimensions of personal privacy

Personal/individual:

- *attentional*, i.e. freedom from receiving intrusive junk mail, phone calls or computer spam;
- *spatial*, i.e. freedom from unwanted observation or photography;
- *anonymity*, i.e. right not to be identified or to have to show identity documents;
- *physical or bodily*, i.e. prohibition on unauthorised drugs testing, fingerprinting or body searches;
- *surveillance*, i.e. control over unwanted access by others, such as members of the public, media representatives.

Relational/interpersonal:

- *relationship*, i.e. freedom from being required to identify associates, friendships or work colleagues;
- *decisional*, i.e. respect for independence and a right to a chosen lifestyle;
- *intimacy*, i.e. right to exercise freedom of choice in relationships with others.

Control over personal data and image:

- *informational*, i.e. control over processing and disclosure of personal and genetic data;
- *proprietary*, i.e. restrictions on commercial use of identity or image by others.

Source: adapted from Pattenden, 2003: 11

Many of these aspects of privacy could apply to therapists and their clients, ranging from intrusive searches of therapists working in custodial settings such as prisons, to unwanted attention by the media with regard to therapeutic work, as in the *Campbell* case. 'In professional–client relationships the issue of confidentiality arises when some personal information has been disclosed and some privacy has, in consequence, been surrendered' (Pattenden, 2003: 12).

Confidentiality required by contract

For therapists, maintaining confidentiality may be a contractual obligation of employment, for example, while carrying out child protection duties or working in a general practice, as well as being a professional obligation. In consequence, a therapist removing files from the office to work at home without first obtaining proper authorisation could well face disciplinary measures from his or her employing agency.

Confidentiality can also be reinforced by being specifically written into a private contract between client and therapist, although the nature of the relationship will itself provide an expectation that confidentiality will be maintained (see Box 5.6).

Contracts can be used to maintain the secrecy of specific training or therapeutic techniques, which are not to be passed on to others. The agency or trainer could protect its investment in the technique by suing for breach of contract, subject to the necessary conditions for this action being met (see Chapter 2).

Box 5.6 Confidentiality and contract

- Confidentiality is a legitimate expectation, whether specifically written into a contract or not, where a relationship of trust arises.
- Contracts can be used to protect trade secrets.
- Therapists working for employers may be required by their employment contract to break confidentiality with employees in order to report malpractice.
- Therapists working in multi-disciplinary or statutory settings should clarify agency limits to confidentiality.
- Confidentiality must be maintained in research and publication.
- Breach of confidence can be met by an injunction and action for damages by the client.

Maintaining confidentiality in research and publication

Research and publication are seen as a necessary part of the development of therapy as a professional activity. Care is needed to avoid inadvertent breaches of confidentiality, which could lead to legal action being taken against the author.

Case study Client identity and case study publication

One case was related by a woman, who had paid £105 for a joint 50-minute session with her mother, with a nationally known therapist who wrote regularly for the quality press.

> *'Then one Saturday morning five weeks later a friend rang me to say I was in a column written by the therapist we had been to see. As I read I realised what I was reading was the session my mother and I had had with him, exactly as it had happened. He hadn't used names but he had put in the type of people we were, our ages, our relationship, so we easily recognised ourselves. In the article, he said 'While the daughter was speaking, the mother was behaving like a manipulative, demanding child.' He described things precisely as they had taken place.*
>
> *When my mother saw the article, she was terribly humiliated and upset. She kept saying 'He didn't like me.' She feels completely destroyed by it, and of course would never go near a therapist again. So this eminent, highly-paid man has not only undone any good he did but has ensured that I will never get my mother to see someone with me again. We are worse off than before we went.'*

Source: Independent on Sunday, 19 April 1992

The client contacted the therapist to make a complaint by phone, but obtained little satisfaction other than to express her anger at what had happened. She could have decided to pursue the matter, either by making a formal complaint to the therapist's professional association, if known, or by taking legal action for breach of confidence. As in the case of Doctors *X v Y* above, a first step could have been to obtain an interlocutory injunction, that is an injunction granted by the court in advance of the trial as a freezing measure. Often, this is not practicable, because the offending article or book may already have been published. In this case, the plaintiff could have brought a legal action for damages, such as an injunction to restrain further breaches, and a case for damages to compensate the plaintiff for any harm caused by the defendant's acts. Therapists writing about their practice should obtain a prior release for publication from clients, and omit any identifying references to them. These steps will go a long way to protecting writers from falling into any legal difficulty.

Conversely, it could be that a client may challenge the tradition of therapists writing about their clinical experience by revealing the practices of an identifiable therapist, without permission. This has occurred with the use of concealed video cameras to film therapists, with the camera operator posing as a client, perhaps anticipating therapist malpractice or an over-hasty diagnosis of childhood sexual abuse. If the material was defamatory and damaging, presumably the therapist could seek to restrain publication, or claim damages for libel, though the adverse publicity so engendered might ultimately prove to be more costly than the client's original breach of confidentiality. Litigation does not come cheap; an alternative might be to make a complaint to the Office of Communications (Ofcom) or to the relevant broadcasting authority (see Resources section for details).

Breaking confidentiality

While the law generally seeks to uphold client–therapist confidentiality, there are circumstances recognised or required by law where a therapist may seek, or be obliged, to break confidentiality. Again, it is repeated that it is expected that therapists will usually first try to discuss this with the client concerned, rather than simply act on their own initiative, unless there are particularly urgent factors to consider. Therapists may be required to break confidentiality either via contract, or by statute. They may seek to break confidence in the wider public interest, as in the case of preventing or reporting serious crime. These situations are described in more detail below.

Legitimate breaches of confidentiality via contract of employment

Apart from unintended breaches of confidentiality, there may be situations where a therapist is required to break confidentiality as part of their contractual obligation, for example to their employer. Counsellors working for an employer such as the nuclear power industry or the police, amongst others, may be expected on occasion to reveal certain confidential information to the employer. An example would be where a client was seriously harming the employer's interests through fraud or incompetence, or by presenting a risk to themselves or to the public. The counsellor's contract of employment could specify that such information must be passed on to the employer.

However, somewhat confusingly, this contractual obligation may not be a defence against action by the employee against the therapist for breach of confidence, unless the client has been specifically warned beforehand about the limitations to confidentiality. This is a 'double bind' situation, where the therapist is caught between the professional and ethical duty to respect the client's confidences, and the contractual duty to reveal sensitive information to the employer (Bond, 2000: 157; Law Commission, 1981: para. 4.56). The best protection here is for the therapist to obtain prior permission from the client to pass on any specific information required by an employer. This does not, unfortunately, remove the double bind where such permission is refused. Any therapist facing this sort of situation should get expert legal advice from their indemnity insurance company or professional association.

The dilemma is not a new one. The medical press at the turn of the century debated the ethics of maintaining or breaking confidentiality in the case of 'the asthmatic signalman'. This was a situation where a doctor treated a railway signalman suffering from asthma, who was prone to falling to the floor, incapable of moving for up to an hour and often being completely alone in the signal box. The signalman was refusing to tell his employers, or to allow the doctor to do so, for fear of dismissal or transfer to lower-paid job (BMA, 1906: 1753). The animated discussion this raised in the letters column does not indicate any outcome, but the principles outlined above suggest a public interest defence would justify disclosure here. As always, there is a risk for the person who breaks confidentiality, with no absolute guarantees as to how their action will be perceived by the courts.

Clearly, the greater the risk to the public, the stronger is the public interest case for disclosing the perceived source of the danger. Therapists facing this difficult dilemma should first seek to discuss the issue with their client, and try to explore avenues such as the client raising the problem him or herself with the relevant authority. If the client is in denial that there is a problem, as perhaps with an alcoholic airline pilot, then the therapist needs to weigh carefully the ethical commitment to the client against the wider duty to society and to potential victims. Careful recording, use of supervision and consultation are recommended precautions.

Confidentiality in multi-disciplinary settings

Therapists working in multi-disciplinary settings, such as primary health care or social services, need to be clear about their agency's expectations regarding the agreed limits and exclusions to client confidentiality. Statutory agencies work on the basis of team confidentiality, meaning that client information may be shared within the clinical or therapeutic team where necessary (Cordess, 2001). This may conflict with the more narrowly client-centred approach to confidentiality of some therapists. Differing perceptions about the status of confidential client material, including records, need to be identified and resolved at an early stage, rather than experienced in the midst of a crisis. Statutory agencies will usually expect team members, including therapists, to pass on information concerning potential suicide by a client, credible threats of harm to a third party or suspected child abuse. It may also be expected that the therapist can recognise and report signs of a client's deteriorating mental health, with a view to facilitating an appropriate response by psychiatric or medical services. While expectations and practice vary according to the nature of the setting and the therapist's actual role, limits to confidentiality need to be clearly communicated and agreed upon by all parties concerned (SDHA/DCC, 1996).

Mandatory reporting requirements

Mandatory reporting requiring a breach of client confidentiality are rare, but one example is the requirement for information on terrorist offences to be passed on to the police. The Terrorism Act 2000, as amended by the Terrorism, Crime and Security Act 2001, places an obligation on the therapist, as a citizen, to pass on information about planned or actual terrorist offences. Failure to do so is a criminal offence under s. 19 of the Act, punishable upon conviction with a prison sentence of up to 14 years. It is a further offence for the therapist to inform the client or any other person that information has been passed to the authorities, where such a disclosure is likely to prejudice any investigation.

Terrorism is defined in broad terms as the use or threat of action designed to influence the government, or to intimidate the public, 'for the purpose of advancing a political, religious or ideological cause'. Action includes serious violence against a person, serious damage to property, a danger to life, a serious risk to the health or safety of the public, or to electronic systems. Terrorism is defined in international terms, rather than referring to activities solely within the UK. Therapists facing the need to report terrorist activity should contact the Anti-Terrorist Branch of Scotland Yard on 0800–789321.

While the Act may be a necessary protection against terrorist incidents, it has been heavily criticised by civil liberties groups. In practice, the Act has been used by the police to stop and search protesters at an international arms fair in Docklands, and to prevent peaceful protest at an RAF station against the Iraq war.

Other forms of mandatory reporting relate to drug money laundering and the proceeds of crime. Under s. 52, Drug Trafficking Act 1994, it is an offence not to disclose information about drug money laundering received in the course of a trade, profession, business or employment. As with mandatory reporting of terrorism, it is an offence, under s. 53 of the Act, to inform the client that the authorities have been notified. The Act is specifically targeted at professionals working in the regulated financial sector, such as accountants and auditors, as with the similar Proceeds of Crime Act 2002. It is much less likely to impact on the work of therapists. It does not require therapists, for example, to report clients who use or sell illegal drugs, as opposed to those clients who are involved in money laundering as such.

The Drug Trafficking Act 1994 was used in 2002 to convict and imprison a solicitor, for failing to report knowledge or suspicion of money laundering (Dabbs, 2002: 1541).

Child protection

The most widely understood cause for breaking confidentiality is where child abuse is suspected. For many therapists working in a statutory setting, this will be a requirement of their employment, as well as a professional expectation. One example is in the case reported in the Court of Appeal (Criminal Division) in 1993, where a psychotherapist was counselling a woman for the results of the sexual abuse she had experienced as a child. During the year's therapy, the woman told the therapist that there might be another younger child in the family who was still being abused by the same abuser, the grandfather. The therapist informed the police, who interviewed the client and the other grandchildren. The man, then aged 79, was tried and sentenced to eight years' imprisonment (*R v C*, 14 January 1993).

The physical and emotional vulnerability of children provides a strong moral argument for breaking confidentiality, which has clear legal backing. The therapeutic needs of clients for disclosure and exploration of their activities may be seen as secondary to the wider need to protect the interests of the public, or more specifically, the interests of children or young people who may continue to be at risk of abuse. A client revealing violent paedophile fantasies in a therapeutic group setting could not, therefore, rely on a contract of confidentiality preventing the facilitators from passing this information on to the relevant authorities.

However, in some instances, breaking confidentiality in cases of child abuse may actually override the wishes and feelings of the child concerned. Under the *Gillick* ruling, doctors have the right to provide confidential advice and treatment for young people under the age of 16 with 'sufficient understanding' (see Chapter 7). In some cases, it may be that the young person him or herself does not wish confidentiality to be broken. Overriding the child's wishes, and informing the authorities, may not always be in the child's best long-term interests, particularly if the investigation into the suspected abuse is inconclusive. For some children and young people, the effect of a mishandled child protection investigation may be quite traumatic in itself. Alternatively, timely and effective social work intervention may release the child from continuing abuse or exploitation.

In practical terms, suspected child abuse can be reported, anonymously if necessary, during office hours to the Local Authority Social Services Department. Outside office hours, it can be reported to the former's Emergency Duty Team, or to the nearest branch of the National Society for the Prevention of Cruelty to Children (see Box 5.7). The police also have powers under s. 17 of the Police and Criminal Evidence Act 1984 to remove and protect children at risk in a case of real emergency. Action on child abuse can be taken for young people upto the age of 18, although policies may vary on the kind of response made in this regard by different local authorities regarding older teenagers.

Box 5.7   Reporting suspected child abuse

- During office hours: contact nearest social services department Child Protection Team for your area.
- In case of an emergency occurring out of hours: contact

  - Social Services Emergency Duty Team, or
  - National Society for Prevention of Cruelty to Children (0808–8005000), or
  - the police.

- The police have powers to remove and protect children at risk in emergency, under s. 17, Police and Criminal Evidence Act 1984.
- Child abuse can be reported in the case of children and young people under 18.
- Child's wishes should be considered, but may be overridden if necessary to avoid 'significant harm' occurring to him or her.

Working with suspected child abuse can present difficult issues for therapists. Many therapists assume that reporting child abuse is mandatory in the UK, as it is in the US (Stewart, 2004; Weir, 2004). However, mandatory reporting of child abuse was rejected as an option in an extensive review of child care law (DHSS, 1985: para. 12.4). The legal situation is that under s. 47 of the Children Act 1989, the Local Authority is required to investigate cases where it is suspected that a child in their area is suffering or is likely to suffer 'significant harm'. Certain agencies, such as the Local Education Authority, Housing and Health Authority are required to assist with inquiries, 'in particular by providing relevant information and advice'. However, apart from those specified or authorised by the Secretary of State, this part of the Act 'does not oblige any person to assist a local authority where doing so would be unreasonable in all the circumstances of the case'. Put more plainly, this means that a therapist has a choice in whether or not to report suspected child abuse, unless they are required to do so by their terms of their contract of employment, or by their own professional code of practice.

The Children Act 2004 and related statutory guidance (HMG, 2006) have not imposed a system of mandatory reporting of child abuse, although there has been a clear policy shift towards encouraging such reporting by all professionals who are in contact with children and young people (DoH, 2003). It may seem obvious that therapists should report any suspected child abuse to the authorities, so that the child can be protected and the alleged offence can be investigated. Therapists reporting such alleged abuse would clearly be working in accordance with the ethical principles of beneficence (welfare) and avoiding harm (non-maleficence). However, the situation may be more complex where the information about abuse is coded in therapeutic terms, ambiguous or unclear. Disclosure of abuse within therapy may be part of an unfolding process, rather than a single, discrete event. Disclosure may also be heavily folded within a developing relationship of trust between client and therapist, where retraction and denial of any abuse may quickly result, if the client is not fully prepared to follow through their allegations (Daniels and Jenkins, 2000).

In working with young people, the client may specifically ask that their a legations *not* be reported, perhaps on the mistaken assumption that they will automatically be taken into care or the family unit will be broken up. In such a situation, the therapist needs to balance the client's right to autonomy, and the need to protect the relationship of trust or fidelity, against the risk of harm to the client, or others, such as younger siblings. Employers have sometimes sought to take a broad-brush policy approach to reporting suspected child abuse, by adopting a 'blanket' reporting stance on child abuse. This does not recognise the complexities of the therapist's role, and the likely adverse impact on the reputation of counselling services which are known by young people to have automatic reporting policies.

In one case, Colleges of Further Education sought to impose a time limit of two hours for reporting alleged abuse to the authorities. The British Association of Counselling (as it was at the time) obtained independent legal opinion to clarify the legal basis for counsellors seeking to protect client confidentiality (Friel, 1998). This clarified that counsellors have a 'fiduciary duty' of trust and confidentiality towards their clients. It also stated that Colleges did not have the legal authority to require reporting of child abuse, in the absence of a clear statutory duty to do so, referring to relevant medical case law in support (*Duncan v Medical Practitioners Disciplinary Committee* [1986]). While counsellors working in Colleges might be required under the terms of their contract of employment to follow such a reporting policy, this was not a formal requirement based on statute. Counsellors deciding not to report abuse on the ethical principles of respecting autonomy and fidelity would, nevertheless, be at risk of being disciplined by their employer for breach of contract of employment. Therapists need to be well informed of agency policies and the law regarding the reporting of child abuse, but also to have a clear sense of the ethical principles involved in complex decision-making on this issue.

'Whistleblowing' in the public interest

Therapists may come across information pointing to malpractice, abuse or exploitation in the course of their work. In the past, legal protection for those wanting to 'whistleblow' on bad practice was limited to the uncertain merits of using 'qualified privilege' to pass information on to the appropriate authorities. Under the Public Interest Disclosure Act 1998, therapists who are employed have legal protection under the Employment Rights Act 1996, if making a 'protected disclosure' to an appropriate person in their organisation.

The disclosure needs to be about a criminal offence, or miscarriage of justice, risk to health or safety, damage to the environment, or a concealment of any of the above. It needs to be made in good faith and to be based on a reasonable belief that it constitutes a protected disclosure under the Act. Disclosures that are made directly to the media, or for personal gain, are not protected under the Act.

Therapists have an ethical responsibility to report malpractice or abuse by their colleagues. Under s. 39 of the BACP *Ethical Framework*, 'practitioners have a responsibility to protect clients when they have good reason for believing that other practitioners are placing them at risk of harm' (2002: 8). In the past, employed therapists in this position have had limited protection under the law.

Reporting malpractice

There are a number of situations in which employed therapists may learn about malpractice or abuse in the course of their work, where

- a client discloses information about malpractice or abuse *by others* within the organisation;
- *a client* presents a high degree of risk to self or others;
- the therapist obtains information about malpractice or abuse about another *therapist*.

In the first situation, it may be that a client discloses information indicating abusive practice on the part of others working in the organisation. For example, Julia Wassell, a Director of Women's Services at a special hospital, became concerned about rape and sexual assault of female patients by male patients, based on the results of a survey carried out on this issue. She was dissatisfied at the hospital's response and took action for constructive dismissal, receiving an out of court settlement without an admission of liability from her employer.

In other situations, it may be that a client discloses information which suggests a high risk of harm to others, particularly vulnerable members of the public. In one case, Beverley Allitt, a nurse, caused the death of several young children in her care on a high dependency unit. The subsequent Clothier Inquiry expressed concern about her apparently 'excessive use of counselling' as a potential warning sign (1994: 84). Therapists working in a staff counselling capacity would be able to pass on information to an appropriate person, where there was a concern that patients or members of the public were at risk from a client.

Therapists may also be well placed to identify abusive practice, particularly where the latter is masked by reference to established theories or therapeutic approaches. In the case of the Beck regime at children's homes in Leicestershire, the sexual abuse and ritual humiliation of children in care was portrayed as a therapeutic approach based on regression therapy. Dr Chris Taylor, a psychiatrist, was brought in to provide group supervision to the mainly junior and untrained staff who operated the regime, and was able to recognise and report the abusive nature of the practice going on (D'Arcy and Gosling, 1998: 110–14).

The Public Interest Disclosure Act 1998 provides a degree of protection to employed therapists who make a protected disclosure concerning malpractice in the appropriate manner. Clearly, clients of staff counselling services need to be informed that this form of disclosure is permitted, or even required, by the organisation. Whether this will lead to an increase in such disclosures on the part of clients, or a significant reduction is, perhaps, an open question. Pattenden, for one, is sceptical about the practical value of the Act in supporting those staff wishing to make a disclosure under the Act. 'Such is the convoluted nature of the Public

Interest Disclosure Act that the employed professional may want to take legal advice before making a disclosure' (2003: 731).

Duty to warn third parties: the *Tarasoff* case in the USA

The *Tarasoff* case is widely recognised and is frequently used on training courses to illustrate the issue of the therapist's apparent 'duty to warn'. It is perhaps not always fully appreciated that its legal significance for therapists does not, as yet, extend to the UK.

Case study   Therapists' duty to warn: the *Tarasoff* case

Prosenjit Poddar was an Indian national studying at the University of California in 1969. While he was receiving therapy from Dr Moore, he made threats against an unnamed girl, who was identifiable as Tatiana Tarasoff. Dr Moore then took steps to have Poddar placed under observation in a psychiatric hospital, and notified the Berkeley campus police. Poddar gave an undertaking to the police that he would stay away from Tarasoff, and he was released. He later went to her flat and killed her. Dr Moore's superior, Dr Powelson, asked the police to return Dr Moore's letter, ordered the destruction of all records and correspondence on the therapy, and finally ordered 'no action' on the decision to place Poddar under psychiatric observation.

Tatiana Tarasoff's parents brought a case against Dr Moore, the campus police and the University of California. The case was lost, but subsequently won on appeal, on the basis that the therapist had a duty of care, in this case to warn the intended victim of any threats, where there was a foreseeable danger. According to the court: 'public policy favouring protection of the confidential character of the patient–psychotherapist relationship must yield in instances in which disclosure is essential to avert danger to others; the protective privilege ends where the public peril begins.'

Source: Tarasoff v Board of Regents of the University of California (1976)

The *Tarasoff* case has had an appreciable impact in the USA on extending the legal liability of therapists for clients' actions. In California, a law was later passed requiring a therapist to break confidentiality and warn another person where there was 'a serious threat of physical violence against a reasonably identifiable victim or victims' (Kermani, 1989: 34). In the ensuing period, a further 14 states enacted legislation on similar lines (Meyer et al., 1988: 47). The *Tarasoff* ruling is capable of different interpretations regarding the therapist's precise duties. Austin et al. distinguish between laws based on the '*Tarasoff* 1 rule', which dictates that it is the therapist's duty to warn the intended victim, and the '*Tarasoff* 2 rule', whereby the therapist is responsible for assessing foreseeable harm, and for exercising a duty to protect foreseeable victims (Austin et al., 1990: 120). The latter places a much wider responsibility on therapists where the danger presented may be to persons as yet unknown. Assessing 'dangerousness' is in itself a complex and imprecise task, which many therapists would feel lies outside their professional remit.

One view on the *Tarasoff* case, however, suggests that US therapists' anxiety about their apparently increased liability is unnecessary. The legislation following *Tarasoff* applies unevenly within a limited number of US states, rather than deriving from a federal requirement, such as the requirement to report suspected child abuse under the US Child Abuse Prevention and Treatment Act 1974. Confusion about the exact import of the *Tarasoff* ruling perhaps derives from the fact that the case was, unusually, taken to court twice, being re-heard in 1976. Whereas the first ruling in 1974 required warning the client's potential victim(s), the second ruling in 1976 actually sets a lesser standard, of the therapist simply exercising 'reasonable care to protect the intended victim against danger'. This could include consulting a supervisor and informing the relevant authorities, rather than necessarily contacting the intended victim. As with any negligence case, the appropriate standard of care would depend crucially upon what was judged to be normal and acceptable practice for a substantial proportion of the professional group in question (see Chapter 3). The main effect of *Tarasoff* is perhaps seen in the doubling of the number of cases where psychiatrists have contacted the police with regard to clients making threats (Mangalmurti, 1994: 391). Otherwise, the effect of *Tarasoff* has not substantially increased therapists' liability in real terms, as measured by successful court cases won against therapists on this issue. 'Twenty years after *Tarasoff*, plaintiffs win few court battles against psychotherapists. Therapists themselves pay little heed to *Tarasoff*, and the practice of psychotherapy thrives' (Mangalmurti, 1994: 404–5).

Developments in the USA since *Tarasoff*

The pattern of findings in US courts regarding the therapist's duty to warn varies significantly from state to state. Another important case, which extended this duty, was that of *Peck v Counseling Service of Addison County* (1985). Here, the plaintiff's son was in therapy, where he claimed that he wanted to burn down his father's barn to get back at him. The therapist extracted a promise from him not to do so, but did not warn the boy's parents of the threat, which was later carried out. The boy's parents then successfully sued the counselling service for negligence, in failing to warn them of the intended threat. This case extended the *Tarasoff* principles to include threats to property, as well as to persons; to all mental health professionals; and underlined the principle of vicarious liability, that organisations bore liability for the actions of their employees (Kermani, 1989: 45). The agency was judged to be at fault in not having established consultation procedures for responding to clients posing a serious threat to life or property.

The outcome of all this for therapists in the USA is that systems for their liability vary from state to state. The *Tarasoff* ruling appears to be about the justification for breaching a professional duty of confidentiality, but this overlooks the fact that the therapist, Dr Moore, had *already* broken confidentiality by approaching the campus police about the threats posed by his client. As Thompson puts it, 'more closely read, the issue is more that of *failure to follow through an already executed breach of confidentiality*, than that of making the breach in the first place' (Thompson, 1983: 84, emphasis added).

Therapists in the UK: a duty to warn?

For therapists in the UK, the implications of *Tarasoff* and subsequent cases indicate one possible line of development, but a hypothetical one. The price that therapists in the USA have had to pay for a limited form of statutory recognition has been a much more extensive form of regulation and liability to litigation. Therapists in the UK are left with the skeleton framework of legal principles outlined above; therapeutic confidentiality is partially recognised, but not protected by the law. Breaking confidentiality in the public interest would be an acceptable defence, provided that the court accepted the definition of the public interest and that it was done in good faith (see Box 5.8). The lack of extensive therapeutic case law in the UK compared with the USA leaves us with the example of the *Egdell* case (*W v Egdell* [1990]) (see p. 108). Here, the public interest supported the doctor's actions in breaking confidentiality with his patient.

Box 5.8   A duty to warn?

- Therapists in the UK are not under a specific obligation to warn third parties as may apply under the *Tarasoff* principle in the USA.
- Therapists warning third parties of a client's AIDS/HIV status would be breaking client confidentiality.
- Therapists may break confidentiality to report or seek help for an attempted suicide.
- It is illegal to assist another person to commit suicide.

Discussion of a therapist's apparent 'duty to warn' reveals that some schools of therapy have major problems with this approach. The need for absolute confidentiality is stressed particularly by psychoanalytic approaches to therapy, which rest on the 'freedom to free associate' (Bollas and Sundelson, 1995: 59). These authors describe the example of a client who regularly fantasised stalking and attacking female victims, but who, apparently, successfully worked through and resolved these violent fantasies by means of intensive psychotherapy. Other therapists might instead have judged the danger posed to these women sufficiently great to take steps to warn either them or the authorities of the threat posed by the client.

Some key aspects of the therapist's responsibilities for risk assessment were considered in the inquiry into the case of Anthony Smith, a psychiatric patient receiving counselling from a therapist working in a primary care setting.

Case study   Managing risk of harm to self and others: the case of Anthony Smith

The report into the care of Anthony Smith was produced by a committee set up in 1996. This was an independent inquiry by Southern Derbyshire Health Authority and Derbyshire County Council, the bodies jointly responsible for his care. It took as its terms of reference a review of the effectiveness of overall arrangements for his care, including primary care, counselling, hospital admission and aftercare in the community.

Issues of client confidentiality were central to the care of Anthony Smith, a psychiatric patient and counselling client. He received counselling from a practice-based counsellor, on a weekly basis, for just over a year. After a year, psychotic symptoms (auditory hallucinations and paranoid features, including weapon-carrying) were detected by the GP, who then referred her patient for psychiatric assessment by a consultant psychiatrist. His mental health deteriorated, and he was admitted to a psychiatric hospital. On his discharge, family relationships continued to worsen. He killed his mother and half-brother four weeks after his discharge.

Source: Jenkins, 1999; SDHA/DCC, 1996

While the inquiry lacked statutory authority, it represented an early attempt to try and grapple with the limits of therapist responsibility for accurate risk assessment and liaison with other professionals when working with vulnerable clients in a multi-disciplinary context. A number of key issues emerge from the report (SDHA/DCC, 1996). These concern the position and role of counsellors working within a system of delegated care, the accurate assessment and management of risk, indicators for breaking client confidentiality, and the role of counselling supervision. The counselling provided by the practice was, presumably, intended to encourage the client's autonomy. Certainly, the report suggests that Anthony Smith found the counselling useful, although the precise objectives or goals of the counselling were not specified to the inquiry. Information on the client was apparently not passed back to the GP, for review or reassessment purposes. The counsellor referred to his professional code of practice to explain his choice not to refer back to the GP information about the client other than 'the most serious matters'.

Therapists working with such clients, who may present a risk to self or to members of the public, need to have a working knowledge of procedures and policy regarding liaison with and referral to psychiatric services. These are governed by the provisions of the Mental Health Act 1983, which is currently subject to major review (see Box 5.9)

> **Box 5.9   Main emergency provisions of the Mental Health Act 1983**
>
> s. 2   *Admission for assessment*: where a patient is seen to be in need of protection from causing harm to self or to others, and they require detaining on the grounds of mental disorder, they can be admitted for 28 days on a compulsory basis. The 'section', as it is called, or being 'sectioned', needs to be authorised by two doctors, such as a consultant psychiatrist and the GP.
>
> s. 3   *Admission for treatment*: authorised on a similar basis to the above, this initially lasts six months, and is extendable for a further six months. It is thereafter renewable on an annual basis, subject to review by the Mental Health Review Tribunal.
>
> s. 4   *Emergency admission for assessment*: this to be used only where it is not possible to obtain a section 2 admission. Authorised usually by the patient's GP, the section can be applied for by the patient's 'nearest relative' (closely defined by the Act), or by an Approved Social Worker from the Local Authority Social Services Department.

A key aspect of establishing a duty to warn would involve extending a professional's legal duty of care to cover third parties, beyond their duty to their immediate client or patient. US law has traditionally been more receptive to widening the therapist's duty of care in this way (see Chapter 4). With the increasing prominence and heightened media interest in mental health inquiries, there has been concern that the courts are now much more likely to impose such a duty to warn third parties on mental health professionals, on the lines of the *Tarasoff* case (Turner and Kennedy, 1997). In one case, following a child's murder by a recently released sex offender, the child's mother sued the Health Authority for breach of duty to care, in failing to warn of the substantial risk posed to children. However, the court found that the Health Authority did not owe a duty of care or a duty to warn of the risk involved (*Palmer v Tees Health Authority* [1998]). A duty to warn a third party would require establishing three conditions, namely that:

- the risk was foreseeable
- the risk was to an identifiable individual
- there was sufficient proximity, or a close and direct relationship, between the defendant and the third party, to warrant a duty of care

While it remains a theoretical possibility for the courts to impose a duty to warn by extending current negligence law along these lines, it seems unlikely to happen in the short term.

AIDS and HIV

One situation where a therapist may be faced with the potential need for breaking confidentiality might be where a client is HIV positive, or has the AIDS virus, and is apparently placing a sexual partner at risk of infection. There have been a number of convictions of persons knowingly passing on the HIV virus by having unprotected sex. The current law in the UK would probably not support a therapist who broke confidentiality to warn a third party of the risk they faced from a sexual partner with HIV or AIDS. However, the situation is different with doctors, as GMC guidelines permit them to breach confidentiality in the case of a patient's partner who is at risk:

> you may disclose information to a known sexual contact of a patient with HIV where you have reason to think that the patient has not informed that person, and cannot be persuaded to do so. In such circumstances you should tell the patient before you make the disclosure, and you must be prepared to justify a decision to disclose information. (GMC, 1997: 9)

Suicidal clients

Under the Suicide Act 1961, suicide ceased to be a crime. However, under s. 2(1) of the Act, 'a person who aids, abets, counsels or procures the suicide of another, or an attempt by another to commit suicide, shall be liable on conviction on indictment to imprisonment for a term not exceeding fourteen years'. Views about suicide as a conscious act vary amongst therapists; one therapist may decide to break confidentiality to warn a third party, for example a GP or psychiatrist, about a client who is seriously depressed and contemplating suicide. Another therapist, perhaps working from a person-centred perspective, might see this more in terms of the client's right to choose to terminate their life according to principles which it is not up to the therapist to deny or seek to change. Diane Pretty, who had progressive motor neurone disease, brought a case in order to protect her husband from criminal prosecution in the event of him assisting her to commit suicide. However, this opportunity to reform the law on assisted suicide was decisively rejected by the courts (*Pretty v DPP* [2001]), as being against the public interest. This case provides a sharp and instructive contrast with that of *Ms B* [2002], discussed in Chapter 1, where the judge's rationale was based on very different grounds, namely empathic respect for patient autonomy.

Where the therapist has a relationship which is perceived by others to be influential, then in the aftermath of a successful suicide the therapist may be called as a witness in the Coroner's Court. The attitude of the deceased person's relatives and of their legal representatives may not be sympathetic to the counsellor's professional stance. Short of actually assisting the client to commit suicide, perhaps via euthanasia for a terminally ill client, the therapist is not liable for failing to prevent its occurrence, or for failing to warn third parties of the client's intentions. However, to break confidentiality in order to prevent or reduce the risk of suicide would not necessarily put the therapist in jeopardy.

From the perspective of the law, suicide needs to be based on evidence of *intention* on the part of the deceased. This is described as 'the essential legal ingredient' for suicide, which would, for example, be explored at a Coroner's Court (*Halsbury's Laws of England*, 1974: 680). For the therapist, part of the professional problem in responding to this issue is trying to distinguish between clients where the risk is of repeated suicide *attempts*, and cases where a client's clear intention is to kill him or herself.

A therapist known to be closely involved in working with a client who succeeds in a suicide attempt may well be called as witness to the Coroner's Court (see Chapter 3). Complaints and legal action by family and relatives against psychiatrists after a successful suicide may also follow on. For the therapist, action intended to reduce the client's potential risk of suicide might include:

– explicitly acknowledging and exploring any suicidal ideas;
– carrying out a thorough risk assessment using established protocols;
– giving information on out-of-hours help, such as the Samaritans (0845–909090);
– referral to the client's GP, psychiatric outreach team, or local community mental health team for medication or possible admission to psychiatric hospital.

The previous discussion has indicated some of the main areas where a therapist may consider breaching client confidentiality. The guidelines in Box 5.10 are not all-embracing, but may provide a starting point for therapists to consider their practice in order to take account of the law, and minimise the risk of complaint or possible future legal action. Key aspects of confidentiality are summarised in Box 5.11.

Box 5.10 Guidelines for professional practice regarding confidentiality

- Carry out an audit of confidentiality within your own practice, and that of your agency, if appropriate.
- Identify strengths and weaknesses.
- Devise an action plan for changes to be made.
- Write and update a policy statement on confidentiality, taking account of case law, and statute, such as the Children Act 1989.
- Discuss this statement with all interested parties:

  – employing agency, or managing committee of voluntary agency
  – counsellors and therapists
  – administrative and reception staff.

- Provide clients with information on your policy on confidentiality:

  – a brief verbal explanation at first interview
  – a leaflet summarising main aspects of your approach
  – access to more detailed policy statement for inspection or photocopy if required.

- Negotiate provision within your policy statement for legitimate professional limitations on confidentiality:

  – consultation and supervision
  – requirements for outline information on client user population by employing or funding agency
  – research and publication.

- Discuss scenarios and develop clear staff understanding on best responses to public interest conflicts with therapeutic confidentiality:

  – criminal activity by clients
  – HIV/AIDS risk to third party
  – threat of harm to third party
  – terrorism
  – child abuse
  – suicidal clients.

Public interest defence for breaking confidentiality

One final note of caution needs to be sounded with regard to therapists seeking to use a public interest defence for breaking confidentiality with a client, for example to report a credible threat to a third party. It is crucial that any intended breaches of confidentiality must be carried out in a thoroughly professional manner, otherwise the public interest defence is invalidated (Bond, 2000: 158–9). Thus the therapist should:

- act in accordance with relevant codes of practice and agency guidelines, including any requirements to seek professional consultation or supervision on the issue;
- restrict disclosure to matters which are directly relevant to the reasons claimed for the disclosure (for instance, a client's intended threat of harm may be relevant to disclose; their sexual orientation may not be relevant);
- restrict disclosure to those persons best able to act in the public interest (for example, by informing the police, rather than the local press).

Again, it is assumed that, wherever possible, the therapist has sought to discuss the matter with the client concerned, in order to gain the client's consent for disclosure.

Box 5.11   Therapists and confidentiality

- Therapists do not possess privilege for client communications, except for some aspects of marital counselling.
- Therapists are required to maintain confidences obtained via their work, e.g. regarding a client's AIDS/HIV status.
- Breach of confidence can be met by

   - disciplinary action by an employer
   - legal action by clients for damages.

- Therapists *may* break confidence in the public interest

   - to report or prevent crime
   - to report malpractice
   - to report suspected child abuse
   - to prevent suicide
   - to report professional misconduct.

- Therapists *must* break confidence

   - to prevent terrorism.

- Therapists in the UK are not under an obligation to warn threatened third parties on the US *Tarasoff* model.

Summary

The emphasis in this chapter has necessarily been on restrictions to therapist–client confidentiality. Hopefully, for most therapists, the need to break confidentiality will be a rare occurrence, but, nevertheless, one for which they are adequately informed and prepared. Confidentiality provides a cornerstone for effective therapeutic practice, both as a pragmatic measure to build trust and rapport, and as an expression of ethical principles supporting the client's right to autonomy and self-determination. This right to confidence is understood and respected by the law, except where the wider public interest requires that it be limited for the benefit of society as a whole.

The therapist's duty of confidentiality arises from both statute and common law, particularly via a relationship of trust with the client. Confidentiality can be endorsed by a contract, whether in the form of a legal contract with the client, or a contract of employment. Therapists do not possess privilege, except in certain limited instances of marital counselling. Breach of confidentiality may be justified, if it is judged to be in the public interest by a court, for example in order to report, or prevent, serious crime. Legal obligations to break client confidentiality are rare, with the exception of reporting terrorism. Child abuse can pose particular dilemmas for therapists, where there may be a tension between respecting the client's autonomy and the need to avoid harm. Breaching client confidentiality to prevent risk to a third party or suicide may be possible in the public interest, but is not required as such by law.

Discussion points

1 Should therapists be afforded 'privilege' to protect the confidentiality of their sessions with clients? What advantages or disadvantages might this present for therapists?

2. How well are therapists prepared by their agency or by their previous training to understand the legal limits of confidentiality? How, in practical terms, might this be improved?

3 Should therapists in the UK have 'a duty to warn' on the US *Tarasoff* model? How can the rights of clients, therapists and vulnerable third parties best be balanced here?

4 When, if ever, have you broken confidentiality without the client's consent? In the light of the information presented in this chapter, would you now revise your past decision or practice in this respect?

5 How might client confidentiality in your own practice best be preserved in order to be consistent with the public interest? What practical steps could be taken to meet the complaint of a client who felt that their confidentiality had been broken without due cause?

Data Protection and Access to Client Records

Issues relating to data protection and access to records clearly impact on the central concept of therapeutic confidentiality, which is discussed in detail in the preceding chapter. With regard to confidentiality, the emphasis is on the therapist as 'custodian' of sensitive client information, as the 'active agent', in deciding whether or not to disclose information to a third party. The focus in this is chapter is on the client or external agencies as the 'active agents', in seeking to obtain access to personal information held by the therapist. Both the therapist disclosing information and the client or other party obtaining such access may infringe confidentiality, but the processes involved are often quite distinct. While this is not a distinction rooted in the law, it is suggested here as a way for therapists to be clear about the different processes and responses involved for them as practitioners.

This chapter considers the processes involved in external bodies obtaining access to records of therapy. Persons with a statutory right of access to personal records include clients, solicitors (in certain situations) and external agencies, such as the police and courts. The legal process of disclosure can involve the therapist in attending court, and being required to answer the court's questions in the witness box. The role of the therapist as witness in court is considered more fully in Chapter 3, but this chapter sets out the wider legal constraints on therapists subject to the processes of the law with regard to access and disclosure of the client's personal information.

Recording therapeutic work

Recording by therapists is influenced by ethical principles, as expressed in professional codes of ethics, and controlled by the law, particularly the Data Protection Act 1998. Access to records is governed by wider principles, namely the powers of the courts to order disclosure in the public interest of otherwise confidential material. The principle of confidentiality of client material is not a valid defence on its own against legal demands for disclosure on judicial grounds, or under statute.

Professional aspects of recording

Therapists are engaged in record-keeping for three sets of reasons: relating to service delivery, therapeutic practice and professional development. In terms of service delivery, record-keeping is useful for the purposes of management and administration, monitoring client progress and measuring outcomes via audit and evaluation. Within agencies, record-keeping maintains a history of client contact and can be used to promote continuity of care and referral to other sources of help if necessary. From a therapeutic perspective, record-keeping may be essential to orient the therapist towards the client's key issues and relationships, and can also play a role in identifying issues to take to supervision. From a professional development point of view, records can be used for personal reflection, or may be needed for accreditation purposes, and to contribute towards research and publication.

Ethical aspects of recording

From an ethical perspective, record-keeping tends to be framed in terms of professional responsibilities to maintain confidentiality and to demonstrate respect for the client (see Box 6.1).

Box 6.1 Professional Codes of Practice and Recording

'Good quality of care:

Practitioners are encouraged to keep appropriate records of their work with clients unless there are adequate reasons for not keeping any records. All records should be accurate, respectful of clients and colleagues and protected from unauthorised disclosure. Practitioners should take into account their responsibilities and their clients' rights under data protection legislation and any other legal requirements.'

(BACP, 2002: 6)

'Confidentiality:

Psychologists shall maintain adequate records, but they shall take all reasonable steps to preserve the confidentiality of information acquired through their professional practice or research and to protect the privacy of individuals or organisations about whom information is collected or held.'

(BPS, 2000: 4)

The British Psychological Society thus requires members to keep 'adequate records', while, conversely, the BACP permits members not to keep any records at all, if there are adequate reasons for doing so. The earlier BAC *Code of Ethics and Practice for Counsellors* required counsellors both to keep records of appointments, and to make clients aware of the nature of the records being kept (BAC, 1998).

Data protection

The ethical justification for record-keeping, as distinct from the professional rationale, has often been unclear. Based on a quasi-medical model, influenced by agency practice and personal preferences, it is likely that therapeutic record-keeping was, in the past, quite varied in its format and content and largely protected from client access. The Data Protection Act (DPA) 1998, derived from European Directive 95/46/EC, has attempted to develop a culture of openness and transparency with regard to personal records kept on citizens. It has had a profound impact on therapeutic recording, not least by challenging the widespread presumption held by therapists that record-keeping is a private, professional task, to be carried out beyond the scrutiny of clients, agency management or the wider society.

According to the Act, personal data is widely defined to cover almost every kind of information related to an identifiable living person, including information recorded electronically. The Act includes within its remit manual or handwritten records, as well as material held on computer, thus capturing for the first time the bulk of therapeutic records. The key principles governing the use of personal data are set out in Box 6.2.

Box 6.2   Principles of data processing: Data Protection Act 1998

Personal data is to be:

1   processed fairly and lawfully
2   obtained only for one or more specified lawful purposes
3   adequate, relevant and not excessive for the record's purpose
4   accurate and kept up to date
5   not kept longer than is necessary
6   processed in accordance with the rights of data subjects
7   protected against unauthorised use or loss
8   not transferred outside the European Economic Area unless subject to similar levels of data protection.

The Act makes a distinction between personal data, and categories of information, such as a person's mental, physical and sexual health, which are termed 'sensitive personal data' and accordingly require higher levels of security, such as the client's explicit consent for any processing.

Format of therapy records

The introduction of the Act has presented a number of difficult challenges to therapists, partly in subjecting to public scrutiny what had previously been assumed to be a largely private professional activity (Jenkins, 2002a). Another source of difficulty is that therapists tend to define record-keeping in terms of the *purpose* of the record. Thus a therapist may distinguish between objective, factual records, kept as part of an official agency record of client contact, and more personal, subjective records, known as process records, identifying the therapist's own personal feelings, counter-transference material, together with notes of issues to take to supervision for discussion with another colleague, either individually or in a group. Data protection law however, defines records on a completely different basis. Records are defined firstly in terms of *context*, so that records kept in health, education and social work settings have separate provisions, deriving from the reforms initiated by the *Gaskin* case (see p. 140). Records are further defined by

Box 6.3 Access to records under the Data Protection Act 1998

Nature of record	Provision for access by client (or solicitor as latter's legal representative) under ss. 7–8, DPA 1998
Accessible records, i.e. health, education and social work	Right of client access, except for risk of 'serious harm'
Computerised records, on their own, or together with:	Right of client access
• relevant filing systems	Right of client access
• unstructured data held by a public authority	Right of client access, under ss. 7–8, DPA, as amended by s. 69, Freedom of Information Act 2000
• unstructured data held by private practitioner or organisation	No right of client access
Manual or handwritten records as *sole* form of recording	No right of client access

Key:

 Data processing formats used by individual or organisation

Data processing formats providing right of client access

Data processing formats <u>without</u> right of client access *format*, rather than by purpose. Thus records are categorised as electronic or manual. Manual, or handwritten, records are further subdivided into those which are part of 'a relevant filing system' and those which are 'unstructured'. These distinctions are crucial for determining issues of client access (see Box 6.3).

Therapists are aware that the major impact of the DPA 1998 has been to facilitate client access. Under ss. 7–8 of the Act, the client, as 'data subject', has a legal right of access to his or her records, in permanent form, with an explanation where the meaning of the record is unclear. Access to material about third parties is to be withheld, in order not to breach their confidentiality. Clients can have inaccurate material corrected, and can seek compensation for damage and associated distress. In the case of health, education and social work records only, access to records can be partially or completely withheld to avoid serious harm to the client or to a third party, such as another family member. For therapy records more generally, it seems that the Act has been instrumental in changing practitioners' recording practice. It is increasingly based on the presumption of client access and has become more factual and less subjective in nature (Jenkins and Potter, 2007). It appears also to have reduced the practice of therapists keeping two sets of notes, one for the agency and one for private reflective purposes, or at least brought this practice into sharp relief.

The purpose of the Act was to develop more transparency in terms of citizen awareness and access to records being kept on them. It is also, however, a complex and rather badly drafted piece of legislation, which has tried, unsuccessfully, to stitch together 'special case' requirements for certain kinds of specialised welfare records, with the overall, far-reaching regulation of computerised and manual records of disparate kinds. The Act has been subject to a steady degree of 'creep' in its scope, gathering in more and more unstructured manual records, well beyond the remit envisaged in its original drafting in Parliament (IDS, 2000: 5). This gradual extension of the application of the Act has been reversed by the decision of the courts in the *Durant* case.

Case study   The *Durant* case

Mr Durant had been involved in a legal case against Barclays Bank, and sought to gain access, as the data subject, to a manual file on his case held by the Financial Services Authority. When this was refused, he took his case to court, but was denied access to this data by the judge. The judge defined 'personal data' as relating to an individual's private information, rather than being open to wider interpretation. In other words, an individual does not have a right of access to a file simply because, as in Mr Durant's case, the file has his name as an identifying label.

The judge set out a clear definition of a 'relevant filing system' for manual records, which returned the definition to its original limited scope. Manual files qualify as a constituting part of a relevant filing system only if they are of sufficient sophistication to provide similar accessibility to a computerised system. This was translated as the 'temp test', namely whether an untrained temporary administrative assistant, without particular knowledge of the kinds of documents or type of work involved, would be able to extract specific knowledge about a named individual. The effect of the Durant case, according to the Information Commissioner, was that very few manual files would be covered by the Data Protection Act 1998.

Source: Durant v FSA [2003]

While the *Durant* case effectively removed much manual recording from the provisions of the Act, the situation was then made more complicated by the introduction of s. 69 of the Freedom of Information Act 2000. This amended the Data Protection Act 1998 to provide for the right of data subject to have access to 'unstructured personal data' held by public authorities. These were defined as including Local Authorities, the NHS, maintained schools and other educational institutions, the police and a long list of public bodies, ranging from the Advisory Committee on NHS Drugs to the Zoo Forum. The effect was to add yet another complicating factor into what has become a patchwork quilt of differing provisions for data protection and client access.

Data protection sets the legal framework for record-keeping and the related provisions for client access. Data subject access, rather confusingly, has been limited, on the one hand, by the *Durant* case and then broadened again, on the other, by the Freedom of Information Act 2000. Some agencies not classed as a 'public authority', or practitioners in private practice, whose records are not held in relevant filing systems, may therefore be exempt from provisions for client access. However, from an ethical and professional perspective, denying client access on legal grounds alone might be seen to be contrary to the move within the profession towards adopting more open and accessible forms of recording, even where these are not formally required by the law.

Many therapists tend to confuse the route of access to client records provided by the DPA 1998 and that available to the courts as part of the legal process. These are, in fact, quite distinct, if slightly overlapping, routes of access to client records (see Box 6.4).

Box 6.4   Access to records

Access to records of therapy by:

- client: ss. 7–8, Data Protection Act 1998
- solicitor (as client's legal representative): ss. 7–8, Data Protection Act 1998
- police (via warrant): s.9, Police and Criminal Evidence Act 1984
- courts: Supreme Court Act 1981; Criminal Procedure and Investigations Act 1996

Client access to records

Clients may seek to gain access to their records for a number of reasons. Therapists have seen growing numbers of clients requesting access to their counselling records, often for use as evidence in civil, rather than criminal, cases (Jenkins, 2003a). Initially, this takes the form of a letter from the client's solicitor, with a signed 'blanket' consent form authorising disclosure of any counselling, health or medical records to the solicitor as the client's duly authorised legal representative (Bond and Sandhu, 2005). Of course, it is no longer automatically the case that the client has a right of data subject access, following the *Durant* case, in which case the request might be legitimately declined by the therapist, after taking sound legal advice.

Alternatively, some counsellors have expressed the view that the client may not be fully aware of the sensitive nature of the material held in their record and the ways in which this might be used to their disadvantage in legal proceedings. The client may have given their consent to disclosure, but this may not necessarily be fully informed consent. The client may not be aware, for example, that the material in their record is disclosed to both parties in any legal case, and that the therapeutic record may be irrelevant or even damaging to their case. Any reference to previous psychiatric illness, alcohol or drug dependency, or major inconsistencies in the therapist's narrative, will tend to discredit the client's credibility as a witness or plaintiff. However, while therapists may be acutely aware of the need for informed consent in their own practice, the law seemingly operates in a rather more blunt manner when it concerns client permission to disclose therapeutic records. According to Pattenden, 'there is no general principle in English law that consent has to be informed to be effective' (2003: 420).

Initial research suggests that therapists tended to find the process of 'contested disclosure' – i.e. where disclosure was mandated by the courts, or sought by the client, in spite of the therapist's misgivings – as being stressful in both personal and professional terms. However, in 'consensual disclosure', where the therapist was fully in support of the client's use of therapeutic records for a court case, the process was less likely to be personally and professionally challenging for the therapist. Consensual disclosure was more likely to occur, for example, in situations where the client was seeking to bring a criminal prosecution for alleged past abuse, and the legal process was seen to have a potential therapeutic and personal benefit for the client (Jenkins, 2003a).

Records as evidence

The process of seeking disclosure of client records for use in civil or criminal cases raises many questions about the nature of therapeutic recording, and its value as evidence in a court of law. Unlike records kept under statute by other professions, such as medicine, nursing and social work, therapists do not generally record in a defensive manner, with a view to the record later being used in evidence in a court of law. Therapists are often not trained to record in a detailed, factual and objective manner, unlike, for example, social workers, who will carefully record detailed observations, dating and timing of each communication in a child abuse investigation. In the US, professional opinion is sharply divided over whether legal considerations should influence or even drive therapeutic recording in this manner. Bollas points out that the

American Psychoanalytic Association, for example, recommends that its members keep no notes, given the danger of court-ordered disclosure, whereas psychologists in the US, in contrast, are required to keep detailed notes on a proactive basis for use in any future litigation (Bollas, 2003: 203). Some of the limitations on therapeutic recording as evidence in legal proceedings are referred to in Box 6.5.

Box 6.5   Limitations of therapy records as evidence

A medical record does not automatically constitute good evidence merely because it has some bearing on an incident that is the subject matter of litigation ... A patient's description of an abusive event in a counselling session, for example, is not provided as evidence of what actually happened, but as part of the process of making sense of his or her feelings, and consequently may not be correct in every factual detail. For example, the tendency for abuse victims to blame themselves could distort the way in which they describe their feelings during counselling. In any event, a counselling record is not a verbatim account of the therapy session but a record of the healthcare provider's interpretation of what was discussed, which includes their biases, clinical observations and speculations. (Tranberg and Rashbass, 2004: 116)

Tranberg and Rashbass clearly point out the limitations of much medical and therapeutic recording as evidence in a court of law. Therapists are not trained to observe and record evidence for legal proceedings, and it could be argued that this would be a distraction from, or even a distortion of, their primary therapeutic role. The authors also refer to the limitations of therapeutic recording where significant evidence is not mentioned or recorded at all (2004: 116):

> It is also unclear how much weight should be attributed to the absence of information from a patient's record. It is tempting, for example, to infer from the fact that no evidence of abuse was recorded that the alleged incident did not take place. This, however, ignores the fact that victims often withhold such information, particularly where domestic violence is involved.

Thus, in one case reported in Canada, the social worker's sessional record did not refer to an alleged sexual assault by a third party. This was then held by the court to be consistent with the plaintiff fabricating the event (*R v Bird* (1999)).

The actual components of a therapeutic record may be very varied, depending on the agency setting where counselling is being provided, the nature of the service being provided, and agency requirements regarding the focus and detail of records kept. Therapy records might include outline client information, referral letters from another agency, details of sessions and e-mails or notes of telephone contact (see Box 6.6).

Box 6.6   Potential components of therapy records

- Client details (age, gender, ethnicity, eligibility for counselling service as employee, patient, etc.)
- Personal details (address, phone number, etc.)
- Pre- and post-counselling questionnaires e.g. CORE, INFORM
- Record of attendance and non-attendance
- Letters, correspondence
- E-mail contact
- Record of consent to counselling
- Counsellor's process notes on therapeutic and helping issues
- Counsellor's personal diaries
- Notes of supervision
- In-session material, e.g. diaries, diagrams, therapeutic writing
- Case summary
- Other

Adapted from Jenkins and Potter (2007)

The list of items is not intended to represent what should be kept in a record of therapy; it is simply a list of items which may constitute part of such a record, depending on the policy of the agency or practitioner concerned. Furthermore, not all aspects of the working client record will automatically be retained in permanent form. One of the data protection principles (Box 6.2) is that personal data be kept no longer than necessary. Therefore some aspects of the record, for example 'process' or supervision notes, might be kept on a short-term basis and then routinely destroyed, rather than kept as a permanent part of the record. A similar point has been made with regard to health records (Box 6.7).

Box 6.7   Health records

Records do not necessarily have to include every piece of paper received in connection with patients or every piece of information. Nor does everything that is added to a record necessarily become a permanent feature of that record that may never be deleted. GPs and trusts (in consultation with doctors) should determine which elements should be considered a permanent part of the record, and which are transient and may be discarded as they cease to be of value. (BMAED, 2004: 201)

Time limits for retaining records

There are conflicting perspectives on how long therapy records should be kept. Some suggested time limits refer to complaints procedures or the various time restrictions on civil litigation. BACP permits professional complaints up to three years after client contact. Litigation for breach of contract can be undertaken up to six years after last contact. On this basis, many organisations recommend keeping therapy records for a minimum of six years. However, the courts can extend this time limit for legal action, so professional indemnity insurers recommend a more cautious stance of keeping records almost indefinitely. This does assume that therapeutic recording is framed in a defensive style, and that it would be effective as evidence in defeating a claim by an aggrieved client. An alternative stance is for agencies and practitioners to routinely shred non-core material, such as notes of supervision, and subjective process notes, keeping minimal, factual records only for a limited period of time, such as a year after last client contact. The latter would be consistent with data protection principles and, incidentally, with standard practice in many commercial companies. Outside of statutory settings, there is no legal requirement for therapists to keep records, or to keep them for a certain length of time. If a client sought to gain access to their record, but it had been routinely destroyed prior to the request being made, then the agency or practitioner could refer to their data protection policy as justification for it no longer being available.

Grounds for disclosure of personal data

The DPA 1998 gives statutory protection to the privacy and confidentiality of personal data. Disclosure of personal data without proper authority or justification is a criminal offence under s. 60 of the Act. There is a limited number of exemptions, which permit the disclosure of personal data relating to taxation and to national security. Otherwise, personal data must not be disclosed unless it is required by law, necessary for the prevention of crime, in the public interest, or based on the consent of the data subject (IC, 2001: para. 9.5). The DPA brings a complex set of regulations to the control and use of personal data and its disclosure. In this, it buttresses the provisions of Article 8 of the Human Rights Act 1998, which affords the individual the right to respect for family and private life, and the wider protection for confidentiality available under common law (see Chapter 5).

Access to client material

In exploring the concept of access to records, there are distinctions to be made between:

- access to therapist's *actual practice with the client*, via direct observation, audio- or videotaping;
- access to the therapist's *records*, such as manual or computerised records, via the process of data subject access or disclosure;
- access to the therapist's *personal experience of practice with the client*, via interview, witness statement or appearance in court.

Furthermore, a number of different agents may seek to gain access to client information. These include employers, client, solicitors, the police and the courts, all of whom are discussed later in this chapter.

Access to therapist's actual practice with the client

Seeking access to the therapist's actual practice with the client may seem a rather remote possibility. However, it has been discussed in the context of Her Majesty's

Inspectorate seeking to observe directly student counsellors at work, under the Inspectorate's statutory powers to inspect schools, colleges and universities. The legal opinion obtained by BAC was that the HMIs appeared to have no statutory authority to insist on a right to observation against the objections of the client (Bond, 2000: 214–19).

It should be borne in mind that access to a therapist's actual practice with a client could also be obtained via access to audio or videotapes of their work. While these methods have decided advantages as recording techniques, the client is also more easily identifiable, especially via video recordings. Other interested parties may thus gain access to the therapist's actual work with the client via this means. Audio and video material could also be copied easily, and made accessible to others well beyond the original intended professional audience.

Access to records by an employer

Therapists providing a service for an employer are usually expected to pass on, at minimum, summary information about their workloads and outline client information. They may also be under a direct contractual obligation to reveal to employers client disclosures which directly damage the employer's interests or present a risk to the public. One example would be that of a client being coun-selled by a therapist from an Employee Assistance Programme, where the client admitted to stealing from an employer, such as a bank. The interest in employ-ers' access to counselling records in health settings has been heightened follow-ing the cases of Beverly Allitt, a nurse convicted after the death of several children in her care (Clothier, 1994), and Amanda Jenkinson, also a nurse, who was convicted of assault after tampering with equipment on an intensive treat-ment unit (Bullock, 1997).

According to the Law Commission, therapists under a contractual obligation to employers should clarify the limits to confidentiality with prospective clients, in order to reduce their parallel liability to the client for possible breach of confidence (Bond, 2000: 157; Law Commission, 1981: 52). Therapists providing a service for employers also need to determine the exact limits of employer access to informa-tion on clients. This might, for example, concern the kinds of summary data or information that will be expected by the employer in order to evaluate the effec-tiveness of the service being provided, or for audit purposes in the NHS.

In one unusual case, the Home Office sought to prevent Dr Bob Johnson, a psy-chiatrist working at Parkhurst Prison, from using videotapes of his successful ther-apeutic work as part of a planned *Panorama* programme. The Home Office claimed ownership of the client material, even though the clients, prisoners convicted of serious offences, had each given their consent for disclosure and for use in the broadcast. In court, the Home Office case for an injunction was rejected, and the tapes were used in the programme in 1997. This was a complex case, pre-dating the introduction of the Data Protection Act 1998, and heard, therefore, according to earlier and now largely superseded legal principles. It suggests, however, that employers' interest in the control of therapeutic material may not always coincide with that of the therapist, particularly in the event of the latter wishing to publicise innovative techniques which run counter to the prevailing political mood (*Home Office v BBC* (1997)).

Case law on access to records by clients

Access to records is usually seen by therapists primarily as access by *clients*. The crucial development accelerating client access to files was brought about by the case of *Graham Gaskin.*

Case study   Access to social work files

Graham Gaskin, born in 1959, spent almost the whole of his life in the care of Liverpool Social Services Department, with frequent moves and disruptions up until leaving care in 1974. He applied to see his case file, intending to bring an action against the Local Authority for negligence, and was refused access on the grounds of previous court rulings protecting such records by social workers, medical practitioners and teachers as confidential. Liverpool City Council took steps to release some, but not all, of the documents, depending upon whether the original authors of the reports would give their permission.

Gaskin's formal application was instrumental in opening up client access to files. He applied under s. 31 of the Administration of Justice Act 1970 for an order requiring disclosure of records by Liverpool City Council to assist in his claim for damages he experienced during his treatment in care (Gaskin v Liverpool C.C. [1980]). He lost the case, but Liverpool City Council responded by developing a plan for all clients to have access to files holding personal information. This spurred the then Department of Health and Social Security (DHSS) to produce a consultative document in 1983, which was followed by a government circular.

Graham Gaskin later took his case to the European Court of Human Rights, and this applied some additional pressure for changes in the legislation. A series of Acts followed, opening up a wider degree of client access to files. After the Access to Personal Files Act 1987, the Access to Personal Files (Social Services) Regulations 1989 came into force, permitting limited access to social work files prior to the date of its effect, and more extensive access to files made subsequently (but excluding full access to adoption records). Gaskin later won compensation of £5,000 for breach of Article 8 of the European Convention on Human Rights, concerning his right to respect for his private and family life but not, significantly, for the alleged violation of Article 10, i.e. the right to receive and impart information.

Source: Gaskin v UK (1988) [1990].

Under the DPA 1998, the client as data subject is entitled to a copy of their record in permanent form, in an intelligible format, unless this would involve disproportionate effort, but excluding reference to material about third parties. In the limited cases of health, education and social work records, access to these records may be denied in part or in full where disclosure would cause 'serious harm' to the client or a third party.

Access to information by the police

Access to client information may also be obtained by external agencies such as the police and the courts (see Box 6.8). Under the Police and Criminal Evidence Act

1984, the police can be authorised to search premises and remove material as evidence if there are reasonable grounds that 'a serious arrestable offence' has been committed. A serious arrestable offence here could include murder, manslaughter, rape, other sexual offences, firearms or explosives offences, terrorist offences or causing death by reckless driving. The Act specifically excludes from police powers what are termed 'personal records'. Under s. 12 of the Act, this refers to:

documentary or other records concerning an individual (whether living or dead) who can be identified from them and relating –

(a) to his physical or mental health;
(b) to spiritual counselling or assistance given or to be given to him; or
(c) to counselling or assistance given or to be given to him, for the purposes of his personal welfare, by any voluntary organisation or by any individual who –

(i) by reason of his office or occupation has responsibilities for his personal welfare; or
(ii) by reason of an order of a court has responsibilities for his supervision.

Box 6.8   Access to confidential therapy records by police or courts

- this may be ordered by the courts in civil or criminal proceedings, as under ss. 33, 34, Supreme Court Act 1981; s. 20, Criminal Procedure and Investigations Act 1996;
- 'private' or second sets of therapeutic notes may still be subject to disclosure, i.e. surrendered in legal processes;
- access by police by warrant may be authorised by a Circuit Judge under s. 12, Police and Criminal Evidence Act 1984;
- defence against discovery of confidential documents is possible on grounds of 'public interest immunity';
- public interest in disclosure as decided by court will override a private or personal interest in confidentiality;
- refusal to surrender documents or to give evidence in legal proceedings can be treated as contempt of court.

The protection afforded to therapeutic records under s. 12, PACE 1984 is both specific and extensive. Authorisation for seizure of such 'excluded material' can only be obtained by the police applying to a Circuit Judge, not simply to a Magistrate ('excluded' here means excluded from the powers of the Magistrate). The warrant needs to refer to specified premises; to be executed within one month of having been authorised; and to apply to one search only (excluding an overnight interruption to observe normal business hours). The advice to practitioners faced with such a search is to get a complete list of all such files or documents removed, to assist in their eventual return.

Case study　Refusal of police access to psychiatric records

Police, investigating a murder close to a psychiatric hospital, applied to access health records, in order to investigate the movements of one of the hospital's in-patients. Dr Kellam, a consultant forensic psychiatrist, refused access to the records, on the grounds that these records constituted 'excluded material' under s. 12, Police and Criminal Evidence Act 1984. Access to this material was then granted by order of Cardiff Crown Court. Dr Kellam successfully applied for a judicial review of this deci-sion, which confirmed that the records were, in fact, excluded material, and therefore not accessible to the police in their inquiries. In Dr Kellam's view, 'the judgement means that the police do not have a right of access to medical records under most cir-cumstances, which is of great importance for reassuring patients about the confiden-tiality of the information they entrust to us' (Kellam, 1994: 100).

Source: R v Cardiff Crown Court, Ex parte Kellam (1993) TLR 3 May

However, the protection of 'excluded material' is limited under the law. The police can remove such material by obtaining a warrant, as detailed above, or may remove it under s. 50, Criminal Justice and Police Act 2001, for the purposes of determining whether or not it falls within their powers of seizure, when it is not practical to examine it on site (Pattenden, 2003: 466).

Police access to client information by covert surveillance

The police may also gain access to client information by means of covert surveillance. Under the Police Act 1997, the police require dual authorisation, from a chief consta-ble and from a Surveillance Commissioner, normally a serving or retired judge, in order to carry out surveillance of a professional consulting room, providing access to private confidential material (Pattenden, 2003: 483). In an Australian case, the police set up a phone tap in a therapist's room, to monitor the therapy with a client under police investigation. For the first six months, the therapist was unaware of the covert surveillance, but thereafter co-operated with the police (Pattenden, 2003: 481).

The main case of police use of surveillance relating to client confidentiality is the *Wintercomfort* case, which led to the conviction and imprisonment of two care workers, Ruth Wyner and John Brock.

Case study　The *Wintercomfort* case

Police concern over alleged drug dealing and illegal use of drugs at the Wintercomfort hostel for homeless people in Cambridge led to a request for police access to a confidential record of the names of those who had been banned for suspected drug

(Continued)

dealing. This request was refused by the management committee of the hostel, on the grounds that to permit access would place staff at risk of reprisals from hostel users, and would breach the principle of client confidentiality, which was an important aspect of their ability to work with marginalised homeless people.

The police then sent two undercover agents – who called themselves 'Ed' and 'Swampy' and posed as homeless persons – into the hostel, to obtain evidence of illegal drug use and dealing. In addition, 300 hours of covert video material was obtained, leading to the conviction of eight alleged drug dealers. Ruth Wyner, Director of the Centre, and John Brock, Day Centre Manager, were convicted and sentenced to five years and four years respectively in 1999, for 'knowingly allowing or suffering to be permitted' the sale of drugs on the premises under s. 8, Misuse of Drugs Act 1971.

The sentences were widely seen as draconian and inappropriate, in that the policy of the Wintercomfort hostel was clearly to prevent the use of illegal drugs on its premises, and to ban access to the hostel for persistent offenders. Ruth Wyner and John Brock were subsequently freed on appeal, but the convictions were not overturned (Wyner, 2003). The government then sought to issue draft guidance to clarify the situation of those working with homeless and vulnerable people, where illegal use of drugs may be involved. This was challenged by independent legal opinion, which maintained that the proposed guidance continued to place workers in a vulnerable and untenable position, at risk of prosecution for illegal drug use, over which they had no effective control (Sinclair Taylor, 2003).

The *Wintercomfort* case is, in many ways, exceptional. It does illustrate, however, the lengths to which the police may go in order to obtain evidence on a matter of public concern. It also demonstrates the limited protection for practitioners, in this case those working with homeless people, in defending client confidentiality from external demands for access to highly sensitive personal information.

Access to information by the courts

Discovery, or disclosure of documents, is a well-established procedure under civil law. Under ss. 33 and 34 of the Supreme Court Act 1981, the High Court has the power to order production of relevant documents in legal proceedings for personal injuries or in respect of a person's death, with regard to litigation or proposed litigation. The detailed provisions for disclosure of documents in civil litigation are set out in the 'White Book', i.e. the *Civil Procedures Rules* (2000). Similarly, the Criminal Procedure and Investigations Act 1996 authorises disclosure of material in criminal cases, including that which has been 'unused' in preparing the prosecution case. Material which is otherwise seen to be confidential must be disclosed to the court in the public interest, in order that the courts can have access to the widest possible range of relevant information when deciding cases. The concept of therapeutic confidentiality therefore provides a very limited defence against the interest of the court in obtaining client material (Foster et al., 1996; Foster and Peacock, 2000).

One of the concerns about the process of disclosure in legal proceedings is its potential misuse as a 'fishing expedition' for material damaging to the opposing side. This concern has been raised by the British Medical Association, in claiming that solicitors were breaching their own code of ethics in asking for full sets of medical records, rather than for specific documents which were known to be relevant to a particular aspect of a given case (BMA, 2001a: 1).

Case study   Use of medical records in a case of alleged rape

It seemed a very strong case – until the defence used the process of disclosure in the run-up to the trial to obtain a copy of Dawn's medical records. Using them, and without ever meeting her, an expert witness for the defence drew up a psychiatric report so damning the Crown Prosecution Service dropped the case just six days before the trial was due to begin.

According to the defence psychiatrist, Dawn had a personality disorder which potentially could make her a compulsive liar. She might also have a tendency to seek out violent sex, which she would later regret. The CPS now says it took the decision after 'long and painstaking consideration', and that it believed the chances of a successful prosecution had been greatly reduced by the report.

Dawn still feels deeply hurt that a psychiatrist could have made such a personal attack on her. 'I was devastated', she says. 'I felt devalued. I was really upset that someone could write something so damning. And I hadn't even met him.' Guardian, 29 May 2001

The outcome illustrates, not only that therapeutic records may be obtained for court proceedings, as shown here in a criminal case, but that records of a psychiatric or therapeutic nature may be used effectively to undermine a client's credibility. Given that clients who have experienced assault or sexual abuse often need psychiatric treatment or therapy to help them to overcome these past experiences, the existence of the relevant records may be used to undermine their very attempts to obtain justice against their alleged abusers or assailants.

A court order for disclosure of records is very wide-ranging in its effects. Therapists are required under the force of law to disclose all material related to the client or case in hand. This can include material which is not formally part of the client's agency file, such as personal diaries, supervision notes and 'process notes', if these are kept separately from the main file. Any attempt to destroy, alter or conceal aspects of the material required by the court is likely to have severe consequences. Pattenden confirms that 'maintaining dual records – one version for the court and another for the use of the professional – is illegal' (2003: 650).

Preparing reports for the court

The courts and other parties in legal proceedings may gain access to information through reports prepared for the court. Therapists may often see preparation of a court report as a way both of assisting the court, and of limiting the disclosure of client information. However, a number of factors need to be borne in mind. Therapists are generally not trained in writing court reports, and their perception of what is a helpful and professional account of their contact with a client may not be judged in a sympathetic light by others involved in the case. Preparing court reports is a highly specialised technical skill, with its own specific conventions and discipline (Bond and Sandhu, 2005; Pollecoff, 2002). On receiving the report, the court may then order disclosure of the original records on which the report is based, completely undermining the therapist's attempts to limit disclosure of sensitive client information, if this was their original intention.

It is worth bearing in mind, when preparing reports for the court, that the final report in effect becomes a public document. Once the report leaves the possession of the therapist, he or she has no control over its future use or distribution, and it may even possibly be read out in open court. The potential readership and impact of very sensitive client information should be carefully considered before inclusion in such reports. Given the complex issues surrounding the preparation and use of court reports, some counselling agencies have adopted the stance that their policy is simply not to prepare reports for legal proceedings on a voluntary basis, but only to comply with court orders for records or witness summons.

Protection of client records under Public Interest Immunity

In certain cases, access to records may be denied on the decision of the court, on the basis of their protected status, if granted 'public interest immunity'.

Case study   Access to client records: 'Public Interest Immunity' defence

An 11-year-old boy in her class seriously assaulted Joyce Campbell, a teacher. She suffered severe injuries as a result, was off work for seven months, and had to take early retirement. To support her legal action against the Local Authority for negligence, she applied for an order for disclosure of all relevant documents, including reports on the pupil made by teachers, psychologists and psychiatrists. This material included a dossier describing previous assaults by the boy in school. A 'green form' was apparently used for making reports on the boy's behaviour, before being passed on to the headteacher. The school log had also been used for the purposes of recording incidents, and in addition there were previous reports on his behaviour from a special school he had attended.

(Continued)

(Continued)

Disclosure was applied for under s. 31 of the Administration of Justice Act 1970. A case for negligence was brought against the Local Authority on the grounds that it was already known that the boy was likely to be violent against members of staff, and inadequate steps had been taken to warn and protect the staff involved. There were three documents which were especially relevant to Joyce Campbell's case: the head-teacher's request for advice, the assessments of the boy's behaviour made by other teachers and the report and recommendations produced by an educational psychologist. The request for access to records was defended by the authorities on the basis of 'public interest immunity'. They requested that the documents be protected from discovery on the grounds that, if released, they would adversely affect the 'candour' of future recordings. In other words, if these professional recordings were made public, then the willingness of professionals to keep full and accurate recordings in future would be undermined by the threat of their use in possible litigation. The Local Authority's case was overruled, however, and access to the records was ordered by the judge as being in the public interest.

Source: Campbell v Tameside Council [1982]

The Local Authority's case in seeking protection for the records was based on the 'candour doctrine', in other words that access would undermine the keeping of full and accurate recordings by professionals. This argument was said by the court no longer to be persuasive, following more recent rulings, as it referred to a private interest which must be subject to the greater public interest in disclosure. Protection in these circumstances can be sought on the basis of either a 'class' or 'contents' argument. In the first, it is claimed that the documents belong to a particular class, in this case statutory records, requiring protection from disclosure. In the second situation, immunity is sought on the basis of the contents of a particular document. This was considered as a 'class' action to restrict access to recordings made under statutory authority, in carrying out the duties of the Local Education Authority, with a claim by the defendants to 'Public Interest Immunity'.

According to Lord Justice Ackner, '(t)he private promise of confidentiality must yield to the general public interest, in that in the administration of justice truth will out, unless by reason of the character of the information or the relationship of the recipient of the information to the informant a more important public interest is served by protecting the information or identity of the informant from disclosure in a court of law' (at 1075). Whether immunity is sought on a class or contents basis, in both cases the courts weigh the balance between justice and the immunity of the nation or public service, and may inspect the documents and order disclosure. Public Interest Immunity is normally held to apply to a very narrow range of records, such as child care cases, and to police informer cases.

Access to client information in the courtroom

The courts may obtain information about clients by requiring a therapist to act as a witness. In this way, the courts gain access not just to written records or documents, but also to the therapist's *experience* of working with the client. While the Samaritans see themselves as a befriending agency rather than as one providing therapy as such, their experience in this area is interesting. Simon Armson, Chief Executive of the Samaritans, clarified the response usually made by the organisation to requests for volunteers to attend court as witnesses.

> whenever this happens (which is very infrequent) we are always careful to ensure that we attend court as a result of a requirement to do so by Court Order (subpoena). We feel that this is important so as to be able to demonstrate that it is only in order to comply with the law that we would cooperate in this way and that we would never voluntarily attend to give evidence about a contact that was made with us by a caller. We generally manage to succeed in gaining the court's co-operation in maintaining the anonymity of the Samaritan volunteer. To do this we usually write to the Crown Prosecution Service and, if appropriate, the defence solicitors seeking their assistance in this matter and to the Clerk of the Court asking for the necessary request to be made to the Judge. (Armson, personal communication)

Normally, it seems courts will respect this arrangement, given that it is based on the need to maintain public confidence in the Samaritans' professionalism and their strict policy of client confidentiality.

Relate (formerly the Marriage Guidance Council) has a different experience of handling requests for therapists to appear as witnesses in court. This is based on the degree of privilege which, unusually, can be claimed for marital or relationship counselling where legal proceedings such as divorce or legal separation may be considered. Derek Hill, former Head of Counselling at Relate, refers to

> situations in which subpoenas, witness orders and less official pressures are applied to Relate counsellors in an effort to get them to disclose information acquired during counselling. In the former cases we have used a barrister several times to argue that privacy and confidentiality outweigh the public interest in securing a disclosure. We have been successful – but not in securing a reasoned judgement, so each time we start anew. (Hill, personal communication)

The limited case law on privilege concerning marital counselling does not appear to carry the full status of legal precedent, which would require courts to recognise therapist privilege in this field. (For a fuller discussion of these issues, see Chapter 5.)

Evidential privilege

The lack of therapist privilege in the UK is not surprising, considering that doctors also do not hold such rights. This is unlike the situation in the US, where medical and therapist privilege is recognised by many states (Bollas and Sundelson, 1995: 11). The term used to describe this situation is 'evidential privilege', namely the right not to have to give evidence in court concerning a patient or client. The most widely cited example of a therapist seeking to obtain evidential privilege is that relating to the case of Dr Anne Hayman.

> ### Case study   Therapists and the arguments for evidential privilege: the *Hayman* case
>
> *Dr Anne Hayman was subpoenaed in 1965 to give evidence in the High Court about one of her patients, thus being faced with a difficult personal and professional dilemma, described originally in an anonymous article in the Lancet.*
>
> > *I had to decide whether to obey the Law or to abide by the rules of professional conduct. I complied with the subpoena by attending Court, but I decided I could not answer any questions about the 'patient', and I made all the arrangements, including having a barrister to plead in mitigation of sentence, for the possibility that I should be sent to prison for contempt of court. In the event, although my silence probably did constitute a contempt, the judge declared he would not sentence me, saying it was obviously a matter of conscience.*
>
> *Part of the strength of Hayman's argument lay in the particular stress placed by her on transference as a therapeutic tool, and on how this professional commitment precluded breaking confidentiality.*
>
> > *To the judge's query whether I would still object if 'the patient' gave permission, I answered with an example: suppose a patient had been in treatment for some time and was going through a temporary phase of admiring and depending on me; he might therefore feel it necessary to sacrifice himself and give permission, but it might not be proper for me to act on this.*
>
> *Source: Hayman, 2002: 21–3*

Dr Hayman's approach was successful, and she was able to convince the judge that justice would not be best served by requiring her to give evidence. The example does not set a legal precedent, however. Refusal to give evidence on the grounds that this infringes client–therapist confidentiality is likely to be treated as contempt of court, as was mooted in a similar case involving a Relate counsellor (Sanctuary, 1965). In another case, a psychiatrist was threatened with contempt for refusing to give evidence, and promptly complied with the judge's instructions (*Nuttall v Nuttall and Twyman* (1964)). In the USA, a Californian psychiatrist, George Romero, was imprisoned in 1977 for three days for refusing to testify about a patient he had seen (Van Hoose and Kottler, 1985: 52).

A therapist cannot simply claim confidentiality as a reason for not providing the court with information, except at the risk of being held to be in contempt of court. However, they might request that sensitive information about a client be disclosed first to the judge, in order to restrict disclosure of information in open court to that which is strictly relevant to the needs of the proceedings in question. This may be more likely to gain a favourable response from the court than a therapist's simple refusal to discuss client material in court. Professional indemnity insurers and professional protection societies may be able to offer expert legal advice in framing an appropriate letter to the court setting out the reasons for limiting disclosure of highly sensitive client information which may be of limited relevance to the case being heard by the court. This has been successful in a number of cases in convincing judges that therapeutic material is of no relevance to the case, or that partial, rather than full, disclosure of therapeutic records is all that is required.

In addition, therapists acting as witnesses should avoid at all costs taking their original case notes with them into the witness box. This might make it easier to refer to notes made at the time, or to check significant dates, but this can be as easily achieved by making a summary of relevant information. The court has a right to inspect the original case notes if taken with the witness into the witness box, thus gaining access to the most direct form of information about the therapeutic process short of a video recording. Acting as a witness may present another way in which the therapist comes into direct contact with the legal system as a result of his or her practice. This is discussed more fully in Chapter 3. Guidelines for professional practice regarding data protection and access to client records are suggested in Box 6.9.

Box 6.9 Guidelines for professional practice regarding data protection and access to client records

- Review your policy on data protection regarding all recordings of therapy, including

  - official or agency records
  - computerised records
  - 'private' or personal notes
  - videos and tape recordings.

- Share policy and procedure on access to records via a brief leaflet given to clients, backed up by a more detailed document.
- Follow good practice concerning the focus and content of client records. Avoid comments which are trivialising, unjustifiable or defamatory.
- Check arrangements for storage and destruction of client records after a set time limit.
- Consider your own responses to:

  - request by a client for access to records
  - request by solicitor with signed client consent for client records
  - request for a court report on therapeutic work with a client
  - witness summons to appear in court.

- In the case of police or court demands for client records or attendance in court as a witness, seek immediate expert legal and professional advice.

Summary

Therapeutic recording is governed by the provisions of the Data Protection Act 1998 and its associated regulations. These have complex provisions for client, or data subject access, depending on the context of the therapeutic work and the nature of the record kept, depending upon whether it is electronic or manual. Case law has defined the status of records kept in 'relevant filing systems', and client access to 'unstructured material' held by public authorities has been introduced by the Freedom of Information Act 2000. Therapeutic records may be of limited value as evidence in legal proceedings because this is not their intended purpose, despite the apparently growing interest in their use as evidence in court.

A number of parties, including employers (to a limited extent), clients, solicitors, the police and the courts, may exercise access to records. The police may have access to client files only with specific judicial authority. The courts have wider powers of access, even to the therapist's 'private' notes, under the process of disclosure. A therapist may request the court's permission to restrict disclosure to material essential for the legal proceedings in hand. However, refusal by a therapist to surrender files, or to give evidence when required by the court under court order or witness summons, can be punished as contempt of court. Some counselling organisations seek to underline their commitment to client confidentiality by requiring that their counsellors only attend court as witnesses when formally summoned, and not on a voluntary basis. In the final analysis, therapeutic confidentiality is subject to the needs of the wider public interest. In the case of conflict or dispute, the courts are the final authority on what constitutes the public interest regarding confidentiality and the disclosure of client material.

Discussion points

1   On what ethical grounds could therapists justify not disclosing therapeutic records to their clients? What types of information might legitimately be withheld from clients as potentially damaging?

2   What are the implications of client access to computerised and manual records held by therapists? How should therapists record information about their personal responses to client material, such as transference and countertransference issues, or material intended for use in supervision?

3   Should therapists seek to acquire 'evidential privilege', as held by some licensed therapists in the USA? What advantages or disadvantages would this entail?

4   How would you respond if required to attend court as a witness in court proceedings concerning your client? How might you prepare yourself for such a role?

5   Does the legal process of disclosure concerning therapy records disadvantage clients, or ensure fairness, by bringing all relevant material into consideration by the court? How might therapists counter the assumption that a client who has received psychiatric treatment or therapy is less reliable as a witness in a court of law?

7 Therapy with Children and Young People

The starting point for this chapter is the view that there is a close relationship between the rights of children and their rights as clients in counselling and psychotherapy. (Children are defined here as being under the age of 18 years, as per the Children Act 1989.) The complexity of the law relating to children mirrors the differing perceptions that adults have of children and of young people's abilities to take an active responsibility for their own lives. For therapists working with children and young people, there is often a degree of urgency in confronting day-to-day issues, such as whether to inform their parents, problems of maintaining confidentiality and in trying to assess the level of responsible decision-making held by the young person. The therapist's decision-making is not helped by the lack of a clear picture of the legal responsibilities of those working in this field.

This chapter links changes in the law relating to therapy for children to corresponding changes in children's rights. Key issues within therapeutic work with children, such as confidentiality, child protection and access to files, are explored. As will be noted, the legal position of therapists working with children and young people may be influenced by the setting in which they work, whether this is in the field of education, health, psychiatry, voluntary agency or private practice. This means that the chapter necessarily explores some material which may at first seem unrelated to the specific needs of therapists who work outside these settings. However, this broader discussion of the issues is needed to provide a more complete picture of the range of possible responses open to therapists. It is also necessary to illustrate the legal anomalies and complexities inherent in therapeutic work with children and young people.

The rights of children and young people

Recognition of the right of children to be treated as independent beings, rather than as the possessions of parents and adult caretakers, has been a major development in society in the last two decades (Jenkins, 2003b). As the landmark Cleveland Report expressed it, 'the child is a person and not an object of concern' (Butler-Sloss, 1988: 245). A wide body of legislative and case law, culminating in the *Gillick* decision, has increasingly emphasised the rights of children to become active decision-makers where their own futures are being decided by the courts and by other authorities. Their right to consideration as an independent party in therapy, rather than simply as a dependent member of the wider family group, is now clearly acknowledged by the law and by statutory codes of practice (see Box 7.1).

The rights of children and young people now represent a distinct specialism in human rights law (Fortin, 1998; Kilkelly, 1999). For the purposes of counselling and psychotherapy, this chapter makes use of the distinction between 'children' and 'young people' suggested by the British Medical Association. This suggests that young people may be judged mature enough to make their own decisions, while children may not be mature enough to do this (BMAED, 2004: 133).

One model of the rights of children and young people (Jenkins, 2003b) distinguishes between rights to:

- welfare
- participation
- autonomy

A right is defined as a claim to treatment, by reference to law or an authoritative official document, such as a statutory code of practice. On this basis, children and young people are entitled to varying sets of rights, depending on their circumstances, and, in some cases, the setting in which they find themselves, such as a health care, education or social work setting.

- *Rights to welfare*: this set of rights entitles children and young people to education, health care and protection from abuse.
- *Rights to participation in decision-making*: this set of rights enables children and young people to have a direct say in decisions being made about them or on their behalf, by courts, social services planning meetings or by child protection conferences.
- *Rights to autonomy*: this set of rights entitles children and young people to autonomous decision-making, or to take legal action on their own behalf, in some cases via an advocate.

Therapists working with children and young people need to be clear about their own ethical stance regarding children's rights. It is likely that, unless the therapist develops a stance of promoting autonomy wherever appropriate, his or her default model of children's rights is likely to be based on welfare and paternalism, rather than promoting participation and the young person's potential for autonomy. Children and young people have a well-developed set of rights, as, for example, under the *Gillick* decision, which offers the potential for independent access to therapy (Box 7.1).

Box 7.1   Children's independent rights to therapy

- *Gillick* decision in House of Lords, 1986
- Article 12, UN Convention on the Rights of the Child 1989
- s. 22, Children Act 1989

The impact of the *Gillick* decision

The development of the right to confidentiality has been a central aspect of this shift in perspective. The right of children and young people to a confidential therapeutic relationship can be traced to the watershed *Gillick* decision, which recognised that young people under 16 are capable of making certain decisions for themselves, without requiring parental knowledge or consent.

Case study   The *Gillick* case

Victoria Gillick, the mother of five daughters under the age of 16, sought assurances from her local area health authority that none of them would receive contraceptive advice or treatment from a doctor without her knowledge. This challenged the existing Department of Health and Social Security advice to doctors that this was a clinical matter solely for the doctor to decide. She then brought an action against the Health Authority, based on the grounds that such advice was unlawful. In effect, she claimed, it amounted to doctors committing an offence, by encouraging unlawful sexual intercourse by a girl under the age of consent. In addition, the action alleged that it constituted a serious infringement of the rights of the parent. The legal action was heard in the House of Lords in 1986. By a majority of three to two, it was held by the Law Lords that children of 'sufficient maturity' were entitled to confidential medical treatment by a doctor, depending upon the doctor's assessment of their degree of maturity and level of understanding.

Source: Gillick v West Norfolk, AHA [1985]

Box 7.2   The 'Fraser guidelines'

The only practicable course is, in my opinion, to entrust the doctor with a discretion to act in accordance with his view of what is best in the interests of the girl who is his patient. He should, of course, always seek to persuade her to tell her parents that she is seeking contraceptive advice, and the nature of the advice that she receives. At least he should seek to persuade her to agree to the doctor's informing the parents. But there may well be cases, and I think there will be some cases, where the girl refuses either to tell the parents herself or to permit the doctor to do so and in such cases the doctor will, in my opinion, be justified in proceeding without the parents' consent or even knowledge provided he is satisfied on the following matters:

(1) that the girl (although under 16 years of age) will understand his advice;
(2) that he cannot persuade her to inform her parents or to allow him to inform the parents that she is seeking contraceptive advice;
(3) that she is very likely to begin or to continue having sexual intercourse with or without contraceptive treatment;
(4) that unless she receives contraceptive advice or treatment her physical or mental health or both are likely to suffer;
(5) that her best interests require him to give her contraceptive advice, treatment or both without the parental consent.

Source: Gillick v West Norfolk AHA [1985], Lord Fraser at 413

Box 7.3 Assessing competence to consent by children and young people

Factors to consider	Checklist for questions
Immediate issues:	
Child's age: '*Gillick*' test:	How *old* is the child or young person? Does the child or young person *understand* the counselling or advice? Are they *refusing* to allow their parents to be informed? Do their *best interests* require that the advice or counselling be given without *parental* consent?
Short-term issues:	
Nature of contact:	Is the *contact* with the counsellor or therapist controlled entirely by the child or young person (e.g. emergency phone call, drop-in centre)?
Support systems:	What *support* does the child or young person have access to alongside or in the place of counselling or therapy Should contact be broken or withdrawn?
Nature of the immediate issue or problem:	What is the degree of *risk*, if any, posed by the child to him or herself or to others (e.g. drugs, abuse, suicide, arson)? Is the risk significant, immediate or longer term?
Child protection responsibilities:	Is the counsellor or therapist *required* by their conditions of employment, or by agency policy, to *report all suspected child abuse* to social services?
Longer-term issues:	
Stage of cognitive and emotional development:	Does the child or young person *understand* • the nature of the issue or problem? • their own needs and the needs of others? • the risks and benefits of counselling or therapy? Does the child or young person have a sense of • their own identity? • time, past, present and future?
Risks and benefits of counselling or therapy being ended:	What *risks or benefits* might ensue if contact with the child or young person were to be broken by him or her, or to be ended by other parties? (e.g. continuation of current abuse)

The Fraser guidelines set out the main circumstances in which the doctor or health professional would be justified in *not* informing a girl's parents of her seeking confidential advice for contraception (see Box 7.2). Lord Scarman also went on to identify other 'exceptional circumstances' where the health professional would be justified in treating the child without parental consent. 'Emergency, parental neglect, abandonment of the child or inability to find the parent are examples of exceptional situations justifying the doctor to treat the child without parental knowledge or consent' (at 424). The guidelines for short- and longer-term issues, set out in Box 7.3, extend this approach to include other relevant factors that therapists may need to consider carefully.

If the *Gillick* principle opens the way to a child-centred therapeutic relationship, a crucial difficulty still remains for therapists and counsellors in deciding how to assess whether the child is of 'sufficient understanding'. Some of the most extensive discussion of the key factors relative to assessing competence has been in the context of decision-making with regard to medical and psychiatric treatment (Ford and Kessel, 2001; Fundudis, 2003; Pearce, 1994). These issues are adapted and extended in Box 7.3 to identify some of the critical factors that a therapist would need to consider, in deciding whether the child or young person was sufficiently competent for a confidential therapeutic relationship to ensue.

These factors obviously do not provide ready-made answers for the therapist trying to decide how best to respond to a child or young person seeking help, but they may indicate some of the main issues to bear in mind. The version of the *Gillick* test above is based on the comments of Lord Scarman and Lord Fraser in the House of Lords decision, and will give therapists a basic framework for deciding whether or not to proceed without parental involvement.

Age as a factor in the *Gillick* principle

The *Gillick* principle applies to young people under the age of 16. Young people aged 16–17 have the same entitlement to confidentiality as would an adult, under both common law and statute. For some counsellors, the key uncertainty is the lower limits of *Gillick*, or the 'cut-off' age for *Gillick* to apply. Of course, the central point of *Gillick* is not to ascribe an arbitrary age for entitlement to a key human right such as confidentiality. The courts have previously listened sympathetically to cogent cases made by articulate and confident young people aged 12. The criterion of 'sufficient understanding' can be linked to the Piagetian concept of formal thinking, which would perhaps be unlikely to develop fully before this age, except in rare cases. Another course of reference comes from the experience of children as young as five or six years quite competently handling their own analgesia or pain relief systems when undergoing medical treatment (Alderson and Montgomery, 1996). Other research into children's decision-making regarding competence and consent to non-critical medical treatment found a rough consensus of children putting the appropriate age at 14 years, with parents deciding on 13.9 years, and health professionals opting for 10.3 years (Shield and Baum, 1994: 1183). None of this is conclusive, but it suggests that there is a wide variation of professional opinion on what remains a difficult issue to decide. Whatever their basis for assessing the child or young person's competence to consent, the therapist's rationale for the decision needs to be clearly worked out, in order to be presented to a court, if necessary.

Child's right to confidential counselling after *Gillick*

The *Gillick* decision lays the basis for working independently with the child or young person as the client, particularly where there is any degree of conflict regarding parental involvement or oversight of the therapeutic relationship. According to Lord Scarman, 'parental right yields to the child's right to make his own decisions when he reaches a sufficient understanding and intelligence to be capable of making up his own mind on the matter requiring decision' (*Gillick* [1986]). The Children's Legal Centre deduced from this that 'mature children have the right to seek independent advice and counselling' (*Childright*, 1989a: 12). This marked a significant step forward for children, and for those who provide a child-centred counselling service. However, it still remains the case that the crucial decision as to whether a child is of sufficient understanding rests with the doctor or therapist. The latter must, in all cases, try to persuade the child to allow their parents to be consulted, unless the child has refused, or where there is a risk of child abuse. The adult needs to be satisfied that the young person understands the implications of the help they are seeking. Even where the child is judged not to be of mature understanding, advice and counselling can be given in the case of emergency, parental neglect, abandonment of the child, or inability to find the parent.

The value of the *Gillick* decision lies in helping the therapist to decide on whether to work with the child or young person where there is an apparent conflict of interest between them and their parent(s). For example, a 15-year-old boy may wish to come for counselling, but without his alcoholic parents being informed of this, in order to discuss his feelings about difficult family relationships. For the parents even to be informed of the fact that he was seeking counselling would perhaps bring pressure on him to disclose what he was discussing, and why he felt the need to go outside the family for help. The therapist here could work with the young person without needing to inform the parents, if the *Gillick* criteria were met, namely the boy understanding the counselling, refusing to let his parents be informed, and the counselling meeting his best interests.

Counselling and the Children Act 1989

The earlier child-centred principles of the Butler-Sloss Report and the *Gillick* decision were further strengthened by the Children Act 1989. The Act provided the response to mounting public and media concern about the exercise of social workers' powers during the preceding two decades. Based on a comprehensive review of child care law, the Act brought together clear and consistent principles about the welfare of children, the related responsibilities of parents, and the duties of Local Authorities. It integrated private law relating to children, as for example with divorce, parental responsibility and contact, with public law, which detailed the responsibilities of the Local Authority in looking after children. Promoting the welfare of 'children in need' was to be based on the principles of partnership and support for families, and on avoiding the need for statutory interventions into family life wherever possible.

The Children Act 1989 made specific reference to counselling as a service for children and families, and to the independent rights of children and young people in decision-making. S. 22 of the Act stated that 'before making any decision with respect to a child whom they are looking after, or proposing to look after, a local authority shall, so far as is reasonably practicable, ascertain the wishes and feelings of...the child'. Building on the welfare principle from earlier legislation such as the Children Act 1975, children were assured some degree of say in the decisions being made about their lives by concerned professionals. This principle was further underlined by the United Nations Convention on the Rights of the Child 1989, ratified by the UK government in 1991 (see Box 7.4).

Box 7.4   UN Convention 1989

Article 12: States Parties shall assure to the child who is capable of forming his or her own views the right to express those views freely in all matters affecting the child, the views of the child being given due weight in accordance with the age and maturity of the child (UNICEF, 1989: 6).

Key issues in therapy with children and young people

Based on the legal framework for counselling children provided by the *Gillick* decision, the Children Act 1989 and the UN Convention on the Rights of the Child, therapists may well confront certain issues of key importance in their work with children. These include:

- confidentiality and its limits
- child protection and the reporting of child abuse
- young people and under-age sexual activity
- young people's rights of access to their personal files
- pre-trial therapy for young people as witnesses in criminal trials
- young people's experiences of abusive therapy

This is followed by an outline of some of the main contexts for counselling young people, including:

- education settings: secondary school
- health settings

- psychiatric care
- voluntary settings
- private practice

Confidentiality and its limits

Confidentiality is widely taken to be a central component of the therapeutic rela-tionship, and this is particularly relevant when working with children and young people. The BACP *Ethical Framework*, for example, stresses the need to consider issues of practitioner ethical awareness and competence, as well as working with the child's developing autonomy, managing confidentiality and parental involve-ment, if any, in the therapeutic work (see Box 7.5).

Box 7.5   Working with young people

15. Working with young people requires specific ethical awareness and compe-tence. The practitioner is required to consider and assess the balance between young people's dependence on adults and carers and their progressive develop-ment towards acting independently. Working with children and young people requires careful consideration of issues concerning their capacity to give consent to receiving any service independently of someone with parental responsibilities and the management of confidences disclosed by clients. (BACP, 2002: 6)

Confidentiality continues to be a matter of the greatest concern and interest to children and young people seeking therapeutic help. According to one qualitative study of young people's perceptions of counselling services: 'For many of the participants, their desire for confidentiality related not so much to concerns for privacy, but to a wish to retain control over the material which they disclosed. The fear that disclosure of a problem would lead to a loss of control over it was common to many participants' (LeSurf and Lynch, 1999: 237). In terms of factors encouraging young people to seek counselling, 'The quality seen as most essential by participants was confidentiality' (1999: 239). Or, as one participant expressed it, 'the confidentiality thing is really important because it means that you've got the freedom to say what you really feel or really think without having it feel that it might go further' (1999: 239). While absolute confidentiality may rarely be promised, it seems that many young people expect high levels of confidentiality to be in place before they will make use of such a service (see Statement by Central Youth Counselling Service in Box 7.6). In fact, fears of a lack of confidentiality may well deter young people from seeking confidential medical advice on contra-ception or on sexually transmitted diseases, even though such services are actually confidential in nature.

Box 7.6   Confidentiality at Central Youth Counselling Service

You can be sure that anything you discuss with any Central Youth workers will stay confidential.

Even if you are under 16 nothing will be said to anyone including parents, other family members, friends, partners, care workers, teachers or police without your permission. The only reason why we might have to consider passing on confidential information would be to protect you or someone else from serious harm. We would always try to discuss this with you first. (Central Youth Statement on Confidentiality)

Confidentiality may need to be qualified where there is perceived to be a high level of risk to the young person, or to others. Childline, a prominent national telephone helpline for children (0800–1111), offers a policy of *qualified* rather than unrestricted confidentiality. Material is confidential unless 'the child is recognised to be in a situation that would lead to the child being in imminent danger of injury or death or a danger to themselves' (*Childright*, 1989b: 19). One such situation is described below.

Case study   Childline's response to a potentially suicidal young person

...a child rang the line after taking an overdose. For three hours, a single counsellor kept talking to the child, who was fading in and out of consciousness. They did not know where the child was ringing from; all the child would tell them was the name of his/her school. While the counsellor kept talking, other staff tried to trace the school. Eventually they found it, and the headteacher searched the school records for the child's address. With the child still talking on the phone to the counsellor, an ambulance arrived.

(Crompton, 1992: 208–17)

Any child-centred approach to confidentiality is subject to certain restrictions. The Butler-Sloss Report, which analysed the taking into care of 121 children in Cleveland in 1987, made this point clear (1988: 245). A child or young person should not be promised confidentiality where the promise cannot be sustained, being overridden, for example, by the need to pass information on to the authorities, or to the courts.

A further set of grounds for overriding confidentiality may lie in the powers held by the courts. Under s. 1 of the Children Act 1989, the welfare of the child is held to be of paramount importance for the court in its decision-making. This gives the court wide powers of access to information which may have a bearing on deciding issues about a child's future. This can include ordering or preventing disclosure of confidential medical reports, therapeutic records or video recordings, if so decided by the court. The power of the court overturns Legal Professional Privilege, which normally protects solicitors' material from disclosure, if the court decides that it is warranted in the interests of the child.

Child protection

In the last two decades, much therapeutic work with children, whether by statutory agencies or by other therapists, has been heavily overshadowed by the issue of child abuse (Trowell, 2001). The reporting of suspected child abuse is mandatory in the USA, an obligation which has led to concern that this inflates the number of reported cases of abuse. It may also place professionals with more discriminating criteria of abuse at risk of negligence claims against them, and may fail to substantially reduce the numbers of those abused (Levine and Doueck, 1995).

Reporting child abuse is not mandatory in England and Wales, but most professionals will be obliged to act on suspected abuse under their terms of employment or professional codes of ethics (Stewart, 2004; Weir, 2004). Under s. 47(1) of the Children Act 1989, the Local Authority is required to investigate cases where it is suspected that a child in their area is suffering or is likely to suffer 'significant harm', which is a key phrase. Certain agencies, such as the Local Education Authority, Health Authority and Housing, are required to assist the Local Authority with their inquiries, 'in particular by providing relevant information and advice'. However, apart from those specified, or those authorised by the Secretary of State, this part of the Act 'does not oblige any person to assist a local authority where doing so would be unreasonable in all the circumstances of the case'.

Some therapists are not bound by agency policy or professional codes of practice to report suspected child abuse. Their position is more complex. In effect, they will have to exercise their professional judgment in deciding whether or not to report child abuse. It also needs to be borne in mind that, according to the key document *Working Together to Safeguard Children*, child protection procedures cover teenagers up to the age of 18, rather than solely being concerned with younger children (HMG, 2006). Statutory guidance on child protection procedures also varies slightly between Northern Ireland, Scotland, Wales and England.

In some cases, concern about the welfare of children may be raised when working with an adult. In one case, a young woman began counselling with a psychotherapist to explore the abuse that she had undergone from her grandfather. She received counselling for about a year, and informed the therapist that she thought another of the grandchildren might still be the subject of abuse. The psychotherapist reported the matter to the police, who brought a prosecution against the grandfather. Although aged 79, he received sentences totalling eight years.' imprisonment for offences against his grandchildren committed over a period of 15 years, ending 10 years before his trial (*R v C* (1993)). Whether, or to what extent, the psychotherapist discussed this course of action with the client is unclear. What is important is that such a breach of client confidentiality will be seen to be justified by the overriding need to protect a potentially vulnerable child from abuse.

Child protection and the Children Act 2004

The Children Act 2004 follows on from the Laming Inquiry into the death of Victoria Climbié, when there were multiple failures in child protection systems designed to protect vulnerable children at risk of abuse. The Green Paper, *Every Child Matters*, was presented as protecting and advancing 'the needs, interests and welfare of children' (HMG, 2003: 4), and as 'putting children at the heart of policy development and service delivery' (2003: 75). The main themes of the Green Paper were the need to:

- reorganise and centralise fragmented systems of child care services;
- reduce professional barriers to inter-disciplinary co-operation;
- increase information-sharing between professionals in order to target and respond to the needs of children at risk;
- introduce new statutory requirements on Local Authorities to promote and safeguard the welfare of children.

The Children Act 2004 replaced the former Area Child Protection Committees with statutory Local Safeguarding Children Boards. These bodies co-ordinate information-sharing between professionals about children, particularly those at risk of abuse, and monitor arrangements to safeguard and promote the welfare of children by a broad range of organisations. A Children's Commissioner was appointed under the Act, with the role of promoting awareness of the views and interests of children, following on from earlier appointments in other parts of the United Kingdom.

The concerns raised by the Victoria Climbié Inquiry (Laming, 2003), and the failures of the child protection system which it revealed have contributed towards the development of a much stronger 'culture of reporting' with regard to child abuse, by health care, social work and education professionals. The clear advice given in the Department of Health guidance summary on *What To Do If You're Worried a Child is Being Abused* is: 'Refer any concerns about child abuse or neglect to social services or the police' (2003: 5). While this document also carried an extensive discussion about the young person's legal rights to confidentiality, this material is, perhaps significantly, missing from more recent statutory guidance on child protection.

Young people and under-age sexual activity

The Sexual Offences Act 2003 provided new definitions for a range of sexual activities, including 'grooming'. It set the age of consent for sexual intercourse at 16 years, so that sexual activity under this age is a criminal offence. Sexual activity with a child under the age of 13 is an absolute offence, for which there is no defence in law. Following the murders of Holly Wells and Jessica Chapman, the Bichard Inquiry recommended that under-age sexual activity be reported to the authorities, unless there are exceptional reasons for not doing so (Home Office, 2004b: 55). Some child protection agencies have interpreted this as authorisation for a blanket reporting of all penetrative sexual activity by under-13-year-olds to social services and the police as a child protection matter (LCPC, 2005: 11).

This may be desirable, or even essential, judged from a child protection viewpoint. However, this stance has been heavily criticised by agencies which provide counselling to young people on sexual issues, such as Brook, and also by the British Medical Association, as being in direct conflict with their wider professional and ethical duties towards young people. Department of Health guidance affirms that, far from automatically overriding a duty of trust towards the young person: 'The Sexual Offences Act 2003 does not affect the duty of care and confidentiality of health professionals to young people under 16' (DoH, 2004a: 1). Clearly, mandatory reporting of under-age sexual activity would protect some young people from abuse and exploitation, but at the potential cost of deterring significant numbers of other young people from seeking help on sensitive issues.

Challenging *Gillick*: The *Axon* case

In 2004, the *Daily Mail* publicised the case of a 14-year-old girl at the Brunts School, Mansfield, who had had an abortion without her mother's knowledge or consent. This case received extensive media coverage, which was largely critical of a policy which apparently permitted a young person to take such a step without parental permission or family support. Subsequent to this, a case was brought for judicial review of the Department of Health guidance, which had authorised the school's health worker to treat the young person concerned as being entitled to confidentiality on the basis of the *Gillick* decision. Sue Axon, a private individual, then brought a case to the High Court, which challenged the guidance as being misleading, and unlawful, in that it excluded parents from the decision-making process and therefore infringed the parents' human rights.

In this respect, her case embodied some of the central philosophical and ethical arguments in favour of a model of 'constrained parental autonomy'. This is a 'decision making model for children that emphasizes parental autonomy constrained by respect for the child's developing personhood' (1998: 3). This approach, as proposed by Ross, claims that US laws providing adolescents with confidential access to contraceptive treatment 'fail to give adequate respect to parental autonomy and the child's need for parental guidance' (1998: 153).

In dismissing the case, the judge carefully considered the arguments behind the original *Gillick* decision. The latter has two quite separate aspects. The first covers the capacity of a young person under 16 with sufficient understanding to *consent* to treatment on their own behalf; the second concerns their entitlement to *confidentiality* (Mason and Laurie, 2006: 273). The *Axon* case sought to challenge directly only the latter, but any change to this condition of *confidentiality* would clearly also have implications for *consent*. The young person faced with a decision would potentially be open, as a result, to additional influence or pressure from a parent to decide, or not, on a certain course of action.

The *Gillick* decision has two distinct rationales. Lord Fraser emphasised the *welfare* aspect of the young person seeking confidential medical treatment, namely that such treatment may be judged to be in their best interests as a protective measure. This theme is quite apparent in the Fraser guidelines. Lord Scarman argued on a different basis for the young person's developing capacity for *autonomous decision-making* (De Cruz, 1987). Given these differing, if complementary, rationales, it becomes essential that *Gillick* not be collapsed into the Fraser guidelines, as this loses sight of the arguments for *autonomy*.

The judge indicated that there was 'a significant public policy dimension' to the case. He attached a good deal of importance to evidence which suggested that a previous reduction in the degree of confidentiality provided to young women seeking contraceptive advice had led to a significant fall, in the order of 30 per cent, in the numbers attending clinics. An assurance of confidentiality was therefore important from a public policy perspective, in order to continue providing a necessary service to young people, one which was particularly important to young people of Indian origin. This consisted, perhaps surprisingly, of a strongly utilitarian argument, where the greater public good would be best served by retaining confidentiality for young people under *Gillick*.

The argument that *Gillick* undermined parental rights, in contrast with law in the United States, was rejected, on the grounds that the European legal tradition attached far greater value to the independent rights of children than did the US. Providing confidentiality for young people was *not* found to breach parents' rights to respect for private and family life, under Article 8 of the Human Rights Act 1998. The judge's conclusion was, therefore, that '*Gillick* remains good law' (Silber, J at 24, para. 93, *Axon v Secretary of State* [2006]).

Access to files by children and young people

Another area where children's rights may have implications for therapists is that of access to files. Children's right of access to counselling or therapeutic files was greatly increased by the *Gaskin* decision by the European Court of Human Rights (see Chapter 6). Graham Gaskin, who spent a large part of his life in Local Authority care, brought an action against Liverpool Social Services Department in order to see his social work file. Refused on the grounds of confidentiality, he was eventually successful in winning his case on the basis of violation of Article 8 of the European Convention on Human Rights (*Gaskin* [1990]). He was awarded £5,000 damages on the grounds that the procedures followed by Liverpool Social Services while he was in their care failed to secure respect for his private and family life, as required by this part of the Convention. (The case for a breach of Article 10, relating to freedom of expression and the right to information, was not found to apply by the court.)

The *Gaskin* case opened up social work health and education records to potential access by clients, both adults and younger people. Under the Data Protection Act 1998, young people have extensive rights to access records, including health, education and social work files, as well as computerised records and manual records kept in a highly structured form, i.e. in 'relevant filing systems'. The Act does not set a minimum age for entitlement to make such a request for access, but guidance from the Information Commissioner suggests that 'by the age of 12 a child can be expected to have sufficient maturity to understand the nature of the request'

(IC, 2001: 35). Information in social work, education and health files may be withheld on the grounds that it may cause 'serious harm' to the data subject, or to a third party, or where it refers to child protection issues or includes third party material. Therapists need to bear in mind that children and young people enjoy extensive rights of access to files, which are backed by statute.

Pre-trial therapy for young people as witnesses in criminal trials

One major example of the potential conflict between therapy and the law is in the case of video-recorded interviews for children subjected to alleged sexual abuse. Under the Criminal Justice Act 1991, video recordings of interviews made by police and social workers may supplement the oral testimony of children in subsequent court proceedings (Ellison, 2001). The format of the interviews is closely defined by detailed guidance from the Home Office, in what was formerly referred to as *Memorandum* interviewing (HO/DoH, 1992) and now is set out in *Achieving Best Evidence* (HO et al., 2002b).

Guidance issued by the Home Office clarified that therapy is appropriate for young people acting as witnesses prior to a criminal trial, for example for child abuse (Home Office et al., 2001). Such therapy needs to be carried out within very clear parameters, so as not to undermine the case being brought by the Crown Prosecution Service. Pre-trial therapy for young people needs to:

- be provided in close liaison with the Crown Prosecution Service;
- avoid rehearsal of evidence or recounting of the original abuse;
- report any fresh allegations or material changes to the young person's evidence;
- maintain careful and accurate records;
- avoid approaches, such as interpretive psychotherapy, hypnotherapy, psychodrama, regression techniques or unstructured groups, which may undermine the credibility of the young person's evidence.

The guidance represents an important step forward in trying to harmonise the sometimes conflicting interests of the criminal justice system and of therapy. It does make very clear that the best interests of the child are of the highest importance. Where these dictate that the young person requires therapy, but that this may conflict with the needs of the prosecution case, then the best interests of the child should come first.

In the past, the policy and practice arising from the former Home Office Memorandum interviewing policy were sharply criticised for the effects on children, whose urgent need for therapy was subordinated to the slow turning of the wheels of justice. In one survey, 81 children who had experienced child sexual abuse were interviewed by researchers from the National Children's Home to explore their perceptions of the treatment they had received from courts, police, social workers and therapists. The children's evaluations of the therapeutic help they had received, whether individual, group or family therapy, was broadly positive, with higher ratings for the two former types of therapy. Where therapy was perceived in negative or critical terms, this was sometimes because the children had experienced the process as one which seemed to repeatedly encourage them to talk about the actual abuse itself (NCH, 1994). More recent research has indicated that the issue of availability of pre-trial therapy continues to be problematic for some families.

Case study Young people's experiences of pre-trial therapy

'I was offered a counsellor after the incident by the police at the local hospital but when I called her to make an appointment she said she didn't really "do" children. The counsellor at school said she'd do it. She has been great.' (Lara, 15)

'I had seen a counsellor but she and the police said I couldn't talk about the case until it was over. I had my first real appointment with the counsellor after the trial and had to cancel it because we thought he might appeal. [He appealed the sentence but not the conviction.] I don't want to go ahead with the counselling now because when we talk about it it's in my head. I hadn't been able to go out and now I have and going out seems normal. It would have helped if I could have talked earlier.' (Mandy, 15)

'My main concern was that my son couldn't have counselling. The police said it might prejudice the trial but I could do it if he was really "falling apart". He was having nightmares and had trouble sleeping. I did too. I tried to follow up anyway but counsellors wouldn't touch him – they said the police wouldn't like it.' (Mother of boy, aged 6)

Source: Plotnikoff and Woolfson, 2004: 64–5

Voluntary organisations such as Barnardo's have, nevertheless, achieved some successful outcomes in their pre-trial therapeutic work with young people. One of these successes has been in terms of protecting the confidentiality of therapeutic records from inappropriate use in legal proceedings. Palmer records that the unit was able to maintain the confidentiality of therapy records through the effective use of Public Interest Immunity applications, which can be used to limit disclosure of sensitive child abuse information in legal proceedings. The unit also referred to supportive judicial comment, which restricted defence applications for material for the purposes of discrediting a witness (*R v Liaqat Hussain* (1996)). According to Palmer:

> despite the previous stated concerns about this area of work, in only 2 of the 42 cases were the therapist's records requested. In both cases the unit staff applied for Public Interest Immunity. On each application, the trial judge viewed the entire file and upheld their request completely in one instance and in the other asked for four sheets of recording to be submitted to the court. These sheets did not convey anything of a personal nature regarding the child and contained purely factual information. (2003: 165)

Research suggests that areas of continuing concern related to the preparation of young people as witnesses prior to criminal proceedings, are in terms of delays and insensitivity to the needs of children and families facing potentially re-traumatising court appearances (Plotnikoff and Woolfson, 2004). This illustrates some of the conflicts, which can occur between therapy and the law, which are further discussed in Chapter 3. The Crown Prosecution Service has indicated that there is emphatically no 'ban' as such on therapeutic work being undertaken with children after they have made videos of evidence for court purposes. However, it does show some of the conflict inherent in the process of promoting abused children's need for therapy and their right to justice.

Young people's experiences of abusive therapy

The experience of abusive therapy is not limited to adult clients. Some of the most closely documented cases have occurred in Local Authority care, as in the Pindown and Beck Reports. This is not to suggest that abuse is unknown in private settings.

Case study   Abusive therapy in residential care

The 'Pindown' regime
The so-called 'Pindown' regime affected 132 children between 1983 and 1989, in children's homes run by Staffordshire Social Services. Pindown was the name for a punitive type of residential care which affected children labelled by the residential system as hard to control. Under this approach, described as 'negative behaviour modification', medicine and hot food were considered to be privileges, as were conversation with staff, reading, contact with parents and daytime clothing (Levy and Kahan, 1991: 40–2). It was described in the official report as 'a regime intrinsically dependent on elements of isolation, humiliation and confrontation' (1991: 124).

The official report into Pindown described the system as 'intrinsically unethical, unprofessional and unacceptable' (Levy and Kahan, 1991: 127). It pointed out that it was 'likely to have stemmed initially from an ill-digested understanding of behavioural psychology; the regime had no theoretical framework and no safeguards' (1991: 167). What is crucial is that the regime was justified as a therapeutic process for those who experienced it, rather than simply existing as a measure of control in its own right. 'Pindown provides a salutary example of the dressing up of oppressive control in the rhetorical garb of therapy, and of the capacity of that rhetoric to convince those running the regime that what they were doing was in the best interests of the children' (Fennell, 1992: 312).

The Beck Report
One of the most alarming and best-documented cases of abusive therapy inflicted upon children can be found in the report on the activities of Frank Beck, who ran a number of Local Authority children's homes in Leicestershire between 1973 and 1986. A qualified and charismatic social worker, Beck ran a regime staffed by junior and untrained workers, with a personal blend of techniques designed to break down and remodel the behaviours of children in care via 'reparenting' them. This technique also acted as a cover for the systematic harassment, humiliation and sexual abuse of children entrusted to his care (D'Arcy and Gosling, 1998). At his trial in 1991, Beck

(Continued)

was found guilty on 17 counts, including sexual and physical assault, for which he was sentenced to life imprisonment. As with the Pindown regime, the pattern of abusive control was dignified with a therapeutic label, in this case that of 'regression therapy'. This 'treatment cocktail' included the 'apparently bizarre use of the paraphernalia of babyhood in the treatment of adolescent boys and girls'.

Management and professional safeguards were either missing or ineffective. There was little outside supervision of practice by external specialists such as psychiatrists. Consequently, 'supervision and counselling were contained within the home and carried out by staff with no training or experience to do it. It was abused by Mr Beck' (Kirkwood, 1993: 62). The young people in residential care 'found the treatment to which they were subjected in the name of therapy abusive in itself' (Kirkwood, 1993: 62).

While these examples relating to Pindown and the Beck regime may be extreme, they illustrate the potential for abuse in residential settings to be masked in a quasi-therapeutic language. Therapists coming across abusive care for young people have a number of options to bring this to the attention of the relevant authorities. If employed, they will be able to make a protected disclosure to management under the Public Interest Disclosure Act 1998. Other disclosure may be made in the public interest to the appropriate authorities, using the defence of 'qualified privilege' (see Chapter 2 for details).

Settings for therapy with children and young people

Children's rights regarding counselling and therapy vary significantly according to the context in which the service is offered. Therapists may be working with young people in an education, health, psychiatric context, voluntary agency setting, or in private practice.

Education settings: secondary school

Children's independent rights within the school setting were eclipsed by the educational reforms of the 1980s (Jeffs, 1995). This legislation stresses that *parents* rather than pupils are the consumers of education, despite the contrary values inherent within the Children Act 1989 and the UN Convention (Harris, 1993: 1).

Counselling services within schools have undergone a significant expansion in the recent past. However, the prevailing culture within schools is often one which does not fully recognise the rights of children and young people to confidentiality. Research suggests that 40 per cent of secondary schools require evidence of parental consent for counselling to take place (Jenkins and Polat,

2006: 8). In effect, this excludes many young people from seeking counselling, as the primary condition of confidentiality is thus missing. Defenders of this position often refer to several supporting propositions: first, that all staff, including counsellors, are required to work 'under the reasonable direction of the headteacher' (Pattenden, 2003: 720). Secondly, the concept of the head acting *in loco parentis* is used in support of the position that the school should not supplant parental authority, but act in ways which are consistent with parental expectations.

These arguments are mistaken. Headteachers could negotiate a confidentiality protocol with school counsellors which fully respected the rights of young people with 'sufficient understanding' to have confidential counselling. 'Reasonable direction' does not necessarily require total knowledge by the headteacher of every child's personal circumstances, but suggests the delegation of specific tasks to other appropriately skilled and qualified professionals. Secondly, the concept of being *in loco parentis* is in danger of being used out of context here, as a way of justifying a parental veto on confidential counselling services in schools. This concept simply refers to the *standard* of care required of school staff in fulfilling their duties regarding schoolchildren in their care, i.e. the standard of a 'careful parent', according to the relevant case law.

Within schools, the other major barrier to maintaining high levels of confidentiality in counselling services is the need to protect children from abuse. Local Education Authorities (LEAs) in England and Wales have a statutory duty under s. 175, Education Act 2002 to safeguard and promote the welfare of children. Part of this duty involves protection from child abuse, as part of a wider overall duty, which includes reference to health and safety, bullying and drug use. The statutory guidance on the implementation of these obligations makes it clear that this duty falls on the LEA, rather than on individual members of staff. Failure to comply with the guidance remains a disciplinary matter, rather than a breach of the substantive law (DfES, 2004: 8).

Health settings

Healthcare professionals have emerged as some of the strongest supporters of the principle of confidentiality in working with children and young people. This is confirmed by the publications and position statements of organisations such as the British Medical Association (BMA, 2001b). Medical practitioners have been concerned to protect medical and therapeutic confidentiality in their work with young people. This applies in a range of settings, whether in primary health settings such as general practice, in outreach work in schools, in drug advice work or in the provision of counselling to young people on sexual health and contraception. Ethical guidance to doctors fully recognises that it is clearly in the public interest to identify and prevent child abuse. However, it also recognises that a duty of confidentiality will be owed to a young person with sufficient understanding under the *Gillick* principle. There may be a conflict of duties, if the young person discloses abuse but also insists that no action be taken, perhaps because of a mistaken fear of breaking up the family. BMA ethical guidance recognises the conflict here, and the need to take time rather than force a hasty decision. 'Doctors must weigh the advantages and disadvantages of disclosure versus non-disclosure and make a decision based on the individual circumstances. Disclosure without consent will be justified in some cases and it follows that doctors should never make promises of secrecy' (BMAED, 2004: 160).

Confidentiality is seen in the Department of Health's *Guidance* (2004a) as valuable for promoting a sense of personal worth and of decision-making skills on the part of the young person faced with dilemmas about sexual activity and contraception. This is consistent with the government's own target of halving the rate of conception among under-18-year-olds by the year 2010 (SEU, 1999: 91). The guidance does acknowledge that breaches of confidentiality may be necessary in order to protect the vulnerable or to protect other children in a family at risk of abuse. 'The duty of confidentiality is not, however, absolute. Where a health professional believes that there is a risk to the health, safety or welfare of a young person or others which is so serious as to outweigh the young person's right to privacy, they should follow locally agreed child protection protocols, as outlined in *Working Together To Safeguard Children*' (DoH, 2004a: 3). Even in this situation, the practitioner is advised to consult with the young person concerned before making any disclosure, and work towards the latter making a disclosure on their own behalf.

The guidance distinguishes between the young person's capacity to *consent* to treatment, and their enduring right to *confidentiality*. Even if the medical practitioner decides not to provide treatment, there is an obligation to maintain confidentiality unless there are exceptional circumstances, such as child abuse. The 2004 guidance was expressly challenged as unlawful in the case brought by Sue Axon, but was upheld by the judge.

Psychiatric treatment

Each year several thousand young people are admitted to psychiatric hospitals for treatment under the Mental Health Act 1983. Therapeutic work represents one of the treatments on offer. In this relatively specialised area of psychiatric care for young people, the *Gillick* decision has had a major influence in the recognition of their independent rights as patients.

Voluntary psychiatric treatment

Provision for psychiatric treatment of young people under 18 is set out in the *Code of Practice* for the Mental Health Act 1983. The Act does not impose a legal duty to follow the Code, but it is noted that failure to do so 'could be referred to in evidence in legal proceedings' (DoH/WO, 1999: Introduction, para 1.) There is no minimum age set for admission to hospital under the Act. Fennell (1992) identified three principles for the operation of the Act in relation to young people: that they should be kept fully informed about their care and treatment; that they should generally be regarded as being able to make their own decisions, with certain provisos;

and that any intervention in the life of a young person should be 'the least restrictive possible', in accordance with the overall philosophy of the Act.

Box 7.7 Medical and psychiatric treatment of children

- s. 8, Family Law Reform Act 1969
- ss. 2, 3, 4, Mental Health Act 1983
- *Gillick* decision by House of Lords [1986]
- ss. 8, 38, 100, Children Act 1989
- Case of *Re R.* [1991]
- Case of *Re W.* [1992]
- Mental Health Act Code of Practice 1999
- *Axon* case [2006]

The legal situation regarding the treatment of young people under the age of 18, and under 16 in particular, is complex and affected by case law decisions and by the principles of the Children Act 1989. Parents or guardians of young people may agree to the admission of a young person under the age of 16 as an informal patient.

Psychiatric assessment for a child may be ordered by the courts, under s. 38 of the Children Act 1989, as part of an Interim Care Order. These orders normally last eight weeks, but can be extended by the court. Under the Mental Health Act 1983, 'medical treatment includes … physical treatment such as ECT and the administration of drugs and psychotherapy' (DoH, 1999: 64 para, 15.4).

Compulsory psychiatric treatment

A range of powers exist for authorising compulsory psychiatric assessment or treatment of children where these measures are thought to be needed. Children may receive compulsory psychiatric treatment under ss. 2, 3 and 4 of the Mental Health Act 1983 (see Chapter 5 for details of this Act). Under the Children Act 1989, a s. 8 'specific issue' order may be sought by the Local Authority, with the parents' consent, to authorise the use of a particular regime in a specialist unit, or the emergency use of medication. Via wardship proceedings under s. 100 of the same Act, the High Court has authorised medical or psychiatric treatment in extreme cases, based on its own powers of inherent jurisdiction.

Impact of medical case law after *Gillick*

Several cases have appeared to qualify the impact of the *Gillick* decision regarding the rights of young people to make decisions regarding their medical care (see Box 7.8).

Box 7.8   Case law after *Gillick*

Re R: a 15-year-old girl refusing anti-psychotic medication

In the case referred to as *Re R* in 1991, a Local Authority sought legal powers to administer anti-psychotic drugs to a 15-year-old girl with a history of severe behaviour problems. The Court of Appeal dismissed the girl's case that she did not consent to the treatment, on the grounds that parents or the courts could override her refusal. Using the analogy of the consent as a 'key' to unlock a door, Lord Donaldson argued that a competent minor could lock the door, or refuse consent, but that other keyholders, such as parents or the courts, could unlock it and override the child's wishes.

Re W: a 16-year-old girl with anorexia nervosa refusing a move to a new unit

In this case, a 16-year-old girl, suffering from anorexia nervosa, was to be moved against her will to a unit specialising in the treatment of this disorder. This move entailed a break in the psychotherapy she was receiving, as the Local Authority seeking her removal preferred the more behaviourally based form of treatment available at the specialist unit. Under s. 8 of the Family Law Reform Act 1969, minors of 16 or over can consent to surgical, medical or dental treatment. In this case, the issue was whether the right of 16-year-olds to consent to treatment meant that they could also veto treatment by withholding their agreement. Rejecting her appeal, the court found against her, claiming that neither the Family Law Reform Act 1969, nor the *Gillick* decision, meant that the rights of young people were absolute with regard to consent to treatment and in fact that W's views 'were of no weight' in the court's decision.

The relevance of this first case to therapists is that it appeared to limit the impact of the *Gillick* decision, and created an air of uncertainty for therapists working with children. This effect is even more evident in the second key legal case, referred to as *Re W* in 1992, to protect the child's anonymity. *Re W* is important because it set some limits on the right of young people aged 16–17 years to decide their own medical or psychotherapeutic treatment in life-threatening circumstances. The effect of the decision in the second case has been to undermine the effect of *Gillick*. Taking the lock analogy a step further, it has been aptly pointed out that 'if the child is inside and has turned the key in the lock, the doctor and a parent may jointly break the door in' (Fennell, 1992: 326). Fortin has pointed out that both cases could have been resolved much more appropriately using the provisions of the Mental Health Act 1983, rather than the powers of the High Court (1998: 76). Alderson notes that both cases 'could have been discussed within provisions made by the Mental Health Act 1983…without needing to refer to *Gillick*' (1993: 49). In other words, both girls could have been treated on a compulsory basis under the Mental Health Act 1983, without the need to take the issues to court. Brazier is less restrained in her judgment of the tortuous judicial reasoning behind the decisions in these two cases and concludes that '*Re R* and *Re W* make nonsense of *Gillick*' (2003: 370).

The limits of autonomy: suicide and self-harm

The cases described above illustrate an important principle, namely that young people under the age of 18 do not have the right to engage in risky behaviour with the potential consequence of inflicting long-term or even fatal damage to themselves. The courts, or a person holding parental responsibility, can intervene decisively in order to prevent a young person known to be risking their health as a consequence of an eating disorder, or through engaging in extensive and serious self-harm. In the past, the courts have, for example, overruled the refusal of a blood transfusion by a young Jehovah's Witness, because of the immediate risk to his life. Of course, in many situations therapists are working with young people engaged in a wide spectrum of risky or potentially self-damaging behaviour, ranging from use of illicit drugs, to self-harm through cutting, to joy-riding in stolen cars. Where there is a clear and significant risk to the young person, or to others, there is presumably a stronger case to be made for reporting such behaviour to the authorities, on the grounds that it is in the public interest to do so. This rather begs the question, however, of what the authorities can realistically do to control the young person's risky behaviour, short of the exceptional case of admission to psychiatric care for a young person meeting the criteria of the Mental Health Act 1983.

It needs to be remembered that, while *Gillick* applies, as case law, to England, Wales and Northern Ireland, young people in Scotland have much more firmly established rights to autonomous decision-making under statute, via the Age of Legal Capacity Act 1991. It has also been suggested that a young person retains the right to refuse treatment under Scottish law, although this has yet to be definitively established in the courts (BMAED, 2004: 139; *Houston (applicant)* (1996)). However, the *Gillick* principle still holds good for the vast majority of children and young people of 'sufficient understanding' who seek counselling or therapy. It is therefore important that therapists know enough about the conflicting case law as outlined above to refute any mistaken claims that *Gillick* has now been overturned or no longer applies with its previous relevance to therapy.

The increasing complexity of the law here is shown by the example of a 14-year-girl who sought counselling from an eating disorders clinic with the full knowledge and permission of her worried parents. While the therapists at the clinic were able to work productively with the girl as the client under *Gillick*, there was also the knowledge that the parents had the option of seeking her admission to a local psychiatric unit for young people, should the clinic's therapy not produce the desired results. Being aware of both options provided a basis of information for trying to establish a therapeutic alliance with the girl, acknowledged and supported by her parents, which would allow the time and space for effective therapeutic work to take place. The law is an uneasy blend of voluntary and coercive elements concerning therapeutic work with children and young people, which therapists need to consider, but without permitting this to side-track them from carrying out their work.

The Mental Health Act 1983 *Code of Practice* takes full account of *Gillick* and the subsequent case law outlined above. As a result, it abides by the principles established that young people under 18 with capacity may consent to medical treatment, but may not refuse it. If the young person does refuse medical treatment, then this treatment can be authorised by one person holding parental responsibility, or by the courts. This sets up a complex matrix of possible scenarios, outlined in the

Box 7.9	Summary of young people's rights and parental consent to informal admission, psychiatric treatment and discharge under the Mental Health Act 1983		
	Status of consent, or refusal of consent, for voluntary psychiatric treatment of young people by persons with parental responsibility		
	Informal admission	**Treatment**	**Discharge**
*'Gillick-*competent' young people under 16*	Parent may arrange young person's admission. Parent cannot override young person's wishes for admission	Young person may consent to treatment, but young person's refusal of consent may be overridden by parent	Young person's wishes for discharge will be 'ordinarily' overridden by parent
Young people aged 16–17*	Young person may arrange own admission, irrespective of parent's wishes	Young person may consent to treatment, but young person's refusal of consent may be overridden by parent	Young person may discharge self, but use of compulsory treatment under the Mental Health Act 1983 is a possible option
*Those deemed capable of expressing their own wishes.			
Source: adapted from DOH/WO, 1999: 143–6			

table above, concerning the rights of young people to give or refuse consent to admission, treatment and discharge from psychiatric care (see Box 7.9).

Confidentiality within psychiatric treatment

The MHA 1983 *Code of Practice* emphasises the importance of confidentiality within the process of providing psychiatric treatment for young people in the mental health system:

> Children's rights to confidentiality should be strictly observed. It is important that all professionals have a clear understanding of their obligations of confidentiality to children and that any limits to such an obligation are made clear to a child who has the capacity to understand them. (DoH/WO, 1999: 147)

Mental health law is undergoing change, with several draft Bills having been substantially revised or discarded. The continuing influence of *Gillick* was expressed by the Expert Committee on the consultative Green Paper. This committee favoured a decisive shift towards clear recognition of 16 as the threshold for capacity for making decisions about treatment. This would be linked to a rebuttable presumption of children's capacity for consent from an age as low as 10 or 12 (DoH, 1999: 112). The Mental Health Act Commission, which oversees the operation of the Act, also recommended that the existing case law on *Gillick* be given clearer legal expression and authority by being incorporated into statute (MHAC, 1999). This would presumably be on the lines of Scottish legislation, such as the Age of Legal Capacity Act 1991. However, these radical proposals have not been included within the government's reform agenda for reshaping mental health services for young people via the *National Service Framework for Children, Young People and Maternity Services* (DoH, 2004b), or via the proposed amendments to the existing Mental Health Act 1983.

Voluntary organisations

There is a wide range of voluntary organisations providing counselling and psychotherapy to children and young people. In many cases, these agencies provide counselling services in school settings, under contract to the school or to the Local Education Authority. Their voluntary status gives them increased freedom to determine policy on access to counselling, confidentiality and child protection reporting procedures. However this degree of latitude may be constrained by two factors. First, the major reorganisation of children's services via the *Every Child Matters* agenda (HMG, 2003) may mean that voluntary organisations are increasingly required to work within the welfare and child protection perspective of Local Safeguarding Children Boards. Secondly, voluntary organisations are becoming more dependent upon local and central government for funding. The risk is that this funding may come at a price, in terms of increasing the tilt towards reporting of suspected child abuse or under-age sexual activity, as opposed to leaving such decisions to individual practitioners' discretion, or to the policy guidance of management committees.

The apparent complexity and unfamiliarity of the law relating to therapy with children and young people may seem daunting at first sight. Some basic guidelines are suggested in Box 7.10 to help therapists who are unsure of how best to base their practice on sound principles.

Box 7.10   Guidelines for professional practice in therapy with children and young people

- Be clear about your helping role and its boundaries, as counsellor, therapist, befriender or advocate.
- Find out about the statute or case law which governs your particular area of work with children, such as the Children Act 1989, *Gillick*, etc.
- Be sure of your agency policy or your own key personal principles in working with children and young people.

(Continued)

- Be clear about who is the main client you are working with – the child/young person, or the family unit as a whole.
- Set and communicate the limits to keeping confidentiality which apply to your work.
- Negotiate and work to a therapeutic agreement with the child or young person as far as possible, covering:

  - risk issues
  - child protection procedures
  - recording and access to files
  - complaints systems

- Be clear about your own working arrangements for:

  - professional supervision
  - personal and agency accountability
  - personal or vicarious liability in the case of legal action
  - obtaining legal advice as required
  - advice from your professional association
  - membership of professional protection society or coverage by indemnity insurance policy

Private practice

A therapist working in private practice will be governed by the law of contract, subject to the usual legal redress for any breach of confidence, or for professional negligence (see Chapters 4 and 5). They are not required to report child abuse under the Children Act 1989, but may choose whether or not to do so in the public interest. The law does not require private citizens as such to report child abuse. However, a therapist, as a private citizen, may safely break confidentiality in order to report child abuse, since it is clearly in the public interest to protect children from 'significant harm'. The key issue for the therapist to decide is who the contract is with: the child or young person, or the parents who may be paying for the therapy. Any contract drawn up needs to specify what rights to information, if any, the parents have regarding the progress or content of the therapeutic work. The danger will be that, if refused information, the parents may end the therapy and withdraw the child. If therapeutic confidentiality is set out in the original contract, it will, in theory at least, be harder for parents to insist later on knowing what is happening in each session.

Summary

The position of children and young people as clients in the therapeutic relationship is closely linked to their rights as set out in law. The right of children and young people to an independent counselling relationship is acknowledged by the

Gillick and *Axon* decisions, and by the Children Act and UN Convention on the Rights of the Child, both of 1989. It follows from the *Gillick* decision that young people have a right to confidentiality, depending upon their level of maturity and understanding as perceived by the adult therapist, independently of the wishes of the parents. Children enjoy rights of access to their files in many situations. Following case law after *Gillick*, young people are now in the slightly contradictory position of being able to consent to, but not refuse, medical treatment, which has complex implications for their admission to psychiatric care, and for their right to refuse essential, life-saving medical treatment. However, the principle remains intact for the vast majority of young people with 'sufficient understanding'.

The duties of therapists in counselling children and young people are perhaps more complex than for counselling adults. Confidentiality can be broken in order to report suspected child abuse, but this is not mandatory for therapists under the law. Therapists have a responsibility to know the appropriate law, and to work within it – not an easy task in this area. Crucially, they need to decide who is their client – child or parent – and to make this explicit in any therapeutic agreement which is drawn up. The problem of determining whether a child is of 'sufficient understanding' for the therapist remains a difficult appraisal, where official guidelines can only complement, rather than replace, the exercise of professional judgment.

Discussion points

1 What do you understand by the *Gillick* principle? How would you go about establishing that a child or young person can show 'sufficient understanding' of what is on offer in a counselling or therapeutic relationship?

2 What policy, if any, does your agency have on counselling children and young people? In what ways does the service differ from that provided for adult clients, and why?

3 How should counsellors and therapists working in schools best meet their professional responsibilities to children, parents and the education authorities? How should the balance be drawn between the principles of the *Gillick* decision and child protection responsibilities where counselling is concerned?

4 Should all therapists be legally obliged to report child abuse, as in the USA? When should the child's right to confidentiality be respected, even if it means that child abuse is not reported?

5 Has the concept of children's rights applied to therapy gone too far? In what circumstances should the therapist seek to work with the child as the client, rather than including parents, or working with the family as a whole?

8 Statutory Regulation of Therapists

Discussion of the law and therapy is inseparable from the issues of professionalisation and statutory regulation. Almost by definition, established professions such as medicine and the law have a recognised status in legislation and case law. This authorises them to carry out certain activities, and delegates some of the responsibility for self-discipline and the maintenance of high standards of practice. Other occupational groups, such as teaching, nursing and social work, have sometimes been described as semi-professions. These groups possess some of the features of established professional groups, but lack unqualified acknowledgement of their professional expertise (Etzioni, 1969). However, unlike these semi-professions, therapists in the UK have been relatively slow to recognise the legal dimension of their practice.

Statutory recognition of therapy

Establishing a clear relationship with the law is one of the elements which is associated with acquiring full professional status. Achieving statutory recognition for psychotherapy and counselling has now emerged as a major goal for the future. Therapy has achieved well-established statutory reference in two main areas, counselling relating to adoption and to infertility treatment, which will now be explored.

Statutory recognition of counselling: adoption

The first statutory recognition of counselling in the UK was in s. 26 of the Children Act 1975. As later outlined in s. 1 of the Adoption Act 1976, it became the duty of every local authority to establish a service for 'counselling for persons with problems relating to adoption'. Adoption has been legal in England and Wales since 1926. Scotland has had a legal form of adoption since 1930, but with the added possibility of adopted persons applying for information on their birth mother and father (if recorded) from the age of 17. The Houghton Committee, set up in 1969 to reform adoption law, was at first reluctant to change the law to widen access to records. It was swayed by the research into the Scottish system of access to birth records undertaken by John Triseliotis of Edinburgh University (HO/SED, 1972; Triseliotis, 1973).

This research demonstrated the value to individuals of acquiring knowledge of their origins, and suggested that the numbers coming forward to use the service would not be overwhelming. A major consideration was that birth mothers had been promised secrecy when initially placing their child for adoption. How would this rewriting of the contract of confidentiality now be managed to the mutual benefit of all parties concerned? The answer to this difficult social and human problem was via the provision of counselling. The Act introduced the somewhat problematic concept of 'compulsory counselling' for those adopted before provision was introduced. For those adopted after 12 November 1975, the counselling was to be offered on a voluntary basis.

Counselling as 'a protective screen'

In the first place, the responsibility for providing the counselling service fell to Local Authority social services departments (DHSS, 1976a). The dilemmas facing the social worker in this counsellor role, as keeper of sensitive personal information, were carefully noted by researchers such as Halmes and Timms. They identified 'the ambiguity inherent in the law: is the law on access and the provision of counselling a law for the provision of information, or a law for the protection of natural parents?' (1985: 27). Counselling was designed here to serve *a protective function*, as a form of screen, to balance the competing rights of the individual to birth record information, and of the birth mother or father to the original compact of confidentiality. Providing only partial access to information, namely information from past circumstances rather than current information, has been one strategy used here to manage the release of information.

The concept of compulsory counselling also underlined the confusing signals being given here to applicants. 'In effect a double message was being given to adopted people: they were entitled by law to the information, but the counselling implied that to use it may be unwise' (Hodgkins, 1991: 7). The counsellor's only statutory obligation is to help the applicant to obtain a birth certificate and the name of the placing agency. Many will go well beyond this narrow remit, in order to help the individual to explore the meaning of their being adopted, and their expectations, if any, of reunion with birth parents.

Purposes of adoption counselling

The original purpose of adoption records counselling was seen as a means of controlling the release of sensitive personal information, rather than having a more enabling or empowering purpose for clients. According to the then Department of Health and Social Security, the aims were to ensure:

(1) that the adopted person has considered the possible effect of any enquiries both on himself and on others; and
(2) that the information he seeks, and to which he now has a legal right, is provided in a helpful and appropriate manner. (DHSS, 1976b)

The original practice remit of adoption counselling was thus set in very narrow terms. However, the personal benefits of counselling and access to birth records information can be enormous, despite the problems detailed above. One adoptee explained that 'You want to know if you are a child of love or lust' (Halmes and Timms, 1985: 2). For another, the experience of being heard was crucial:

> For my part, being asked how it felt, over and over, by someone who looked genuinely interested, someone who didn't back off when I was not immediately able to respond, helped me to appreciate the significance of this process, and allowed me to connect with my feelings of outrage, pain, excitement and apprehension. (Marks, 1995: 49)

Adoption Support Agencies

Recent legislation in the form of the Adoption and Children Act 2002 closely regulates and controls the provision of adoption counselling. Adoption support may only be provided by Adoption Support Agencies (ASAs), which need to be registered. Providing adoption support without being registered is an offence under s. 11 of the Care Standards Act 2003. However, this is not intended to prohibit any form of counselling which merely touches on a client's experience of adoption. A therapist discussing adoption with a client does not necessarily take on the functions of an Adoption Support Agency, and does not necessarily need to register with the authorities. The activities of adoption support services are closely defined as assisting persons over 18 either to obtain birth records information, or to facilitate contact with their relatives. An adoption support service may consist of a voluntary or profit-making organisation, or a sole practitioner. Nevertheless, such a body 'is not an ASA merely because it provides information in connection with adoption ... [it] does not extend to a self-help group meeting in a person's house' (Bridge and Swindells, 2003: 273).

Dilemmas in adoption counselling

From the counsellor's point of view, the ethical and legal dilemmas may arise in the form of balancing competing rights, namely the right of the individual to obtain birth records information, and the earlier, original right of the birth parent to privacy. In one case, the counsellor was faced with the need to assess the degree of personal risk posed to the birth mother by the request for information. Here the rights of the parties were in direct conflict, with little in the way of precedent to guide the counsellor towards a final decision.

The client's right of data access is not absolute, as was made clear in one of the few cases involving therapy to be heard at Appeal Court level.

Case study   Client's right of access to adoption records denied

This case concerns the correct interpretation of a statutory duty to provide counselling and information to an applicant concerning their adoptive parent. Under s. 51 of the Adoption Act 1976, counselling was provided for persons who were adopted and who wished to obtain information about their birth records. In this particular case, the

(Continued)

(Continued)

request for information was from R., a psychiatric patient at Broadmoor Hospital, who had a history of extreme violence, and who had expressed aggressive feelings towards the birth mother who had placed him for adoption at the age of nine weeks. His request for information could have revealed his mother's identity. This request was refused by the Registrar General, after first obtaining medical reports. The applicant then requested a judicial review of this administrative decision, but his case was dismissed by the Court of Appeal.

Source: R. v Registrar General ex parte Smith [1991]

The clash here was between the rights under statute of the individual to information, and the rights of the birth mother to safety and privacy. When this request was refused, the client applied for a judicial review, to clarify the grounds for this administrative decision. Greater priority, however, was given to the protection required by his birth mother. It was decided that to release the information would have placed her under substantial threat of attack, based on the client's past behaviour as interpreted by expert medical witnesses.

The Court of Appeal's decision confirmed the correctness of the Registrar General's decision to deny access to the information. It also provided, incidentally, a degree of protection for the counselling staff who would have had to respond directly to R.'s request for the information, and who themselves might have been at some degree of personal risk in doing so. The court's decision set a clear path through a tangle of conflicting legal principles concerning the rights of the individual, on the one hand, and the need to prevent serious breaches of the law on the other. Its conclusion was that 'the performance of the statutory duty would not be enforced, even when framed in absolute terms, if to do so would enable someone to cause serious harm to others in the future' (at 255). From an ethical perspective, the client's right to obtain personal information, from a liberal individualist approach, was therefore judged to be subject to wider considerations of the public good, based on a utilitarian model.

Conflicts within adoption counselling

For therapists, this case is a reminder that their work is not carried on in a social vacuum. Activities which are by their nature highly intimate and private can be charged with a wider social responsibility, as demonstrated here, albeit with rather an extreme example. The case also underlines some of the special problems associated with adoption records counselling, and the ambiguous position it can be seen to occupy. In addition, adoption records counselling places a strain on the therapist's usual primary allegiance to the client as the recipient of their service. As illustrated by this example, there can be a threat of violence to a third party. There is a need here for the interests of other interested parties, besides the client, to be fully explored in each situation. 'The counsellor does have a responsibility to represent to the adopted person the interests of other people involved ...', which is not necessarily standard practice with all schools of therapy. However, 'this should always be done on the basis of researched facts and not assumptions' (Hodgkins, 1991: 14).

To summarise, the judgment established a point of law about the subordination of a statutory duty to the wider principle of preventing serious crime. It raises the issue for therapists of their responsibilities to third parties not present in the consulting room, and of the added pressures that this expectation may place on their therapeutic work.

Statutory recognition of counselling: infertility counselling

The second area of clear statutory recognition of counselling has been in the field of infertility treatment. Rapid technological advances in the treatment of infertile couples prompted the setting up of the Warnock Committee. This took a positive and generally understanding view of the role that counselling could play in helping donors and couples make difficult emotional decisions. In contrast with the earlier, hesitant approach to adoption counselling, the Warnock Report made a number of striking recommendations, which laid out a clear and purposeful agenda for counselling. It argued for recognition of its distinct professional expertise, linked to appropriate training and qualification (Warnock, 1985: 16).

Under s. 3 of the Human Fertilisation and Embryology Act 1990, an offer of counselling to potential donors or recipients of the service is mandatory. For example, under Schedule 3 of the Act:

(1)   Before a person gives consent under this Schedule –
(a)   he must be given a suitable opportunity to receive proper counselling about the implications of taking the proposed steps...

Counselling is of key importance in establishing the necessary basis of informed consent by the donor or recipient of treatment.

Code of practice

The details of how counselling is to be provided are set out in the statutory *Code of Practice* issued by the Human Fertilisation and Embryology Authority (HFEA, 2003). In the Code, counselling as an activity is distinguished from the processes of:

- giving information
- establishing the normal clinical relationship
- assessing people for treatment

It goes on to identify three different types of counselling:

- *counselling as information-giving*, about the implications of the proposed course of action;
- *supportive counselling*, through providing emotional support, for example when a client is failing to become pregnant;

- *therapeutic counselling*: 'to assist people in developing successful coping strategies for dealing with both the short and long term consequences of infertility and treatment. It includes helping people to try to adjust to their expectations and to come to terms with their particular situation' (HFEA, 2003: 71).

The resources needed to achieve this are set out in detail. 'Treatment centres are expected to create an atmosphere that is conducive to discussion and allows sufficient time for counselling to be conducted sensitively' (2003: 71). Requirements for counselling practice are specified to include either a social work qualification, counselling diploma, infertility counselling award, or chartered psychologist status. Relevant criminal convictions, for example for violence, dishonesty, blackmail, sexual offences against children, drugs offences and breaches of regulatory machinery, are to be considered when making appointments.

Several points stand out in the way that counselling is introduced into the process of providing infertility treatment. First, it is identified as a distinct area of expertise, deliberately separated out from the clinical responsibilities of the doctor organising the treatment (para. 7.7). Secondly, the specific boundaries of counselling confidentiality, based on the primacy of information shared between client and counsellor, rather than making information available to any member of the team as a whole, are carefully demarcated and preserved. Under para. 7.26: 'Information obtained in the course of counselling is expected to be confidential'. In turn, the Code further elaborates:

> 3.22: Where adverse information has been provided in confidence to a member of staff at the treatment centre. Consent is expected to be sought from the information provider to discuss it with other members of staff. Where such consent is refused but the member of staff considers the matter as crucial to the decision being taken treatment centres are expected to use their discretion, based on good professional practice, before breaking that confidence. (HFEA, 2003)

The Code set out a distinct role for counsellors and established fresh boundaries for handling confidential information, based on a counselling, rather than a medical, model.

Practice issues in infertility counselling

From a practice point of view, the Code sets out an admirable standard to follow. The need for counselling within the treatment and decision-making process is presented as one which should not be restricted to the early contact with the service, but, as with adoption, needs to extend throughout the contact with the centre. Thus 'it may be imperative for the counselling to which patients are likely to be directed...to apprise patients of the results which they are likely to meet, and for the counselling to be available throughout the treatment cycle programme, and even afterwards' (Morgan and Lee, 1991: 17). In addition, 'It is possible that after many repeated, unsuccessful attempts to establish a pregnancy, counselling is more necessary than at the beginning' (1991: 150–1).

The crucial function of counselling in relation to proposed infertility treatment lies in relation to the concept of informed consent by the applicant or patient.

Counselling is not obligatory, and may be refused, but it must be offered to the person seeking treatment, to enable them to make an informed choice. This was demonstrated in the case brought by Diane Blood against the HFEA over its refusal of her request to use her deceased husband's sperm in order to become pregnant.

Case study   Status of informed consent in the absence of counselling

In 1996, Diane Blood brought legal proceedings against the Human Fertilisation and Embryology Authority (HFEA) in order to be able to use her deceased husband's sperm to start a pregnancy. The sperm had been taken from her husband just prior to his death from meningitis. Mrs Blood's request was refused by the HFEA, on the grounds that her husband had not given his written consent, had not received information and had not had the opportunity for counselling, as required by law.

Diane Blood argued that she and her late husband were committed to starting a family, and had discussed the possibility of his dying before this happened. The HFEA refused permission for the use of the stored sample either in the UK, or in another European country. The Appeal Court upheld the HFEA's decision not to permit use of the sample in the UK, but considered that Mrs Blood had a right under European law to seek treatment in another country. It referred the matter back to the HFEA, which withdrew its objection to her using the sample in another country. She then went on to have two successful pregnancies, following treatment in Europe using the stored sample.

Source: R v HFEA, ex parte Blood [1997]

The case illustrates the crucial role perceived for counselling in the process of establishing informed consent to treatment. From an ethical point of view, in this situation the law places a high value on promoting autonomy, given the sensitivity of issues around infertility and assisted conception. It also perhaps illustrates the rather cumbersome nature of the law in attempting to deal with difficult dilemmas which were never anticipated in the original drafting of the legislation.

Developments in the provision of therapy

The first full statutory recognition of counselling has been in the fields of adoption and infertility. Starting from a rather narrow conception of counselling in adoption, and moving towards a more rounded one in infertility counselling, the comparison suggests how public perceptions of counselling are now more informed by the views of counsellors themselves, for example regarding roles and confidentiality. Thus the legislation on adoption counselling was influenced by the views of the British Association of Social Workers, whereas the law concerning the provision of infertility counselling bore the stamp of the British Association for Counselling. In both cases, the potential for a widening of the original brief, or what sociologists call 'net-widening', has occurred. New needs are identified and the pressure for counselling to respond to a wider range of situations begins to develop. It is striking that both instances of statutory counselling provision revolve around the processes of releasing information and of decision-making in the context of family relationships, either from the past or the intended future.

Professionalisation of therapy

The drive for statutory recognition of psychotherapy and counselling is under way, a declared part of the therapeutic community's agenda for the next decade. The process is often presented as a series of measures or steps that organised groups of therapists need to take in order both to obtain full recognition for their work, and to protect the public against untrained or incompetent practitioners. This approach is heavily influenced by what is described as the 'trait' model of professionalisation, namely that professional groups are distinguished by possession of key characteristics or traits. The acquisition of the full range of traits signals that the process of professionalisation is complete. Johnson (1972: 23), notes that professional status according to the trait model includes most of the following characteristics:

- skill based on theoretical knowledge
- provision of training and education
- testing the competence of members
- organisation of members
- adherence to a professional code of conduct
- altruistic service
- complaints and disciplinary procedures
- statutory recognition

The next section describes some of the main aspects of statutory regulation of therapists in the USA and UK, and notes key developments towards regulation.

Statutory regulation of therapists

Statutory recognition would entail the use of legal sanctions concerning the authorised use of a specific *title*, or possessing the right to *practise*. Disciplinary measures could entail the removal of the individual's right to use the title or to practise the profession, as in the case of doctors disciplined by the General Medical Council.

Alberding has identified five potentially negative and five potentially positive consequences of regulation, based on the US experience (see Box 8.1).

The table lists many of the standard arguments for and against statutory regulation currently rehearsed with regard to therapy in the UK. In the USA, regulation at state level entails the right for counsellors to privileged communication, which is not applicable to therapists in the UK. Under this privilege, counsellors in the USA are not required to disclose information to the courts, or to act as a witness concerning a client. There is an added importance for US counsellors in achieving

---

Box 8.1   Potential positive and negative consequences of counsellor regulation in the USA

Positive consequences	Negative consequences
• Protects public from incompetent practitioners	• Discriminates against some competent practitioners
• Profession increases power and prestige	• Public may lose some power and control
• Counsellors more likely to receive third party insurance payments for providing service	• Cost of service to consumers may rise.
• Right of privileged communication acquired by law	• Regulation may lead to a stagnating profession
• Protects right of counsellors to practise from encroachment by potential competitors in mental health field	• Regulation lulls consumers into unwary and vulnerable state

Source: Alberding et al., 1993: 35

---

legal regulation, in that this status can provide access to funding by insurance companies for therapy or mental health care as a reliable source of income. This is an issue of major concern to therapists in the USA, where public provision of therapy or mental health care is limited, compared with the UK.

Purpose of statutory regulation in the UK

Attempts to achieve statutory regulation of therapy in the UK have been under way for some years. The purpose of therapists achieving statutory regulation is twofold. First, there is seen to be a need to protect the public and other consumers from incompetent or fraudulent practitioners. Secondly, regulation provides a degree of formal recognition of the status and value of the profession's contribution to society (Sieghart, 1978: iv). Thus, it follows that, under regulation, an individual's ability to practise would be tied to their having to follow a stringent code of ethics. Breach of the Code could result in removal from a list of qualified practitioners, which would debar the erring individual from future practice.

Developments towards achieving professional status

Of the range of therapists' professional associations, only the British Psychological Society currently possesses statutory recognition in the form of Chartered Status. Chartered Status can be awarded to psychologists with six years' training, made up of three years of study at degree level plus three years' postgraduate training and professional supervision. They are also subject to a code of ethics, where the ultimate decision-makers about breaches of the code and disciplinary measures include non-psychologists.

The BPS has been a Chartered Body since its incorporation by Royal Charter in 1965. It has been authorised to maintain a Register of Chartered Psychologists since 1987. This step was achieved through an order of the Privy Council, rather than via primary legislation, such as a Bill placed before Parliament. Statutory recognition is thus available for Chartered Psychologists via membership of the BPS. It also applies to medically qualified psychotherapists, via their status as medical practitioners regulated by the General Medical Council. For non-medical (or lay) therapists, the search for full professional recognition has been a long process. Landmarks in this drive for recognition include those listed in Box 8.2.

Box 8.2   Developments towards statutory regulation by therapists

1960:   Professions Supplementary to Medicine Act (PSMA) 1960, regulating professions such as occupational therapists, physiotherapists and radiographers
1971:   *Foster Report* on Scientology
1978:   *Sieghart Report* on the statutory regulation of psychotherapy
1981:   Psychotherapy (Registration) Bill presented by Graham Bright, MP
1982:   Rugby conference of psychotherapy groups, under BAC auspices
1989:   UK Standing Conference for Psychotherapy set up (later to become the UKCP)
1993:   Voluntary Register of UKCP psychotherapists
1995:   Voluntary Register of BCP psychotherapists
1996:   Voluntary Register of BAC/COSCA counsellors
1999:   Health Act 1999, with provision under s. 60 for statutory regulation of professions allied to medicine via the Health Professions Council
2001:   Psychotherapy Bill presented by Lord Alderdice
2005:   Department of Health 'mapping' exercise of counselling and psychotherapy, preparatory to statutory regulation by Health Professions Council

---

The policy adopted by therapists' organisations in seeking government approval for statutory recognition has been a gradualist one. The Foster Report in 1971 broached the issue of regulating 'psychological medicine' or therapeutic treatment, as a consequence of its investigation of the Church of Scientology. The Sieghart Report in 1978 represented the response made to this encouraging signal by a wide range of professional organisations. However, the latter failed to provide a united response, and the government then took more of a 'wait and see' approach towards implementing legislation: 'the DHSS stated that legislation would not be possible until a coherent picture of the psychotherapy profession could be presented' (Abram, 1992: 14). The policy adopted by the therapeutic community has since sought to operate in a number of ways. The movement towards regulation has focused on achieving greater coherence and unity within the different sectors of the therapy community, for example under the broad umbrella of the UKCP. However, the underlying split between psychotherapy and counselling has yet to be resolved. There have been moves to establish voluntary registers of competent practitioners, which will indicate a high degree of professional commitment to self-regulation, and demonstrate an ability to identify and maintain standards of good practice. The next stage would be for this process to be crowned by formal statutory recognition. This could take the form of a Practice Act or a Title Act, either restricting the practice of therapy, or the use of specified terms such as 'counsellor', 'therapist' or 'psychotherapist'.

The Foster Report

The Foster Report represented a landmark in the process of acquiring statutory recognition. Its terms of reference were announced in 1969 by Richard Crossman as being 'to enquire into the practice and effects of scientology' (Foster, 1971: v). This followed growing public concern about the secretive practices allegedly used by the Church of Scientology, and its use of psychological measures to recruit, retain and control its membership. Moving from its original focus on Scientology, the Report went on to explore the benefits of regulating psychological treatments in a more general form.

Amongst its principal recommendations was the following statement:

(a) that psychotherapy (in the general sense of the treatment, for fee or reward, of illnesses, complaints by psychological means) should be organised as a restricted profession open only to those who undergo an appropriate training and are willing to adhere to a proper code of ethics, and that the necessary legislation should be drafted and presented to Parliament as soon as possible. (Foster, 1971: v)

Chapter 9 of the Report provided a detailed case for the regulation of 'psychological medicine' (1971: 176–81). The author's conclusion was that 'the intervention of Parliament has become necessary' (1971: 17). Intervention and regulation were justified on the grounds of therapy's capacity to cause harm: 'the danger in anything other than the most skilled hands is great and, what is worse, the possibilities of abuse by the unscrupulous are immense' (Foster, 1971: 177).

The conclusion was that:

it is high time that the practice of psychotherapy for reward should be restricted to members of a profession properly qualified in its techniques and trained – as all organised professions are trained – to use the patient's dependence which flows from the inherent inequality of the relationship only for the good of the patient himself, and never for the exploitation of his weakness to the therapist's profit. (1971: 179)

However, the Report betrays a marked degree of confusion about the distinctions to be drawn between different psychological therapies. It founders on a recurrent problem, that of producing definitions of the types of therapy which are acceptable to the professionals concerned and understandable by the wider public. Foster thus tried to differentiate between psychiatry, psychology, counselling and psychotherapy. 'Psychiatry' dealt with emotional or mental problems, 'psychology' mainly with problems of the intellect (1971: 176). 'Counselling' was widely practised in everyday life, as was 'psychotherapy without a fee'. There was, therefore, no compelling case for restricting the practice of either counselling or psychology as such. Given that almost everyone practised some form of psychotherapy on others in terms of personal relationships, the Report concluded that only psychotherapy which was based on a fee or reward in cash or in kind should be subject to statutory control (1971: 180). The problem of definition may have proved intractable, but the overall message to the relevant professions was clear: steps towards the formal regulation of psychotherapy would now be favourably received by the authorities.

The Sieghart Report

The next development was in the form of the Sieghart Report (1978), the product of a two-year working party, following the recommendations of the Foster Report on Scientology. The working party grew out of discussions between the Department of Health and Social Security, the British Psycho-Analytical Society and six other practitioner organisations in the field of psychotherapy (Mowbray, 1995: 42). The Report limited itself to the law relating to England and Wales. It picked up, but failed to resolve, the problem of *definition* bequeathed to it by the Foster Report. Thus, the Report commented:

> we have serious doubts whether psychotherapy as a function could be defined precisely enough by statutory language to prevent evasion, without at the same time casting the net so wide as to catch many people who are outside the mischief which the statute is designed to meet. We have in mind here professions as diverse as general medical practitioners, applied psychologists, clergymen, counsellors and educators who do not present themselves as specialised psychotherapists, but many of whom use interpersonal techniques in the course of their ordinary work which could be interpreted as falling within the definition of 'psychotherapy' if that definition were made sufficiently wide to prevent evasion by the unscrupulous. (Sieghart, 1978: 6)

A further problem was acknowledged in that there were other professional groups, such as social workers, who were not necessarily psychotherapists as such, but who might possess and use some similar skills. The role of the proposed Council was accordingly 'to encourage continued variety and innovation, rather than attempt to impose any kind of uniformity' (1978: 8).

The Report came up with an elegant organisational solution to the problem of controlling a profession which resisted easy or comprehensive definition. This was in the form of a preference for regulation by means of a Title Act, rather than a Practice Act. The working party described the use of a Title Act as 'indicative registration', and a Practice Act as 'functional registration'.

> we were driven to the conclusion that functional regulation was not feasible in our case, because there is simply no way of defining the practice of psychotherapy with enough certainty to make it possible for, say, a Magistrates' Court to decide whether someone has been practising it or not ... only `indicative' regulation would be feasible. (1978: vi)

A crucial role in operating statutory regulation would be performed by the adoption of a code of ethics. It was envisaged that there would be a single code to cover all registered practitioners, which would specify the kinds of professional misconduct requiring disciplinary action, such as the following examples:

- breach of professional confidence;
- sexual or financial exploitation of a patient;
- commercial advertising;
- 'fee-splitting', or the making of any payments for the referral of patients;
- failure to obtain the patient's informed consent to treatment;
- conviction of a crime rendering the practitioner unfit to remain on the register;
- dishonestly claiming possession of qualifications in psychotherapy, or of specialised skills, for example in behavioural techniques.

The Report was based on the model of the Professions Supplementary to Medicine Act 1960, with the exception that the relevant powers would be held by one council rather than by a series of separate boards. The Report 'recommended a substantial "lay" membership for the Council'. 'Ideally, there should be someone who can represent the interests of the profession's patients, but we have not been able to suggest how such a representation could be easily identified' (Sieghart, 1978: ix–x). Any appeal against erasure from the register would be made to the Privy Council, 'a wholly independent body within the British Constitution which has wide experience in exercising ultimate supervision over bodies of this kind' (1978: x).

Differences between therapists' organisations

The problems in achieving statutory recognition were brought to a head by the expression of unresolved differences within the field of therapy. The British Association for Behavioural Psychotherapy sounded an interesting (and ultimately persuasive) note of dissent to the otherwise unanimous Sieghart Report. The former group presented an argument for treatments to be evaluated on the basis of their proven *effectiveness*, rather than on the basis of their practitioners simply having completed a recognised form of training. Hence, it claimed that 'registration in the main report is suggested on the basis of training which is largely of unproven value at the present time' (1978: 18). This reflected more than just the well-known tension between psychoanalytic and behavioural methods within therapy. It actually goes to the very heart of the stated rationale for professional organisation. Professional organisation contains conflicting pressures towards, on the one hand, protecting the interests of members as a guild or quasi-monopoly, and, on the other, defending the interests of the public or consumer in receiving a service of proven effectiveness. This note of dissent revealed the existence of continuing differences in the camp of psychotherapy, which have taken more than two decades to overcome, and which, to a certain extent, may still remain.

Psychotherapy Bill

In 2001, Lord Alderdice introduced a Bill to the House of Lords, seeking to establish statutory regulation of psychotherapy, along the lines of earlier legislation such as the Osteopaths Act 1993. The rationale for the Bill was to protect the public from what he termed 'wild psychotherapy', where therapists could practise without control over their qualification or standard of professional work. Regulation was to be on the now accepted model of indicative registration, in order to protect the title of 'psychotherapist' by law. Other therapists might seek to practise psychotherapy, but would not be legally permitted to use the title 'psychotherapist' in their advertising or publicity. The alternative route to regulation, of functional registration, would rely on defining and controlling the practice of psychotherapy, the very reef which had been narrowly avoided by the earlier Foster and Sieghart Reports.

Lord Alderdice argued that the Bill would ensure that 'ethical responsibility to the public would be upheld' (Hansard, 2001: col. 1337). Despite this, the Bill was criticised in the debate, principally on the grounds that it excluded counsellors from its remit. Lord Burlison did not disagree with the proposed Bill's principles, but with its detail, arguing that: 'I cannot accept that where counselling is offered by a trained practitioner to the high standards set by the leading professional bodies it is distinguishable from psychotherapy in anything but name' (Hansard, 2001: col. 1353). Statutory regulation of psychotherapy on its own was rejected as no more than a partial solution to the problem of monitoring the field of psychological therapy as a whole. The Bill would privilege one group of practitioners, psychotherapists, at the expense of the wider profession of counselling. The way forward proposed by the government, following the withdrawal of the Bill, was via statutory regulation of both counsellors and psychotherapists by the newly established Health Professions Council, under s. 60 of the Health Act 1999.

The Department of Health emerged as the key government body driving the process of statutory regulation, on an indicative basis, of both counsellors and psychotherapists. In 2005, it commissioned a 'mapping' exercise from the main therapists' associations, the BACP and the UKCP, as an information-gathering process, preparatory to formal regulation. The main findings are summarised in Box 8.3.

Box 8.3   Department of Health 'mapping' of counselling and psychotherapy

Main findings of DoH mapping exercise:

- Numbers of counsellors and psychotherapists are increasingly rapidly
- There is a wide diversity of training routes and qualifications for counselling and psychotherapy
- A large number of small counselling and psychotherapy organisations can be identified
- In many therapy organisations there is a lack of separation between regulatory and disciplinary functions
- Complaints procedures often have limited lay representation and public accountability
- Many similarities can be found between counselling and psychotherapy, but there remain some significant differences in terms of their traditions, training and practice
- Ethical codes of conduct for counsellors and psychotherapists fulfil or exceed requirements of Health Professions Council

Source: Aldridge and Pollard, 2005.

The results of the mapping exercise point to the complexity of the terrain covered by a diverse professional community of therapists. While the current drive is towards achieving indicative statutory regulation of the titles 'counsellor' and 'psychotherapist', there is also concern over whether the Health Professions Council, working on a quasi-medical model, is the most appropriate agency to act as regulator. In the meantime, therapists' associations have achieved a significant amount of convergence and voluntary self-regulation regarding standards for professional practice and establishing effective complaints procedures. However, this degree of progress could itself become a barrier to achieving intervention by government agencies, and formal regulation by the law. Indeed, if it can be demonstrated that voluntary registration can resolve the problem of defining practice boundaries and policing standards, then, from a government perspective, it may actually *reduce*, rather than increase, the perceived need for legislation in the future.

Therapy, professional power and society

The debate about statutory regulation of therapy goes to the heart of the problematic status of therapy in society at the present time. However, even its staunchest defenders acknowledge that it may be some way away from convincing the wider public of the rightness of its claims to full professional status. Therapy is undeniably growing in popularity. The media's sceptical treatment of therapy does not seem to undermine its increasing appeal and application, however, in employment, post-trauma situations or for facilitating personal growth. Giddens suggests that the growing demand for therapy reflects the pressures on individuals in a postmodern society, where former support systems of community, family and established values have been eroded. This has led to the growth of 'expert systems'. Problems of coping with modernity have led to a reliance by individuals on expert systems, such as psychotherapy and counselling, to manage and cope with problems concerning intimacy, trust and interpersonal relationships. Giddens refers to 'the transformation of intimacy', and the widening interest in self-reflection and self-actualisation in modern society (Giddens, 1990: 124). Increasingly, individuals come to rely on 'experts of the personal', whether therapists or lawyers, to help them negotiate and resolve problems in living in a complex and ever-changing society.

Yet increasing levels of demand for therapy do not necessarily translate into a dynamic process which ends with the achievement of full professional status for therapists. What is sometimes lacking in discussions about the professionalisation of therapy is placing such a process in its wider social context. Critics of professionalisation, such as Mowbray (1995) argue that it is fundamentally about *power relationships* relative to the client, and to other professional groups. Becoming a profession is not a gradual process of refining codes of ethics, or of improving selection and training, but is fundamentally a question of power and occupational control. The new profession needs to possess and maintain a monopoly of a crucial form of expertise and decision-making power (Johnson, 1972: 37-8).

Furthermore, professionalisation is a historically specific process. The period following the Industrial Revolution, which saw emergence of this form of social power for doctors and lawyers, has quite possibly passed. New, aspiring professions now have the disadvantage of competing for power with more powerful and well-established social groupings which do not wish to cede power to newcomers.

Finally, there is the social policy argument. Moves to recognise the professional status of new professional groups form part of a wider political canvas. Recognition depends upon the gaining of wide public support and the backing of powerful groups in society. This is suggested by the example of social work as another aspiring professional group. The slow process of social workers in acquiring a modest exercise of power, since diminished, hinged in the first stage on the revelation of public care scandals in 1944. In the second stage, it was accelerated by government departments wishing to extend their influence in 1970, following a major government report by the Seebohm Committee. This led to the growth of social work as a major resource controller in local and national government. The reduction of the legal and resource powers of social workers has shown this model working in reverse, following the unrelenting series of child care inquiries in the 1970s, and, more recently, by the recasting of social services, via the reforms introduced by the Children Act 2004. For therapists to be granted full professional status, there would need to be other supporting interests who would benefit from this development by acquiring organisational power or prestige as a result. It is not yet clear who these interests might be, or how they would benefit from devolving professional status to therapists.

Summary

Formal recognition by the law of therapy's contribution is a key element in therapy's move towards achieving greater status as a profession or semi-profession. The model of professional status which the therapeutic community seems to have adopted is that of a 'trait' approach. This model focuses on the main qualities of established professional groups such as medicine and the law. Each stage in the group's development, such as producing a detailed code of ethics, represents a step towards achieving recognition by society as a fully fledged profession. To date, in the UK, statutory recognition has been achieved chiefly in the areas of adoption counselling and infertility counselling. Therapists are committed, through the work of their professional associations, to achieving the legal protection of the titles of 'counsellor' and 'psychotherapist' via the gradualist route of indicative statutory regulation by government agency.

Conclusion

At various stages, this book has emphasised the contrasting and even conflicting natures of therapy and the law. They are concerned with different dimensions of human experience, with private as opposed to public spheres of discourse and interaction, and with the dimensions of feeling and experience versus those of evidence and logic. However, these opposing elements may sometimes be over-stated. Bond (2000: 49) has suggested that the law is a crucial cornerstone of safe, ethical and competent therapeutic practice. According to Giddens (1990), therapy, like the law, is an 'expert system' which helps people to make sense of their experience, and to adapt more purposefully to the challenge of contemporary living. Both law and therapy are crucially concerned with the ideas of rights, justice and the peaceful resolution of conflict. One possible danger may be the accelerating process of the 'legalisation of therapy'. It is hoped that, rather than this scenario occurring, therapeutic values and experience may reach some kind of closer interplay and co-existence, influencing and informing the quality of justice in the future.

Discussion points

1   Is therapy a full profession, like law or medicine, or more of a semi-profession, like nursing or social work? Could achieving full professional status for therapy lead to other benefits, such as increased recognition of its status by society, and a degree of legal privilege, as in the US?
2   Can therapy achieve professional status without statutory regulation? Should all therapy be controlled, or is there a place for 'wild psychotherapy', as described by Lord Alderdice in his Psychotherapy Bill?
3   What does the comparison of adoption records counselling and infertility counselling suggest about the changing status of counselling and therapy? What other areas of counselling practice deserve specific recognition by the law?
4   Should the use of specific terms such as 'counsellor' and 'psychotherapist' be restricted by law? What positive or negative effects might this have on the status of therapeutic practice in society?
5   What are the advantages and disadvantages of statutory regulation of counselling and psychotherapy? What is your view of the current gradualist approach to achieving regulation via government agency?

Resources

Professional Indemnity Insurance

Balen Specialist Insurance Brokers
2 Nimrod House, Sandy's Road,
Malvern
Worcs WR14 1JJ
(01684 893006)
(Fax: 01684 893416)
www.balen.co.uk

Howden Professional Liability Insurance
1200 Century Way
Thorpe Park Business Centre
Colton
Leeds LS15 8ZA
(0113 251 5011)
professionals@howdenins.co.uk
www.howdenins.co.uk/professionals

Towergate Professional Risks
31 Clarendon Road
Leeds LS2 9PA
(0113 294 4000)
(Fax: 0113 294 4100)
professionalrisks@towergate.co.uk
www.professionalrisks.co.uk.

Professional Protection Societies

Psychologists' Protection Society
Standalane House
Kincardine
Alloa
Clacks FK10 4NX
(01259 730785)

info@ppsweb.info
www.ppsweb.info

Official Organisations

Children's Commissioner (England)
1 London Bridge
London SE1 9BG
(0844 8009113)
www.childrenscommissioner.org
info.request@childrenscommissioner.org

Commissioner for Children and Young People (Scotland)
85 Holyrood Road
Edinburgh EH8 8AU
(0131 558 3733)
(Fax: 0131 556 3378)
www.cypcommissioner.org
info@ccyp.org.uk

Children's Commissioner (Northern Ireland)
Children's Law Centre
3rd Floor, Philip House
123–137 York Street
Belfast BT15 1AB
(028 902 45704)
(Fax: 028 902 245609)
www.childrenslawcentre.org

Children's Commissioner (Wales)
 Oystermouth House
 Charter Court, Phoenix Way
 Llansamlet
 Swansea SA7 9FS
 (01792 765600)
 (Fax: 01792 765601)

 Pehrhos Manor, Oak Drive
 Colwyn Bay
 Conwy LL29 7YW
 (01492 523333)
 www.childcomwales.org.uk
 post@childcom.org.uk

Commission for Racial Equality (England)
St Dunstan's House

201–211 Borough High Street
London SE1 1GZ
(020 7939 0000)
(Fax: 020 7939 0001)
www.cre.gov.uk

Commission for Racial Equality (Scotland)
The Tun
12 Jackson's Entry
off Holyrood Road
Edinburgh EH8 8PJ
(0131 524 2000)
(Fax: 0131 524 2001)
scotland@cre.gov.uk

Commission for Racial Equality (Wales)
3rd Floor, Capital Tower
Greyfriars Road
Cardiff CF1 3AG
(02920 729200)
(Fax: 02920 729220)
informationwales@cre.gov.uk

Criminal Injuries Compensation Board
(London and South East UK):
Morley House
26–30 Holborn Viaduct
London EC1A 2JQ
(020 7482 6800)
(Fax: 020 7436 0804)

Criminal Injuries Compensation Board
(Rest of UK):
Tay House
300 Bath Street
Glasgow G2 4LN
(0141 331 2726)
(Fax: 0141 331 2287)
www.cica.gov.uk

Crown Prosecution Service
50 Ludgate Hill
London EC4M 7EX
(020 7796 8000)
www.cps.gov.uk

Department for Constitutional Affairs
Selbourne House

54–60 Victoria Street
London SW1E 6QW
(020 7210 8510)
www.dca.gov.uk

Disability Rights Commission
DRC Helpline
Freepost MID 02164
Stratford-upon-Avon
CV37 9HY
(08457 622633)
(Textphone 08457 622644)
Enquiry@drc.org.uk
www.drc.org.uk

Equal Opportunities Commission (England)
Arndale House
Arndale Centre
Manchester M4 3EQ
(0845 601 5901)
(Fax: 0161 838 8312)
www.eoc.org.uk

Equal Opportunities Commission (Scotland)
St Stephens House
279 Bath Street
Glasgow G2 4JL
(0845 601 5901)
(Fax: 0141 248 5834)
scotland@eoc.org.uk

Equal Opportunities Commission (Wales)
Windsor House
Windsor Lane
Cardiff CF10 3GE
(0845 601 5901)
(Fax: 029 2064 1079)
wales@eoc.org.uk

European Commission of Human Rights
Council of Europe
BP 431 R6
67075 Strasbourg-Cedex
France
(+33(0) 388 41 20 18)
(Fax: +33(0) 388 41 27 30)
www.echr.coe.int

Home Office
50 Queen Anne's Gate
London SW1H 9AT
(020 7273 3400)
www.homeoffice.gov.uk

Information Commissioner
Wycliffe House
Water Lane
Wilmslow
Cheshire SK9 5AF
(Enquiries: 01625 545745)
(Admin: 01625 535711)
www.dataprotection.gov.uk

Law Commission
Conquest House
37–38 John Street
Theobald's Road
London WC1N 2BQ
(020 7453 1220)
(Fax: 020 7453 1297)
www.lawcomm.gov.uk

Law Society
113 Chancery Lane
London WC2A 1PL
(020 7242 1222)
(Fax: 020 7831 0344)
www.lawsociety.org.uk

Legal Services Commission
85 Gray's Inn Road
London WC1X 8TX
(020 7759 0000)
www.legalservices.gov.uk

Mental Health Act Commission
Floor 3, Maid Marian House
56 Houndsgate
Nottingham NG1 6BG
(0115 943 7100)
(Fax: 0115 943 7101)
www.mhac.org.uk

National Health Service Litigation Authority
Family Health Services Appeal Unit

30 Victoria Avenue
Harrogate HG1 5PR
(01423 530280)
(Fax: 01423 522034)

NHSLA
Napier House
24 High Holborn
London WC1V 6AZ
(020 7430 8700)
(Fax: 020 7405 4286)
www.nhsla.com

Office of Communications (Ofcom)
Ofcom Contact Centre
Riverside House
2a Southwark Bridge Road
London SE1 9HA
(0845 456 3000)
www.ofcom.org.uk

Parliamentary and Health Service Ombudsman
Millbank Tower
Millbank
London SW1P 4QP
(0845 015 4033)
(Fax: 020 7217 4000)
www.ombudsman.org.uk

Therapists' organisations

British Association for Counselling and Psychotherapy
BACP House
15 St John's Business Park
Lutterworth LE17 4HB
(0870 443 5252)
www.bacp.co.uk

British Psychoanalytic Council
West Hill House
6 Swains Lane
London N6 6QS
(020 7267 3626)
(Fax: 020 7267 4772)
www.bcp.org.uk
mail@psychoanalytic-council.org

British Psychological Society
St Andrew's House
48 Princess Road East
Leicester LE1 7DR
(01162 549 568)
www.bps.org.uk

COSCA: Counselling and Psychotherapy in Scotland
18 Viewfield Street
Stirling FK8 1UA
(01786 475140)
(Fax: 01786 446207)
www.cosca.org.uk
cosca@compuserve.com

General Medical Council
44 Hallam Street
London W1N 6AE
(020 7580 7642)
www.gmc-uk.org

Independent Practitioners Network (IPNOSIS)
www.ipnet.org.uk

Royal College of Psychiatrists
17 Belgrave Square
London SW1X 8PG
(020 7235 2351)
(Fax: 020 7245 1231)
www.rcpsych.ac.uk

United Kingdom Council for Psychotherapy
2nd Floor, Edward House
2 Wakley Street
Islington
London EC1V 7LT
(020 7014 9966)
www.ukcp.org.uk
www.psychotherapy.org.uk

Specialist, advocacy or consumer support organisations

Academy of Experts
3 Gray's Inn Square

London WC1R 5AH
(020 7430 0333)
(Fax: 020 7430 0666)
www.academy-experts.org.uk
admin@academy-experts.org

Accuracy About Abuse
www.accuracyaboutabuse.org

Action For Advocacy
PO Box 31856
Lorrimore Square
London SE17 3XR
(020 7820 7868)
(Fax: 020 7820 9947)
www.actionforadvocacy.org.uk
info@actionforadvocacy.org.uk

Association of Child Abuse Lawyers
Suite 5, Claremont House
22–24 Claremont Road
Surbiton KT6 4QU
(020 8399 1152)
www.childabuselawyers.com

Bar Pro Bono Unit/Free Representation Unit
289–293 High Holborn
London WC1V 7HZ
(020 7611 9500)
(Fax: 020 7611 9505)
www.probono.org.uk
www.freerepresentationunit.org.uk

British False Memory Society
Bradford-on-Avon
Wiltshire BA15 1NFA
(01225 868682)
(Fax: 01225 862251)
www.bfms.org.uk

Children's Legal Centre
University of Essex
Wivenhoe Park
Colchester
Essex CO4 3SQ
(01206 872466)
(Fax: 01206 974026)

(Advice line: 01206 873820)
www.childrenslegalcentre.com
clc@essex.ac.uk

Consumers' Association (Publishers of *Which?*)
Castlemead
Gascoyne Way
Hertford SG14 1LH
(01992 822800)
(Fax: 020 7770 7485)
www.which.co.uk

Freedom to Care (Whistleblowers)
PO Box 125
West Molesey
Surrey KT8 1YE
(020 8224 1022)
freedomtocare@aol.com

Immunity Legal Centre (HIV+/AIDS)
1st Floor, 32–38 Osnaburgh Street
London NW1 3ND
(020 7388 6776)
www.disabilityuk.com

Inquest (Campaign on Coroners' Courts)
89–93 Fonthill Road
London N4 3HJ
(020 7263 1111)
(Fax: 020 7561 0799)
www.inquest.org.uk
inquest@inquest.org.uk

Law Centres Federation
Duchess House
18–19 Warren Street
London W1P 5LR
(020 7387 8570)
(Fax: 020 7387 8368)
www.lawcentres.org.uk
info@lawcentres.org.uk

Legal Action Group
242 Pentonville Road
London N1 9UN
(020 7833 2931)
(Fax: 020 7837 6094)

www.lag.org.uk
lag@lag.org.uk

MIND (The Mental Health Charity)
15–19 Broadway
Stratford
London E15 4BQ
(020 8519 2122)
(Fax: 020 8522 1725)
(Information line: 0845 7660163)
www.mind.org.uk
contact@mind.org.uk

National Association of Citizens Advice Bureaux
Myddleton House
115–123 Pentonville Road
London N1 9LZ
www.nacab.org.uk

National Consumer Council
20 Grosvenor Gardens
London SW1W 0DH
(020 7730 3469)
(Fax: 020 7730 0191)
www.ncc.org.uk
info@nacab.org.uk

National Youth Advisory Service
99–105 Argyle Street
Birkenhead
Wirrall CH41 6AD
(0151 649 8700)
(Fax: 0151 649 8701)
www.nyas.net
main@nyas.net

Public Concern at Work (Whistleblowers)
Suite 301
16 Baldwin Gardens
London EC1N 7RJ
(020 7404 6609)
(Fax: 020 7404 6576)
www.pcaw.co.uk
whistle@pcaw.co.uk

Public Law Project (Support for Judicial Review procedures)
150 Caledonian Road

London N1 9RD
(020 7697 2190)
(Fax: 020 7837 7048)
www.publiclawproject.org.uk
admin@publiclawproject.org.uk

Refugee Legal Centre
153–157 Commercial Road
London E1 2DA
(020 7780 3200)
(Fax: 020 7780 3201)
www.refugee-legal-centre.org.uk
RLC@Refugee-Legal-Centre.org.uk

Rights of Women (Legal advice on domestic violence)
52–54 Featherstone Street
London EC1Y 8RT
(020 7251 6575)
(Fax: 020 7490 5377)
www.rightsofwomen.org.uk
info@row.org.uk

Stonewall (Gay and lesbian rights)
Tower Building, York Road
London SE1 7NX
(020 7593 1850)
(Fax: 020 7593 1877)
www.stonewall.org.uk
info@stonewall.org.uk

Suzy Lamplugh Trust (National Centre for Personal Safety)
Hampton House, 20 Albert Embankment
London SE1 7TJ
(020 7091 0014)
(Fax: 020 7091 0015)
www.suzylamplugh.org
info@suzylamplugh.org

United Kingdom Advocacy Network (Mental Health Survivors)
Volserve House
14–18 West Bar Green
Sheffield S1 2DA
www.u-kan.co.uk
office@u-kan.co.uk

Witness (Against abuse by health and care workers)
32–36 Loman Street

Southwark
London SE1 OEE
(020 7922 7802)
(Helpline: 08454 500 300)
www.witnessagainstabuse.org.uk

Witness Support Programme
Victim Support
Cranmer House
39 Brixton Road
London SW9 6DZ
(020 7735 9166)
(Fax: 020 7582 5712)
www.victimsupport.org.uk
contact@victimsupport.org.uk

Complaints concerning legal representation

General Council of the Bar (Barristers)
289–293 High Holborn
London WC1V 7HZ
(020 7242 0082)
(Fax: 020 7831 9217)
www.barcouncil.org.uk

Legal Services Ombudsman
3rd Floor, Sunlight House
Quay Street
Manchester M3 3JZ
(0161 839 7262)
(Fax: 0161 832 5446)
www.oslo.org

Solicitors: Consumers Complaints Service
Victoria Court
8 Dormer Place
Leamington Spa
Warwickshire CV32 5AE
(0845 608 6565)
www.lawsociety.org.uk
enquiries@lawsociety.org.uk

Mediation

Advisory, Conciliation and Arbitration Service
Brandon House
180 Borough High Street
London SE1 1LW
(020 7210 3613)
www.acas.org.uk

Centre for Effective Dispute Resolution
70 Fleet Street
London EC4Y 1EU
(020 7536 6000)
(Fax: 020 7536 6001)
www.cedr.co.uk
info@cedr.co.uk

Family Mediators Association
Grove House
Grove Road
Bristol BS6 6UN
(0117 946 7062)
(Fax: 0117 946 7181)
www.thefma.co.uk

Mediation UK (Alternative Dispute Resolution)
Alexander House
Telephone Avenue
Bristol BS1 4BS
(0117 904 6661)
(Fax: 0117 904 3331)
www.mediationuk.org.uk
enquiry@mediationuk.org.uk

Glossary of Terms and Abbreviations

Actus reus Guilty act; combined with guilty intent (***mens rea***), an indication of a crime having been committed.

Amicus curiae Friend of the court; adviser to the court on specialist points of law.

Analytic treatment Shorthand for psychoanalytic therapy, based on an exploration of unconscious drives.

Approved Social Worker Social worker authorised to make compulsory admissions of patients under the Mental Health Act 1983.

Arbitration Dispute resolution process, where parties agree to the outcome decided by an independent body.

Assault Reasonable fear of violence, or threat of uninvited physical contact.

BAC British Association for Counselling: see **BACP**.

BACP British Association for Counselling and Psychotherapy. The main professional body representing the interests of counsellors, psychotherapists and those using counselling skills; known as British Association for Counselling until 2001.

Barrister Qualified advocate, specialising in legal representation in higher courts.

Battery Actual violence or uninvited physical contact, other than everyday touching.

Bipolar disorder Mental illness characterised by violent mood swings between elation and profound sadness, formerly termed manic depression.

BMA British Medical Association; the main representative body for doctors as a profession.

***Bolam* test** Standard of care applied in medical or therapist negligence cases; standard of a reasonably competent practitioner.

BPS British Psychological Society; the main body representing interests of psychologists; holds the Royal Charter.

Chartered Psychologist Member of the British Psychological Society, holding a degree plus three years' supervised clinical work.

Child Legal term for a person aged under 18 years.

Child in need Target group for services provided under Children Act 1989.

Childline Confidential telephone helpline for children.

Circuit judge Judge at Crown Court or County Court level.

Civil law Law dealing with disputes between private individuals or organisations.

Cognitive therapy Form of treatment focusing on clients' thinking patterns.

Common law Body of law based on tradition; law made by judges, rather than law made by Parliament.

Community Legal Service Funding State-funded assistance with costs of legal representation, formerly termed Legal Aid.

Conciliation Voluntary process for resolving disputes concerning custody or contact with children in divorce or separation.

Conciliation privilege Legally recognised form of confidentiality for marital counselling involving advice on divorce and separation.

Conditional fee Legal representation for increased fee if the case is won; also known as 'no win, no fee'.

Contempt of court Sanction for failure to recognise due authority of court.

Contract Legally binding agreement to exchange goods or services for payment.

Counselling Contracted therapeutic work with a group or individual.

Counselling skills Use of defined responses, such as active listening or paraphrasing, often as part of another work-role, such as nurse or teacher.

Court order Authoritative decision of the court, requiring, for example, a person to attend court and give evidence.

Criminal law Law relating to offences against the person, property or the state.

Cross-examination Questioning of a witness's evidence by the opposing lawyer, after the examination-in-chief.

Crown Prosecution Service State agency leading prosecution in criminal cases.

De Clerambault's syndrome An erotic obsession with a therapist.

Defamation Comment which is damaging to the reputation or interests of its subject.

Deliberate self-harm Damaging behaviour such as cutting or overdosing with medication, probably intended to fall short of suicide.

Deontological Approach to ethics based on following rules or imperatives, derived from work of the German philosopher, Kant.

DES Department of Education and Science.

DfEE Department for Education and Employment.

DfES Department for Education and Skills.

DHSS Department of Health and Social Security, later Department of Health.

Disclosure Legal term for release of confidential documents required by court.

DoH Department of Health.

DSM *Diagnostic and Statistical Manual*: main assessment and treatment manual in use for mental health problems; currently in its fourth edition; see also *ICD*.

EAP Employment Assistance Programme; professional counselling firm contracted to provide a service to an organisation's workforce.

Eating disorders Severe problems in maintaining a normal diet or body weight, associated with anorexia nervosa or bulimia nervosa.

EC European Community (formerly Common Market; European Economic Community).

ECHR European Court of Human Rights.

ECT Electro-convulsive therapy; also known as electric shock treatment; treatment used for severe clinical depression.

Emergency Protection Order Power authorising a social worker to remove a child at risk, authorised by a magistrate under section 44 Children Act 1989.

EU European Union (formerly Common Market; European Economic Community).

Evidential privilege Legal protection from the requirement to give evidence about confidential matters in a court of law.

Examination-in-chief Main presentation of the body of evidence by a witness, via responding to questions by a lawyer representing the party calling the witness.

Ex parte Court hearing in the absence of one party, such as the defendant.

Expert witness Witness accepted by the court as qualified to give opinion on matters before the court, based on special knowledge, qualifications or experience.

False memory Contested memory of earlier childhood sexual abuse, returning in therapy but lacking supporting evidence. Also referred to as 'recovered memory'.

Fiduciary Relationship of trust and responsibility, as in professional contract with a therapist.

Forensic Relating to crime and offenders, as in forensic psychiatry.

Foster Report 1971 Report of Inquiry into the Church of Scientology, recommending the regulation of psychotherapy.

Fraser guidelines Rationale for House of Lords decision in the *Gillick* case, from a welfare perspective.

Gillick Court decision in 1986 indicating when a child under 16 can be treated in a confidential relationship by a doctor or a therapist without requiring parental permission.

GMC General Medical Council; statutory regulatory body for doctors.

GP General practitioner; family doctor.

Hearsay evidence Second-hand observation or recounting of what another person has seen or experienced.

HFEA Human Fertilisation and Embryology Authority.

HMI Her Majesty's Inspectorate; former body for inspecting schools and colleges.

HRA Human Rights Act 1998, incorporating European Convention on Human Rights.

Hypnotherapist Therapist using hypnosis as main treatment.

ICD *International Classification of Diseases*; manual for the assessment and treatment of mental health, similar to *DSM*; currently in its 10th edition.

Indemnity insurance Coverage against the cost of legal representation and payment of damages in case of court action.

Informed consent Client's voluntary agreement to treatment, based on a knowledge of the risks and benefits involved.

Injunction Court order requiring the subject to follow certain action, such as to stop harassment of a former marital partner.

In loco parentis Standard of care applied to teachers and headteachers; duty to act as a careful or reasonable parent.

Interlocutory Hearing held before a judge, as a temporary 'holding' action.

Judicial review Legal process where decisions of courts or public bodies are examined for procedural fairness.

Law Commission Reform body set up in 1965 to simplify and modernise the law.

Law Society Professional body representing solicitors.

Legal Aid See **Community Legal Service Funding**.

Legal professional privilege Immunity or protection from enforced disclosure by the courts.

Liability Responsibility to act according to a certain standard; failure to do so determines vulnerability to legal action.

Libel Permanent form of defamation, as in an article or on TV.

Liberal individualism Ethical approach based on rights of individual, balanced against needs of others; derived from work of J.S. Mill, a Victorian philosopher.

Litigant in person Person acting without legal representation.

Litigation Taking civil legal action, such as suing another person for breach of contract.

Litigation friend Unofficial adviser for a party in court, formerly a *McKenzie*.

Local Safeguarding Children Board Body linking police, health and social services to co-ordinate responses to child abuse, set up by Children Act 2004.

McNaughten rules Procedure for making legal defence based on insanity.

Malice Legal term indicating lack of due authority.

Malpractice Lack of care to client involving the use of an actively damaging approach, such as sexual contact.

Manic depression See **Bipolar disorder**.

Mediation Voluntary agreement to resolve disputes using an outside negotiator, as in financial matters following divorce.

Memorandum interviewing Video interview with a child to present evidence of sexual abuse to a court in criminal proceedings against the alleged abuser, now covered by *Achieving Best Evidence* protocols.

Mens rea Guilty mind or criminal intent; required with guilty act (***actus reus***) to qualify as a crime.

Negligence Lack of care to client, involving failure to follow accepted professional standards.

Nervous shock Dated legal term for psychological injury.

NHS National Health Service.

NSPCC National Society for the Prevention of Cruelty to Children; leading voluntary organisation in the field of child protection.

Paradoxical injunction Technique in therapy of highlighting a problem area for the client by appearing to give contradictory advice about it.

Personality disorder Psychiatric term for abnormal, deeply ingrained behaviours causing distress to the patient or client and disruption to relationships with others.

Person-centred Form of therapy focusing on exploration of the client's feelings and experiencing, based on the work of Carl Rogers.

Post-Traumatic Stress Disorder Legally recognised term for the state where a person relives a distressing incident such as a disaster via flashbacks or persistent intrusive images.

Precedent Legally binding decision by a higher, more authoritative court on the same issue.

Prima facie Based on the immediate known facts of the case.

Private law Action taken by a citizen to pursue his or her rights or seek redress, for example by suing an individual or organisation; includes **tort**, **contract** and divorce.

Privilege Legally recognised form of confidentiality; immunity from enforced disclosure.

Privity of contract Rule that persons not directly party to a contract cannot sue for breach of that contract.

Pro bono Free legal advice or representation.

Professional protection society Defence organisation providing legal advice and representation for its members.

Psychiatrist Medically qualified therapist, able to diagnose mental illness, prescribe medication and authorise treatment.

Psychoanalysis Classical form of therapy focusing on the exploration of unconscious material, based on the work of Sigmund Freud.

Psychodynamic As in psychoanalysis; may be short-term; sometimes shortened, as in 'dynamic therapy'.

Psychologist Term for wide range of therapists, academics and researchers covering all aspects of human interaction and behaviour.

Psychosis Form of mental illness characterised by delusions and a seriously flawed perception of consensual reality.

Psychotherapy Contracted therapeutic work with a group or individual.

Public authority Public agency, such as NHS, or publicly owned company.

Public interest Judicial standard of the public good, used for deciding issues such as breach of confidentiality.

Public Interest Immunity Form of legal protection from enforced disclosure for documents or confidential sources of information.

Public law Statute and case law concerning the responsibilities of local and central government bodies; includes criminal, constitutional and administrative law.

QC Queen's Counsel: elite barrister.

Qualified privilege Limited form of legal protection against defamation for professionals in releasing information or reporting a colleague's misconduct.

Ramona Key false memory case in California in 1994, where therapists were successfully sued by a third party, the client's father.

Regression therapy Therapeutic approach based on client returning to earlier stage of development in order to resolve physical and emotional dependency issues.

Relate Formerly National Marriage Guidance Council.

Samaritans Major voluntary telephone and on-line crisis befriending service.

Schizophrenia Serious and enduring form of mental illness, involving disintegration of personality and reduced social functioning.

Sectioning Compulsory admission of patient to a psychiatric hospital under Mental Health Act 1983.

Sieghart Report Document produced in 1978 by a broad range of psychotherapy associations on the need for statutory regulation.

Significant harm Trigger for the investigation by social workers of alleged child abuse, under s. 47 Children Act 1989.

Slander Damaging statement about another person made in temporary form, such as speech.

Small Claims Court Branch of the County Court providing access to civil action over claims up to £3,000 without requiring a lawyer.

Solicitor Qualified lawyer; may be specialist in particular area, such as medical negligence.

Specialling Placing a potentially suicidal psychiatric patient under special observation, such as constant nursing supervision.

Spent convictions Convictions no longer requiring disclosure after a prescribed lapse of time for certain occupations.

SSD Social Services Department; social work division of local government.

Stalking Intrusive and unwanted following, contact or attention, covered by civil and criminal law under the Protection from Harassment Act 1997.

Statute Act of Parliament, such as Children Act 2004.

Statutory duty Compulsory requirement under Act of Parliament.

Statutory Instrument Secondary legislation, under powers delegated to relevant government minister.

Strict liability Responsibility for damage held by the manufacturer or distributor of a product, once the fact of damage is proven by the claimant.

Subpoena Court order requiring action, such as attending court as a witness.

Tarasoff Key legal case in California, requiring therapists to take reasonable steps to warn intended victims of the danger posed by a client.

Teleological Approach to ethics based on considering likely or desired outcomes of an action.

Therapeutic privilege Potential for withholding certain information from a client or patient in establishing informed consent, to avoid harm to the client caused by that information.

Therapy Generic term for psychological treatment.

Third party Interested party who is not directly involved in the primary relationship between the client and the therapist, such as a parent or partner.

Tort Civil wrong; legal term for a broad range of actions, such as negligence or personal injury.

Transference Arousal of powerful emotion directed at the therapist during therapy, associated with psychoanalytic approaches.

UKCP United Kingdom Council for Psychotherapy; major umbrella organisation for psychotherapists.

Utilitarianism Ethical approach based on achieving the greatest good of the greatest number, highly influential in English law; based on work of Jeremy Bentham, a Victorian philosopher.

Vicarious liability Liability or legal responsibility for the staff's actions held by an employer, such as the NHS.

Virtue Term for ethical conduct, based on high ideals or sound moral character, derived from work of Aristotle, an ancient Greek philosopher.

Whistleblowing Disclosure of otherwise confidential material in the public interest, to report or prevent malpractice or crime.

References

Abram, J. (1992) *Individual Psychotherapy Trainings: A Guide.* Free Association: London.

Academy of Experts (2002) 'Model form of expert's report', pp. 173–5, in Jenkins, P. (ed.) *Legal Issues in Counselling and Psychotherapy.* Sage: London.

Academy of Medical Royal Colleges (2005) *Medical Expert Witnesses: Guidance from the Academy of Medical Royal Colleges.* AMRC: London.

Alberding, B., Lauver, P. and Patnoe, J. (1993) 'Counselor awareness of the consequences of certification and licensure', *Journal of Counseling and Development*, September/October, 72: 33–8.

Alderson, P. (1993) *Children's Consent to Surgery.* Open University Press: Buckingham.

Alderson, P. and Montgomery, J. (1996) *Health Care Choices: Making Decisions with Children.* Institute for Public Policy Research: London.

Aldridge, S. and Pollard, J. (2005) *Interim Report to Department of Health on Initial Mapping Project for Psychotherapy and Counselling.* BACP/UKCP: Rugby.

Alexander, R. (1995) *Folie à Deux: An Experience of One-to-one Therapy.* Free Association: London.

American Psychiatric Association (APA) (1994) *Diagnostic and Statistical Manual of Mental Disorders.* Fourth edition. APA: Washington, DC.

Armson, S. (1995) Chief Executive, Samaritan, personal communication.

Atkins, K. (2000) 'Autonomy and the subjective character of experience', *Journal of Applied Philosophy*, 17(1): 71–80.

Austin, K., Moline, M. and Williams, G. (1990) *Confronting Malpractice: Legal and Ethical Dilemmas in Psychotherapy.* Sage: London.

Balen, D. (1995) 'Professionalism in practice insurance', *The Therapist*, 3(2): 15–17.

Bass, E. and Davis, L. (1991) *The Courage to Heal: A Guide for Women Survivors of Child Sexual Abuse.* Cedar: London.

Bazire, S. (1995) *Psychotropic Drugs Directory.* Quay: Salisbury.

Beamish, S., Melanson, M. and Oladimeji, M. (1998) *Client Rights in Psychotherapy and Counselling: A Handbook of Client Rights and Therapist Responsibility.* Client Rights Project: Toronto.

Beauchamp, T. and Childress, J. (2001) *Principles of Biomedical Ethics.* Fifth edition. Oxford University Press: Oxford.

Bellah, R., Madsen, R., Sullivan, W. and Swidler, A. (1996) *Habits of the Heart: Individualism and Commitment in American Life.* University of California: Berkeley, CA.

Blom-Cooper, L., Grounds, A., Guinan, P., Parker, A. and Taylor, M. (1996) *The Case of Jason Mitchell: Report of the Independent Panel of Inquiry.* Duckworth: London.

Bollas, C. (2003) 'Confidentiality and professionalism', pp. 202–10, in Levin, C., Furlong, A. and O'Neil, M.K. (eds) *Confidentiality: Ethical Perspectives and Clinical Dilemmas.* Analytic Press: Hillsdale, NJ.

Bollas, C. and Sundelson, D. (1995) *The New Informants: Betrayal of Confidentiality in Psychoanalysis and Psychotherapy*. Karnac: London.

Bond, C., Solon, M. and Harper, P. (1999) *The Expert Witness in Court: A Practical Guide*. Second edition. Shaw: Glasgow.

Bond, T. (1991) 'Suicide and sex in the development of ethics for counsellors', *Changes: An International Journal of Psychology and Psychotherapy*, 9(4): 284–93.

Bond, T. (2000) *Standards and Ethics for Counselling in Action*. Second edition. Sage: London.

Bond, T. (2002) 'The law of confidentiality – a solution or part of the problem?', pp. 123–43, in Jenkins, P. (ed.) *Legal Issues in Counselling and Psychotherapy*. Sage: London.

Bond, T. and Sandhu, A. (2005) *Therapists in Court: Providing Evidence and Supporting Witnesses*. BACP/Sage: London.

Bond, T., Higgins, R. and Jamieson, A. (2001) *Confidentiality: Counselling, Psychotherapy and the Law in Scotland*. BACP: Rugby.

Bowman, C.G. and Mertz, E.E. (1996) 'A dangerous direction: Legal intervention in sexual abuse therapy', *Harvard Law Review*, January, 109(3): 551–639.

Bradley, J. (1989) 'Malpractice in psychiatry', *Medico-Legal Journal,* 57(3): 164–73.

Brandon, S., Boakes, J., Glaser, D. and Green, R. (1997) 'Recovered memories of childhood sexual abuse: Implications for clinical practice', *British Journal of Psychiatry*, 172: 296–307.

Bray, J.H., Shepherd, J.N. and Hays, J.R. (1985) 'Legal and ethical issues in informed consent to psychotherapy', *American Journal of Family Therapy*, 13(2): 50–60.

Brazier, M. (1992) *Medicine, Patients and the Law*. Second edition. Penguin: Harmondsworth.

Brazier, M. (2003) *Medicine, Patients and the Law*. Third edition. Penguin: Harmondsworth.

Bridge, C. and Swindells, H. (2003) *Adoption: The Modern Law*. Jordan: Bristol.

Brinkley, A. (1993) 'Families hit by a wall of silence', *Legal Aid News*, October.

British Association for Counselling (BAC) (1992) *Code of Ethics and Practice for Counsellors*. BAC: Rugby.

British Association for Counselling (1998) *Code of Ethics and Practice for Counsellors*. BAC: Rugby.

British Association for Counselling and Psychotherapy (BACP) (2002) *Ethical Framework for Good Practice in Counselling and Psychotherapy*. BACP: Rugby.

British Broadcasting Corporation (2006) *Taking a Stand*. Radio 4, 12 September.

British Medical Association (BMA) (1906) 'Railway signalman: Professional secrecy', *British Medical Journal*, 15 December: 1753.

British Medical Association (2001a) 'Lawyers to probe records claims', *BMA News*, 19 May: I.

British Medical Association (2001b) *Consent, Rights and Choices in Health Care for Children and Young People*. BMA: London.

British Medical Association Ethics Department (BMAED) (2004) *Medical Ethics Today: The BMA's Handbook of Ethics and Law*. BMA: London.

British Psychological Society (BPS) (1995a) *Expert Testimony: Developing Witness Skills*. Training Video. BPS: Leicester.

British Psychological Society (1995b) *Recovered Memories*. BPS: Leicester.

British Psychological Society (2000) *Code of Conduct, Ethical Principles and Guidelines*. BPS: Leicester.

Brodsky, S. (1998) *Testifying in Court: Guidelines and Maxims for the Expert Witness*. American Psychological Association: Washington, DC.

Brown, D. and Pedder, J. (1979) *Introduction to Psychotherapy*. Tavistock: London.

Brown, L. (1995) 'The therapy client as plaintiff: Clinical and legal issues for the treating therapist', pp. 337–60, in Alpert, J. (ed.) *Sexual Abuse Recalled: Treating Trauma in the Era of the Recovered Memory Debate*. Aronson: London.

Bruner, J. (2002) *Making Stories: Law, Literature and Life*. Harvard University Press: London.

Bullock, R. (1997) *Report of the Independent Inquiry into the Major Employment and Ethical Issues Arising from the Events Leading to the Trial of Amanda Jenkinson*. North Nottinghamshire Health Authority: Mansfield.

Burnett, D. (2002) *A Trial by Jury*. Bloomsbury: London.

Butler-Sloss, E. (1988) *Report of the Inquiry into Child Abuse in Cleveland 1987*. Cm 412. HMSO: London.

Carson, D. (1990) *Professionals and the Court: A Handbook for Expert Witnesses*. Venture: Birmingham.

Childright (1989a) No. 57: 7–10.

Childright (1989b) No. 58: 11–14.

Civil Procedures Rules (2000) Sweet and Maxwell: London.

Clarkson, P. (2000) *Ethics: Working with Ethical and Moral Dilemmas in Psychotherapy*. Whurr: London.

Clarkson, P. and Keter, V. (2000) 'Judicial review of psychotherapy self-regulation', pp. 242–9, in Clarkson, P. *Ethics: Working with Ethical and Moral Dilemmas in Psychotherapy*. Whurr: London.

Clothier, C. (1994) *The Allitt Inquiry: An Independent Inquiry Relating to Deaths and Injuries on the Children's Ward at Grantham and Kesteven General Hospital during the Period February to April 1991*. HMSO: London.

Cohen, J. (1995) 'The independent?', *Supplement to New Law Journal*, 14 July.

Cohen, K. (1992) 'Some legal issues in counselling and psychotherapy', *British Journal of Guidance and Counselling*, 20(1): 10–26.

Coles, D. and Shaw, H. (2002) *How the Inquest System Fails Bereaved People: INQUEST's Response to the Fundamental Review of Coroner Services*. INQUEST: London.

Conaghan, J. and Mansell, W. (1993) *The Wrongs of Tort*. Pluto: London.

Cordess, C. (ed.) (2001) *Confidentiality in Mental Health*. Jessica Kingsley: London.

Costigan, R. (2004) 'Why bother about the Human Rights Act?', *Counselling and Psychotherapy Journal*, 15(10): 42–61.

Cristofoli, G. (2002) 'Legal pitfalls in counselling and psychotherapy practice, and how to avoid them', pp. 24–33, in Jenkins, P. (ed.) *Legal Issues in Counselling and Psychotherapy*. Sage: London.

Crompton, M. (1992) *Counselling and Children*. Edward Arnold: London.

D'Arcy, M. and Gosling, P. (1998) *Abuse of Trust: Frank Beck and the Leicestershire Children's Homes Scandal*. Bowerdean: London.

Dabbs, D. (2002) 'Rope-walking in a strait-jacket', *New Law Journal*, 11 October: 1537, 1541.

Daniels, D. and Jenkins, P. (2000) *Therapy with Children: Children's Rights, Confidentiality and the Law*. Sage: London.

Daniluk, J.C. and Haverkamp, B.E. (1993) 'Ethical issues in counseling adult survivors of incest', *Journal of Counseling and Development*, 72: 16–22.

De Cruz, P. (1987) 'Parents, doctors and children: The *Gillick* case and beyond', *Journal of Social Welfare Law*, March: 93–108.

Department for Constitutional Affairs (2006a) *Getting the Best Deal from Your Lawyer*. DCA News Release 019/06. 19 January.

Department for Constitutional Affairs (2006b) *Coroners Service Reform: Briefing Note*. DCA: London.

Department for Education and Skills (DfES) (2004) *DfES/0027/2004 Safeguarding Children in Education*. DfES: London.

Department of Health (DoH) (1991) *Guidelines for Ethics Committees*. DoH: London.

Department of Health (1999) *Reform of the Mental Health Act 1983: Proposals for Consultation*. Cm 4480. Stationery Office: London.

Department of Health (2001a) *Treatment Choice in Psychological Therapies and Counselling: Evidence Based Clinical Practice Guidelines*. DoH: London.

Department of Health (2001b) *Good Practice Implementation Guide: Consent to Examination or Treatment*. DoH: London.

Department of Health (2003) *What To Do If You're Worried a Child is Being Abused*. Stationery Office: London.

Department of Health (2004a) *Best Practice Guidance for Doctors and Other Health Professionals on the Provision of Advice and Treatment to Young People under 16 on Contraception, Sexual and Reproductive Health*. DoH: London.

Department of Health (2004b) *National Service Framework for Children, Young People and Maternity Services*. DoH: London.

Department of Health (2007) *Trust, Assurance and Safety – The Regulation of Health Professionals in the 21st century*. Cm 7013. Stationary Office: London.

Department of Health and Social Security (DHSS) (1976a) *Children Act 1975: Implementation of Section 26, Access by Adopted Children to Birth Records*. LAC (76)21. DHSS: London.

Department of Health and Social Security (1976b) *Access to Birth Records: Notes for Counsellors*. HMSO: London.

Department of Health and Social Security (1985) *Review of Child Care Law*. HMSO: London.

Department of Health and Welsh Office (DoH/WO) (1999) *Mental Health Act 1983: Code of Practice*. HMSO: London.

Dryden, W. (ed.) (1997) *Therapists' Dilemmas*. Second edition. Open University Press: Buckingham.

Ellison, L. (2001) *The Adversarial Process and the Vulnerable Witness*. Oxford University Press: Oxford.

Enns, C.Z., McNeilly, C.L., Corkery, J.M. and Gilbert, M.S. (1995) 'The debate about delayed memories of childhood sexual abuse: A feminist perspective', *The Counseling Psychologist*, 23(2): 181–279.

Etzioni, A. (1969) *The Semi-Professions and their Organization*. Free Press: New York.

Feldman, S. and Ward, T. (1979) 'Psychotherapeutic injury: Reshaping the implied contract as an alternative to malpractice', *North Carolina Law Review*, 58: 63–96.

Fennell, P. (1992) 'Informal compulsion: The psychiatric treatment of juveniles under common law', *Journal of Social Welfare and Family Law*, 4: 311–33.

Fine, R. (1997) *Being Stalked: A Memoir*. Chatto and Windus: London.

Fishwick, C. (1988) *Court Work*. Pepar: Birmingham.

Flaxman, R.H. (1989) *How to Protect Your Reputation: A Guide to Professional Indemnity Insurance*. ICSA: Cambridge.

Fleming, J. (1994) *Barbarism to Verdict: A History of the Common Law*. Angus and Robertson: NSW, Australia.

Ford, T. and Kessel, A. (2001) 'Feeling the way: Childhood mental illness and consent to treatment', *British Journal of Psychiatry*, 179: 384–6.

Fortin, J. (1998) *Children's Rights and the Developing Law*. Butterworths: London.

Foster, C. and Peacock, N. (2000) *Clinical Confidentiality*. Monitor: Suffolk.

Foster, C., Wynn, T. and Ainley, N. (1996) *Disclosure and Confidentiality: A Practitioner's Guide*. Sweet and Maxwell: London.

Foster, J.G. (1971) *Enquiry into the Practice and Effects of Scientology*. HMSO: London.

Foucault, M. (1991) *Discipline and Punish: The Birth of the Prison*. Penguin: Harmondsworth.

Freud, S. (1906/1971) 'Psycho-analysis and the establishment of the facts in legal proceedings', in *Jensen's 'Gradiva' and Other Works*, pp. 103–14, Vol. 9. *Standard Edition of the Complete Works*. Hogarth/Institute of Psycho-Analysis: London.

Freud, S. (1931/1971) 'The expert opinion in the *Halsmann* case', in *The Future of an Illusion: Civilisation and its Discontents*, pp. 251–3, Vol. 21. *Standard Edition of the Complete Works*. Hogarth/Institute of Psycho-Analysis: London.

Friel, J. Q.C. (1998) *In the Matter of the British Association for Counselling, The Association for Student Counselling and The Association of Colleges*. Unpublished legal opinion.

Fundudis, T. (2003) 'Consent issues in medico-legal procedures: How competent are children to make their own decisions?', *Child and Adolescent Mental Health*, 8(1): 18–22.

Gabbard, G. (1995) 'Transference and counter transference in the psychotherapy of therapists charged with sexual misconduct', *Journal of Psychotherapy Practice and Research*, 4(1): 10–17.

Garvey, P. and Layton, A. (eds) (2005) *Comparative Confidentiality in Psychoanalysis*. British Institute of International and Comparative Law/International Psychoanalytical Association: King's Lynn.

General Medical Council (1997) *Serious Communicable Diseases*. GMC: London.

Giddens, A. (1990) *The Consequences of Modernity*. Stanford University Press: Stanford, CA.

Gilligan, C. (1993) *In a Different Voice: Psychological Theory and Women's Development*. Harvard University Press: Cambridge, MA.

Griffin, G. (2001) 'Vicarious liability', *Counselling and Psychotherapy Journal*, 12(4): 8–9.

Grunebaum, H. (1986) 'Harmful psychotherapy experience', *American Journal of Psychotherapy*, April, 40(2): 165–76.

Halmes, E. and Timms, N. (1985) *Adoption, Identity and Social Policy*. Gower: Aldershot.

Halsbury's Laws of England (1974) Fourth edition. Butterworth: London.

Hammond, D.C. (1995) 'Hypnosis, false memories and guidelines for using hypnosis with potential victims of abuse', pp. 101–31, in Alpert, J. (ed.) *Sexual Abuse Recalled: Treating Trauma in the Era of the Recovered Memory Debate*. Aronson: London.

Hansard (2001) *House of Lords Psychotherapy Bill Debate*, 19 January, cols 1333–59.

Harris, B. (1976) *A Guide to the Rehabilitation of Offenders Act 1974*. Barry Rose: London.

Harris, N. (1993) *Law and Education: Regulation, Consumerism and the Education System*. Sweet and Maxwell: London.

Harrison, S. and Westergaard, J. (2006) 'Developing a meaningful relationship: A conversation about supervision from the supervisor's perspective', pp. 97–109, in Reid, H. and Westergaard, J. (eds) *Providing Support and Supervision: An Introduction for Professionals Working with Young People*. Routledge: London.

Hawkins, C. (1985) *Mishap or Malpractice?* Blackwell Scientific Publications: London.

Hayman, A. (2002) 'Psychoanalyst subpoenaed', pp. 21–3, in Jenkins, P. (ed.) *Legal Issues in Counselling and Psychotherapy*. Sage: London.

Her Majesty's Government (2003) *Every Child Matters*. Cm 5860. Stationery Office: London.

Her Majesty's Government (2006) *Working Together to Safeguard Children: A Guide to Inter-Agency Working to Safeguard and Promote the Welfare of Children*. Stationery Office: London.

Hill, D. (1995) Relate, Personal communication.

Hodgkins, P. (1991) *Birth Records Counselling: A Practical Guide*. British Agencies for Adoption and Fostering: London.

Holmes, D., Taylor, M. and Saeed, A. (2000) 'Stalking and the therapeutic relationship', *Forensic Update*, 60: 31–5.

Holmes, J. and Lindley, R. (1989) *The Values of Psychotherapy*. Oxford University Press: Oxford.

Holmes, J., Adshead, G. and Smith, J. (1994) 'An ethical dilemma in psychotherapy', *Psychiatric Bulletin*, 18(8): 466–8.

Home Office (2004a) *Police And Criminal Evidence Act 1984 (PACE): Code of Practice for the Detention, Treatment and Questioning of Persons by Police Officers: Code C.* Home Office: London.

Home Office (2004b) *Bichard Inquiry Recommendations: Progress Report*. Home Office: London.

Home Office/Department of Health (1992) *Memorandum of Good Practice on Video Recorded Interviews with Child Witnesses in Criminal Proceedings*. HMSO: London.

Home Office, Crown Prosecution Service and Department of Health (2001) *Provision of Therapy for Child Witnesses Prior to a Criminal Trial: Practice Guidance*. CPS: Bolton.

Home Office, Crown Prosecution Service and Department of Health (2002a) *Provision of Therapy for Vulnerable or Intimidated Witnesses Prior to a Criminal Trial: Practice Guidance*. Home Office Communications Directorate: London.

Home Office, Lord Chancellor's Department, Crown Prosecution Service, Department of Health, National Assembly for Wales (2002b) *Achieving Best Evidence in Criminal Proceedings: Guidance for Vulnerable or Intimidated Witnesses, Including Children*. Home Office Communications Directorate: London.

Home Office/Scottish Education Department (1972) *Report of the Departmental Committee on the Adoption of Children*. Cmnd 5107. HMSO: London.

Hubble, M., Duncan, B. and Miller, S. (eds) (2002) *The Heart and Soul of Change: What Works in Therapy*. American Psychological Association: Washington, DC.

Human Fertilisation and Embryology Authority (HFEA) (1993) *Code of Practice*. HFEA: London.

Human Fertilisation and Embryology Authority (HFEA) (2003) *Code of Practice*. HFEA: London.

Income Data Services (2000) *Data Protection Act 1998*. IDS: London.

Information Commissioner (2001) *The Data Protection Act 1998: Legal Guidance*. IC: Wilmslow.

Ingram, K. and Roy, L. (1995) 'Complaints against psychiatrists: A five year study', *Psychiatric Bulletin*, 19: 620–22.

Jakobi, S. and Pratt, D. (2002) 'Therapy notes and the law', pp. 175–82, in Jenkins, P. (ed.) *Legal Issues in Counselling and Psychotherapy*. Sage: London.

Jeffs, T. (1995) 'Children's educational rights in a new ERA?', pp. 25–39, in Franklin, B. (ed.), *Handbook of Children's Rights: Comparative Policy and Practice*. Routledge: London.

Jehu, D., Davis, J., Garrett, T., Jorgensen, L.M. and Schoener, G.R. (1994) *Patients as Victims: Sexual Abuse in Psychotherapy and Counselling*. Wiley: Chichester.

Jenkins, P. (1999) 'Client or patient? Contrasts between medical and counselling models of confidentiality', *Counselling Psychology Quarterly*, 12(2): 169–81.

Jenkins, P. (2001) 'Supervisor responsibility and the law', pp. 22–40, in Wheeler, S. and King, D. (eds) *Supervising Counsellors: Issues of Responsibility*. Sage: London.

Jenkins, P. (2002a) 'Transparent recording: Therapists and the Data Protection Act 1998', pp. 45–56, in Jenkins, P. (ed.) *Legal Issues in Counselling and Psychotherapy*. Sage: London.

Jenkins, P. (2002b) 'False memories or recovered memories? Legal and ethical implications for therapists', pp. 144–64, in Jenkins, P. (ed.) *Legal Issues in Counselling and Psychotherapy*. Sage: London.

Jenkins, P. (2003a) 'Therapist responses to requests for disclosure of therapeutic records: An introductory study', *Counselling and Psychotherapy Research*, 3(3): 232–8.

Jenkins, P. (2003b) *Exploring Children's Rights: A Participative Exercise to Introduce the Issues around Children's Rights in England and Wales.* Pavilion: Brighton.

Jenkins, P. (2005) 'Aspects of the external frame: Psychodynamic psychotherapy and the law', *Psychodynamic Practice*, 11(1): 41–56.

Jenkins, P. (2006) 'Contracts, ethics and the law', pp. 109–16, in Sills, C. (ed.) *Contracts in Counselling and Psychotherapy.* Second edition. Sage: London.

Jenkins, P. (in press) 'Supervisors in the dock? Supervisors and the law', in Tudor, K. and Worrall, M. (eds) *Freedom to Practise*, Vol. 2. PCCS: Ross-on-Wye.

Jenkins, P. and Polat, F. (2006) 'The Children Act 2004 and implications for counselling in schools in England and Wales', *Pastoral Care in Education*, 24(2): 7–14.

Jenkins, P. and Potter, S. (2007) 'No more "personal notes"? Data protection policy and practice in Higher Education counselling services in the UK', *British Journal of Guidance and Counselling*, 35(1): 131–46.

Johnson, S. (2006) 'Professional liability insurance', pp. 208–13, in Hooper, D. and Weitz, P. (eds) *Psychological Therapies in Primary Care: Training and Training Standards.* Karnac: London.

Johnson, T.J. (1972) *Professions and Power.* Macmillan: London.

Johnston, M. (1997) *Spectral Evidence: The Ramona Case: Incest, Memory, and Truth on Trial in Napa Valley.* Westview: Oxford.

Jones, C., Shillito-Clarke, C., Syme, G., Hill, D., Casemore, R. and Murdin, L. (2000) *Questions of Ethics in Counselling and Therapy.* Open University Press: Buckingham.

Kamphuis, J. and Emmelkamp, P. (2000) 'Stalking – a contemporary challenge for forensic and clinical psychiatry', *British Journal of Psychiatry*, 176: 206–9.

Kellam, A. (1994) 'Police power to obtain information about patients', *Psychiatric Bulletin*, 18: 99–100.

Kermani, E.J. (1989) *Handbook of Psychiatry and the Law.* Year Book Medical Publishers: London.

Keter, V. (2002) 'The implications of the Human Rights Act 1998 for counsellors and psychotherapists', pp. 165–72, in Jenkins, P. (ed.) *Legal Issues in Counselling and Psychotherapy.* Sage: London.

Kilkelly, U. (1999) *The Child and the European Convention on Human Rights.* Ashgate: Aldershot.

Kirkwood, A. (1993) *The Leicestershire Inquiry 1992.* Leicestershire County Council: Derby.

Knight, B.H. and Palmer, R.N. (1992) *Medico-Legal Reports and Appearing in Court.* Medical Protection Society: London.

Kohlberg, L. (1981) *Essays on Moral Development: The Philosophy of Moral Development*, Vol. 1. Harper and Row: New York.

Kohlberg, L. (1984) *Essays on Moral Development: The Philosophy of Moral Development*, Vol. 2. Harper and Row: New York.

Laing, R.D. (1985) *Wisdom, Madness and Folly: The Making of a Psychiatrist.* Macmillan: London.

Lambert, M. and Ogles, B. (2004) 'The efficacy and effectiveness of psychotherapy', pp. 139–93, in *Bergin and Garfield's Handbook of Psychotherapy and Behaviour Change.* Fifth edition. Wiley: New York.

Lambert, M.J., Bergin, A.E. and Collins, J.L. (1977) 'Therapist induced deterioration in psychotherapy', pp. 452–81, in Gurman, A. and Razin, A. (eds) *Effective Psychotherapy: A Handbook.* Pergamon: Oxford.

Laming, Lord (2003) *Victoria Climbié Inquiry.* Cm 5730. Stationery Office: London.

Langs, R. (1998) *Ground Rules in Counselling and Psychotherapy.* Karnac: London.

Law Commission (1981) *Breach of Confidence.* Cmnd 8388. HMSO: London.

Law Commission (1995a) *Liability for Psychiatric Illness*. Consultation Paper 137. HMSO: London.

Law Commission (1995b) *Damages for Personal Injury: Non-pecuniary Loss.* Consultation Paper 140. HMSO: London.

Law Commission (1998) *Making the Law on Civil Limitation Periods Simpler and Fairer.* Law Commission Consultation Paper 151. Law Commission: London.

Layard, R. (2006) *Happiness: Lessons from a New Science*. Penguin: Harmondsworth.

Lees, S. (1997) *Carnal Knowledge: Rape on Trial*. Penguin: Harmondsworth.

Leonard, G. and Beazley Richards, J. (2001) 'How supervisors can protect themselves from complaints and litigation', pp. 192–7, in Carroll, M. and Tholstrup, M. (eds) *Integrative Approaches to Supervision*. Jessica Kingsley: London.

LeSurf, A. and Lynch, G. (1999) 'Exploring young people's perceptions relevant to counselling: A qualitative study', *British Journal of Guidance and Counselling*, 27(2): 231–43.

Levine, M. and Doueck, H.J. (1995) *The Impact of Mandated Reporting on the Therapeutic Process*. Sage: London.

Levy, A. and Kahan, B. (1991) *The Pindown Experience and the Protection of Children: The Report of the Staffordshire Child Care Enquiry 1990*. Staffordshire County Council: Stafford.

Levy, S. (2003) 'The lesser of two evils: A contextual view of the English case of the conjoined twins', *Medicine and Law*, 22(1): 1–9.

London Child Protection Committee (LCPC) (2005) *Working with Sexually Active Young People under the Age of 18 – A Pan-London Protocol*. LCPC: London.

McKendrick, E. (2000) *Contract Law*. Fourth edition. Macmillan: London.

Macpherson, W. (1999) *The Stephen Lawrence Inquiry: Report by Sir William Macpherson*. Cm 4262–1. Stationery Office: London.

Major, M. (2002) *Guide to Small Claims in the County Court*. Second edition. Easyway: London.

Malcolm, J. (1997) *In the Freud Archives*. Macmillan: London.

Mangalmurti, V.S. (1994) 'Psychotherapists' fear of *Tarasoff*: All in the mind?', *Journal of Psychiatry and Law*, Fall, 22(3): 379–409.

Manson-Smith, D. (2004) *The Legal System of Scotland*. Third edition. Stationery Office: Edinburgh.

Marks, L. (1995) 'Adopted and at home in the world: A message for counsellors', *Counselling*, 6(1): 48–50.

Mason, J.K. and Laurie, G. (2006) *Mason & McCall Smith's Law and Medical Ethics*. Seventh edition. Oxford University Press: Oxford.

Masson, J. (1992) *Against Therapy*. Fontana: London.

Mayberry, M. and Mayberry, J. (2003) *Consent in Clinical Practice*. Radcliffe: Oxford.

Meara, N., Schmidt, L. and Day, J. (1996) 'Principles and virtues: A foundation for ethical decisions, policies and character', *The Counseling Psychologist*, 24(1): 4–77.

Mearns, D. (1993) 'Against indemnity insurance', pp. 161–4, in Dryden, W. (ed.) *Questions and Answers on Counselling in Action*. Sage: London.

Memon, A., Vrij, A. and Bull, R. (2003) *Psychology and Law: Truthfulness, Accuracy and Credibility*. Second edition. Wiley: Chichester.

Mental Health Act Commission (1999) *Mental Health Act Commission: 8th Biennial Report*. Stationery Office: London.

Meyer, G., Landis, E. and Hays, J. (1988) *Law for the Psychotherapist*. Norton: New York.

Morgan, D. and Lee, R. (1991) *Human Fertilisation and Embryology Act 1990: Abortion and Embryo Research, The New Law*. Blackstone: London.

Mowbray, R. (1995) *The Case against Psychotherapy Registration*. Trans Marginal Press: London.

Mr and Mrs E. (2004) 'The *Bournewood* Gap', *Open Mind*, 132, March/April: 23.

Mullaney, N.J. and Handford, P.R. (1993) *Tort Liability for Psychiatric Damage: The Law of 'Nervous Shock'*. Law Book Company: Sydney.

Mullis, A. and Oliphant, K. (1993) *Torts*. Macmillan: London.

National Children's Home: Action for Children (NCH) (1994) *Messages from Children: Children's Evaluations of the Professional Response to Child Sexual Abuse*. NCH: London.

Nijboer, H. (1995) 'Expert evidence', pp. 555–64, in Bull, R. and Carson D. (eds) *Handbook of Psychology in Legal Contexts*. Wiley: Chichester.

O'Dowd, J. (2001) 'Online counselling and the law', *Counselling and Psychotherapy Journal*, 12 (5): 27–9.

Otto, R. and Schmidt, W. (1991) 'Malpractice in verbal psychotherapy: Problems and some solutions', *Forensic Reports*, 4: 309–36.

Packman, W.L., Cabot, M.G. and Bongar, B. (1994) 'Malpractice arising from negligent psychotherapy: Ethical, legal and clinical implications of *Osheroff v. Chestnut Lodge*', *Ethics and Behaviour*, 4(3): 175–97.

Palmer, S. and Szymanska, K. (2001) 'Therapy checklist for potential clients and those already in therapy', pp. 323–6, in Milner, P. and Palmer, S. (eds) *Counselling: The BACP Counselling Reader: Volume 2*. Sage/BACP: London.

Palmer, T. (2003) 'Pre-trial therapy with children who have been sexually abused', pp. 152–66, in Richardson, S. and Bacon, H. (eds) *Creative Responses to Child Sexual Abuse: Challenges and Dilemmas*. Jessica Kingsley: London.

Pannett, A.J. (1992) *Law of Torts*. Sixth edition. Longman: London.

Pattenden, R. (2003) *The Law of Professional–Client Confidentiality: Regulating the Disclosure of Personal Information*. Oxford University Press: Oxford.

Pavela, G. (2006) *ASJA Law and Policy Report* 203, 19 January (gpavela@umd.edu).

Pearce, J. (1994) 'Consent to treatment during childhood: The assessment of competence and the avoidance of conflict', *British Journal of Psychiatry*, 165: 713–16.

Pearce, P. (1988) 'The law', pp. 1–27, in Pearce, P., Parsloe, P., Francis, H., Maccara, A. and Watson, D. (eds) *Personal Data Protection in Health and Social Services*. Croom Helm: London.

Pearson Commission (1978) *Royal Commission on Civil Liability and Compensation for Personal Injury*. Cmnd 7504. Report Vol. 1. HMSO: London.

Perry, J.C. and Jacobs, D. (1982) 'Overview: Clinical applications of the amytal interview in psychiatric emergency settings', *American Journal of Psychiatry*, 139(5): 552–9.

Piaget, J. (1965) *The Moral Judgement of the Child*. Free Press: Glencoe, IL.

Plotnikoff, J. and Woolfson, R. (2004) *In Their Own Words: The Experiences of Fifty Young Witnesses in Criminal Proceedings*. NSPCC: London.

Pollecoff, P. (2002) 'Preparing reports and presenting evidence in court', pp. 57–71, in Jenkins, P. (ed.) *Legal Issues in Counselling and Psychotherapy*. Sage: London.

Proctor, G. (2002) *The Dynamics of Power in Counselling and Psychotherapy: Ethics, Politics and Practice*. PCCS: Ross-on-Wye.

Pugh, C. and Trimble, M.R. (1993) 'Psychiatric injury after Hillsborough', *British Journal of Psychiatry*, 163: 425–9.

Putnam, F.W. (1992) 'Using hypnosis for therapeutic abreactions', *Psychiatric Medicine*, 10: 51–65.

Pyles, R. (2003) 'The American Psychiatric Association's fight for privacy', pp. 252–60, in Levin, C., Furlong, A. and O'Neil, M.K. (eds) *Confidentiality: Ethical Perspectives and Clinical Dilemmas*. Analytic Press: Hillsdale, NJ.

Reynolds, M.P. and King, P.S.D. (1989) *The Expert Witness and His Evidence*. Blackwell Scientific Publications: London.

Ross, L.F. (1998) *Children, Families and Health Care Decision Making*. Clarendon: Oxford.

Roth, A. and Fonagy, P. (2006) *What Works for Whom? A Critical Review of Psychotherapy Research.* Second edition. New York: Guilford.

Rowley, W.J. and MacDonald, D. (2001) 'Counseling and the law: A cross-cultural perspective', *Journal of Counseling and Development,* 79: 422–9.

Russell, B. (1969) *History of Western Philosophy.* Allen and Unwin: London.

Russell, J. (1993) *Out of Bounds: Sexual Exploitation in Counselling and Therapy.* Sage: London.

Rutter, P. (1991) *Sex in the Forbidden Zone.* Mandala: London.

Sanctuary, G. (1965) 'The work of the National Marriage Guidance Council', *Law Society Gazette,* October: 566–70.

Sands, A. (2000) *Falling for Therapy: Psychotherapy from a Client's Point of View.* Macmillan: London.

Scottish Law Commission (2004) *Report on Damages for Psychiatric Injury.* Report 196. Stationery Office: Edinburgh.

Scraton, P., Jemphrey, A. and Coleman, S. (1995) *No Last Rites: The Denial of Justice and the Promotion of Myth in the Aftermath of the Hillsborough Disaster.* Liverpool City Council: Liverpool.

Shield, J. and Baum, J. (1994) 'Children's consent to treatment', *British Medical Journal,* 7 May, 308: 1182–3.

Sieghart, P. (1978) *Statutory Registration of Psychotherapists: A Report of Professions Joint Working Party.* Tavistock: London.

Sim, J. (1996) 'Client confidentiality: Ethical issues in Occupational Therapy', *British Journal of Occupational Therapy,* 59(2): 56–61.

Simons, A. and Harmer, C. (2002) *A Practical Guide to the Small Claims Court.* Third edition. Tolley: London.

Sinclair Taylor, J. (2003) *Independent Legal Opinion on Government Consultation on Guidance Related to s.8(d) Misuse of Drugs Act 1971.* Homeless Link: London.

Smith, J. (2003) *The Shipman Inquiry: Third Report – Death Certification and the Investigation of Deaths by Coroners.* Cm 5854. Stationery Office: London.

Social Exclusion Unit (1999) *Teenage Pregnancy.* Cm 4342. SEU: London.

Southern Derbyshire Health Authority and Derbyshire County Council (SHDA/DCC) (1996) *Report of the Inquiry into the Care of Anthony Smith.* SDHA/DCC: Derby.

Stewart, H. (2004) *Child Abuse Reporting Laws.* Social Work Monograph 202. University of East Anglia: Norwich.

Striano, J. (1988) *Can Psychotherapists Hurt You?* Professional Press: Santa Barbara.

Sumerling, R. (1996) 'Violence and harassment against medical practitioners', *Medical Protection Society Casebook,* 8: 8–10.

Sutherland, S. (1977) *Breakdown.* Paladin: St Albans.

Szasz, T. (1974) *The Ethics of Psychoanalysis: The Theory and Methods of Autonomous Psychotherapy.* Routledge and Kegan Paul: London.

Thompson, A. (1983) *Ethical Concerns in Psychotherapy and their Legal Ramifications.* University Press of America: Lanham.

Tranberg, H. and Rashbass, J. (2004) *Medical Records: Use and Abuse.* Radcliffe: Oxford.

Traynor, B. and Clarkson, P. (2000) 'What happens if a psychotherapist dies?', pp. 168–72, in Clarkson, P. *Ethics: Working with Ethical and Moral Dilemmas in Psychotherapy.* Whurr: London.

Triseliotis, J. (1973) *In Search of Origins: The Experience of Adopted People.* Routledge and Kegan Paul: London.

Trowell, J. (2001) 'Confidentiality and child protection', pp. 85–94, in Cordess, C. (ed.) *Confidentiality and Mental Health.* Jessica Kingsley: London.

Turner, M. and Kennedy, M. (1997) '*Tarasoff* and the duty to warn third parties', *Psychiatric Bulletin,* 21: 465–6.

UNICEF (1989) *The United Nations Convention on the Rights of the Child 1989*. Children's Rights Development Unit: London.

Van Hoose, W.H. and Kottler, J.A. (1985) *Ethical and Legal Issues in Counseling and Psychotherapy*. Second edition. Jossey-Bass: London.

Ward, S. (1995) 'Laying down the law on medical evidence', *BMA News Review*, June: 21–2.

Warnock, W. (1985) *A Question of Life: The Warnock Report on Human Fertilisation and Embryology*. Basil Blackwell: Oxford.

Weir, A. (2004) 'Parenting and mental illness. Legal frameworks and issues – some international comparisons', pp. 271–84, in Gopfert, M., Webster, J. and Seeman, M. (eds) *Parental Psychiatric Disorder: Distressed Parents and their Families*. Second edition. Cambridge University Press: Cambridge.

Wells, C. (1994) 'Disasters: The role of institutional responses in shaping public perceptions of death', pp. 196–222, in Lee, R. and Morgan, D. (eds) *Death Rites: Law and Ethics at the End of Life*. Routledge: London.

Whimster, P. (2000) *A Straightforward Guide to Small Claims in the County Court*. Third edition. Straightforward Publications: London.

World Health Organisation (WHO) (1992) *ICD–10: Classification of Mental and Behavioural Disorders*. WHO: Geneva.

Wyner, R. (2003) *From the Inside: Dispatches from a Women's Prison*. Aurum: London.

Yalom, I. (1991) *Love's Executioner and Other Tales of Psychotherapy*. Penguin: Harmondsworth.

Internet sources

www.the-hutton-enquiry.org.uk/content/transcripts/hearing-trans36.htm

Table of Cases

Note: Law references follow a format which may be unfamiliar to most therapists. Case reports are written in the following way:

R v Emery (1993), Criminal Appeals Reports (Sentencing) 14 394–400;
Bolam v Friern HMC [1957] 2 All ER 118

The first case is a criminal case. The second case, probably more relevant to therapists, is a civil case, with the full report available in Volume 2 of the *All England Law Reports* (All ER) for 1957, starting at page 118. Where a number of judges comment on a case, the style of quotation will be 'per Lord Ackner at 569', rather than the usual Harvard system (such as Egan, 2006: 214). Other abbreviations include TLR (*Times Law Reports*) or refer to the court involved, e.g. HL for House of Lords, CA for Court of Appeal.

Most public reference libraries will have Acts of Parliament, and either the *All England Law Reports*, or *Weekly Law Reports* (WLR), together with CD-ROM or internet access to newspaper reports and relevant government publications referred to in this text. Many key recent case reports are available via the web, on www.bailii.org and Acts of Parliament from 1998 are available via www.parliament.uk. On-line computer access to unreported cases can be made via Lexis, but this will only be available to paying subscribers, such as law firms or university law departments. Journals which carry up-to-date commentary on the law include *Childright*, *Community Care* and *New Law Journal*.

UK

Canada

US

Table of Statutes

Tables of Boxes

Index

For individual legal cases, refer to **Table of Cases;** for Acts of Parliament, refer to **Table of Statutes.**